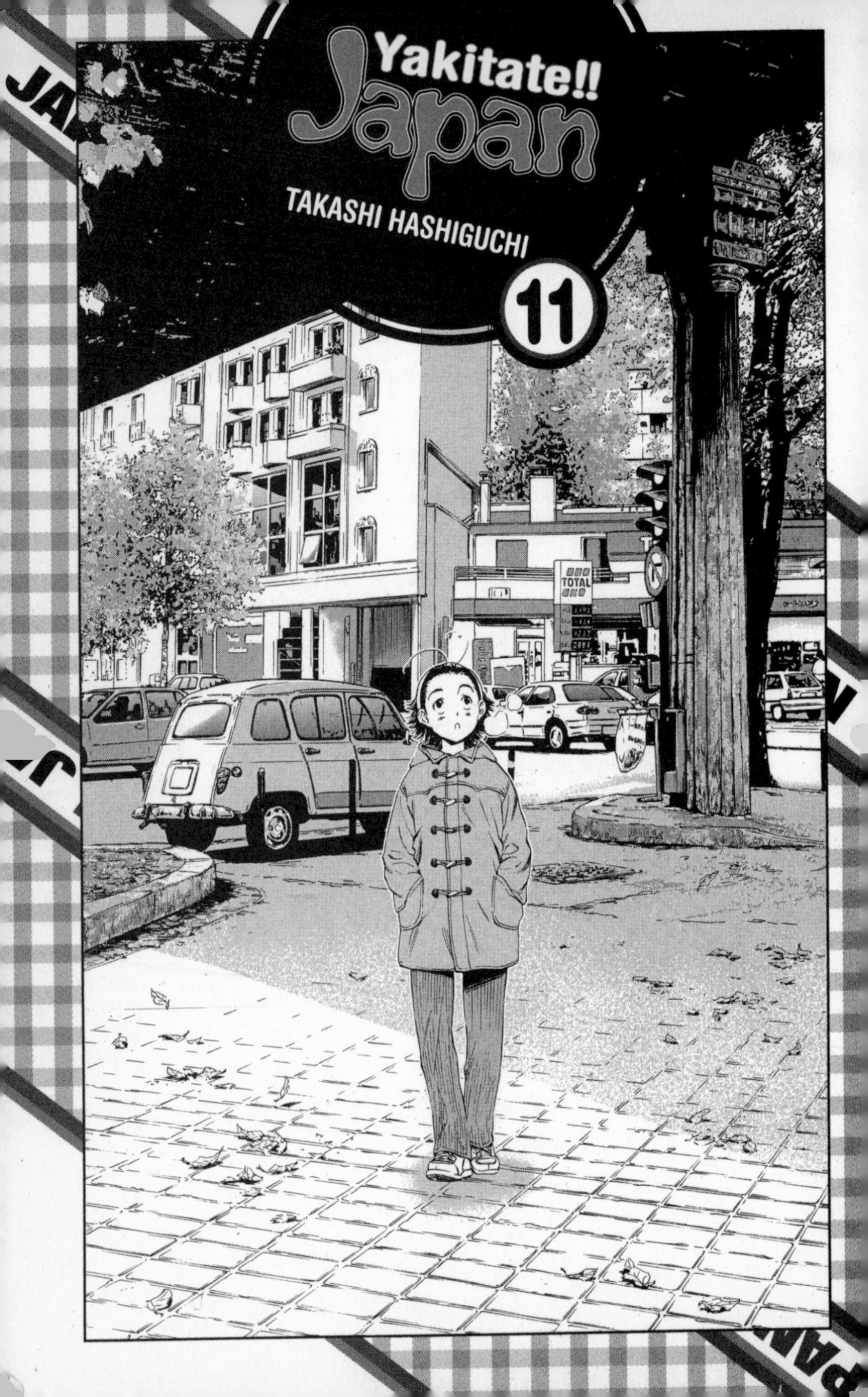
Yakitate!! Japan
TAKASHI HASHIGUCHI
11
TOTAL

YAKITATE!! JAPAN
11
VIZ Media Edition

★The Story Thus Far★

The Japanese representatives brilliantly advance to the Monaco Cup semifinals with a taiyaki bread filled with delectable potato paste. But the competition on the deserted island is nullified, and it is decided that there will be a rematch.

However, at this new venue, the Japanese team—along with Pierrot, who decided to do the judging on-site—are plummeted into a horrifically deep cave that appears to be impossible to escape from.

Despite this desperate situation, and with a little bit of Pierrot's trickery, Azuma and his team complete the bread for their assignment. Moreover, with the help of Pharaoh, who has been monitoring the tournament for cheating, they are able to safely escape the cave. This time, Pantasia really clinches its advancement to the semifinals.

Azuma and his partners look forward to their next battle with renewed vigor, but they also become concerned about the actions of St. Pierre's owner, Kirisaki, the man who may have driven the tournament steering committee chairman to commit suicide after he failed to crush Team Japan!!

CONTENTS

Research Assistance/Bakery Consultant:
Koichi Uchimura.

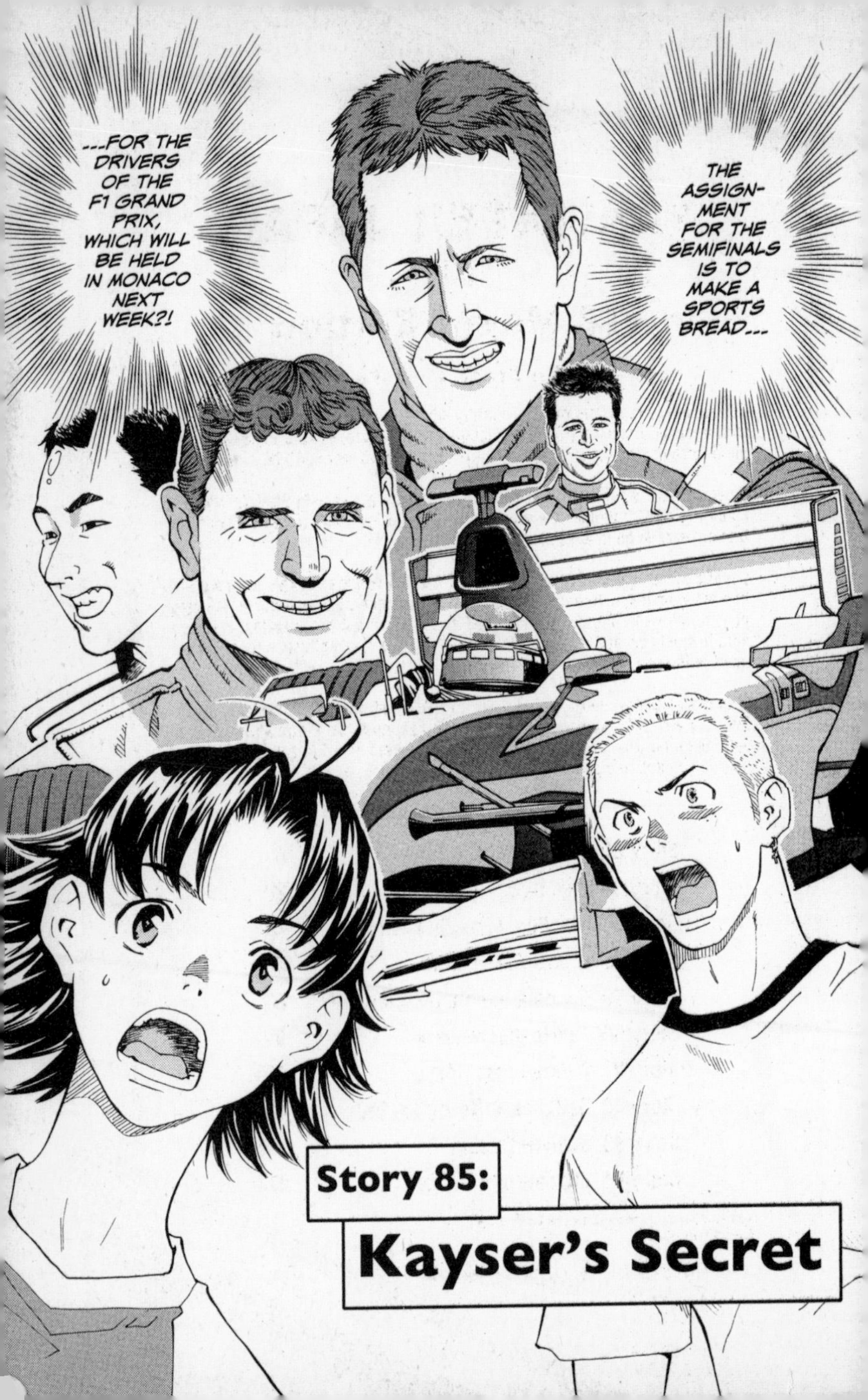
THE ASSIGNMENT FOR THE SEMIFINALS IS TO MAKE A SPORTS BREAD...
...FOR THE DRIVERS OF THE F1 GRAND PRIX, WHICH WILL BE HELD IN MONACO NEXT WEEK?!
Story 85:
Kayser's Secret

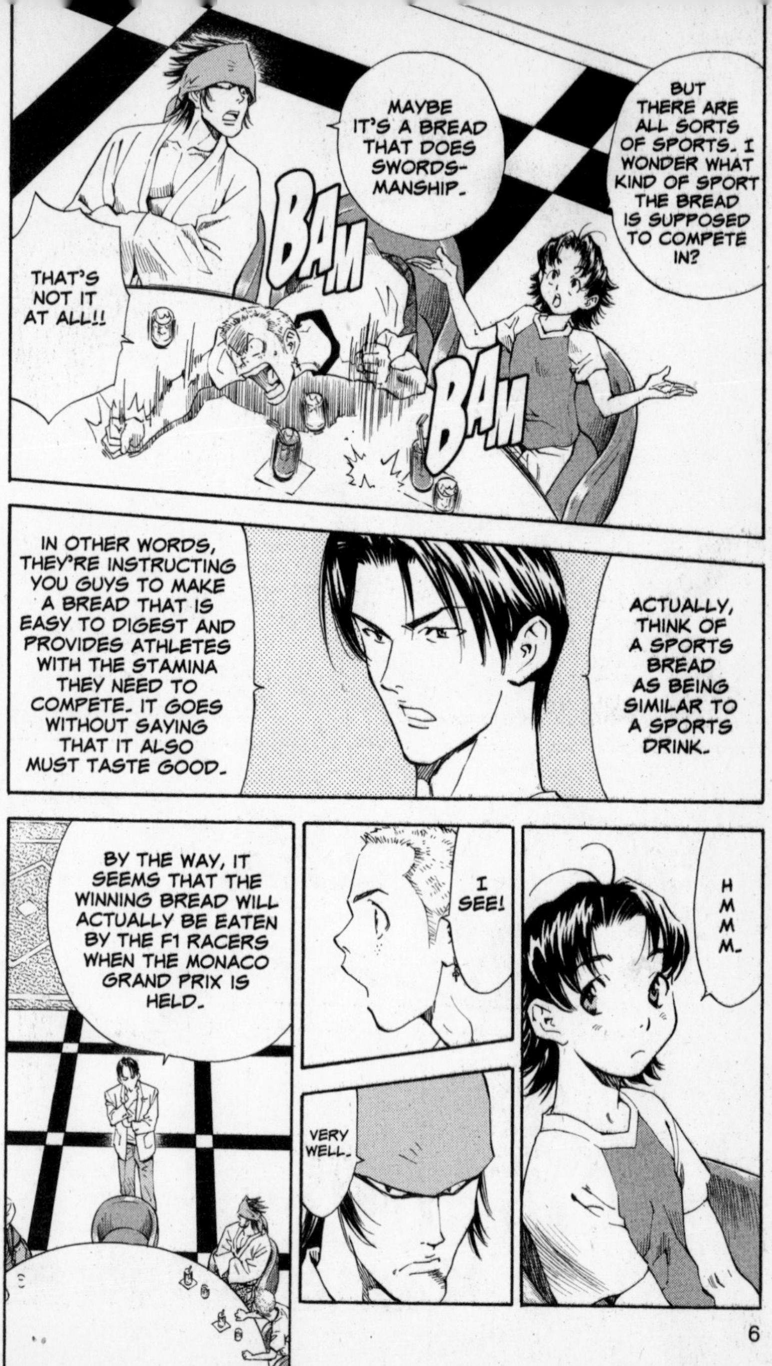
BUT THERE ARE ALL SORTS OF SPORTS. I WONDER WHAT KIND OF SPORT THE BREAD IS SUPPOSED TO COMPETE IN?
MAYBE IT'S A BREAD THAT DOES SWORDS-MANSHIP.
BAM
BAM
THAT'S NOT IT AT ALL!!
ACTUALLY, THINK OF A SPORTS BREAD AS BEING SIMILAR TO A SPORTS DRINK.
IN OTHER WORDS, THEY'RE INSTRUCTING YOU GUYS TO MAKE A BREAD THAT IS EASY TO DIGEST AND PROVIDES ATHLETES WITH THE STAMINA THEY NEED TO COMPETE. IT GOES WITHOUT SAYING THAT IT ALSO MUST TASTE GOOD.
HMMM.
VERY WELL.
I SEE!
BY THE WAY, IT SEEMS THAT THE WINNING BREAD WILL ACTUALLY BE EATEN BY THE F1 RACERS WHEN THE MONACO GRAND PRIX IS HELD.

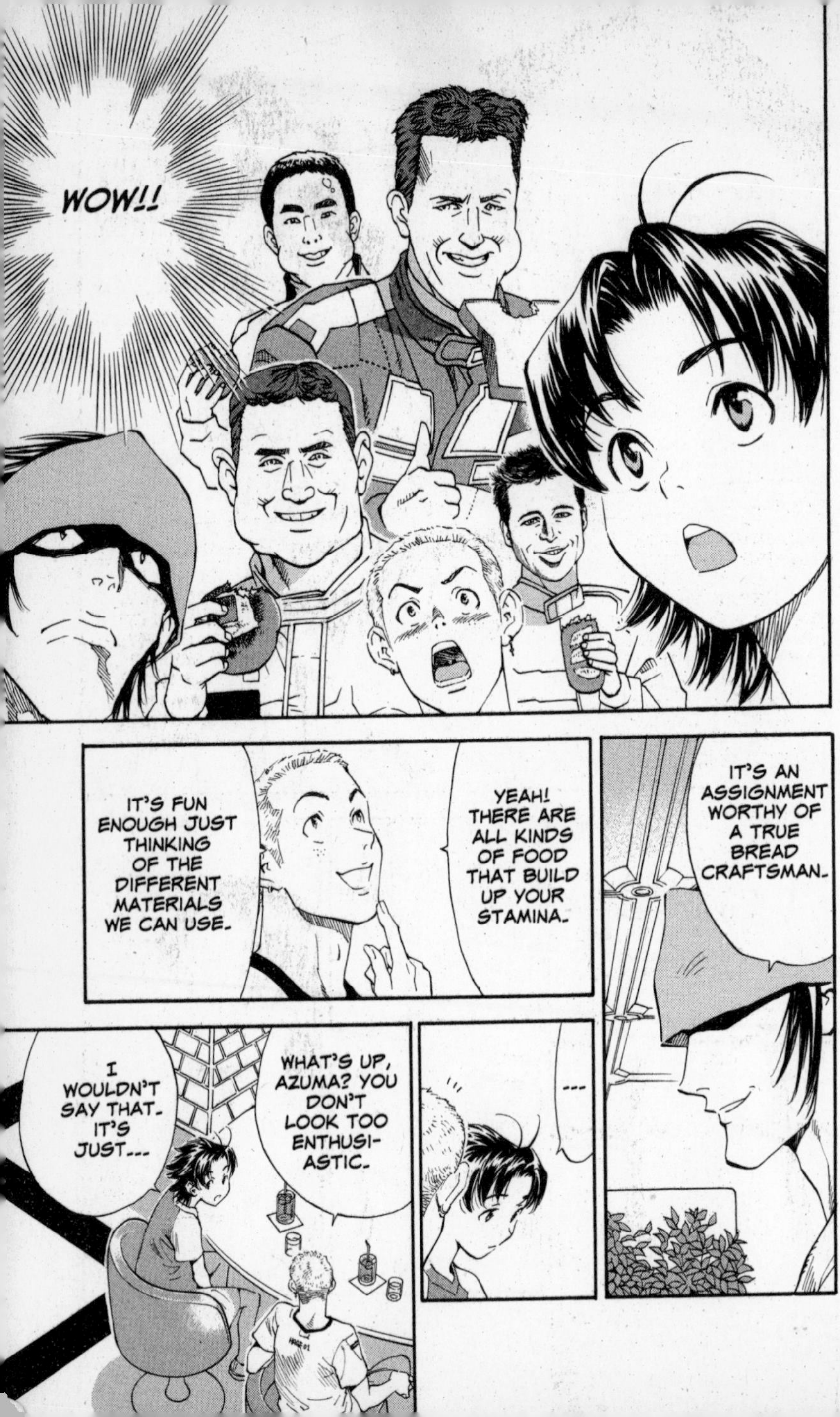
WOW!!
IT'S AN ASSIGNMENT WORTHY OF A TRUE BREAD CRAFTSMAN.
YEAH! THERE ARE ALL KINDS OF FOOD THAT BUILD UP YOUR STAMINA.
IT'S FUN ENOUGH JUST THINKING OF THE DIFFERENT MATERIALS WE CAN USE.
...
WHAT'S UP, AZUMA? YOU DON'T LOOK TOO ENTHUSI-ASTIC.
I WOULDN'T SAY THAT. IT'S JUST...

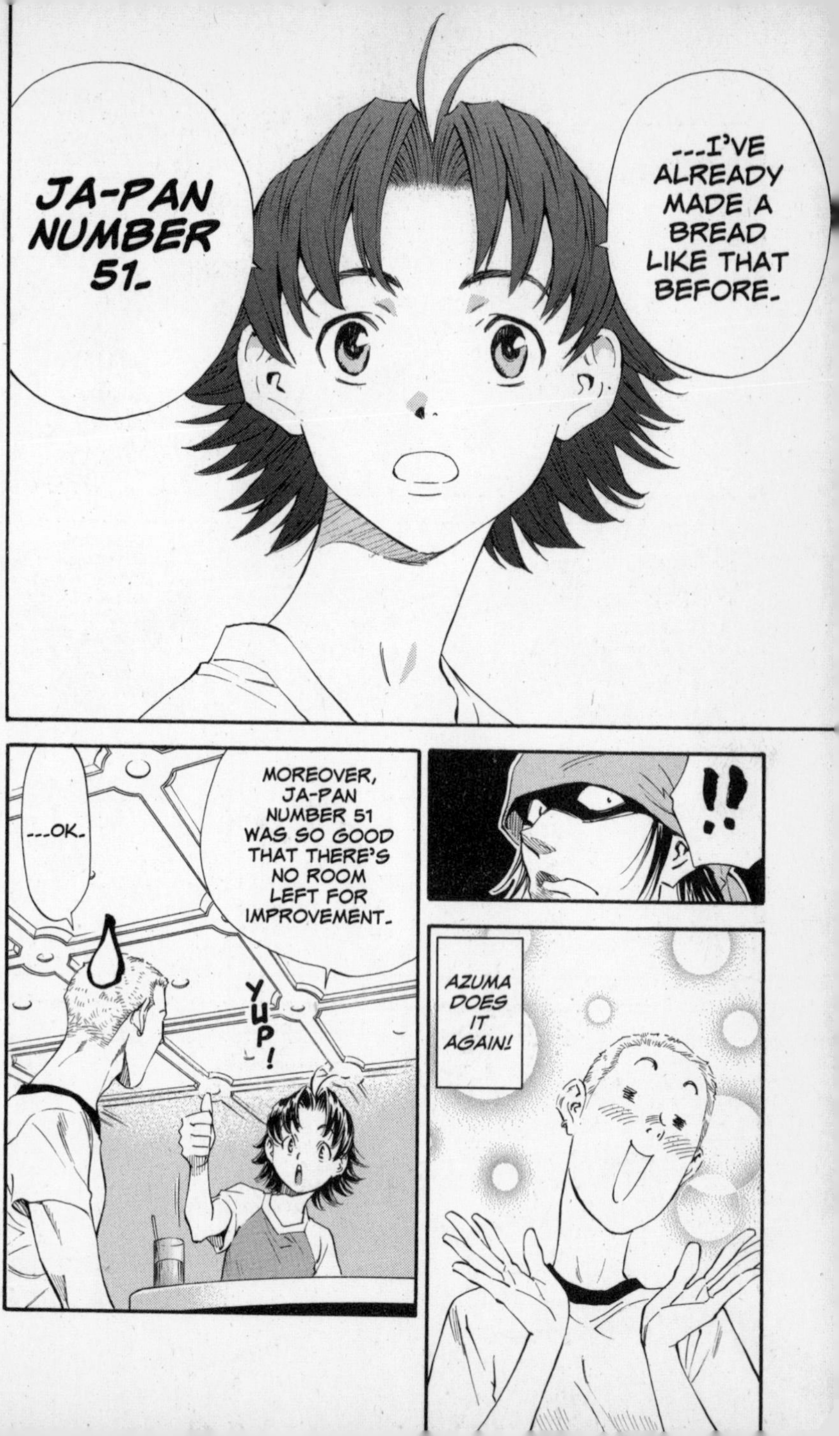
---I'VE ALREADY MADE A BREAD LIKE THAT BEFORE.
JA-PAN NUMBER 51.
!!
AZUMA DOES IT AGAIN!
MOREOVER, JA-PAN NUMBER 51 WAS SO GOOD THAT THERE'S NO ROOM LEFT FOR IMPROVEMENT.
YUP!
---OK.

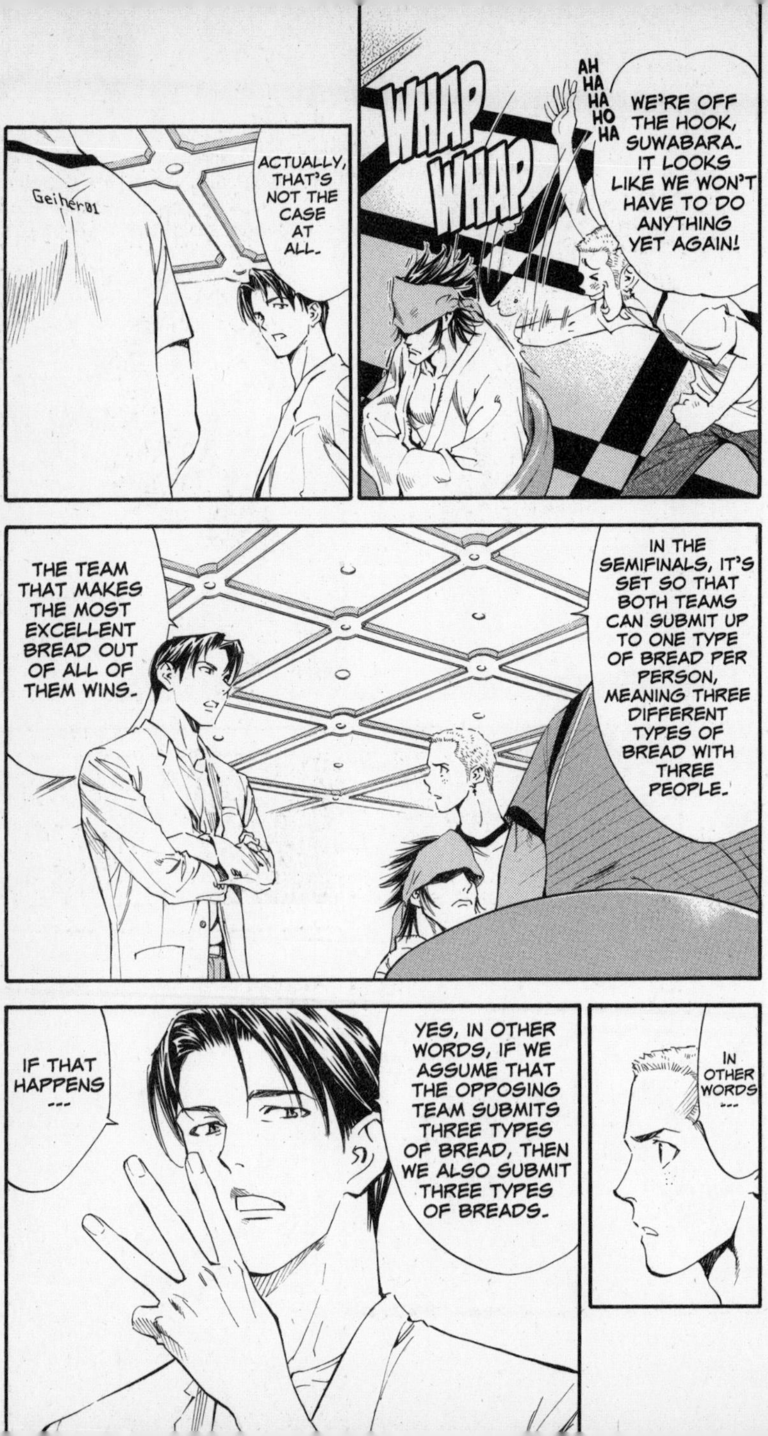
WE'RE OFF THE HOOK, SUWABARA. IT LOOKS LIKE WE WON'T HAVE TO DO ANYTHING YET AGAIN!
AH HA HA HO HA
WHAP WHAP
ACTUALLY, THAT'S NOT THE CASE AT ALL.
Geiher01
IN THE SEMIFINALS, IT'S SET SO THAT BOTH TEAMS CAN SUBMIT UP TO ONE TYPE OF BREAD PER PERSON, MEANING THREE DIFFERENT TYPES OF BREAD WITH THREE PEOPLE.
THE TEAM THAT MAKES THE MOST EXCELLENT BREAD OUT OF ALL OF THEM WINS.
IN OTHER WORDS ---
YES, IN OTHER WORDS, IF WE ASSUME THAT THE OPPOSING TEAM SUBMITS THREE TYPES OF BREAD, THEN WE ALSO SUBMIT THREE TYPES OF BREADS.
IF THAT HAPPENS ---

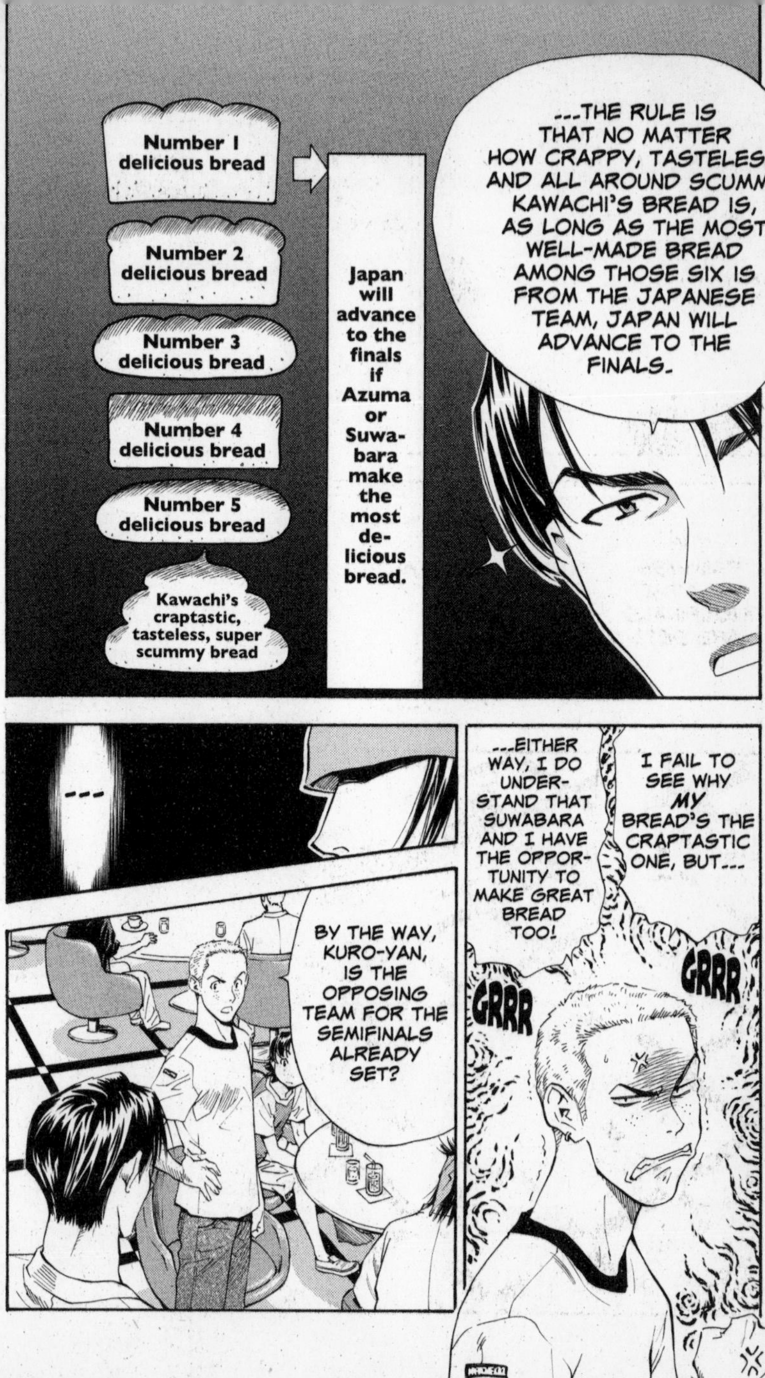
---THE RULE IS THAT NO MATTER HOW CRAPPY, TASTELESS AND ALL AROUND SCUMMY KAWACHI'S BREAD IS, AS LONG AS THE MOST WELL-MADE BREAD AMONG THOSE SIX IS FROM THE JAPANESE TEAM, JAPAN WILL ADVANCE TO THE FINALS.
Japan will advance to the finals if Azuma or Suwabara make the most delicious bread.
Number 1 delicious bread
Number 2 delicious bread
Number 3 delicious bread
Number 4 delicious bread
Number 5 delicious bread
Kawachi's craptastic, tasteless, super scummy bread
I FAIL TO SEE WHY *MY* BREAD'S THE CRAPTASTIC ONE, BUT---
---EITHER WAY, I DO UNDERSTAND THAT SUWABARA AND I HAVE THE OPPORTUNITY TO MAKE GREAT BREAD TOO!
GRRR
GRRR

BY THE WAY, KURO-YAN, IS THE OPPOSING TEAM FOR THE SEMIFINALS ALREADY SET?

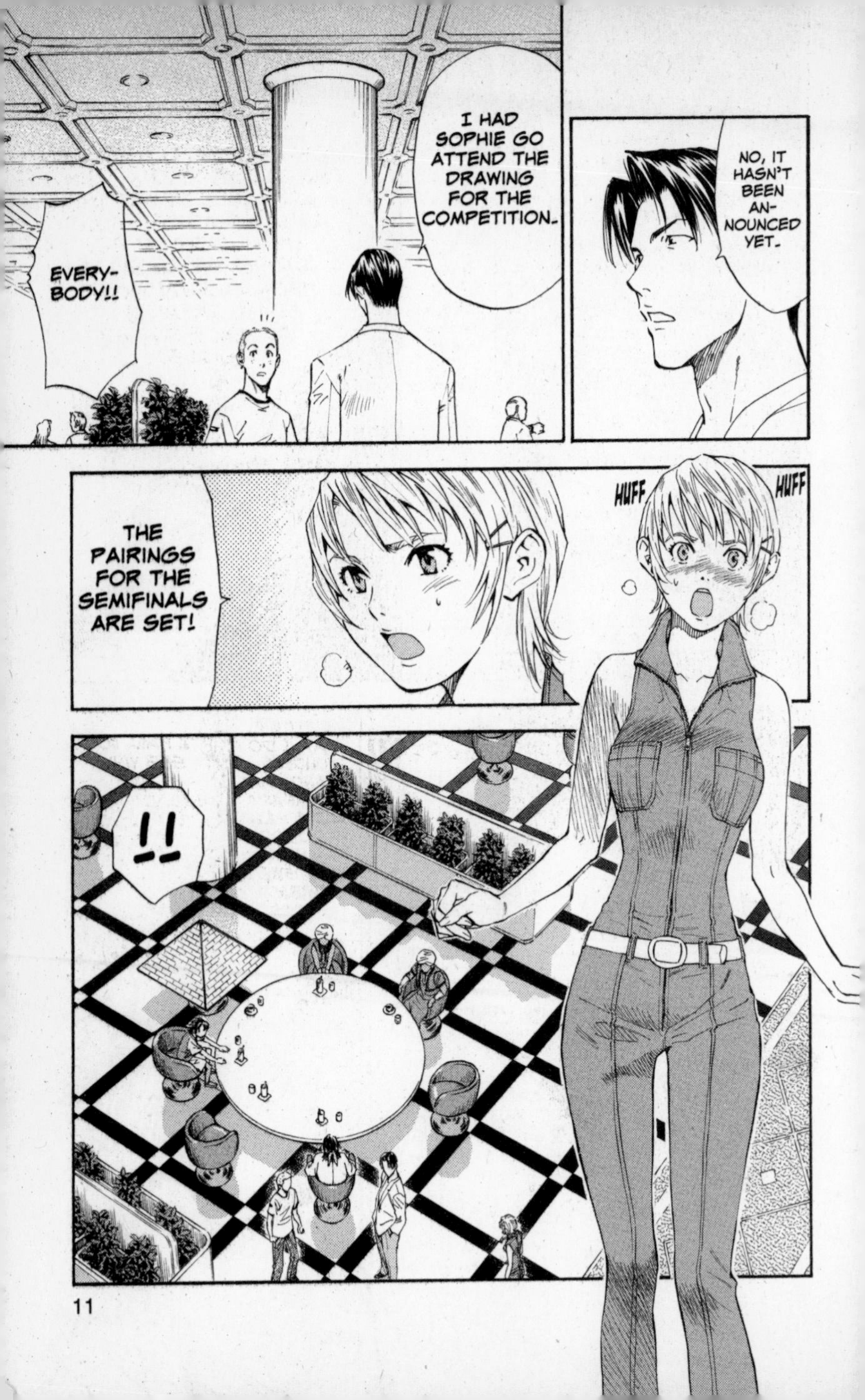
NO, IT HASN'T BEEN AN-NOUNCED YET.
I HAD SOPHIE GO ATTEND THE DRAWING FOR THE COMPETITION.
EVERY-BODY!!
HUFF
HUFF
THE PAIRINGS FOR THE SEMIFINALS ARE SET!
!!

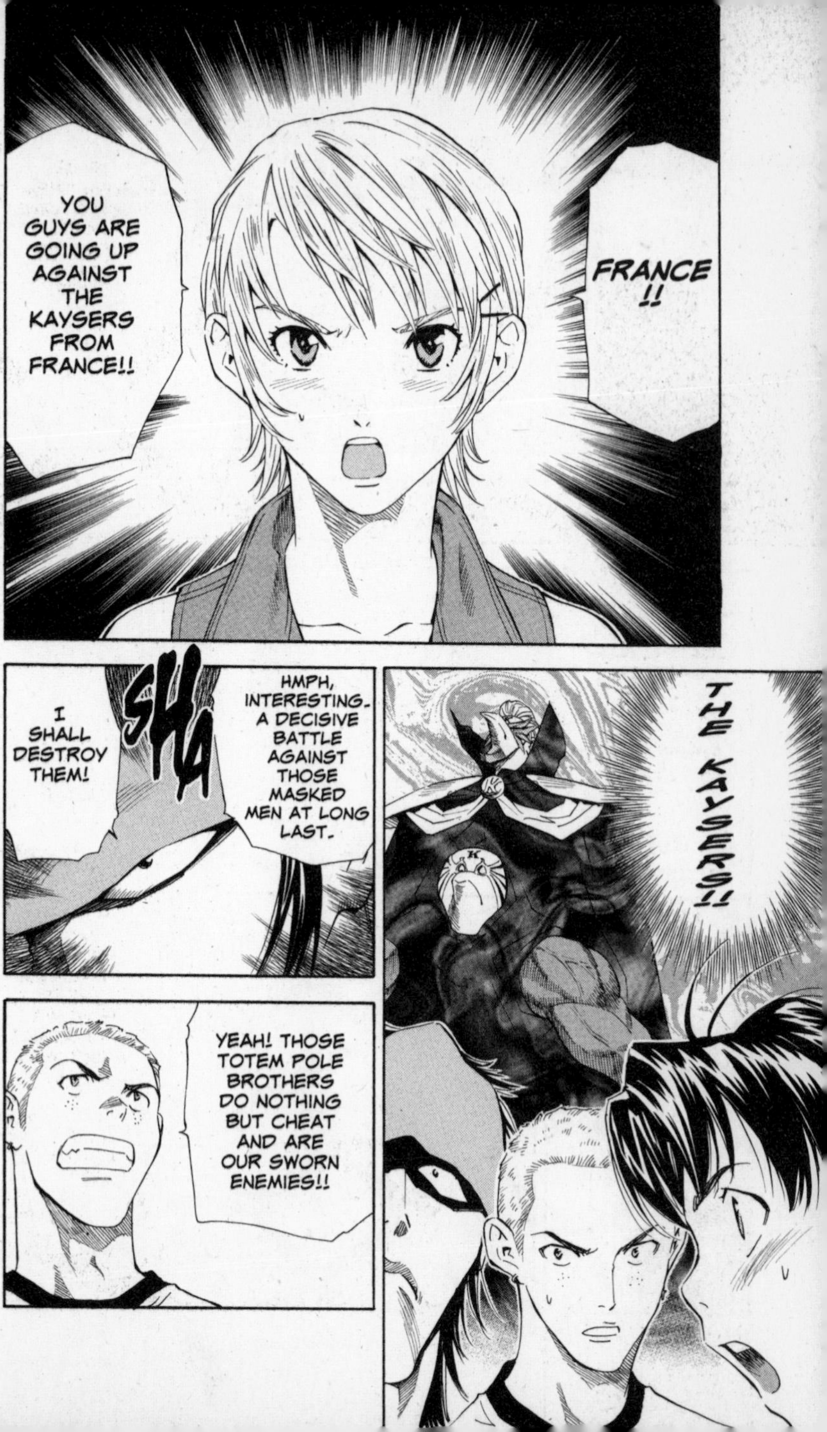
FRANCE!!
YOU GUYS ARE GOING UP AGAINST THE KAYSERS FROM FRANCE!!
THE KAYSERS!!
HMPH, INTERESTING... A DECISIVE BATTLE AGAINST THOSE MASKED MEN AT LONG LAST...
SHA
I SHALL DESTROY THEM!
YEAH! THOSE TOTEM POLE BROTHERS DO NOTHING BUT CHEAT AND ARE OUR SWORN ENEMIES!!

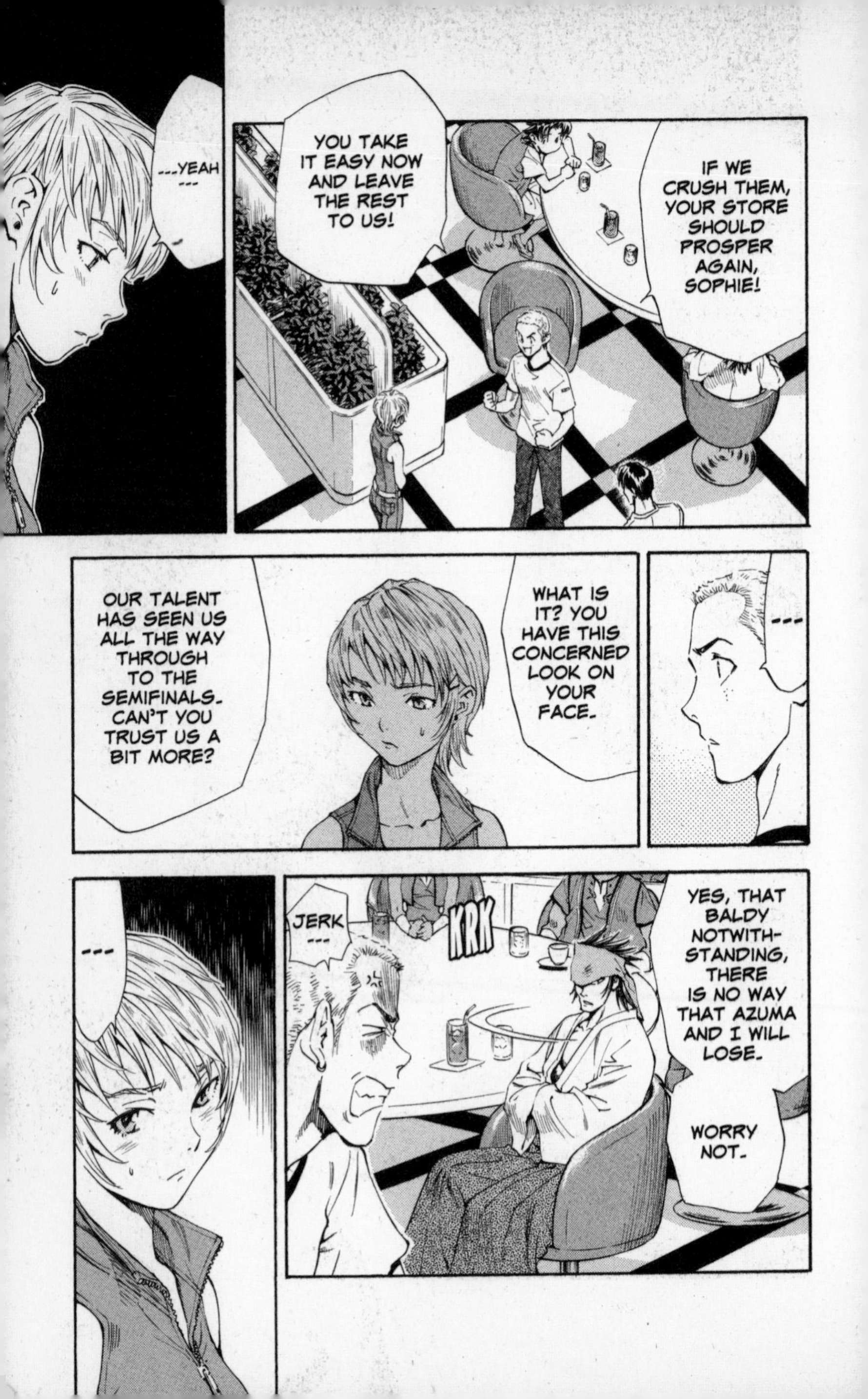
IF WE CRUSH THEM, YOUR STORE SHOULD PROSPER AGAIN, SOPHIE!
YOU TAKE IT EASY NOW AND LEAVE THE REST TO US!
---YEAH---

WHAT IS IT? YOU HAVE THIS CONCERNED LOOK ON YOUR FACE.
OUR TALENT HAS SEEN US ALL THE WAY THROUGH TO THE SEMIFINALS. CAN'T YOU TRUST US A BIT MORE?
YES, THAT BALDY NOTWITH-STANDING, THERE IS NO WAY THAT AZUMA AND I WILL LOSE.
WORRY NOT.
KRK
JERK---

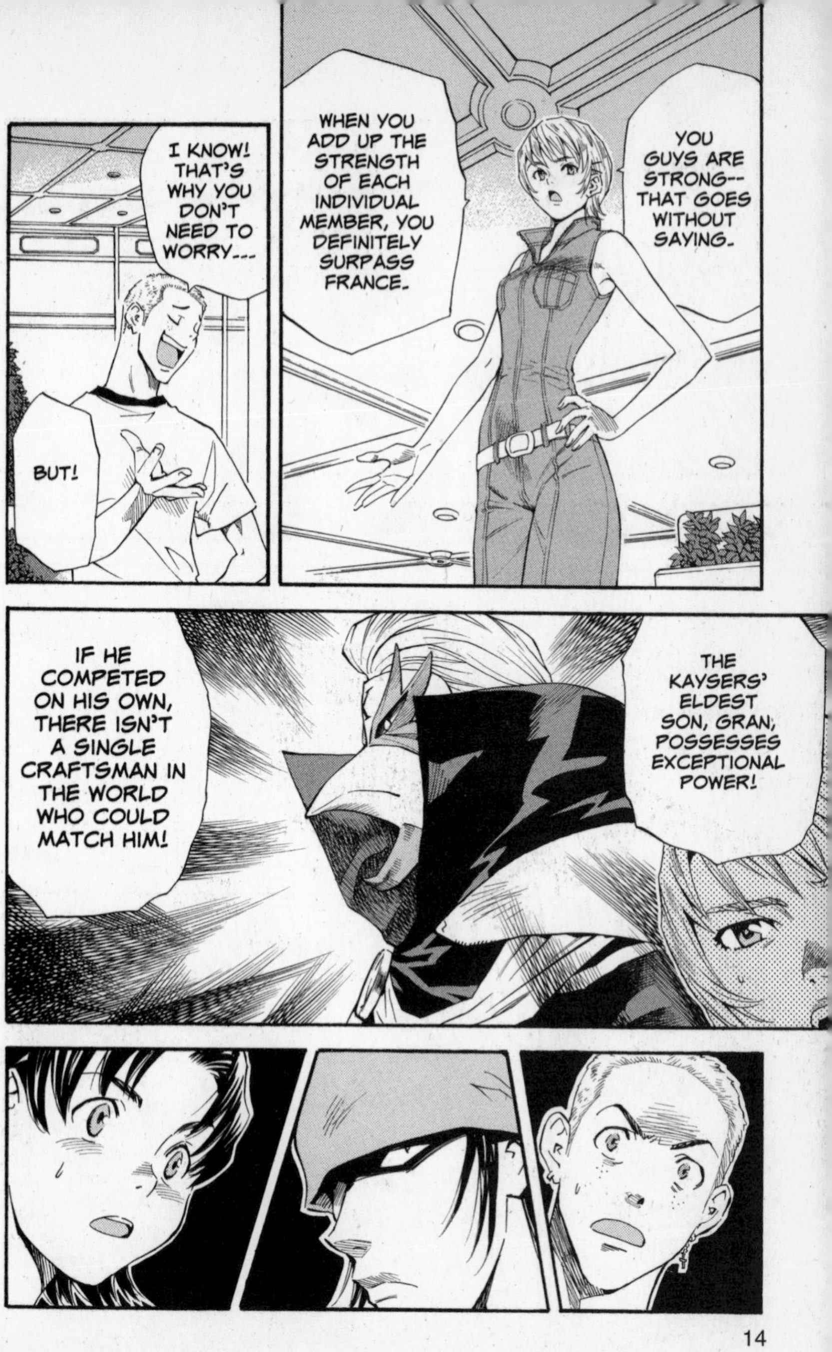
YOU GUYS ARE STRONG--THAT GOES WITHOUT SAYING.
WHEN YOU ADD UP THE STRENGTH OF EACH INDIVIDUAL MEMBER, YOU DEFINITELY SURPASS FRANCE.
I KNOW! THAT'S WHY YOU DON'T NEED TO WORRY...
BUT!
THE KAYSERS' ELDEST SON, GRAN, POSSESSES EXCEPTIONAL POWER!
IF HE COMPETED ON HIS OWN, THERE ISN'T A SINGLE CRAFTSMAN IN THE WORLD WHO COULD MATCH HIM!

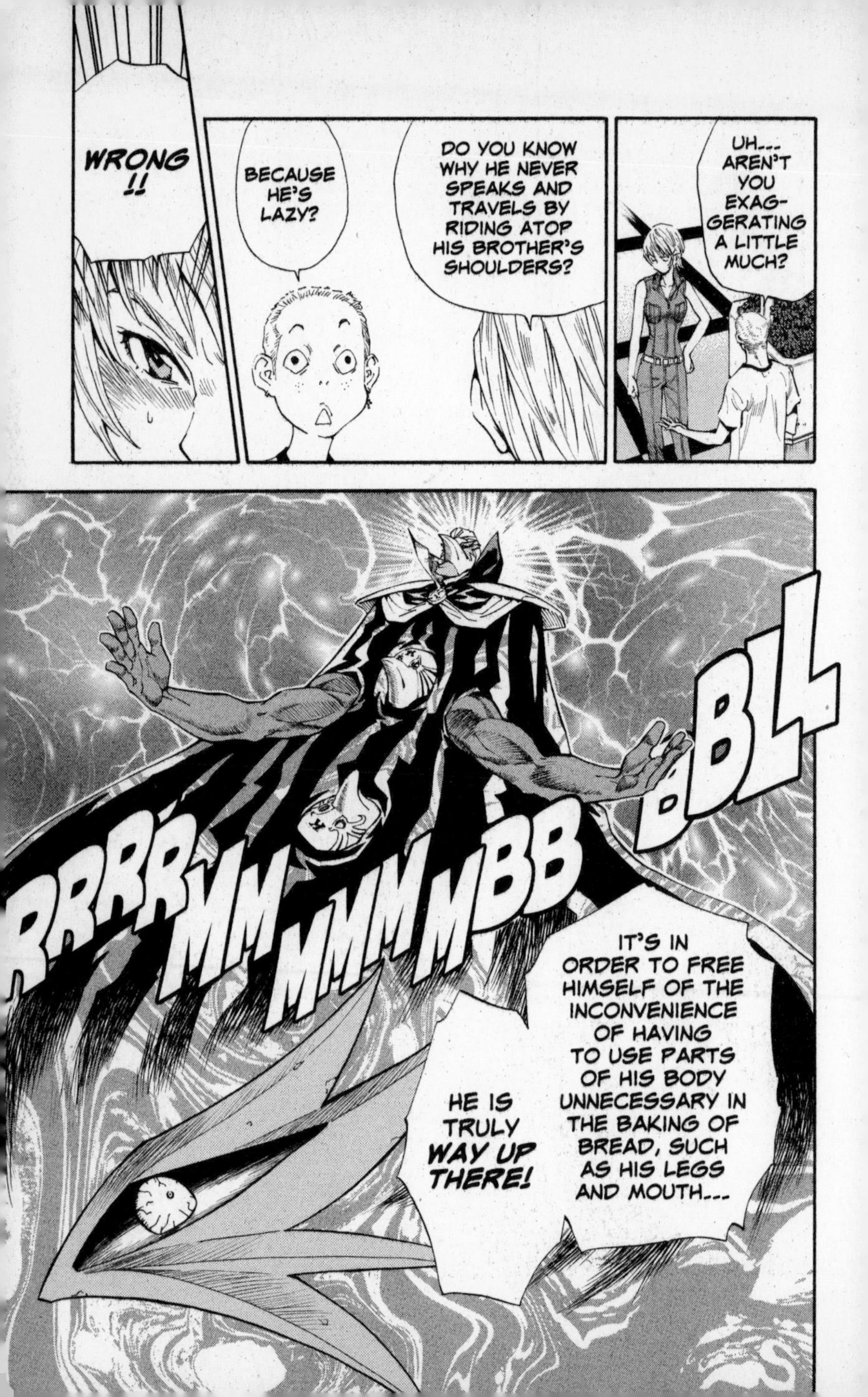
UH... AREN'T YOU EXAG-GERATING A LITTLE MUCH?
DO YOU KNOW WHY HE NEVER SPEAKS AND TRAVELS BY RIDING ATOP HIS BROTHER'S SHOULDERS?
BECAUSE HE'S LAZY?
WRONG !!
BBLL
RRRRMM MMMMBB
IT'S IN ORDER TO FREE HIMSELF OF THE INCONVENIENCE OF HAVING TO USE PARTS OF HIS BODY UNNECESSARY IN THE BAKING OF BREAD, SUCH AS HIS LEGS AND MOUTH...
HE IS TRULY WAY UP THERE!

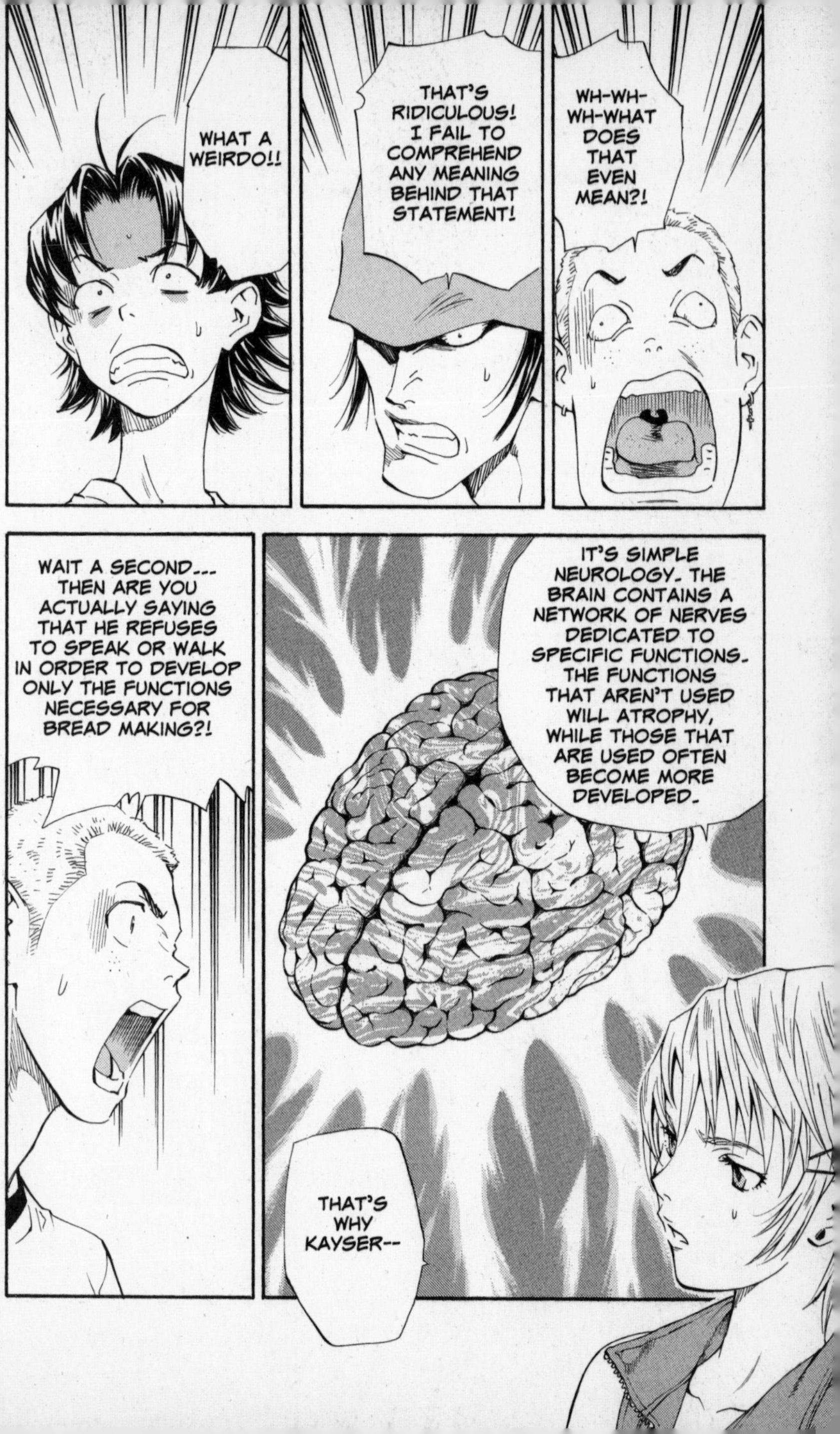
WH-WH-WH-WHAT DOES THAT EVEN MEAN?!
THAT'S RIDICULOUS! I FAIL TO COMPREHEND ANY MEANING BEHIND THAT STATEMENT!
WHAT A WEIRDO!!
IT'S SIMPLE NEUROLOGY. THE BRAIN CONTAINS A NETWORK OF NERVES DEDICATED TO SPECIFIC FUNCTIONS. THE FUNCTIONS THAT AREN'T USED WILL ATROPHY, WHILE THOSE THAT ARE USED OFTEN BECOME MORE DEVELOPED.
THAT'S WHY KAYSER--
WAIT A SECOND... THEN ARE YOU ACTUALLY SAYING THAT HE REFUSES TO SPEAK OR WALK IN ORDER TO DEVELOP ONLY THE FUNCTIONS NECESSARY FOR BREAD MAKING?!

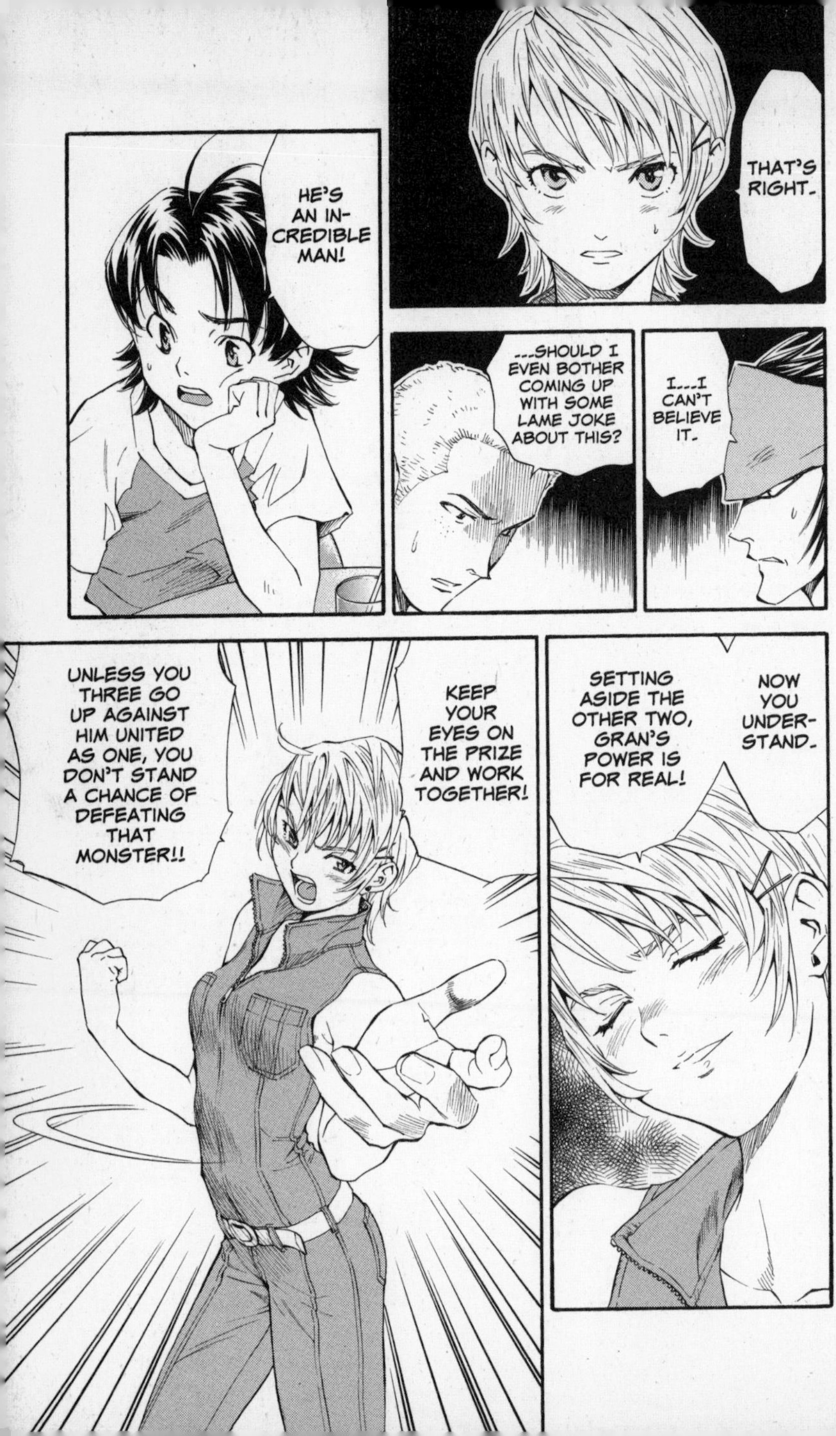
THAT'S RIGHT.
HE'S AN IN-CREDIBLE MAN!
I...I CAN'T BELIEVE IT.
...SHOULD I EVEN BOTHER COMING UP WITH SOME LAME JOKE ABOUT THIS?
NOW YOU UNDER-STAND.
SETTING ASIDE THE OTHER TWO, GRAN'S POWER IS FOR REAL!
KEEP YOUR EYES ON THE PRIZE AND WORK TOGETHER!
UNLESS YOU THREE GO UP AGAINST HIM UNITED AS ONE, YOU DON'T STAND A CHANCE OF DEFEATING THAT MONSTER!!

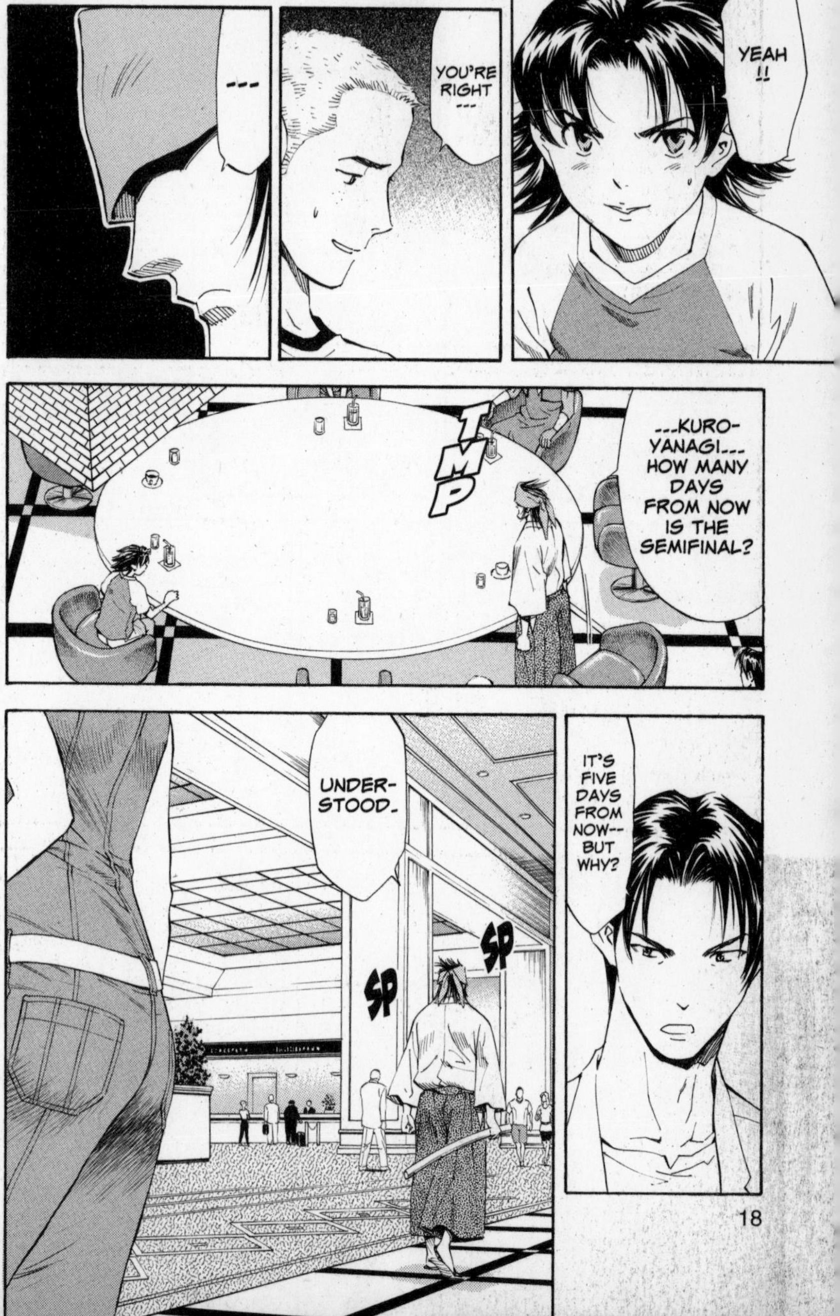
YEAH !!
YOU'RE RIGHT ...
...
...KURO-YANAGI... HOW MANY DAYS FROM NOW IS THE SEMIFINAL?
TMP
IT'S FIVE DAYS FROM NOW-- BUT WHY?
UNDER-STOOD.
SP
SP

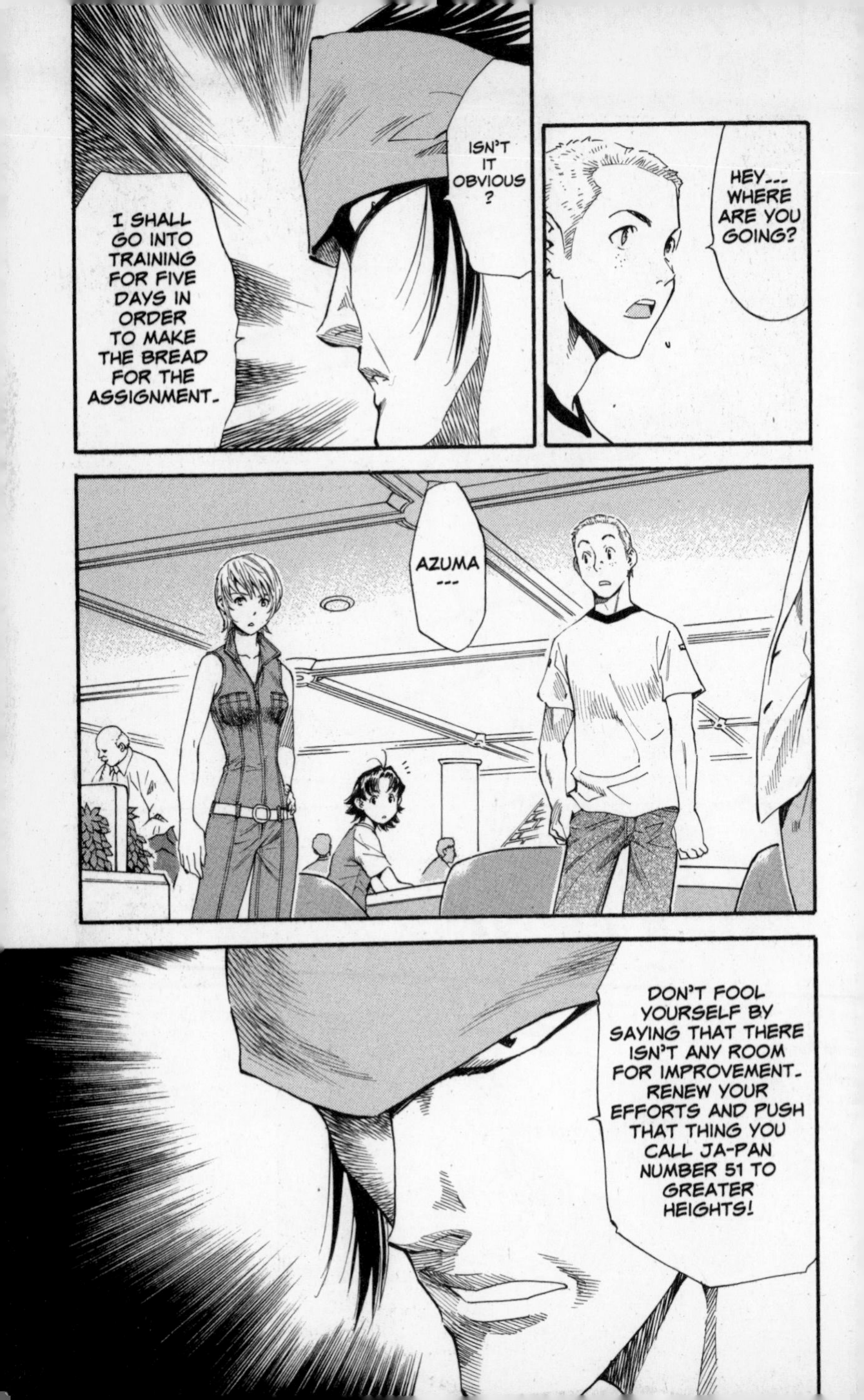
HEY... WHERE ARE YOU GOING?
ISN'T IT OBVIOUS?
I SHALL GO INTO TRAINING FOR FIVE DAYS IN ORDER TO MAKE THE BREAD FOR THE ASSIGNMENT.
AZUMA...
DON'T FOOL YOURSELF BY SAYING THAT THERE ISN'T ANY ROOM FOR IMPROVEMENT. RENEW YOUR EFFORTS AND PUSH THAT THING YOU CALL JA-PAN NUMBER 51 TO GREATER HEIGHTS!

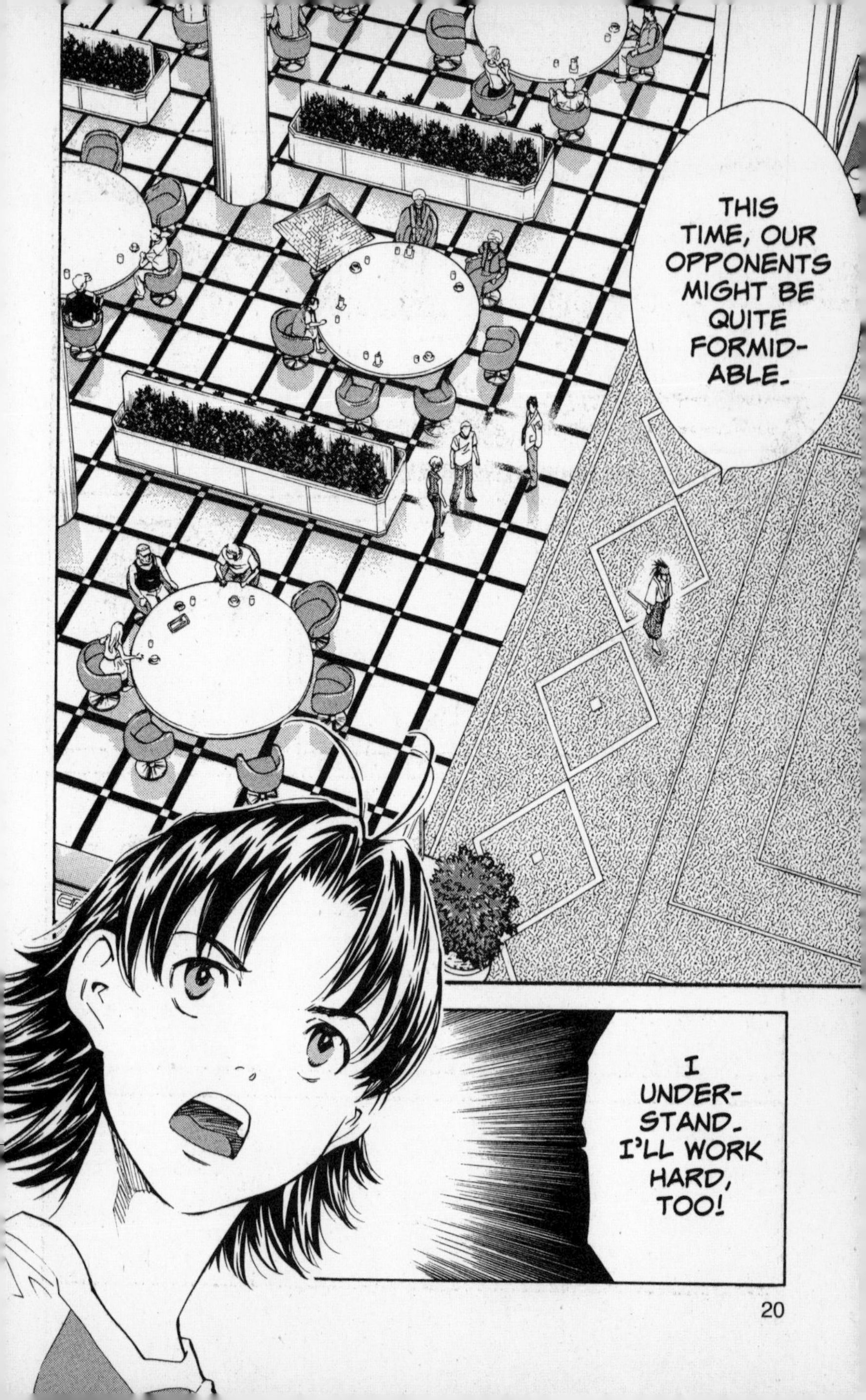
THIS TIME, OUR OPPONENTS MIGHT BE QUITE FORMIDABLE.
I UNDERSTAND. I'LL WORK HARD, TOO!

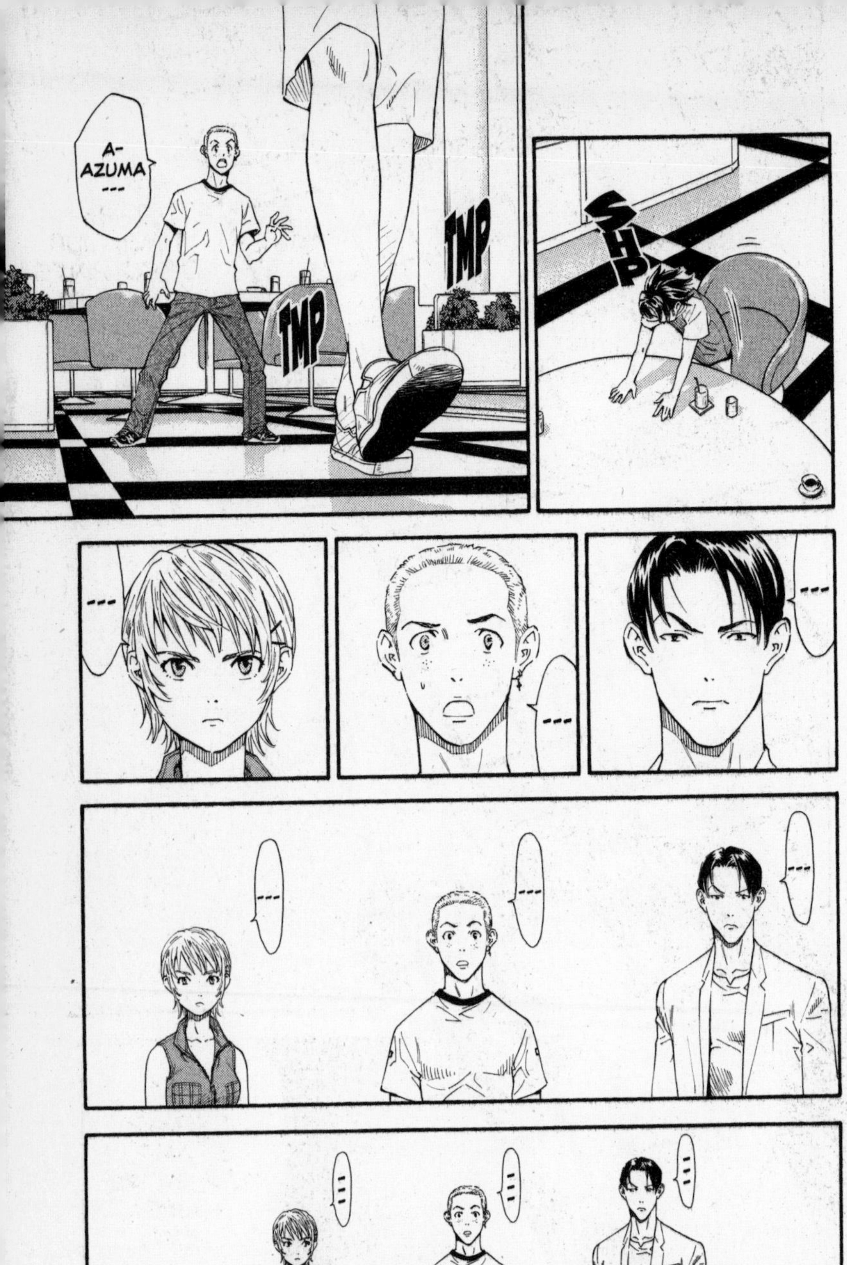
SHP
TMP
TMP
A-AZUMA---

...
...
...

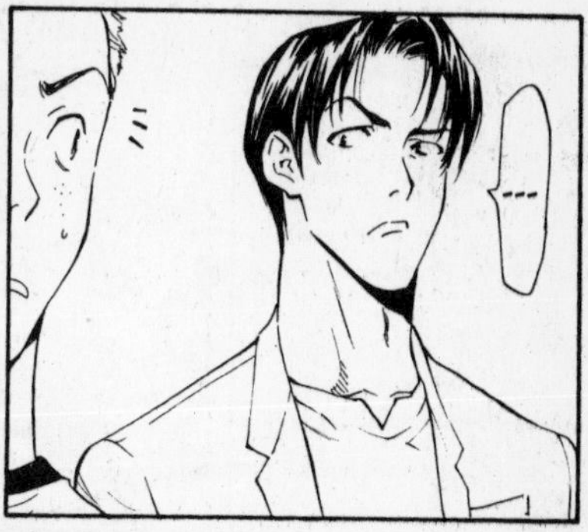
...

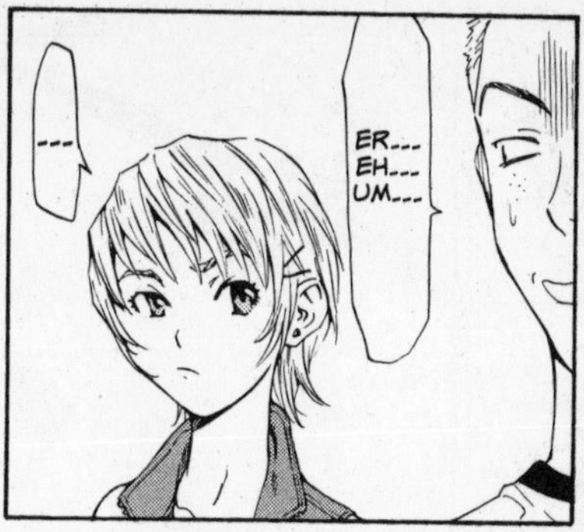
ER...
EH...
UM...
...

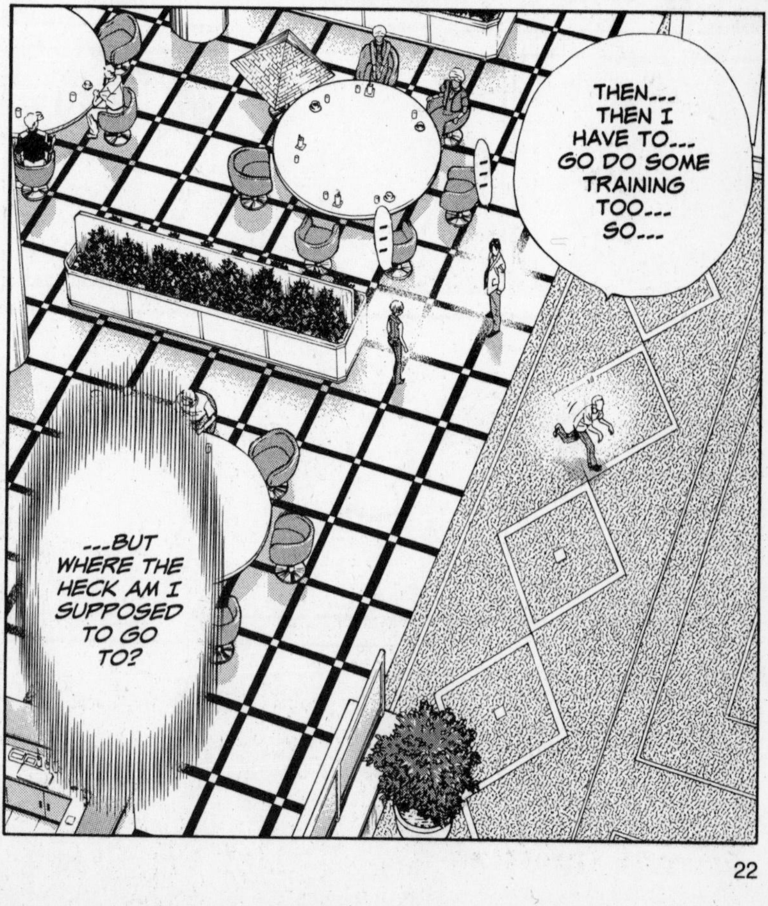
THEN... THEN I HAVE TO... GO DO SOME TRAINING TOO... SO...
...
...
...BUT WHERE THE HECK AM I SUPPOSED TO GO TO?

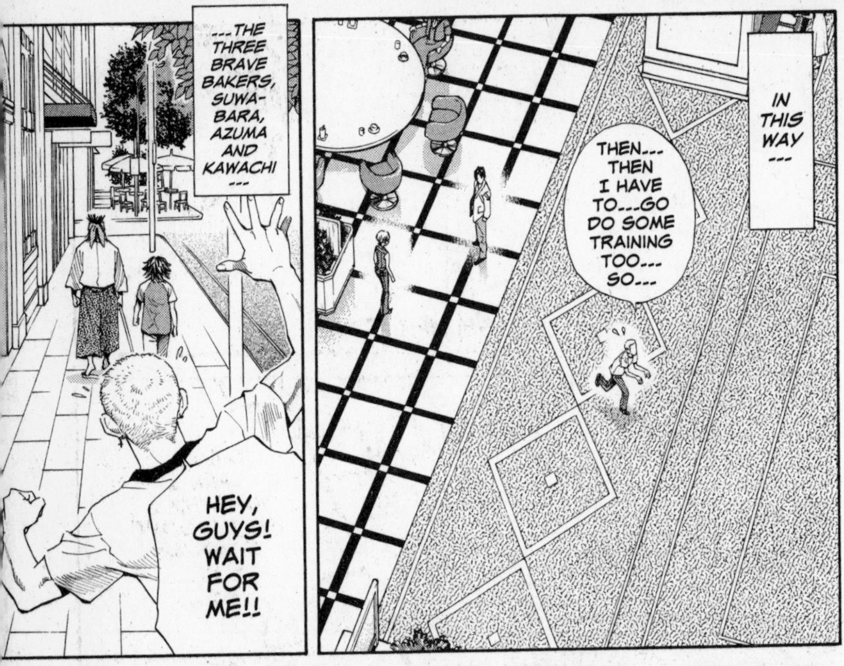
IN THIS WAY ---
THEN--- THEN I HAVE TO---GO DO SOME TRAINING TOO--- SO---
---THE THREE BRAVE BAKERS, SUWA-BARA, AZUMA AND KAWACHI ---
HEY, GUYS! WAIT FOR ME!!

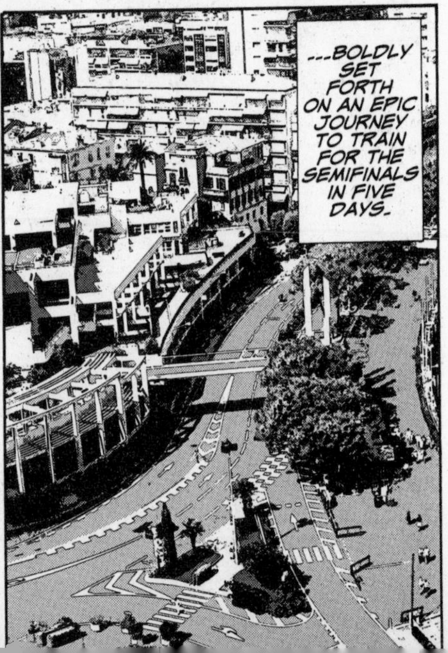
---BOLDLY SET FORTH ON AN EPIC JOURNEY TO TRAIN FOR THE SEMIFINALS IN FIVE DAYS.

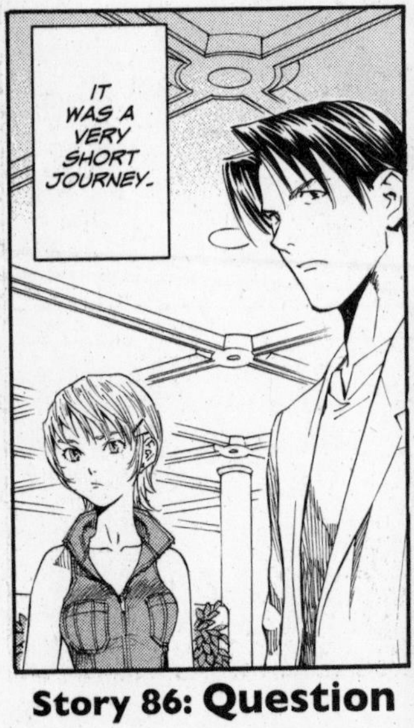
IT WAS A VERY SHORT JOURNEY.

Story 86: Question

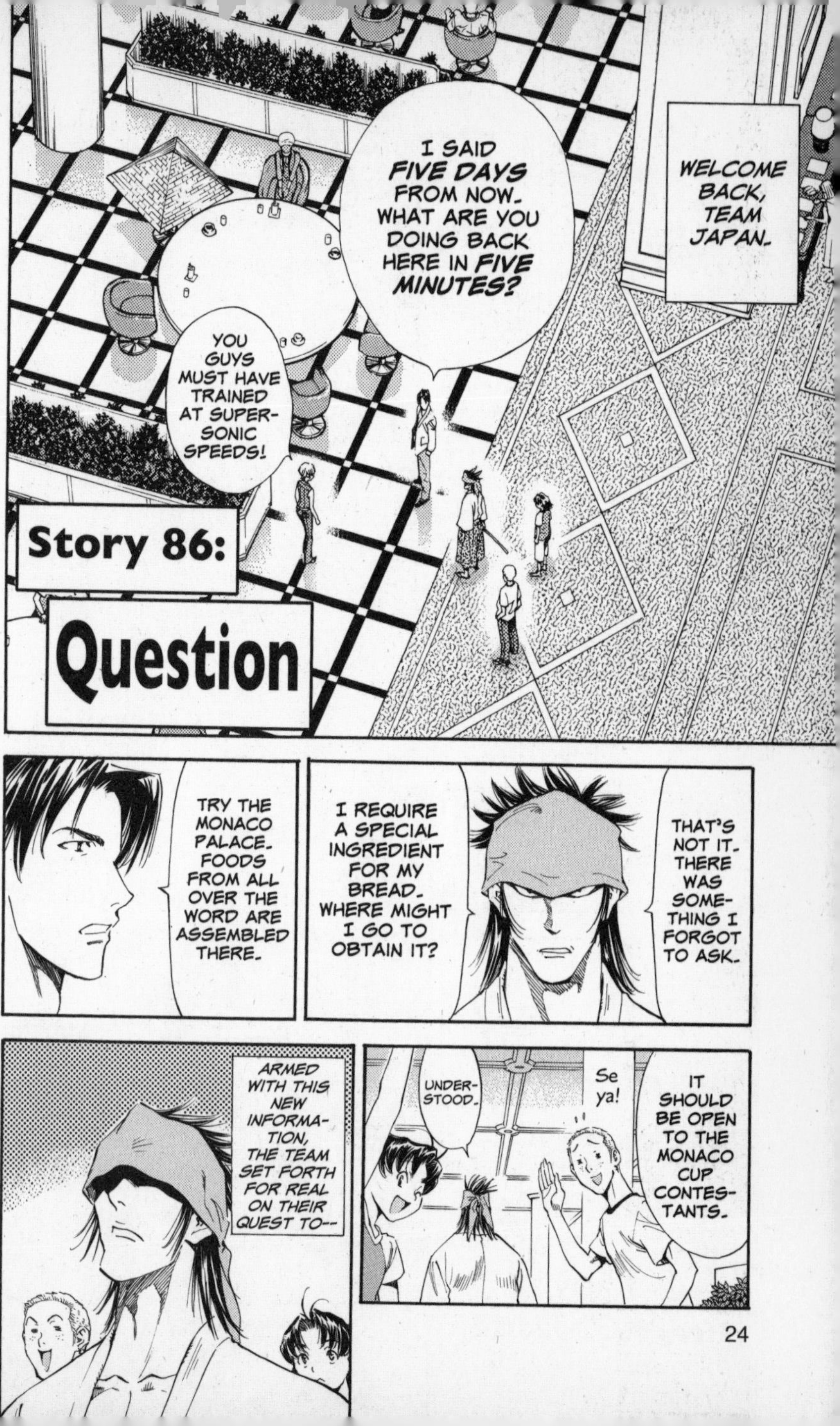
WELCOME BACK, TEAM JAPAN.
I SAID FIVE DAYS FROM NOW. WHAT ARE YOU DOING BACK HERE IN FIVE MINUTES?
YOU GUYS MUST HAVE TRAINED AT SUPER-SONIC SPEEDS!
Story 86:
Question
THAT'S NOT IT. THERE WAS SOME-THING I FORGOT TO ASK.
I REQUIRE A SPECIAL INGREDIENT FOR MY BREAD. WHERE MIGHT I GO TO OBTAIN IT?
TRY THE MONACO PALACE. FOODS FROM ALL OVER THE WORD ARE ASSEMBLED THERE.
IT SHOULD BE OPEN TO THE MONACO CUP CONTES-TANTS.
Se ya!
UNDER-STOOD.
ARMED WITH THIS NEW INFORMA-TION, THE TEAM SET FORTH FOR REAL ON THEIR QUEST TO--

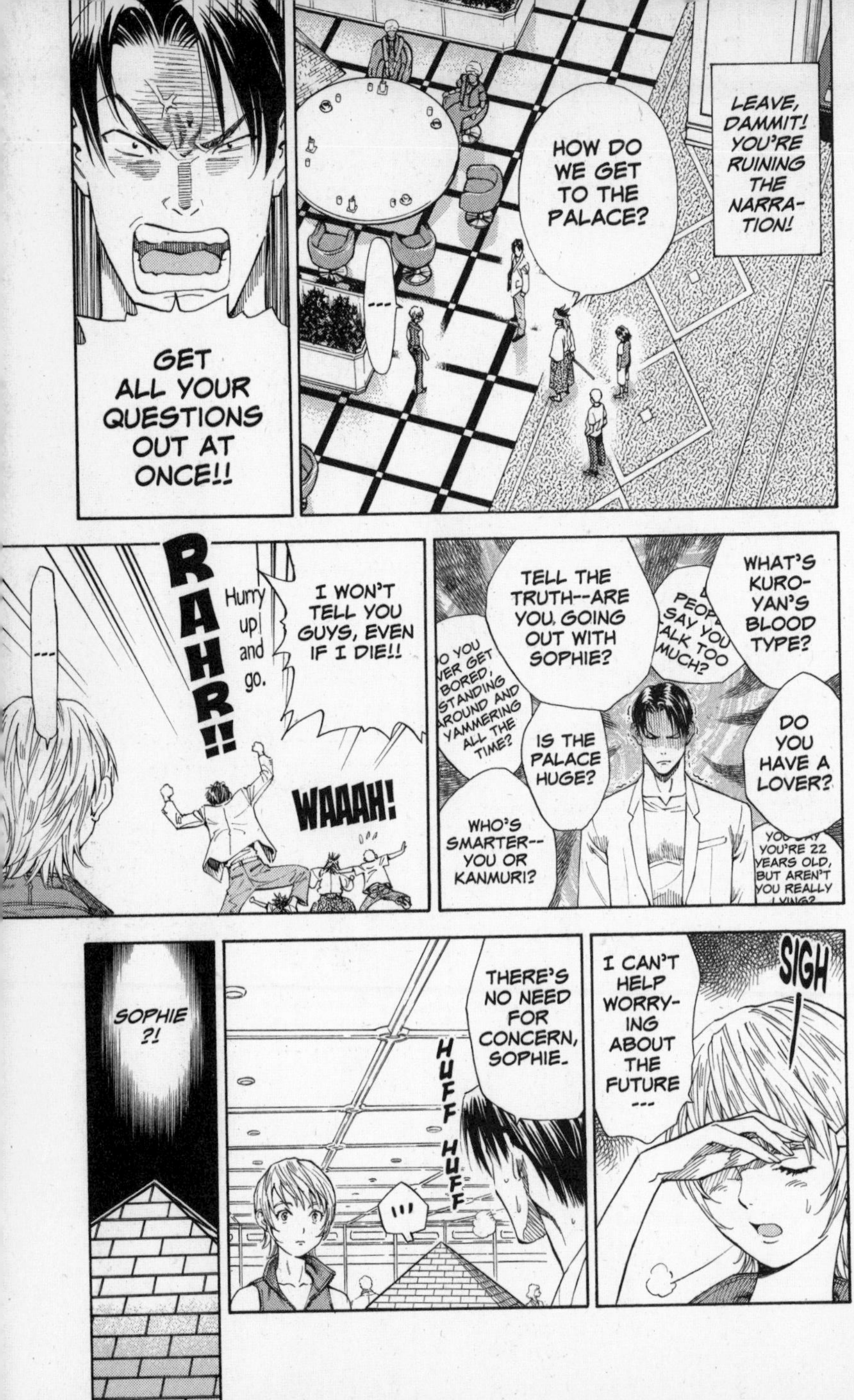
LEAVE, DAMMIT! YOU'RE RUINING THE NARRATION!
HOW DO WE GET TO THE PALACE?
...
GET ALL YOUR QUESTIONS OUT AT ONCE!!
WHAT'S KURO-YAN'S BLOOD TYPE?
DO YOU HAVE A LOVER?
YOU'RE 22 YEARS OLD, BUT AREN'T YOU REALLY
SAY YOU TALK TOO MUCH?
TELL THE TRUTH--ARE YOU GOING OUT WITH SOPHIE?
IS THE PALACE HUGE?
STANDING AROUND AND YAMMERING ALL THE TIME?
WHO'S SMARTER--YOU OR KANMURI?
I WON'T TELL YOU GUYS, EVEN IF I DIE!!
Hurry up! and go.
RAHR!!
WAAAH!
...
SIGH
I CAN'T HELP WORRYING ABOUT THE FUTURE...
THERE'S NO NEED FOR CONCERN, SOPHIE.
HUFF HUFF
!!
SOPHIE?!

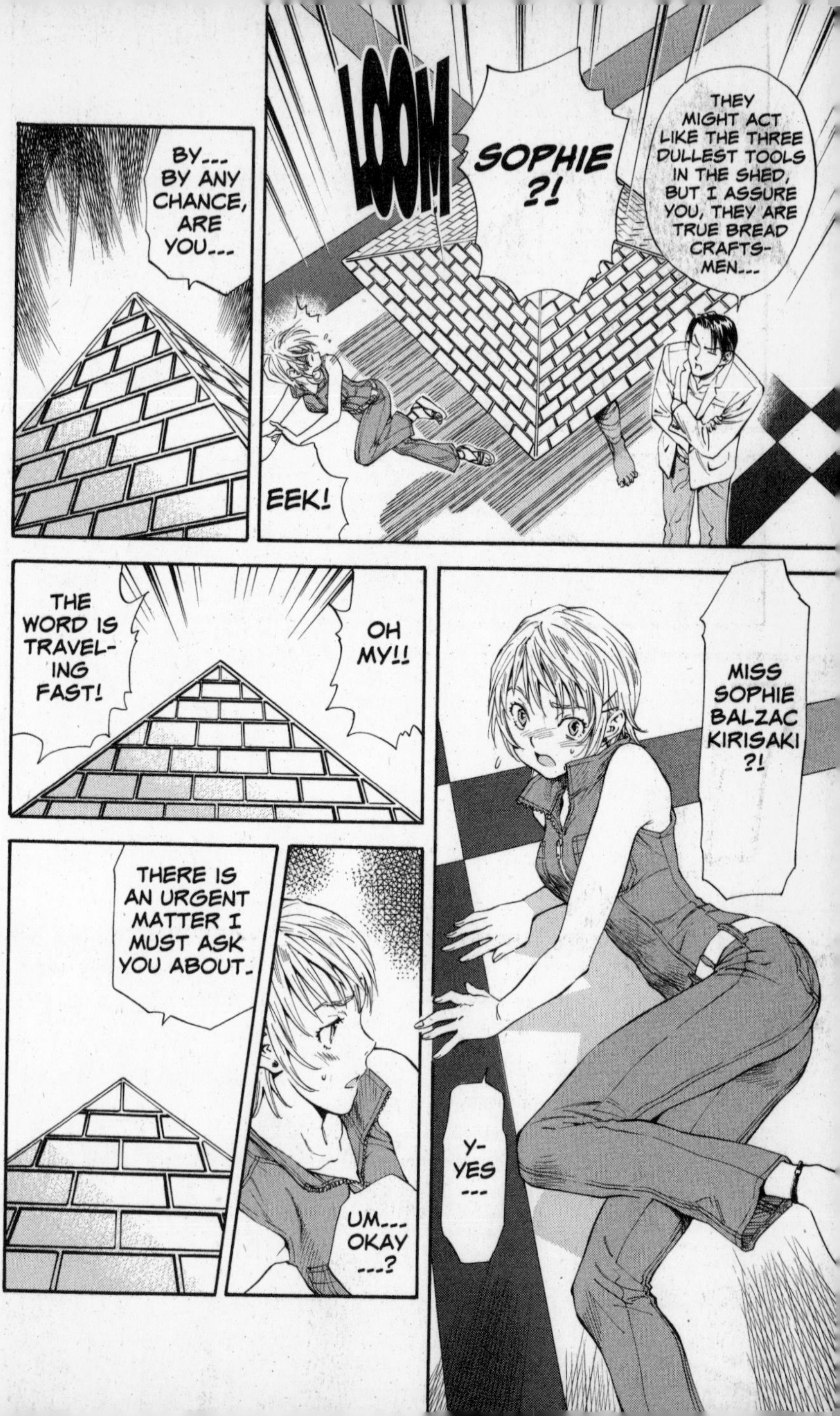
THEY MIGHT ACT LIKE THE THREE DULLEST TOOLS IN THE SHED, BUT I ASSURE YOU, THEY ARE TRUE BREAD CRAFTS-MEN...
SOPHIE ?!
LOOM
EEK!
BY... BY ANY CHANCE, ARE YOU...
MISS SOPHIE BALZAC KIRISAKI ?!
OH MY!!
THE WORD IS TRAVEL-ING FAST!
Y-YES ...
UM... OKAY ...?
THERE IS AN URGENT MATTER I MUST ASK YOU ABOUT.

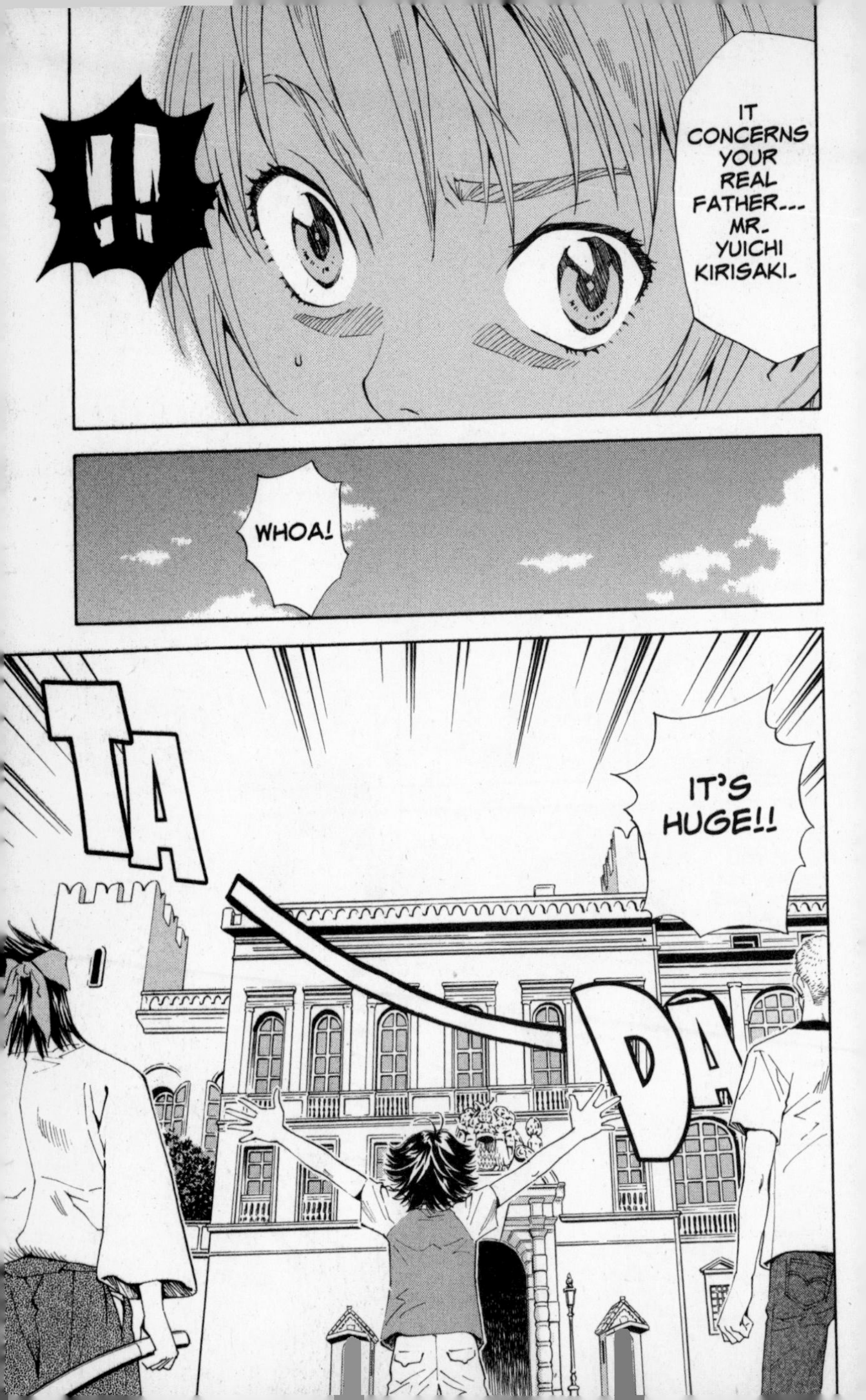
IT CONCERNS YOUR REAL FATHER... MR. YUICHI KIRISAKI.
!!
WHOA!
IT'S HUGE!!
TA
DA

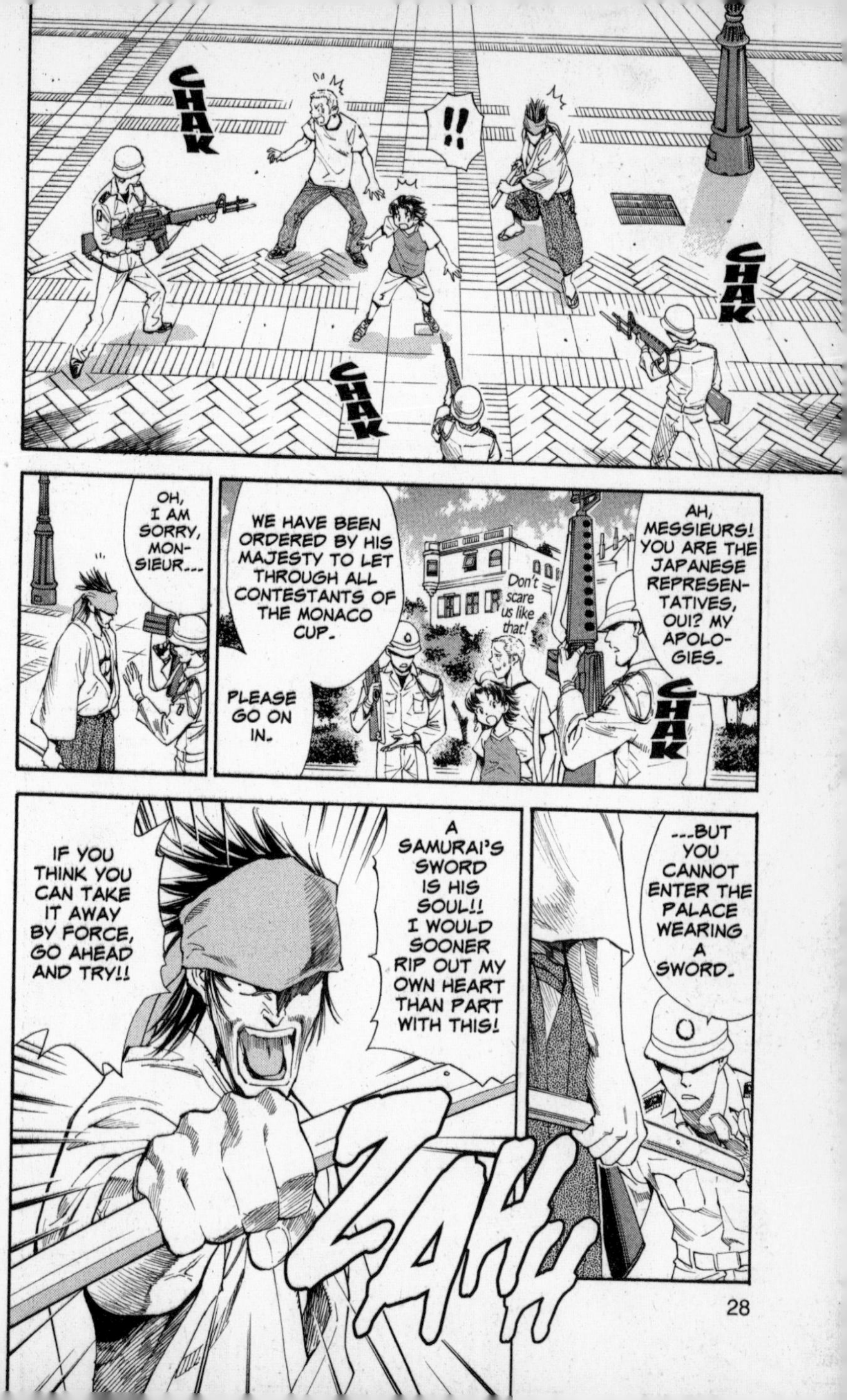
CHAK
!!
CHAK
CHAK
AH, MESSIEURS! YOU ARE THE JAPANESE REPRESEN-TATIVES, OUI? MY APOLO-GIES.
CHAK
Don't scare us like that!
WE HAVE BEEN ORDERED BY HIS MAJESTY TO LET THROUGH ALL CONTESTANTS OF THE MONACO CUP.
PLEASE GO ON IN.
OH, I AM SORRY, MON-SIEUR...
...BUT YOU CANNOT ENTER THE PALACE WEARING A SWORD.
A SAMURAI'S SWORD IS HIS SOUL!! I WOULD SOONER RIP OUT MY OWN HEART THAN PART WITH THIS!
IF YOU THINK YOU CAN TAKE IT AWAY BY FORCE, GO AHEAD AND TRY!!
ZAH

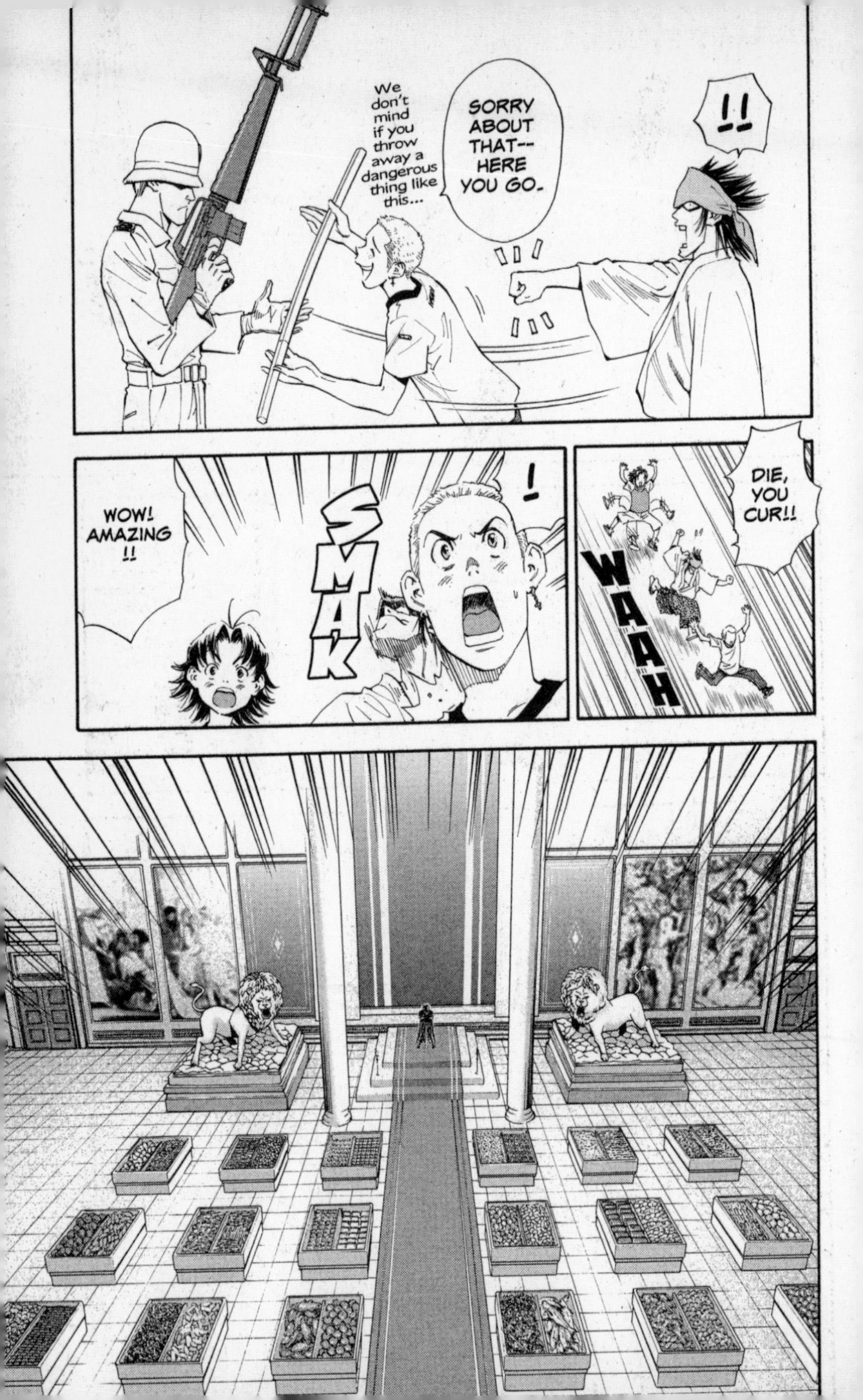
!!
SORRY ABOUT THAT-- HERE YOU GO.
We don't mind if you throw away a dangerous thing like this...
DIE, YOU CUR!!
WAAH
!
SMAK
WOW! AMAZING !!

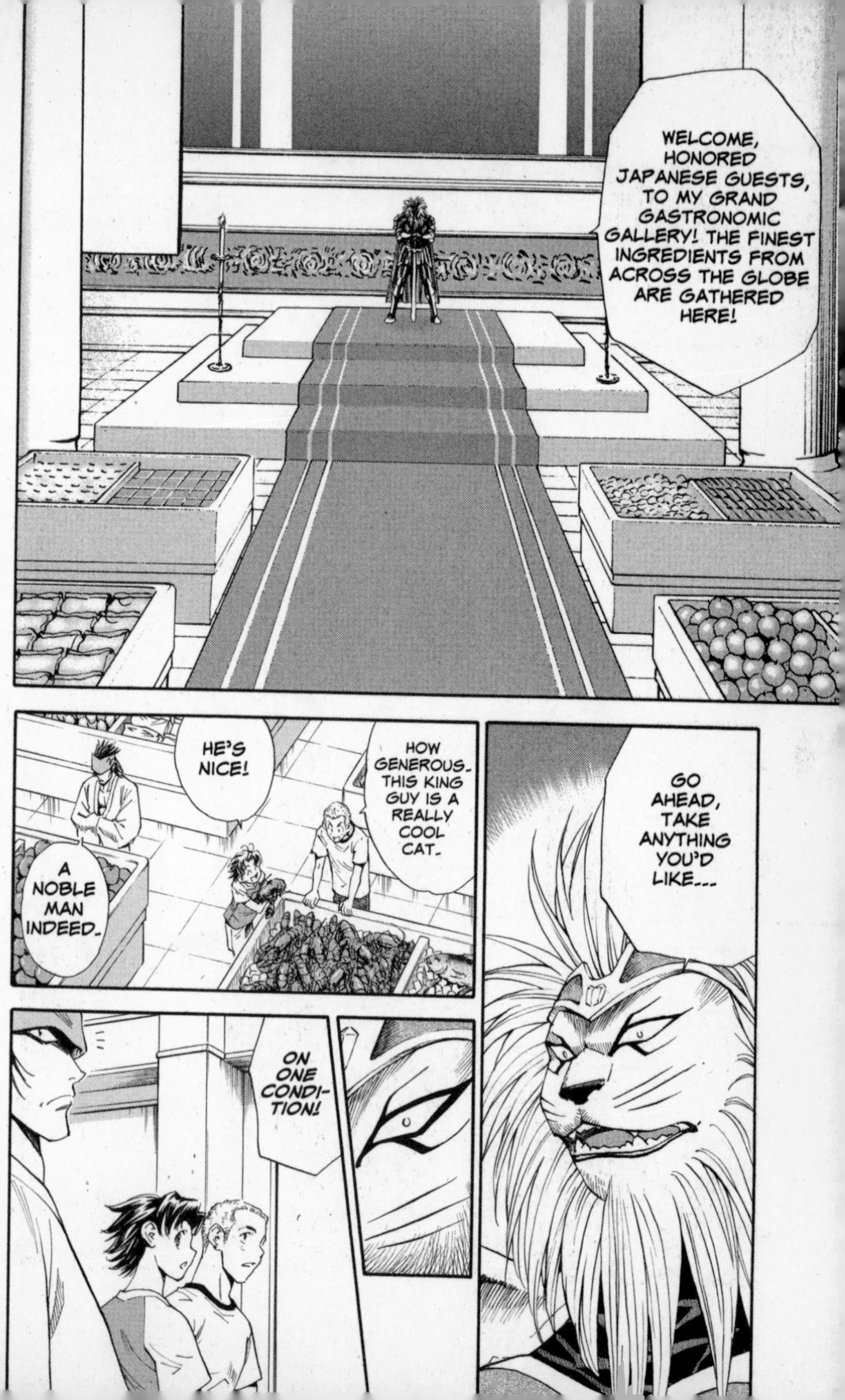
WELCOME, HONORED JAPANESE GUESTS, TO MY GRAND GASTRONOMIC GALLERY! THE FINEST INGREDIENTS FROM ACROSS THE GLOBE ARE GATHERED HERE!
GO AHEAD, TAKE ANYTHING YOU'D LIKE...
HOW GENEROUS. THIS KING GUY IS A REALLY COOL CAT.
HE'S NICE!
A NOBLE MAN INDEED.
ON ONE CONDITION!

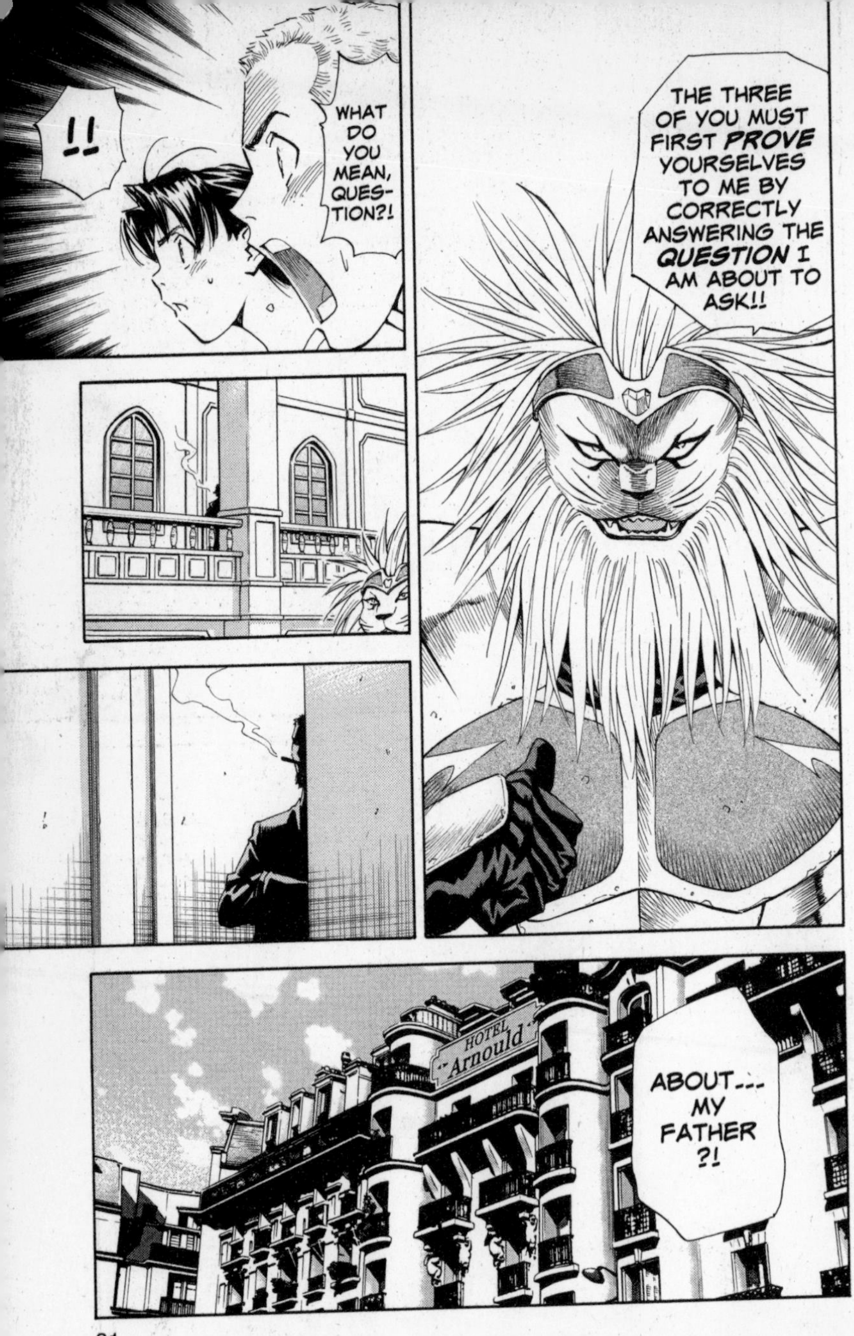
THE THREE OF YOU MUST FIRST PROVE YOURSELVES TO ME BY CORRECTLY ANSWERING THE QUESTION I AM ABOUT TO ASK!!
WHAT DO YOU MEAN, QUES-TION?!
!!
HOTEL "Arnould"
ABOUT--- MY FATHER ?!

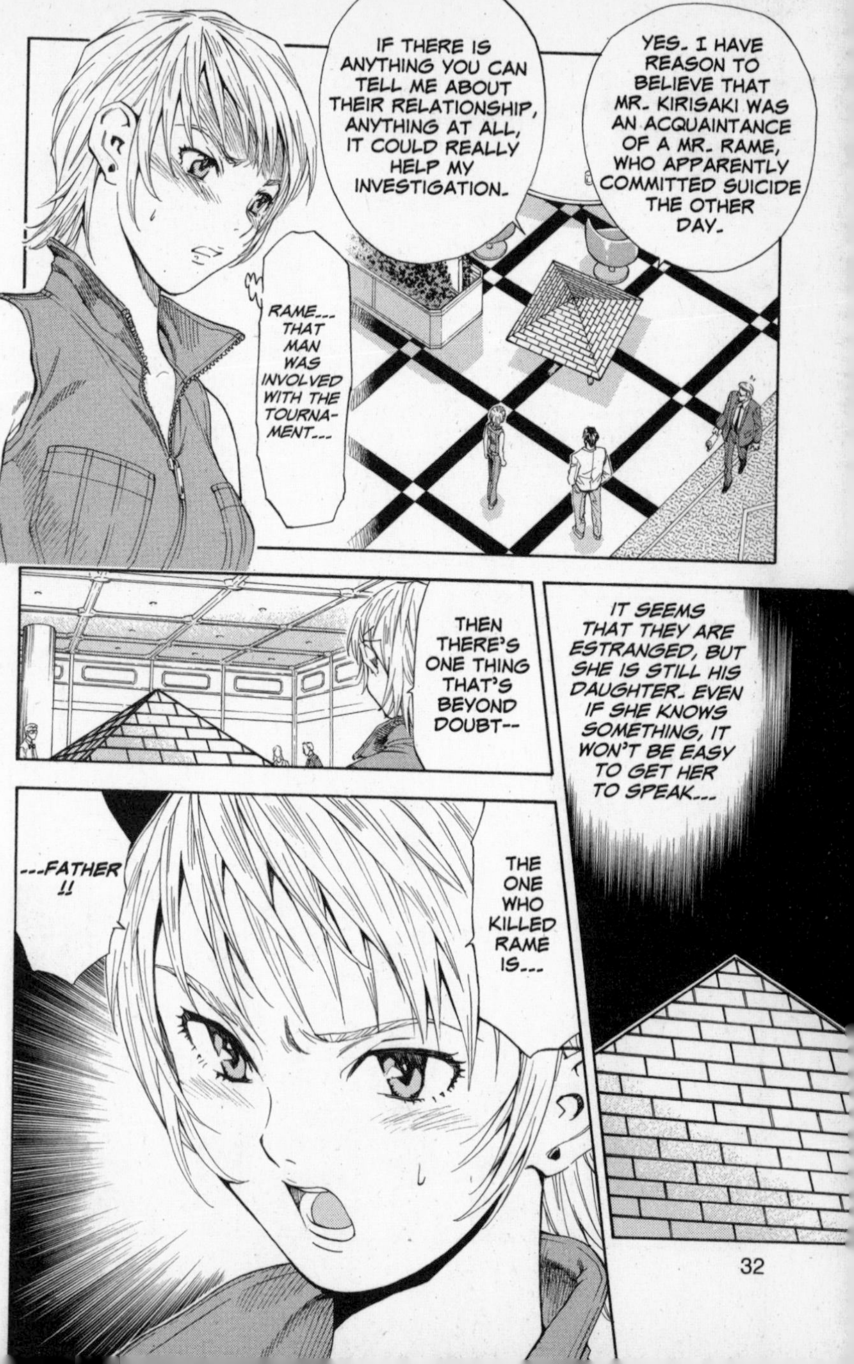
YES. I HAVE REASON TO BELIEVE THAT MR. KIRISAKI WAS AN ACQUAINTANCE OF A MR. RAME, WHO APPARENTLY COMMITTED SUICIDE THE OTHER DAY.
IF THERE IS ANYTHING YOU CAN TELL ME ABOUT THEIR RELATIONSHIP, ANYTHING AT ALL, IT COULD REALLY HELP MY INVESTIGATION.
RAME... THAT MAN WAS INVOLVED WITH THE TOURNAMENT...
IT SEEMS THAT THEY ARE ESTRANGED, BUT SHE IS STILL HIS DAUGHTER. EVEN IF SHE KNOWS SOMETHING, IT WON'T BE EASY TO GET HER TO SPEAK...
THEN THERE'S ONE THING THAT'S BEYOND DOUBT--
THE ONE WHO KILLED RAME IS...
...FATHER !!

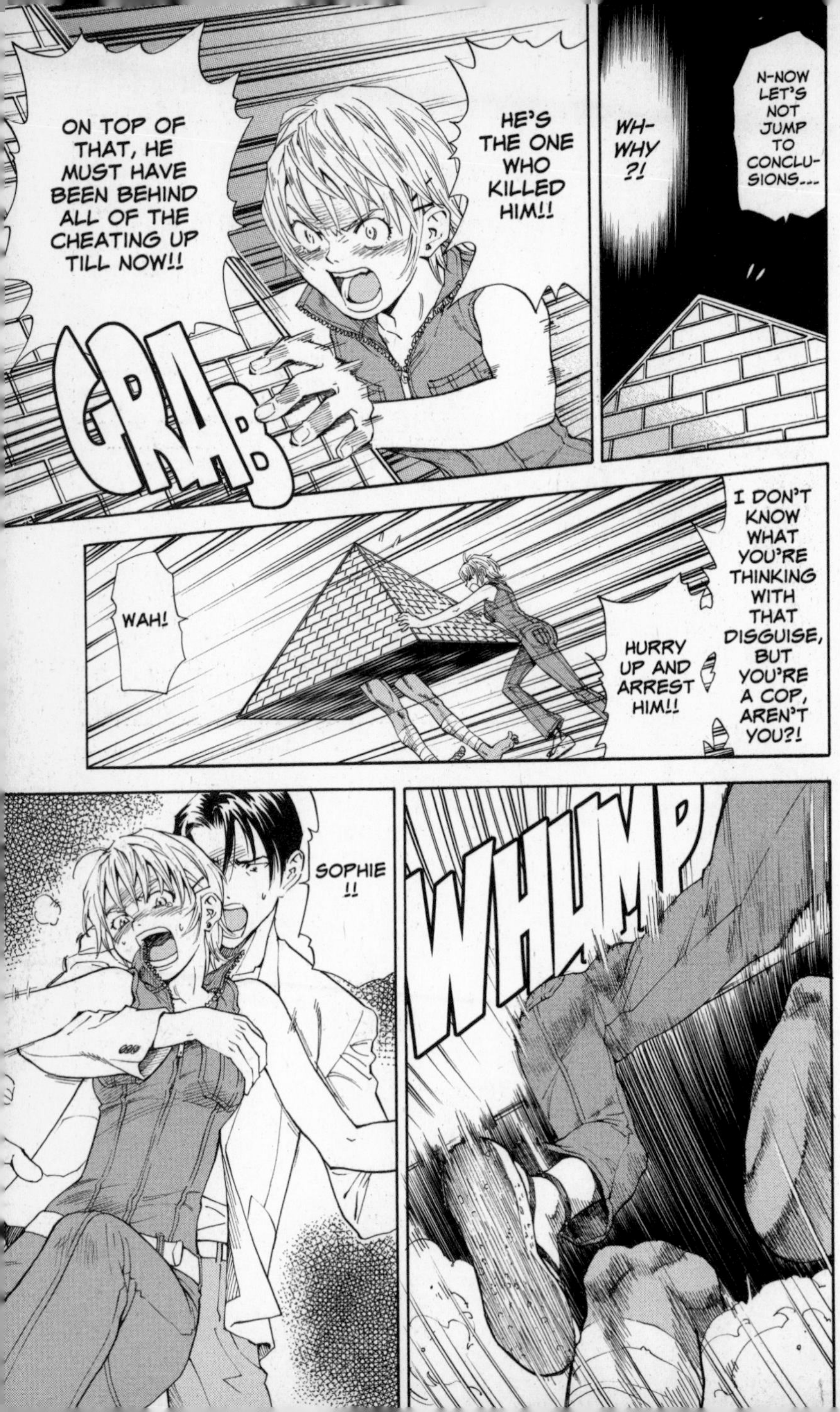
N-NOW LET'S NOT JUMP TO CONCLUSIONS...
WH-WHY?!
HE'S THE ONE WHO KILLED HIM!!
ON TOP OF THAT, HE MUST HAVE BEEN BEHIND ALL OF THE CHEATING UP TILL NOW!!
GRAB
I DON'T KNOW WHAT YOU'RE THINKING WITH THAT DISGUISE, BUT YOU'RE A COP, AREN'T YOU?!
HURRY UP AND ARREST HIM!!
WAH!
WHUMP
SOPHIE!!

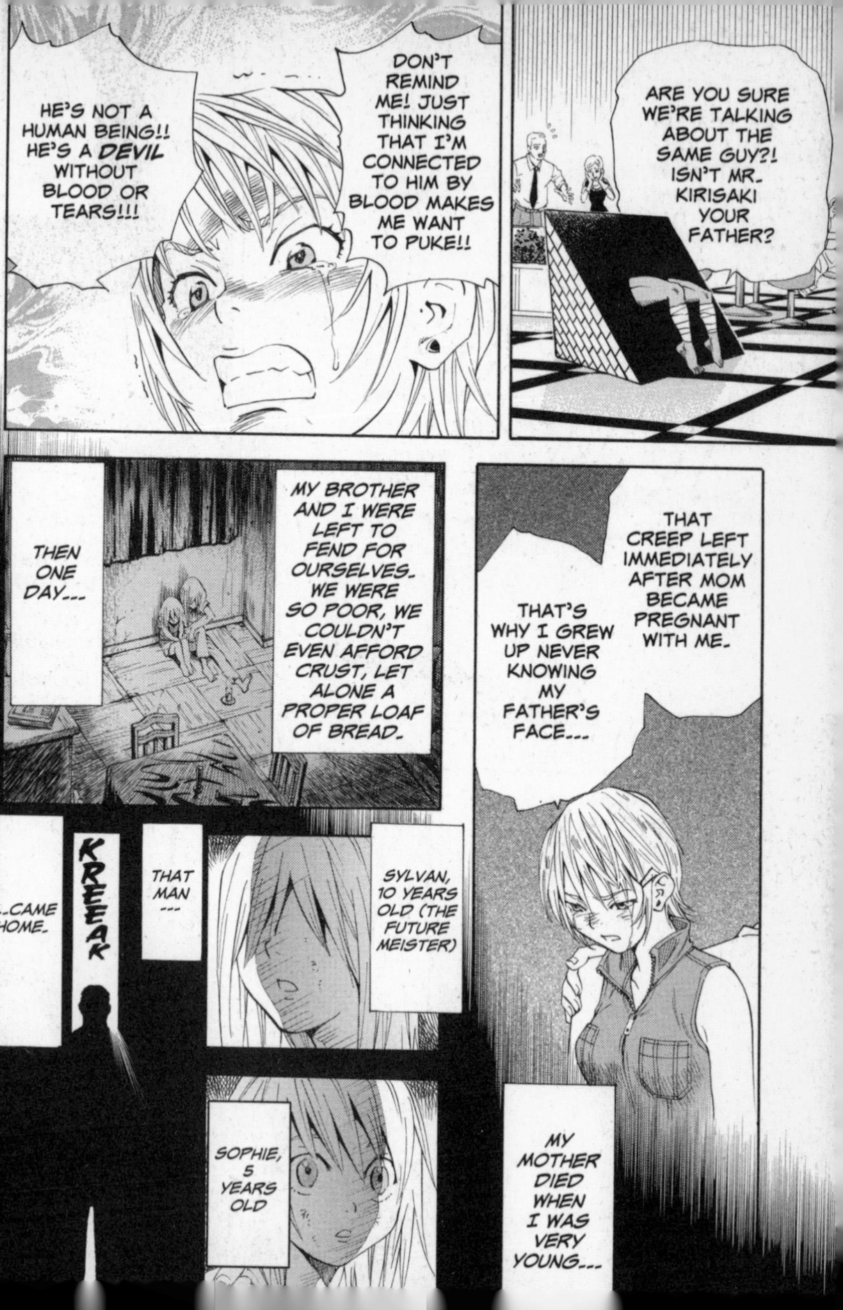
ARE YOU SURE WE'RE TALKING ABOUT THE SAME GUY?! ISN'T MR. KIRISAKI YOUR FATHER?
DON'T REMIND ME! JUST THINKING THAT I'M CONNECTED TO HIM BY BLOOD MAKES ME WANT TO PUKE!!
HE'S NOT A HUMAN BEING!! HE'S A DEVIL WITHOUT BLOOD OR TEARS!!!
THAT CREEP LEFT IMMEDIATELY AFTER MOM BECAME PREGNANT WITH ME.
THAT'S WHY I GREW UP NEVER KNOWING MY FATHER'S FACE...
MY MOTHER DIED WHEN I WAS VERY YOUNG...
MY BROTHER AND I WERE LEFT TO FEND FOR OURSELVES. WE WERE SO POOR, WE COULDN'T EVEN AFFORD CRUST, LET ALONE A PROPER LOAF OF BREAD.
THEN ONE DAY...
SYLVAN, 10 YEARS OLD (THE FUTURE MEISTER)
SOPHIE, 5 YEARS OLD
THAT MAN ...
KREEAK
...CAME HOME.

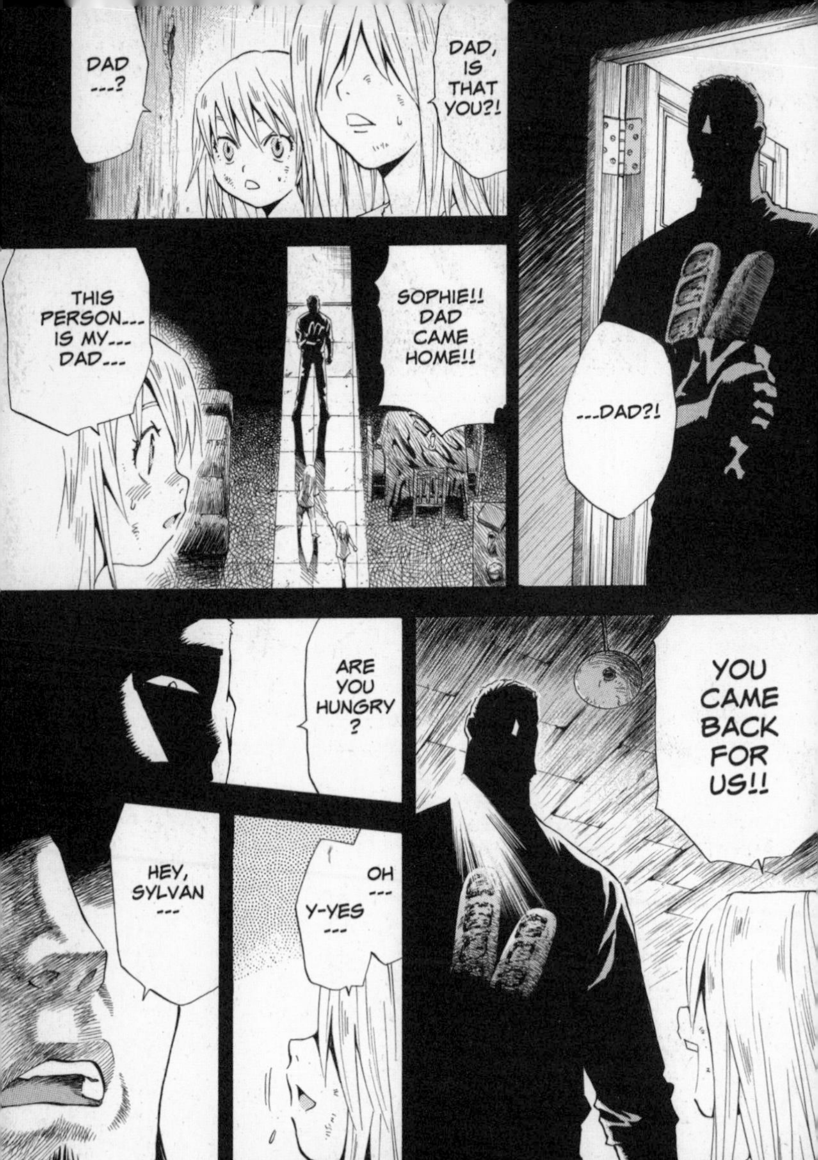
---DAD?!
DAD, IS THAT YOU?!
DAD---?
SOPHIE!! DAD CAME HOME!!
THIS PERSON--- IS MY--- DAD---
YOU CAME BACK FOR US!!
ARE YOU HUNGRY?
OH--- Y-YES---
HEY, SYLVAN---

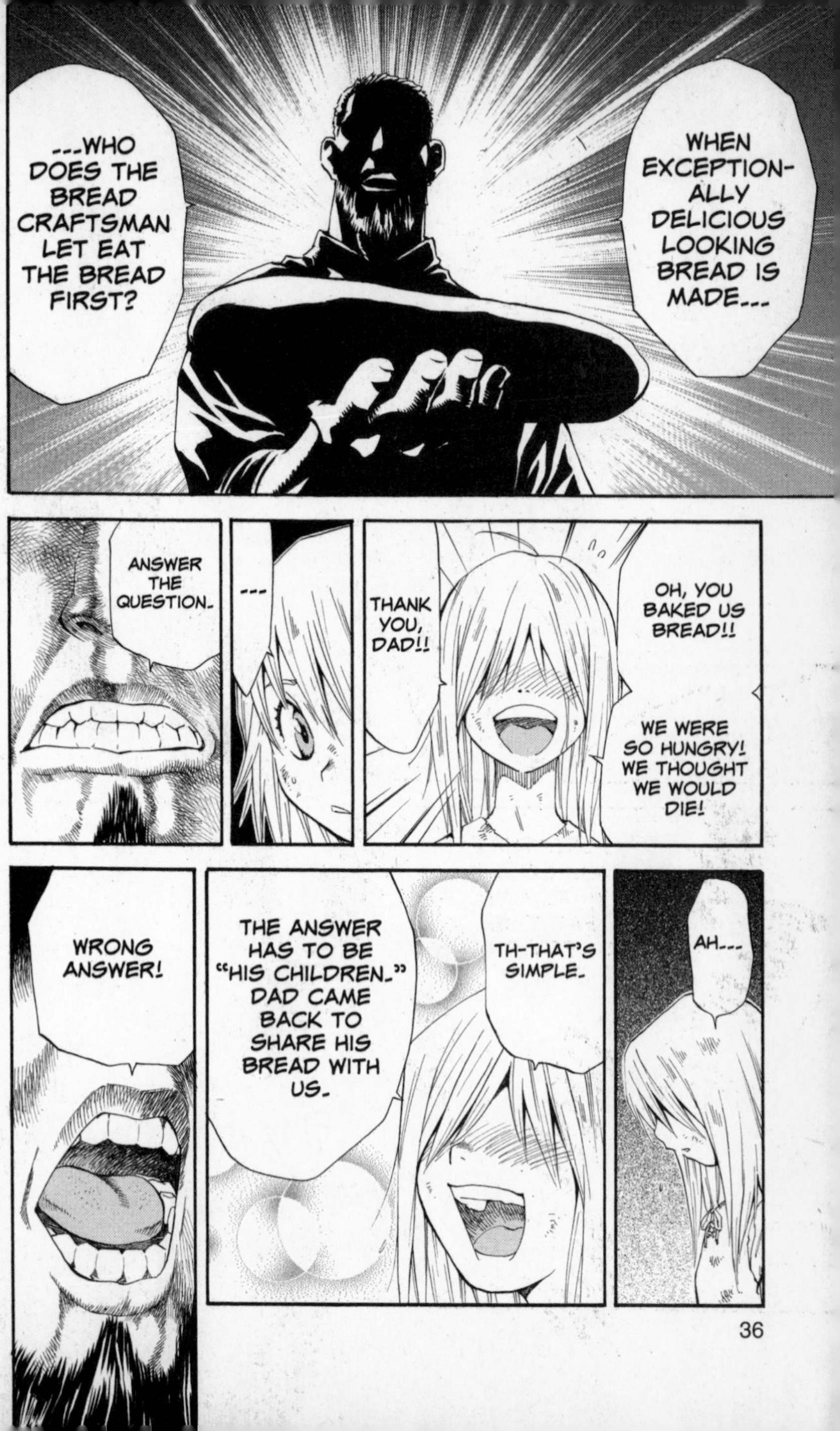
WHEN EXCEPTION-ALLY DELICIOUS LOOKING BREAD IS MADE...
...WHO DOES THE BREAD CRAFTSMAN LET EAT THE BREAD FIRST?
OH, YOU BAKED US BREAD!!
WE WERE SO HUNGRY! WE THOUGHT WE WOULD DIE!
THANK YOU, DAD!!
...
ANSWER THE QUESTION.
AH...
TH-THAT'S SIMPLE.
THE ANSWER HAS TO BE "HIS CHILDREN." DAD CAME BACK TO SHARE HIS BREAD WITH US.
WRONG ANSWER!

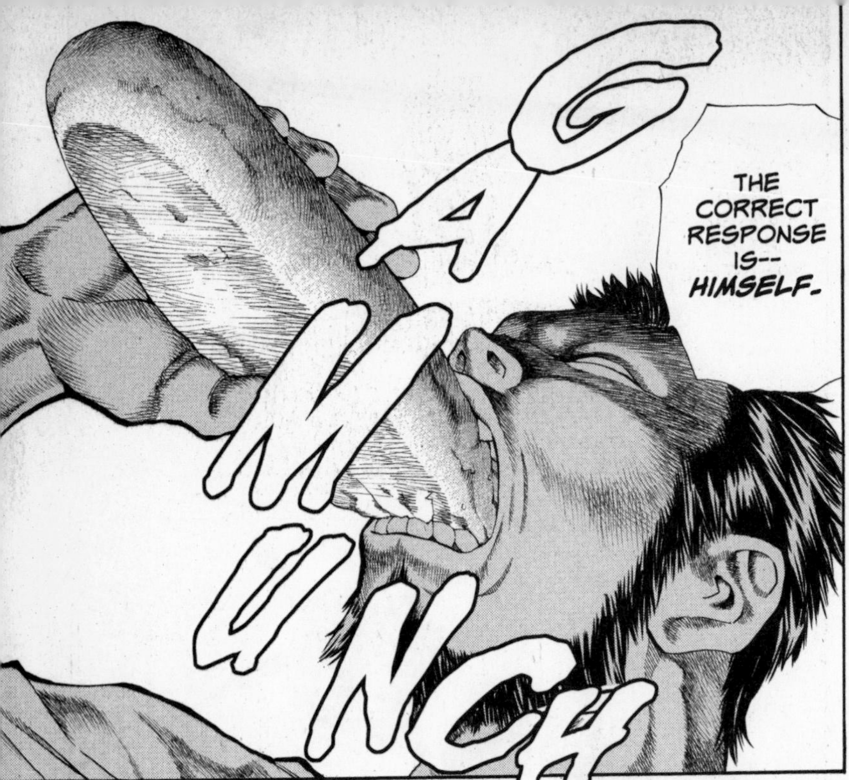
GAMUNCH
THE CORRECT RESPONSE IS-- HIMSELF.

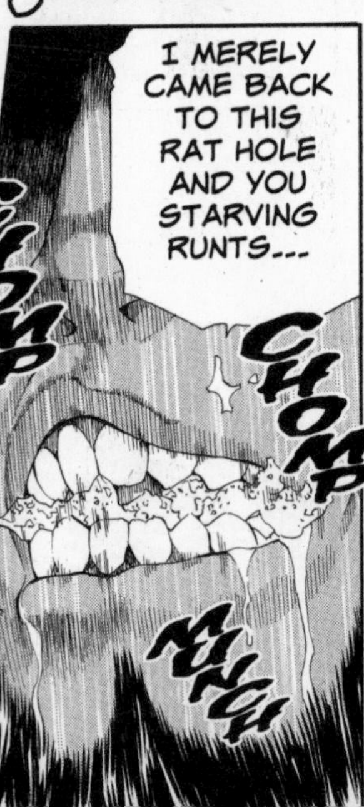
I MERELY CAME BACK TO THIS RAT HOLE AND YOU STARVING RUNTS...
CHOMP
MUNCH

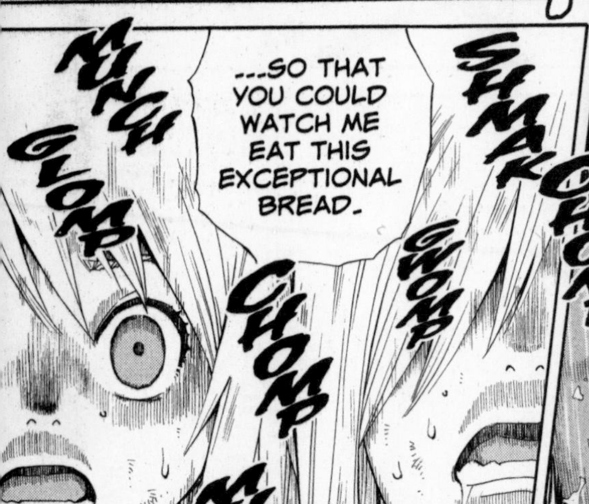
SHMAK
CHOMP
GNOMP
...SO THAT YOU COULD WATCH ME EAT THIS EXCEPTIONAL BREAD.
CHOMP
MUNCH
MUNCH
GLOMP

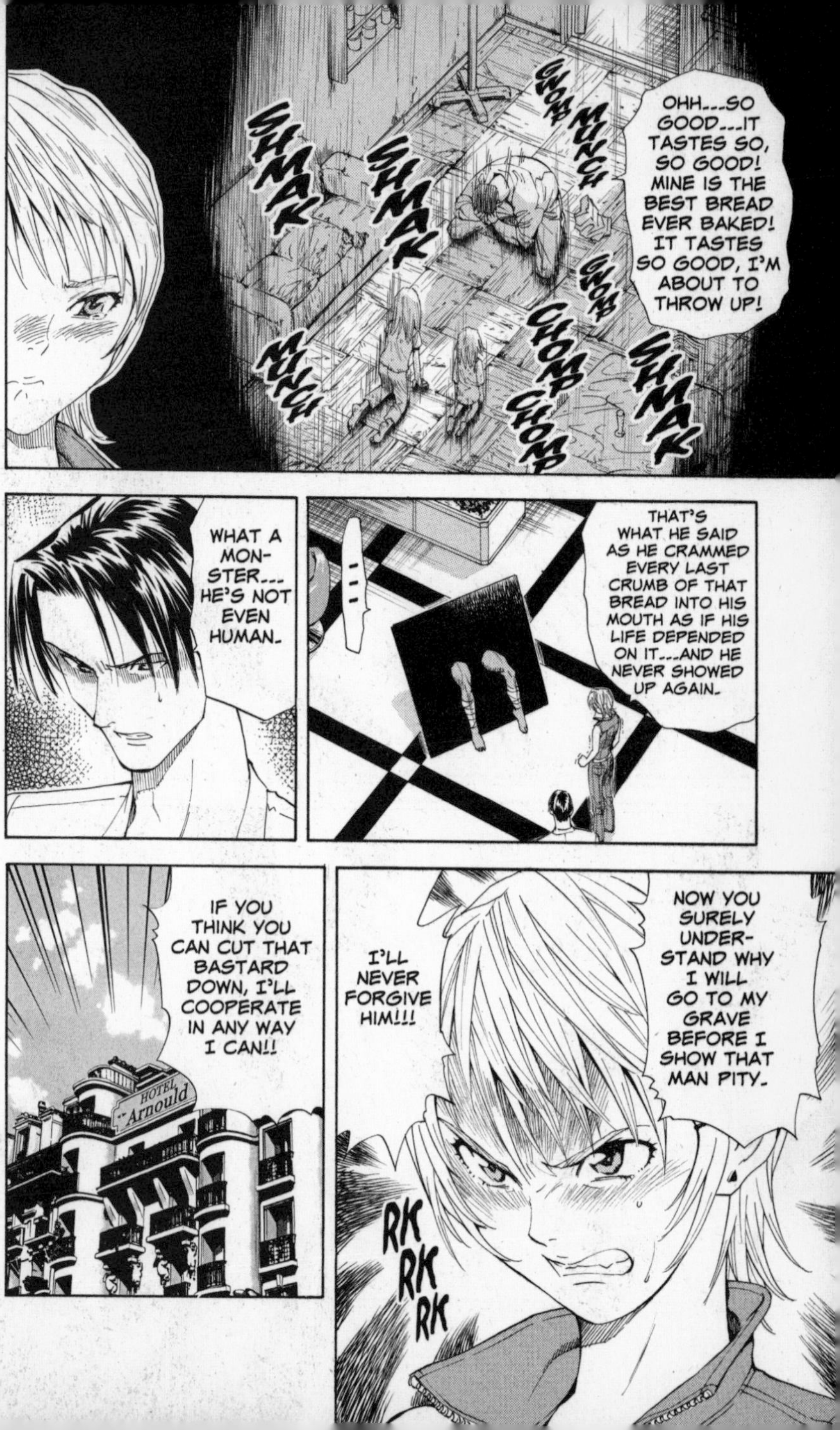
OHH...SO GOOD...IT TASTES SO, SO GOOD! MINE IS THE BEST BREAD EVER BAKED! IT TASTES SO GOOD, I'M ABOUT TO THROW UP!
SHMAK
GNOM MUNCH
GNOM
CHOMP CHOMP
SHMAK
SHMAK
MUNCH
THAT'S WHAT HE SAID AS HE CRAMMED EVERY LAST CRUMB OF THAT BREAD INTO HIS MOUTH AS IF HIS LIFE DEPENDED ON IT...AND HE NEVER SHOWED UP AGAIN.
...
WHAT A MON-STER... HE'S NOT EVEN HUMAN.
NOW YOU SURELY UNDER-STAND WHY I WILL GO TO MY GRAVE BEFORE I SHOW THAT MAN PITY.
I'LL NEVER FORGIVE HIM!!!
RK RK RK
IF YOU THINK YOU CAN CUT THAT BASTARD DOWN, I'LL COOPERATE IN ANY WAY I CAN!!
HOTEL Arnould

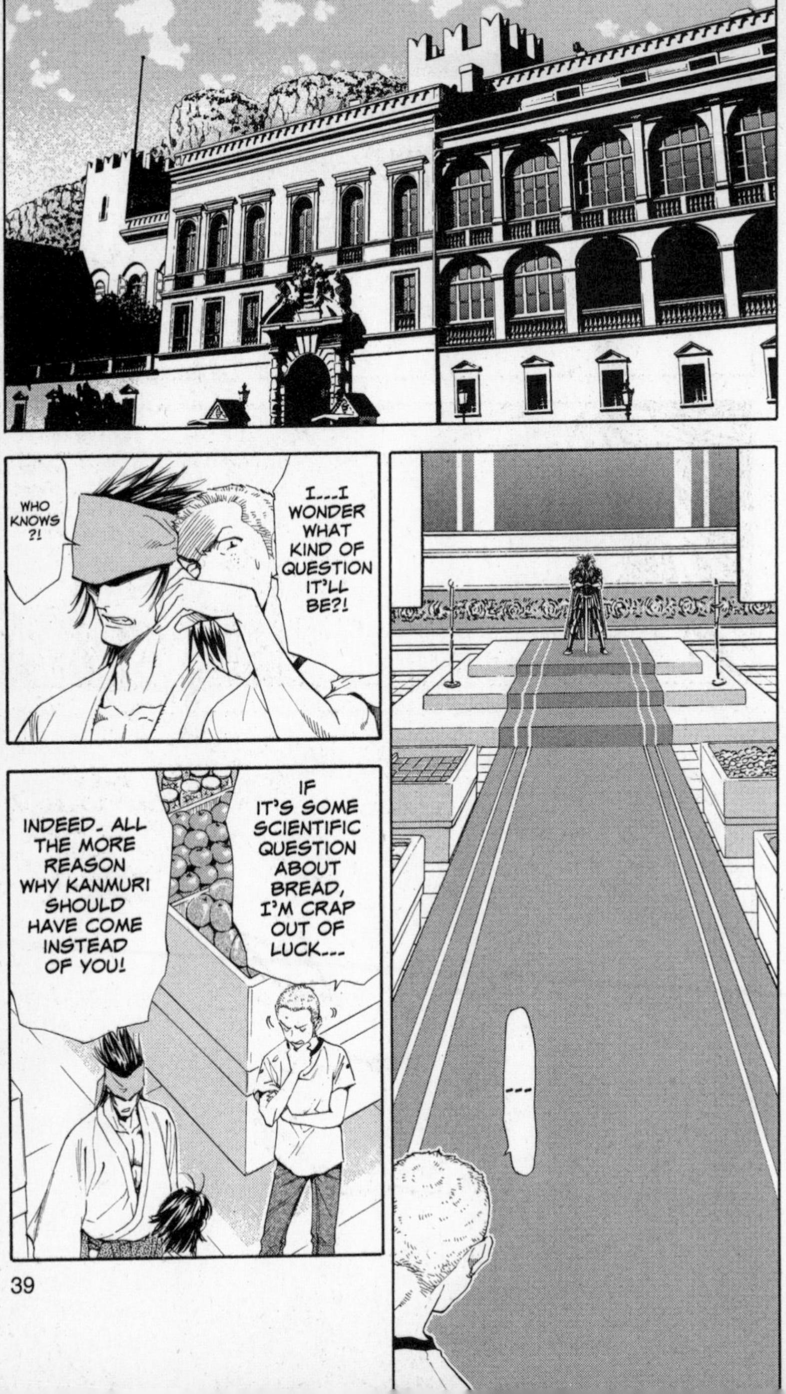
...
I...I WONDER WHAT KIND OF QUESTION IT'LL BE?!
WHO KNOWS ?!
IF IT'S SOME SCIENTIFIC QUESTION ABOUT BREAD, I'M CRAP OUT OF LUCK...
INDEED. ALL THE MORE REASON WHY KANMURI SHOULD HAVE COME INSTEAD OF YOU!

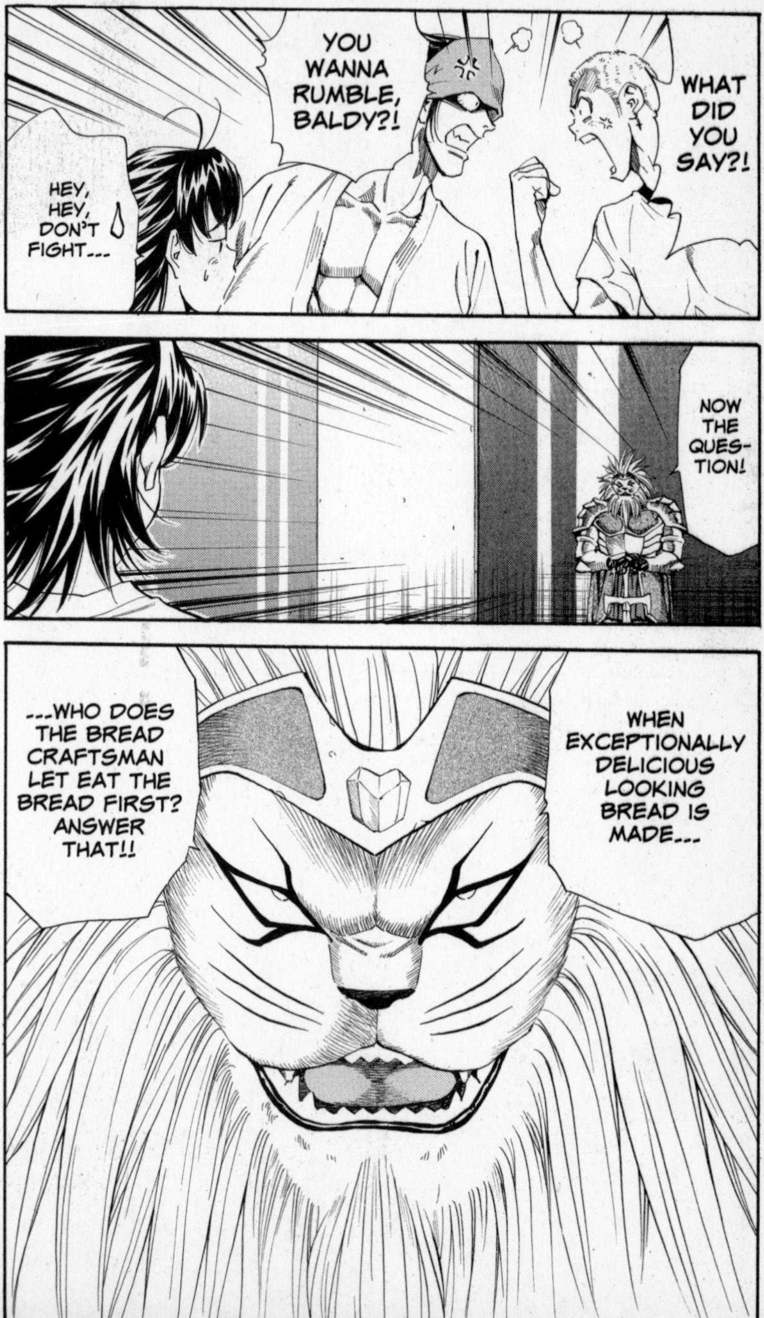
WHAT DID YOU SAY?!
YOU WANNA RUMBLE, BALDY?!
HEY, HEY, DON'T FIGHT...
NOW THE QUES-TION!
WHEN EXCEPTIONALLY DELICIOUS LOOKING BREAD IS MADE...
...WHO DOES THE BREAD CRAFTSMAN LET EAT THE BREAD FIRST? ANSWER THAT!!

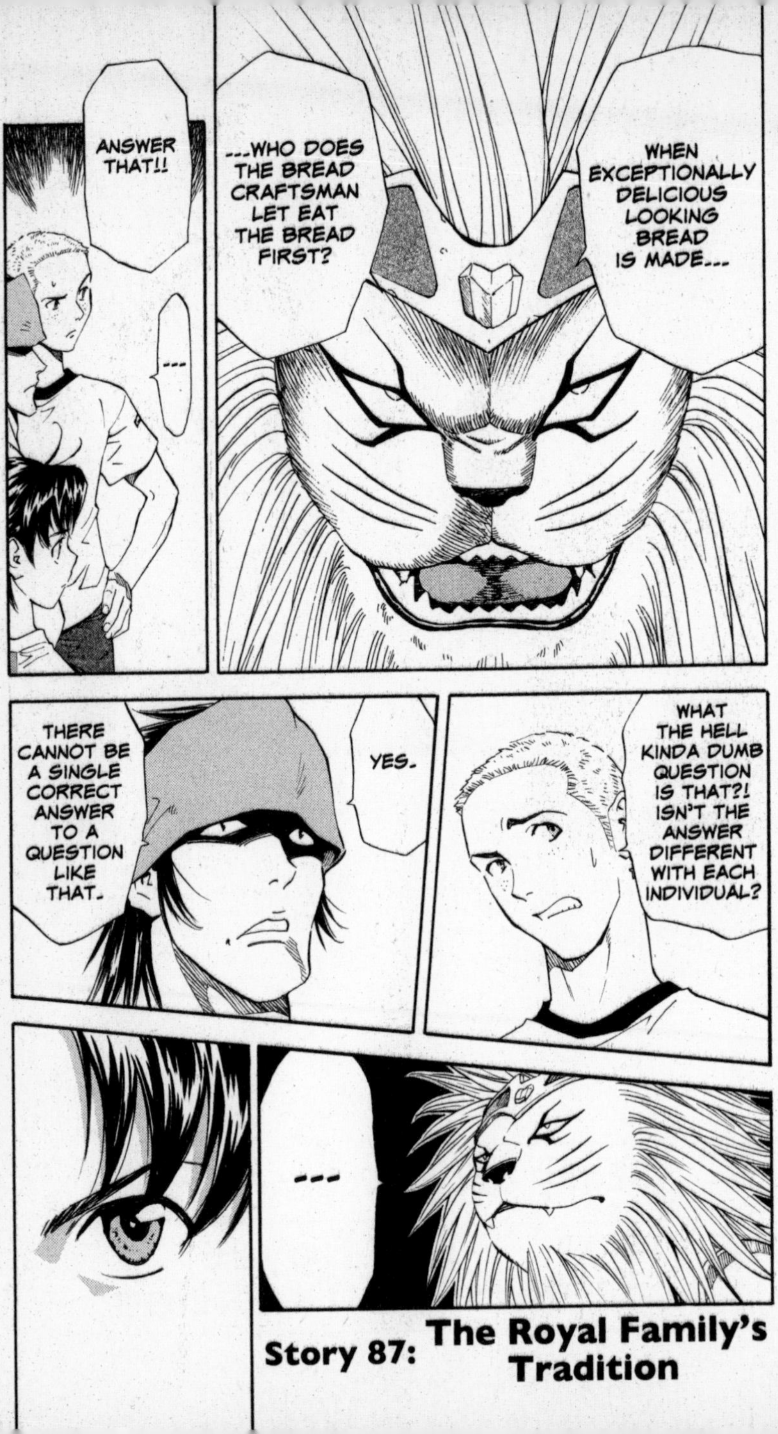
WHEN EXCEPTIONALLY DELICIOUS LOOKING BREAD IS MADE...
...WHO DOES THE BREAD CRAFTSMAN LET EAT THE BREAD FIRST?
ANSWER THAT!!
...
WHAT THE HELL KINDA DUMB QUESTION IS THAT?! ISN'T THE ANSWER DIFFERENT WITH EACH INDIVIDUAL?
YES.
THERE CANNOT BE A SINGLE CORRECT ANSWER TO A QUESTION LIKE THAT.
...

Story 87: The Royal Family's Tradition

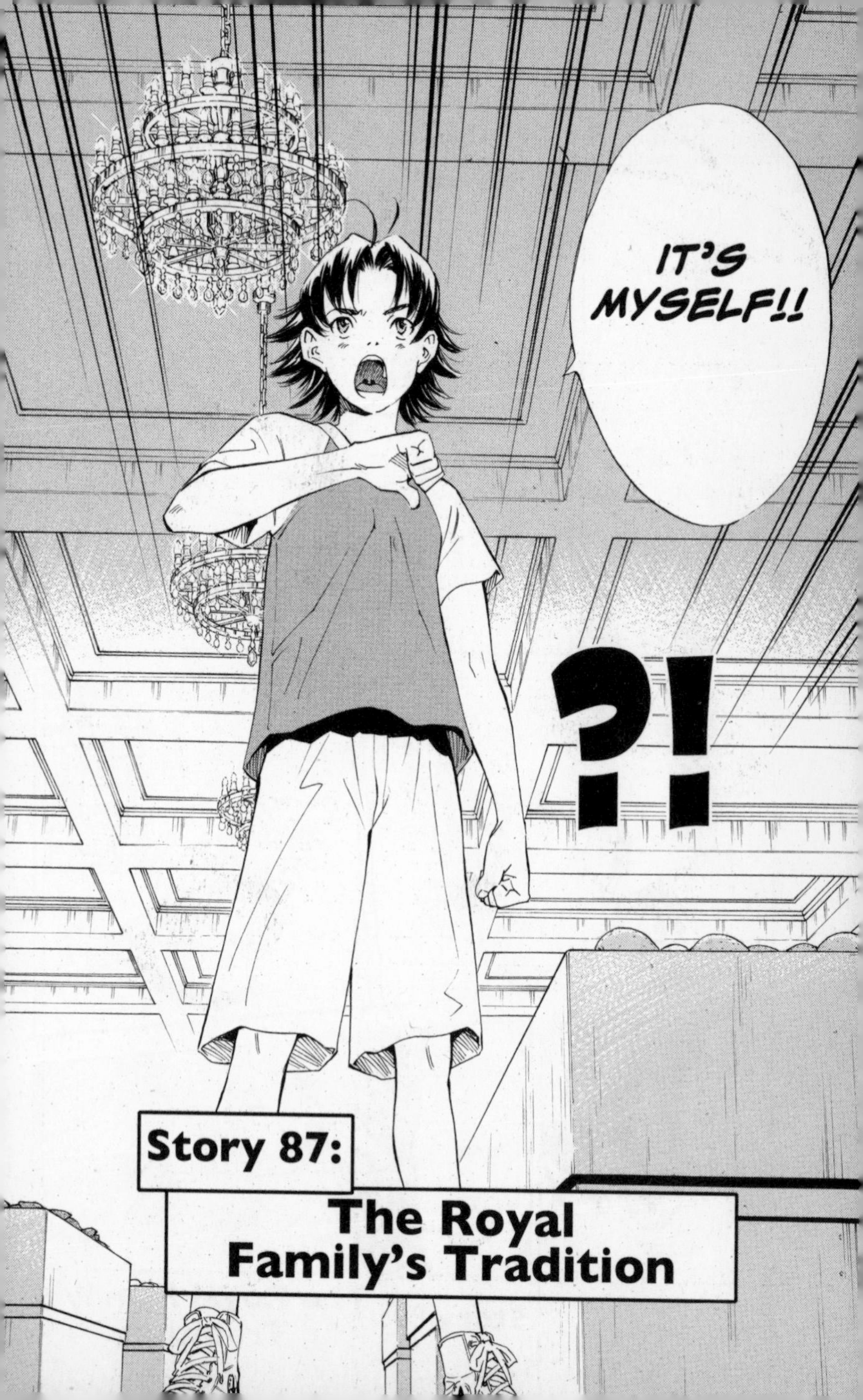
IT'S MYSELF!!
?!

Story 87: The Royal Family's Tradition

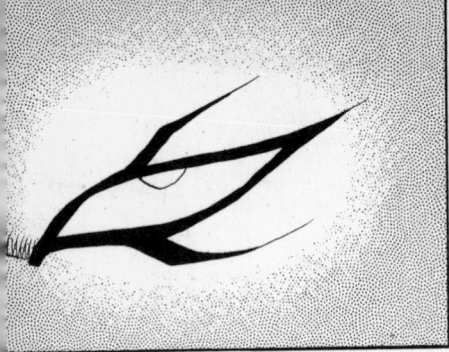

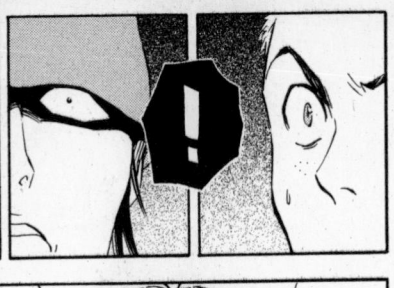

!
THE FIRST TO EAT IT---
---IS ME!
HMM--- YOUNG BOY ---
WHY DO YOU SAY THAT?
BECAUSE IT'S AN EXCEP-TIONALLY DELICIOUS "LOOKING" BREAD, RIGHT?
IF THAT'S THE CASE, YOU STILL DON'T KNOW WHETHER OR NOT IT TASTES GOOD.
YOU CAN'T LET ANOTHER PERSON EAT THAT KIND OF THING. IT'S ONLY NATURAL TO EAT IT YOURSELF!
NOW THAT HE PUTS IT THAT WAY, HE'S RIGHT---

OF ALL PEOPLE--- I WAS THOUGHT-LESS.

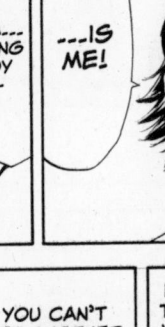

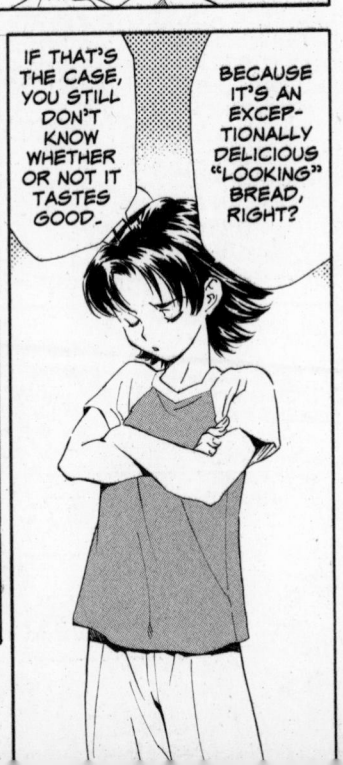

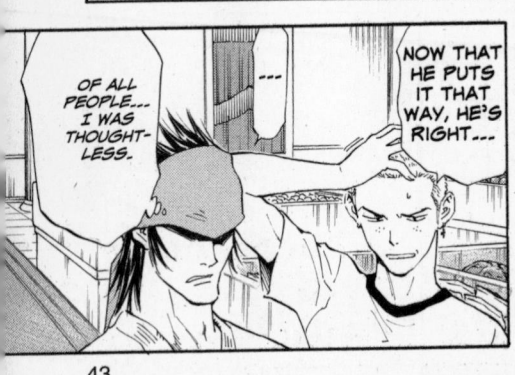

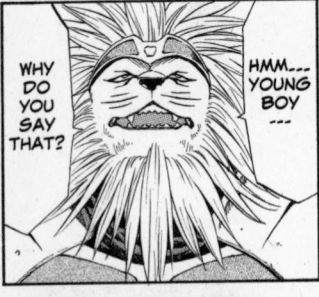

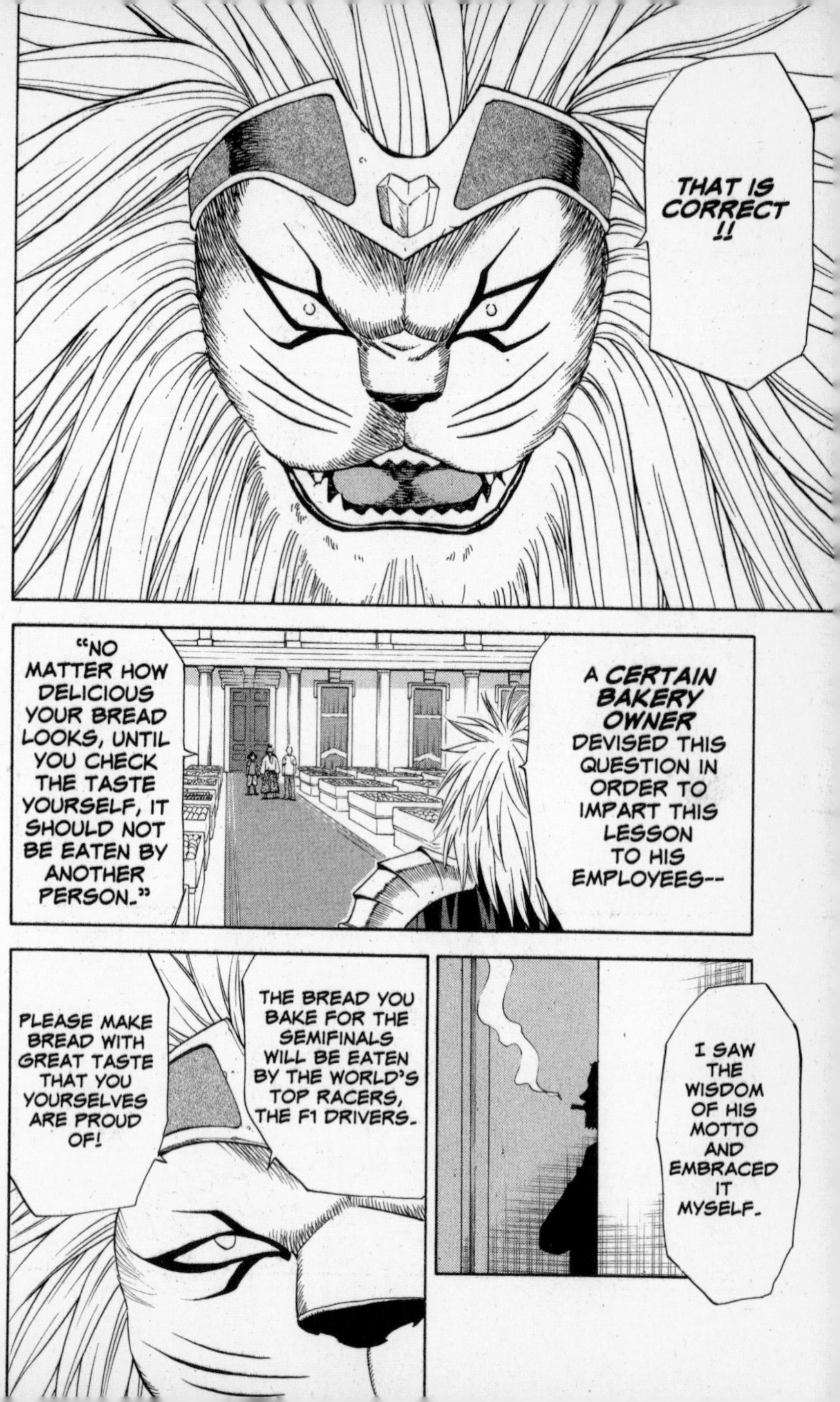
THAT IS CORRECT !!
A *CERTAIN BAKERY OWNER* DEVISED THIS QUESTION IN ORDER TO IMPART THIS LESSON TO HIS EMPLOYEES--
"NO MATTER HOW DELICIOUS YOUR BREAD LOOKS, UNTIL YOU CHECK THE TASTE YOURSELF, IT SHOULD NOT BE EATEN BY ANOTHER PERSON."
I SAW THE WISDOM OF HIS MOTTO AND EMBRACED IT MYSELF.
THE BREAD YOU BAKE FOR THE SEMIFINALS WILL BE EATEN BY THE WORLD'S TOP RACERS, THE F1 DRIVERS.
PLEASE MAKE BREAD WITH GREAT TASTE THAT YOU YOURSELVES ARE PROUD OF!

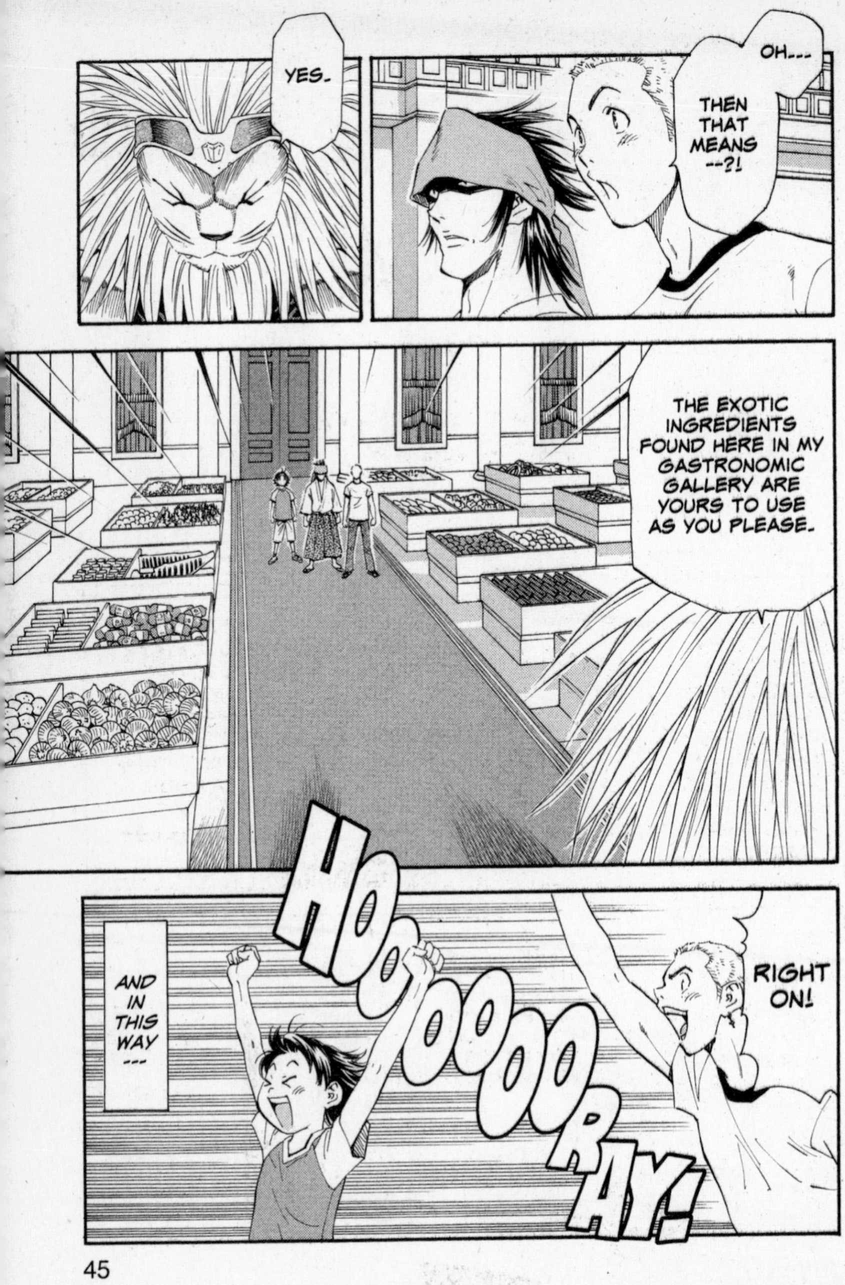
OH...
THEN THAT MEANS --?!
YES.
THE EXOTIC INGREDIENTS FOUND HERE IN MY GASTRONOMIC GALLERY ARE YOURS TO USE AS YOU PLEASE.
RIGHT ON!
HOOOOOOORAY!
AND IN THIS WAY ---

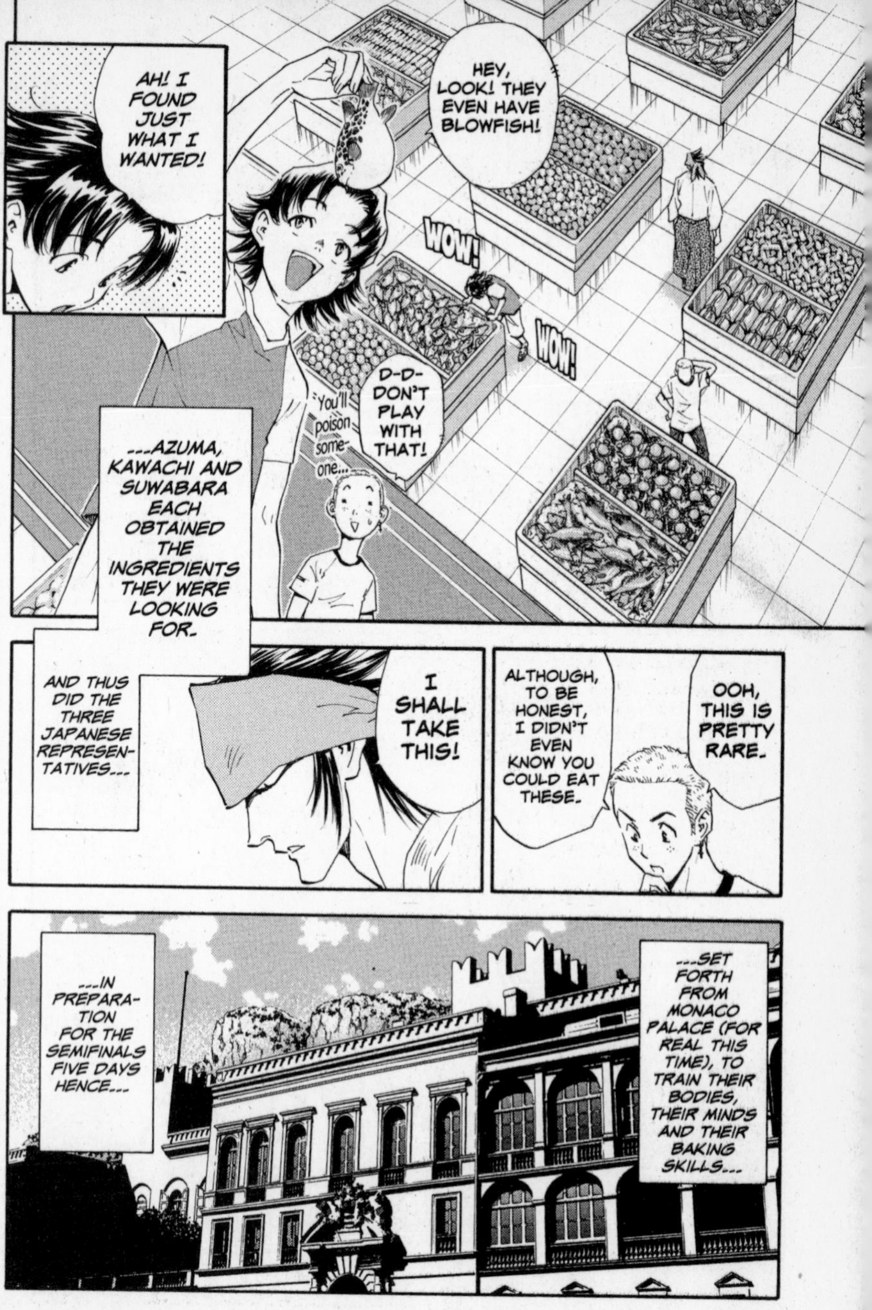
HEY, LOOK! THEY EVEN HAVE BLOWFISH!
WOW!
AH! I FOUND JUST WHAT I WANTED!
WOW!
D-D-DON'T PLAY WITH THAT!
You'll poison some-one...
...AZUMA, KAWACHI AND SUWABARA EACH OBTAINED THE INGREDIENTS THEY WERE LOOKING FOR.
OOH, THIS IS PRETTY RARE.
ALTHOUGH, TO BE HONEST, I DIDN'T EVEN KNOW YOU COULD EAT THESE.
I SHALL TAKE THIS!
AND THUS DID THE THREE JAPANESE REPRESEN-TATIVES...
...SET FORTH FROM MONACO PALACE (FOR REAL THIS TIME), TO TRAIN THEIR BODIES, THEIR MINDS AND THEIR BAKING SKILLS...
...IN PREPARA-TION FOR THE SEMIFINALS FIVE DAYS HENCE...

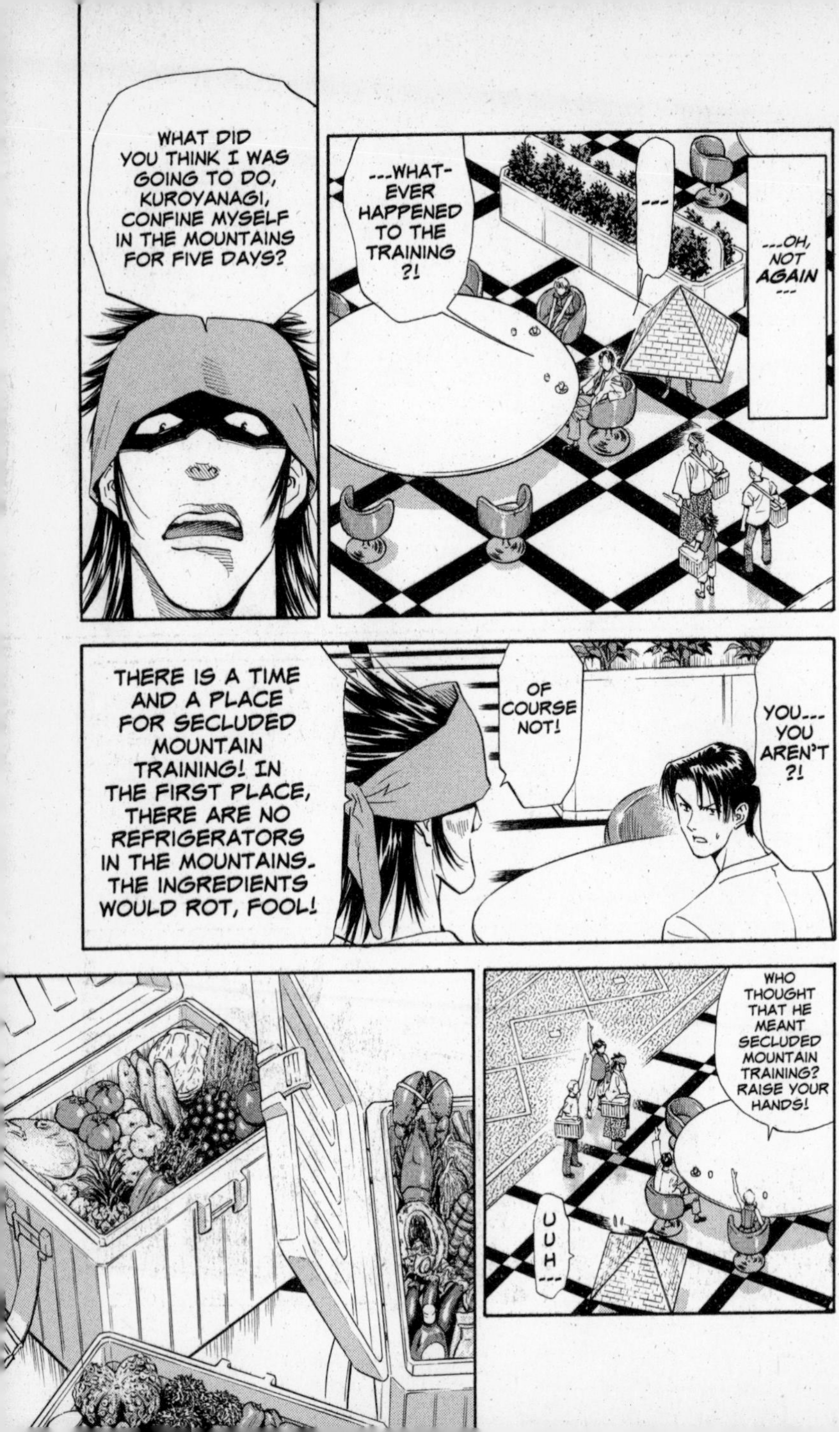
---OH, NOT AGAIN ---

---WHAT-EVER HAPPENED TO THE TRAINING ?!
WHAT DID YOU THINK I WAS GOING TO DO, KUROYANAGI, CONFINE MYSELF IN THE MOUNTAINS FOR FIVE DAYS?
YOU--- YOU AREN'T ?!
OF COURSE NOT!
THERE IS A TIME AND A PLACE FOR SECLUDED MOUNTAIN TRAINING! IN THE FIRST PLACE, THERE ARE NO REFRIGERATORS IN THE MOUNTAINS. THE INGREDIENTS WOULD ROT, FOOL!
WHO THOUGHT THAT HE MEANT SECLUDED MOUNTAIN TRAINING? RAISE YOUR HANDS!
UUH ---

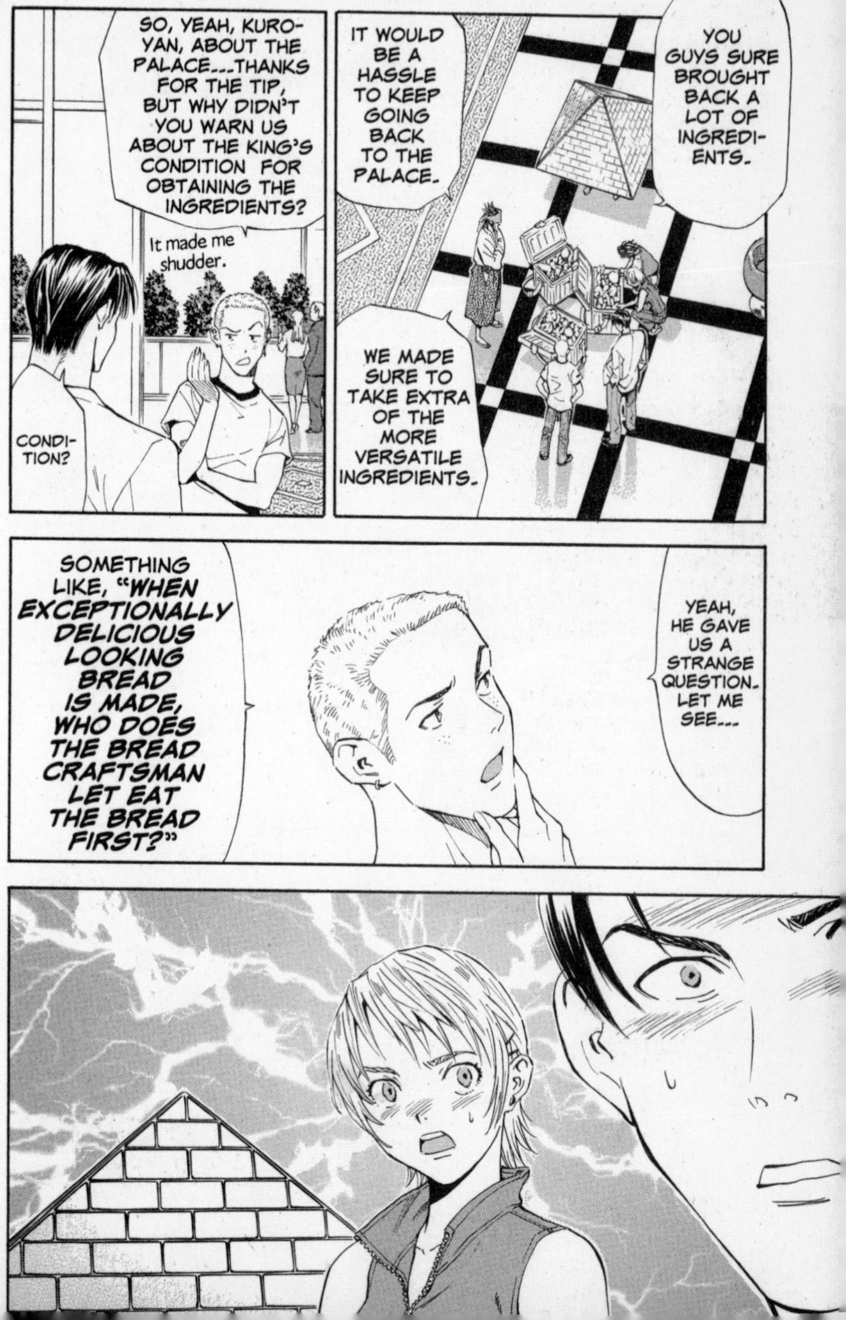
YOU GUYS SURE BROUGHT BACK A LOT OF INGREDI-ENTS.
IT WOULD BE A HASSLE TO KEEP GOING BACK TO THE PALACE.
WE MADE SURE TO TAKE EXTRA OF THE MORE VERSATILE INGREDIENTS.
SO, YEAH, KURO-YAN, ABOUT THE PALACE...THANKS FOR THE TIP, BUT WHY DIDN'T YOU WARN US ABOUT THE KING'S CONDITION FOR OBTAINING THE INGREDIENTS?
It made me shudder.
CONDI-TION?
YEAH, HE GAVE US A STRANGE QUESTION. LET ME SEE...
SOMETHING LIKE, "WHEN EXCEPTIONALLY DELICIOUS LOOKING BREAD IS MADE, WHO DOES THE BREAD CRAFTSMAN LET EAT THE BREAD FIRST?"

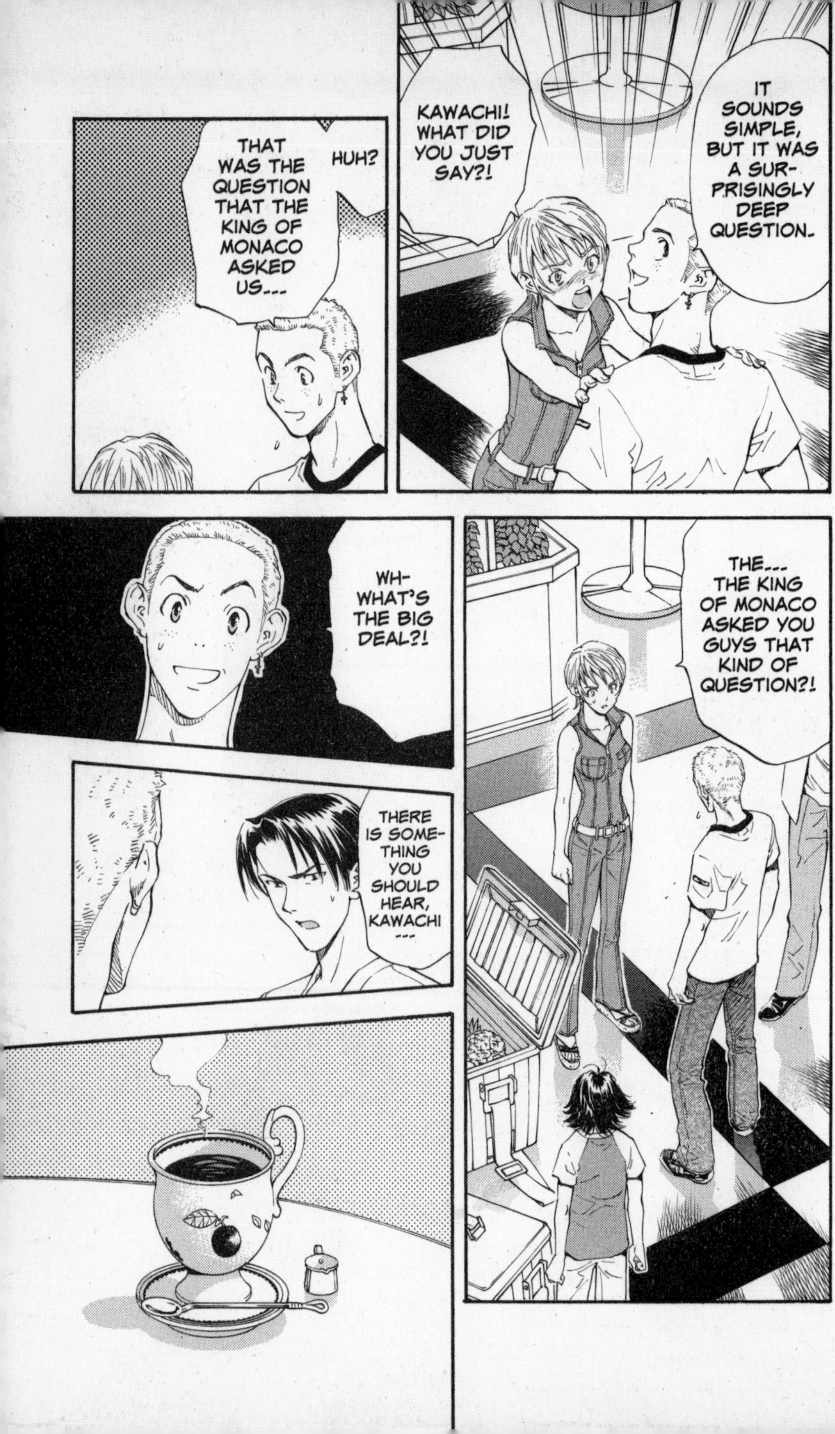
IT SOUNDS SIMPLE, BUT IT WAS A SUR-PRISINGLY DEEP QUESTION.
KAWACHI! WHAT DID YOU JUST SAY?!
HUH?
THAT WAS THE QUESTION THAT THE KING OF MONACO ASKED US...
THE... THE KING OF MONACO ASKED YOU GUYS THAT KIND OF QUESTION?!
WH-WHAT'S THE BIG DEAL?!
THERE IS SOME-THING YOU SHOULD HEAR, KAWACHI...

HOTEL Arnould
YOU'VE GOT TO BE KIDDING!
IS...IS THERE REALLY A PARENT WHO WOULD DO SUCH A THING TO HIS OWN CHILDREN?!
WHY WOULD HE DO SOMETHING THAT CRUEL?!
IF THAT'S A FACT, THIS MAN CALLED YUICHI KIRISAKI IS NO LONGER HUMAN!
THAT GUY... I...
I TOTALLY CAN'T FORGIVE HIM!!

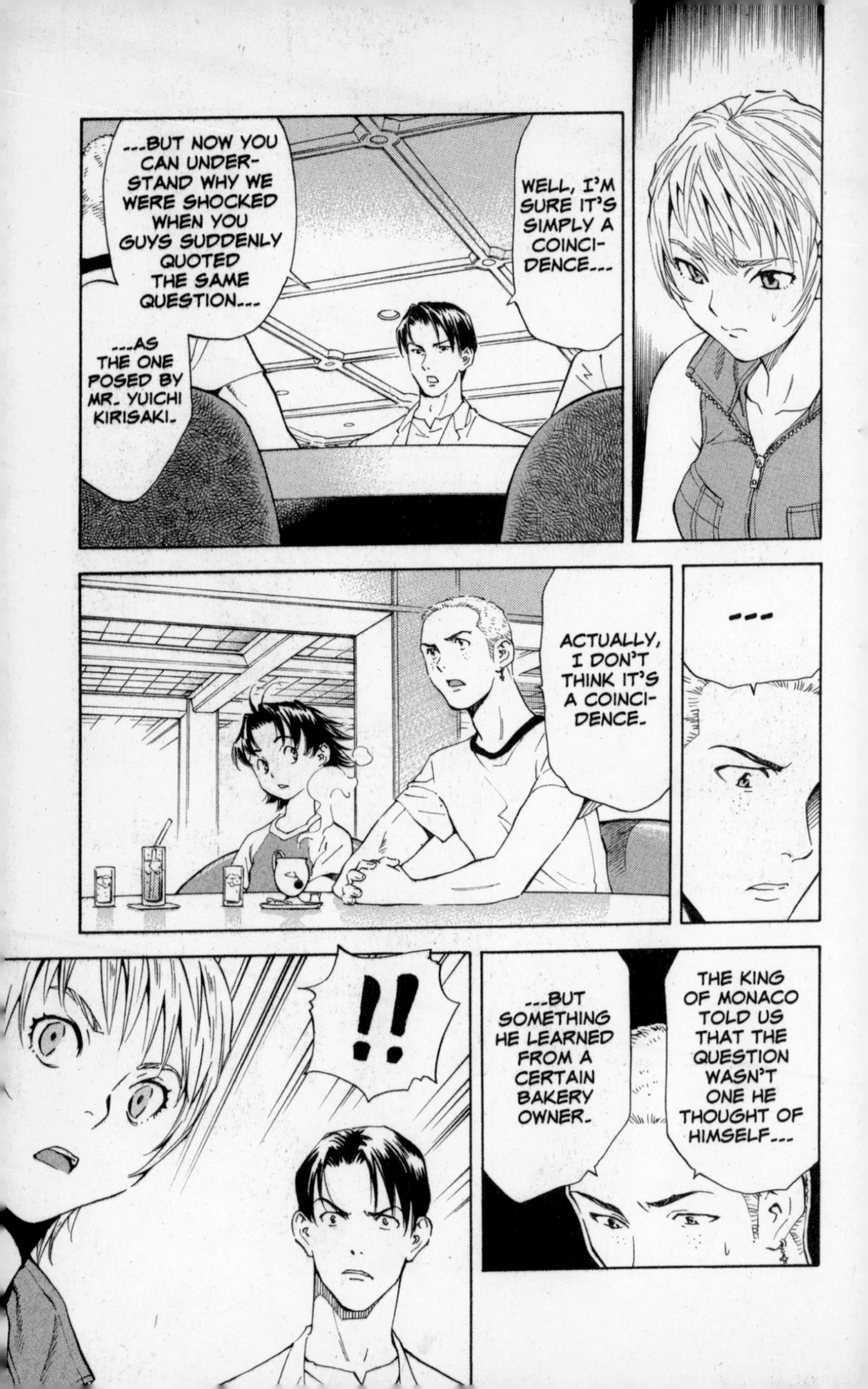
WELL, I'M SURE IT'S SIMPLY A COINCIDENCE...
...BUT NOW YOU CAN UNDERSTAND WHY WE WERE SHOCKED WHEN YOU GUYS SUDDENLY QUOTED THE SAME QUESTION...
...AS THE ONE POSED BY MR. YUICHI KIRISAKI.
...
ACTUALLY, I DON'T THINK IT'S A COINCIDENCE.
THE KING OF MONACO TOLD US THAT THE QUESTION WASN'T ONE HE THOUGHT OF HIMSELF...
...BUT SOMETHING HE LEARNED FROM A CERTAIN BAKERY OWNER.
!!

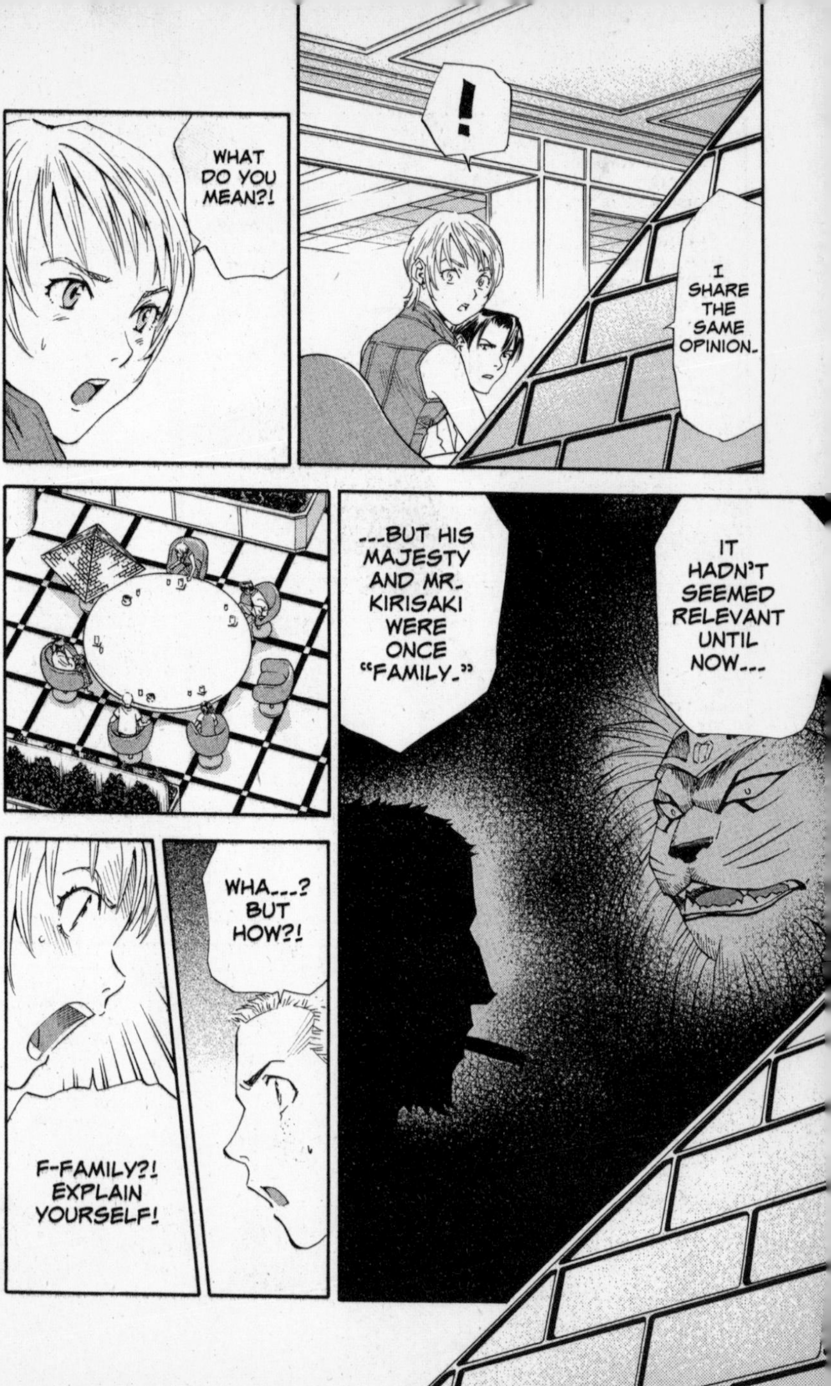
I SHARE THE SAME OPINION.
!
WHAT DO YOU MEAN?!
IT HADN'T SEEMED RELEVANT UNTIL NOW...
...BUT HIS MAJESTY AND MR. KIRISAKI WERE ONCE "FAMILY."
WHA...? BUT HOW?!
F-FAMILY?! EXPLAIN YOURSELF!

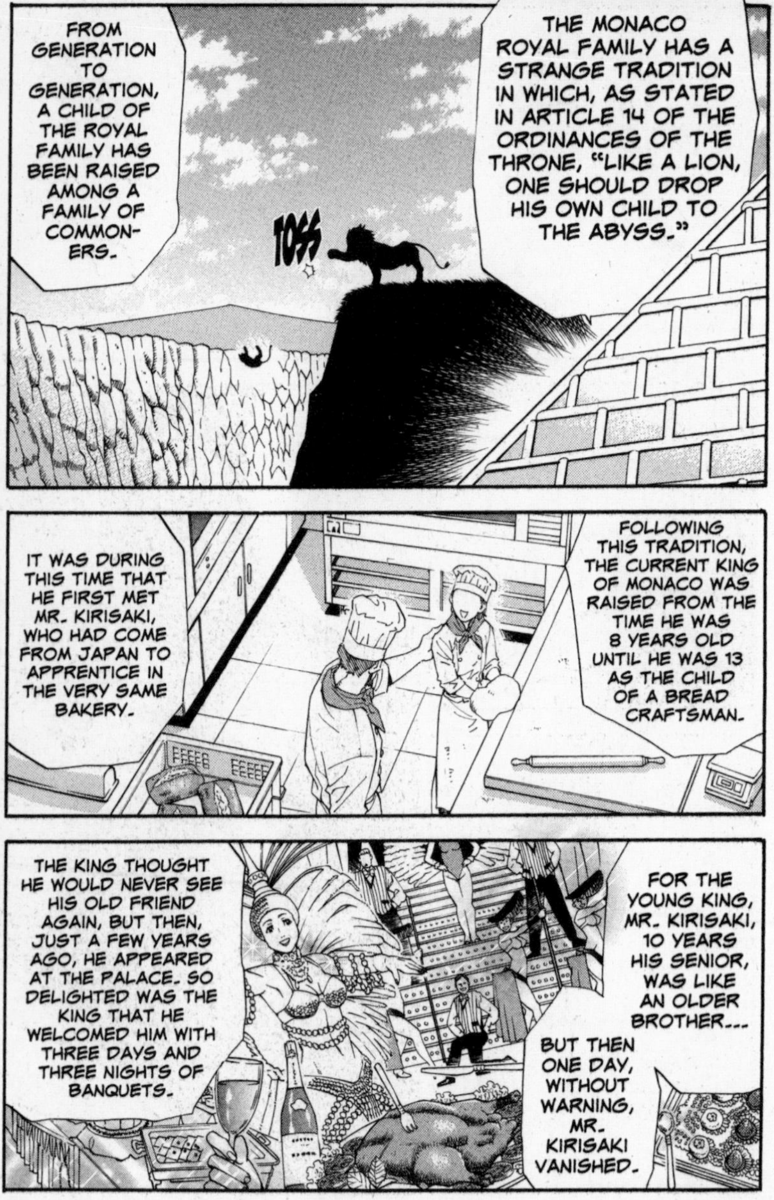
THE MONACO ROYAL FAMILY HAS A STRANGE TRADITION IN WHICH, AS STATED IN ARTICLE 14 OF THE ORDINANCES OF THE THRONE, "LIKE A LION, ONE SHOULD DROP HIS OWN CHILD TO THE ABYSS."
TOSS
FROM GENERATION TO GENERATION, A CHILD OF THE ROYAL FAMILY HAS BEEN RAISED AMONG A FAMILY OF COMMON-ERS.
FOLLOWING THIS TRADITION, THE CURRENT KING OF MONACO WAS RAISED FROM THE TIME HE WAS 8 YEARS OLD UNTIL HE WAS 13 AS THE CHILD OF A BREAD CRAFTSMAN.
IT WAS DURING THIS TIME THAT HE FIRST MET MR. KIRISAKI, WHO HAD COME FROM JAPAN TO APPRENTICE IN THE VERY SAME BAKERY.
FOR THE YOUNG KING, MR. KIRISAKI, 10 YEARS HIS SENIOR, WAS LIKE AN OLDER BROTHER...
BUT THEN ONE DAY, WITHOUT WARNING, MR. KIRISAKI VANISHED.
THE KING THOUGHT HE WOULD NEVER SEE HIS OLD FRIEND AGAIN, BUT THEN, JUST A FEW YEARS AGO, HE APPEARED AT THE PALACE. SO DELIGHTED WAS THE KING THAT HE WELCOMED HIM WITH THREE DAYS AND THREE NIGHTS OF BANQUETS.

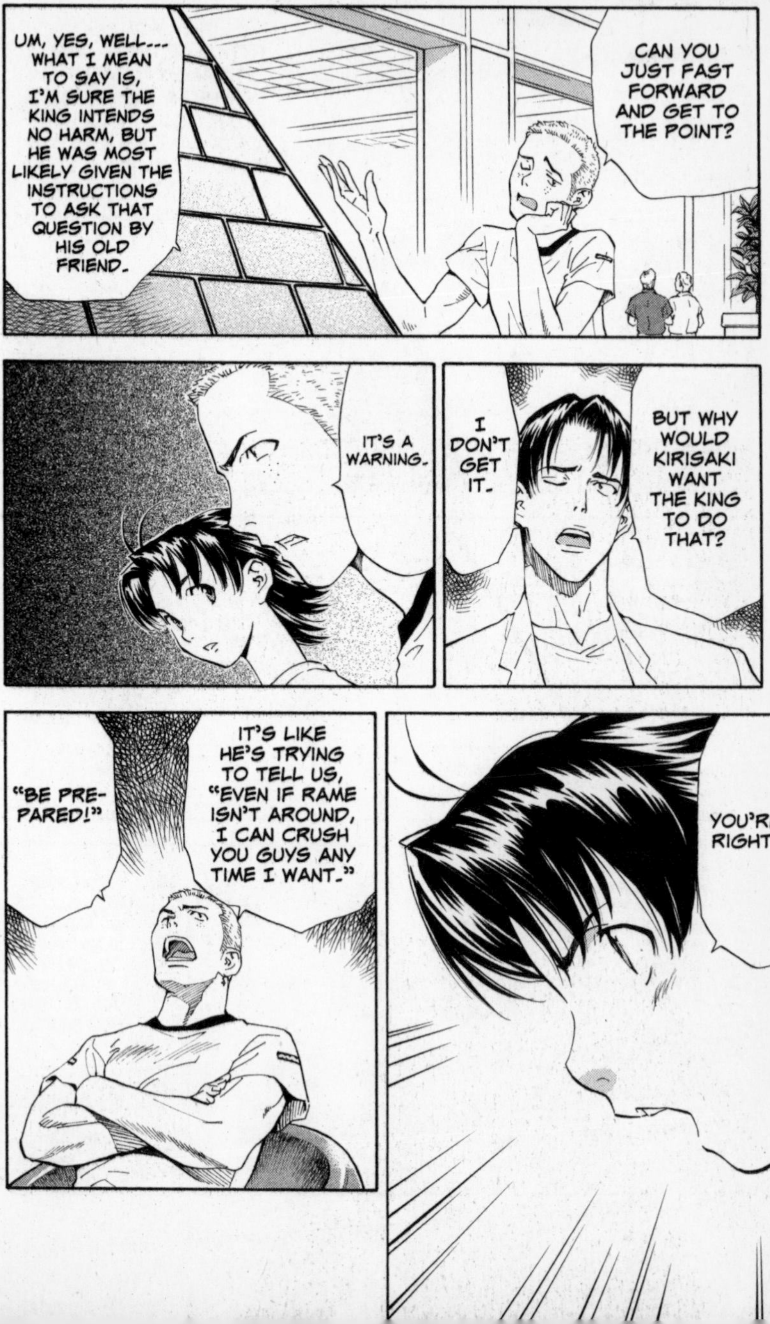
CAN YOU JUST FAST FORWARD AND GET TO THE POINT?
UM, YES, WELL... WHAT I MEAN TO SAY IS, I'M SURE THE KING INTENDS NO HARM, BUT HE WAS MOST LIKELY GIVEN THE INSTRUCTIONS TO ASK THAT QUESTION BY HIS OLD FRIEND.
BUT WHY WOULD KIRISAKI WANT THE KING TO DO THAT?
I DON'T GET IT.
IT'S A WARNING.
YOU'RE RIGHT!
IT'S LIKE HE'S TRYING TO TELL US, "EVEN IF RAME ISN'T AROUND, I CAN CRUSH YOU GUYS ANY TIME I WANT."
"BE PREPARED!"

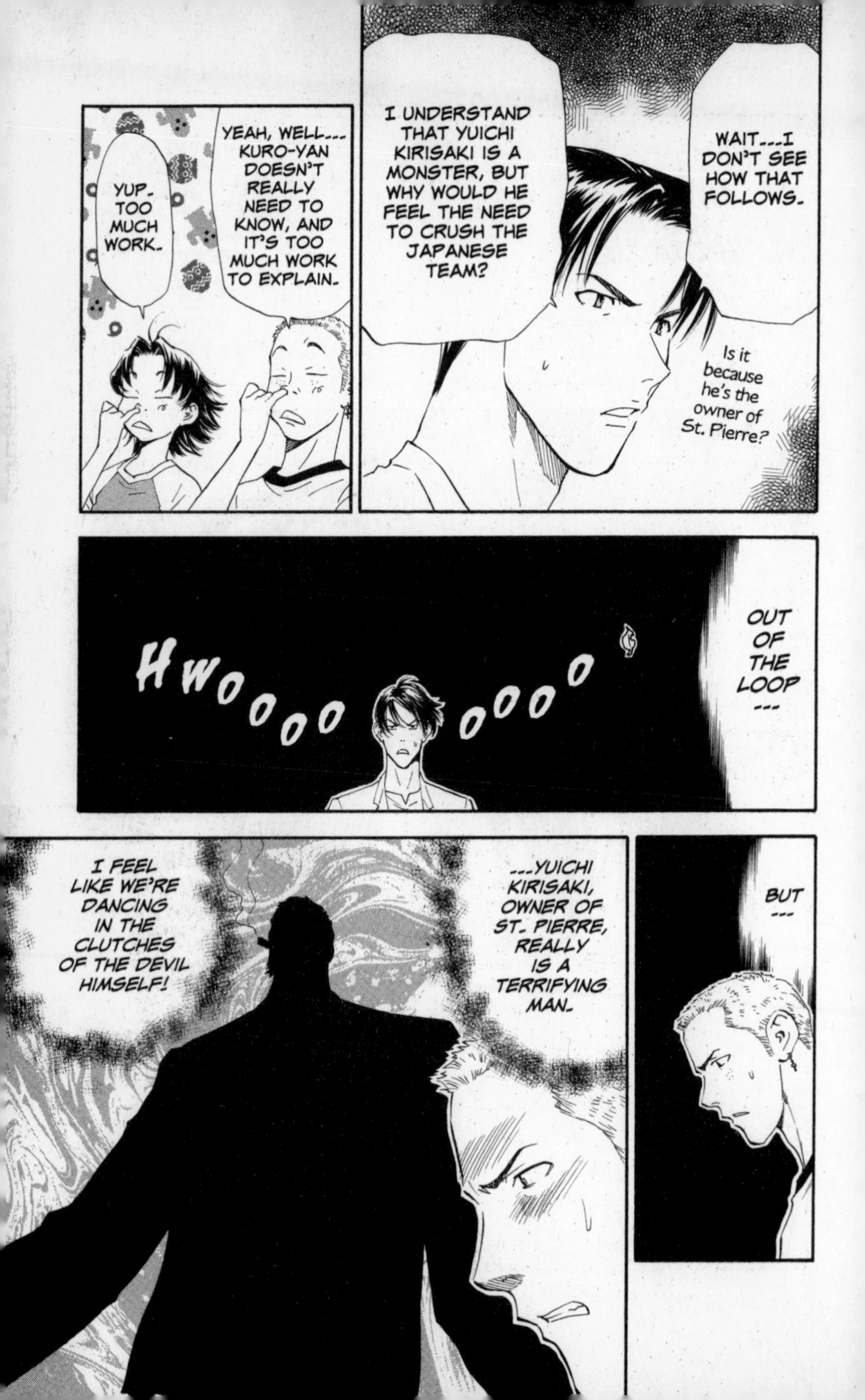
WAIT...I DON'T SEE HOW THAT FOLLOWS.
I UNDERSTAND THAT YUICHI KIRISAKI IS A MONSTER, BUT WHY WOULD HE FEEL THE NEED TO CRUSH THE JAPANESE TEAM?
Is it because he's the owner of St. Pierre?
YEAH, WELL... KURO-YAN DOESN'T REALLY NEED TO KNOW, AND IT'S TOO MUCH WORK TO EXPLAIN.
YUP. TOO MUCH WORK.
OUT OF THE LOOP ...
HWOOOOOOOOO
BUT ...
...YUICHI KIRISAKI, OWNER OF ST. PIERRE, REALLY IS A TERRIFYING MAN.
I FEEL LIKE WE'RE DANCING IN THE CLUTCHES OF THE DEVIL HIMSELF!

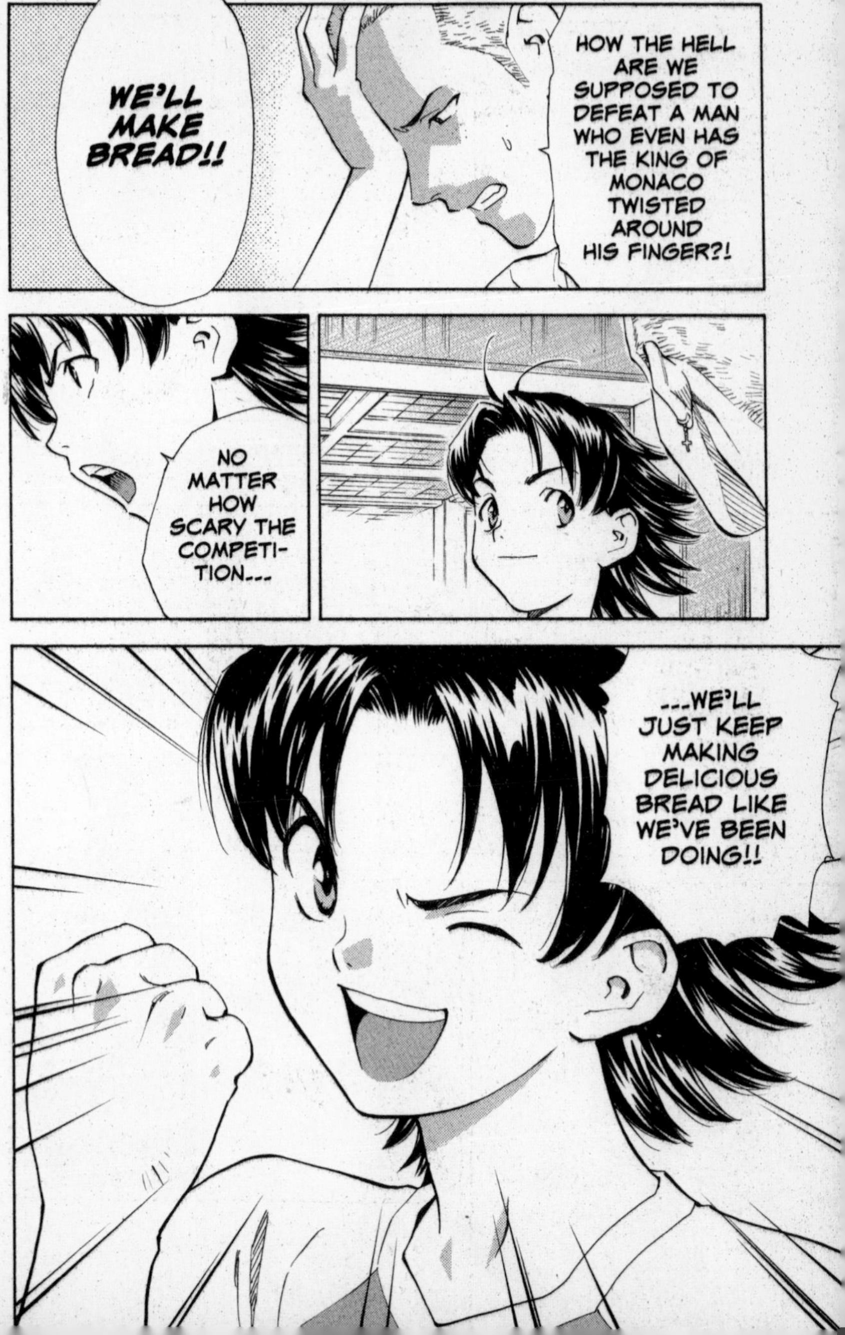
HOW THE HELL ARE WE SUPPOSED TO DEFEAT A MAN WHO EVEN HAS THE KING OF MONACO TWISTED AROUND HIS FINGER?!
WE'LL MAKE BREAD!!
NO MATTER HOW SCARY THE COMPETITION...
...WE'LL JUST KEEP MAKING DELICIOUS BREAD LIKE WE'VE BEEN DOING!!

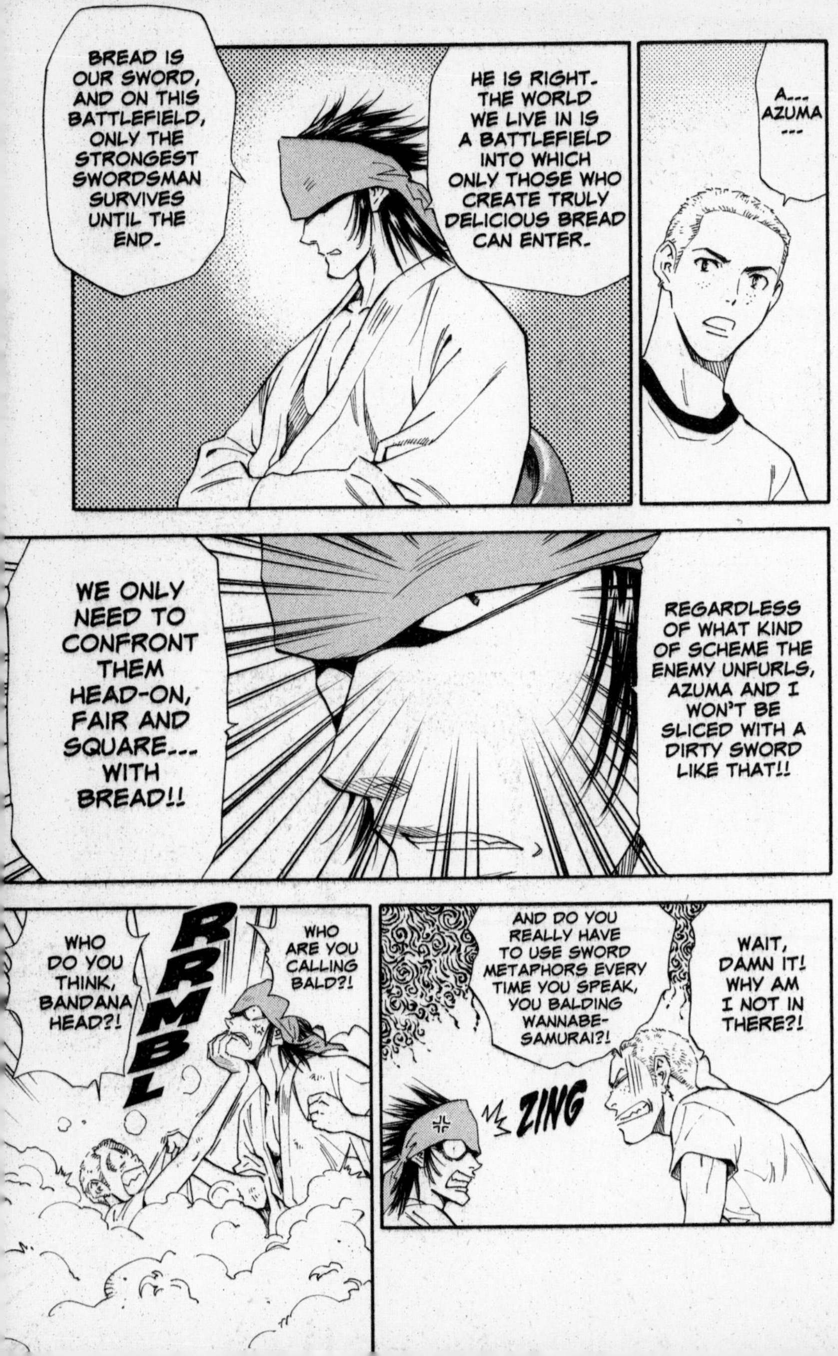
A... AZUMA ...
HE IS RIGHT. THE WORLD WE LIVE IN IS A BATTLEFIELD INTO WHICH ONLY THOSE WHO CREATE TRULY DELICIOUS BREAD CAN ENTER.
BREAD IS OUR SWORD, AND ON THIS BATTLEFIELD, ONLY THE STRONGEST SWORDSMAN SURVIVES UNTIL THE END.
REGARDLESS OF WHAT KIND OF SCHEME THE ENEMY UNFURLS, AZUMA AND I WON'T BE SLICED WITH A DIRTY SWORD LIKE THAT!!
WE ONLY NEED TO CONFRONT THEM HEAD-ON, FAIR AND SQUARE... WITH BREAD!!
WAIT, DAMN IT! WHY AM I NOT IN THERE?!
AND DO YOU REALLY HAVE TO USE SWORD METAPHORS EVERY TIME YOU SPEAK, YOU BALDING WANNABE-SAMURAI?!
ZING
WHO ARE YOU CALLING BALD?!
RRMBL
WHO DO YOU THINK, BANDANA HEAD?!

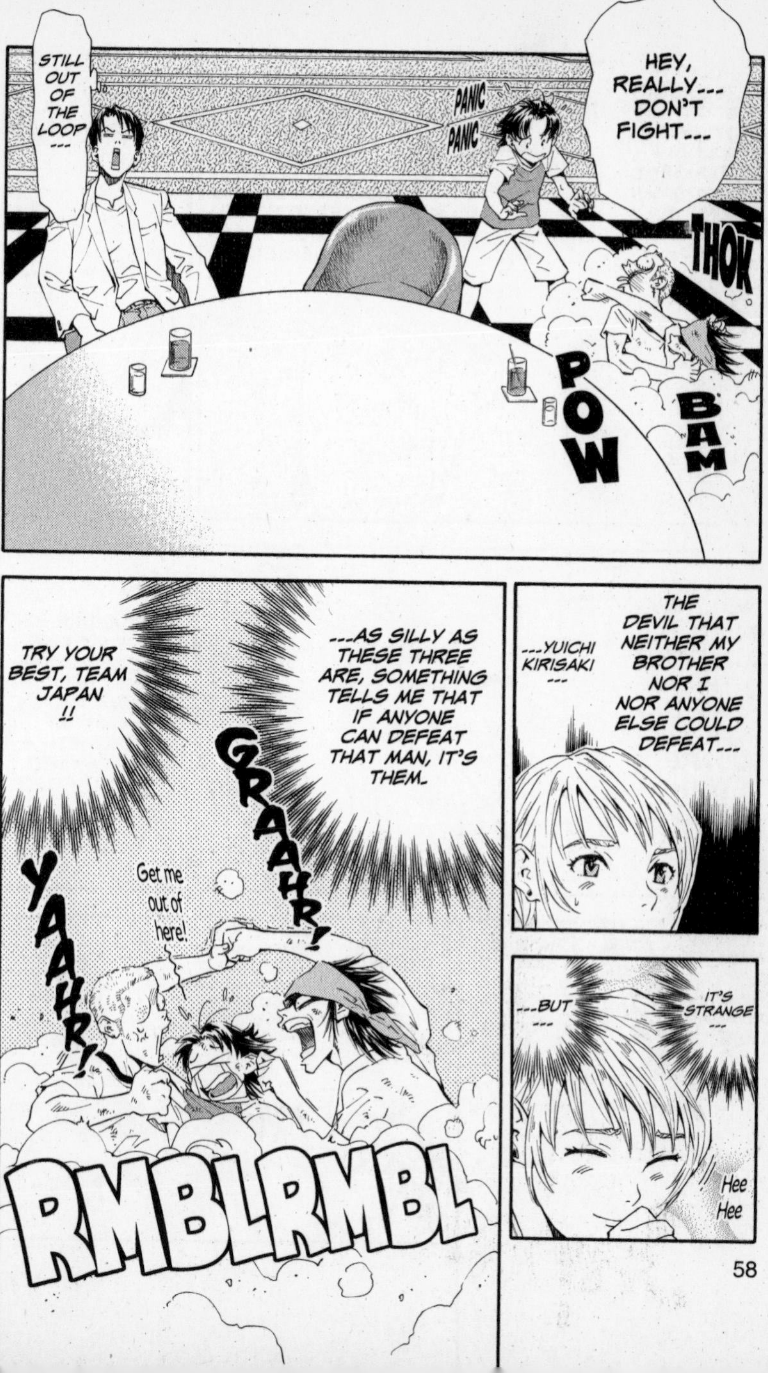
HEY, REALLY... DON'T FIGHT...
PANIC PANIC
STILL OUT OF THE LOOP...
THOK
POW
BAM
THE DEVIL THAT NEITHER MY BROTHER NOR I NOR ANYONE ELSE COULD DEFEAT...
...YUICHI KIRISAKI...
...AS SILLY AS THESE THREE ARE, SOMETHING TELLS ME THAT IF ANYONE CAN DEFEAT THAT MAN, IT'S THEM.
TRY YOUR BEST, TEAM JAPAN !!
GRAAHR!
YAAHR!
Get me out of here!
RMBLRMBL
IT'S STRANGE...
...BUT...
Hee Hee

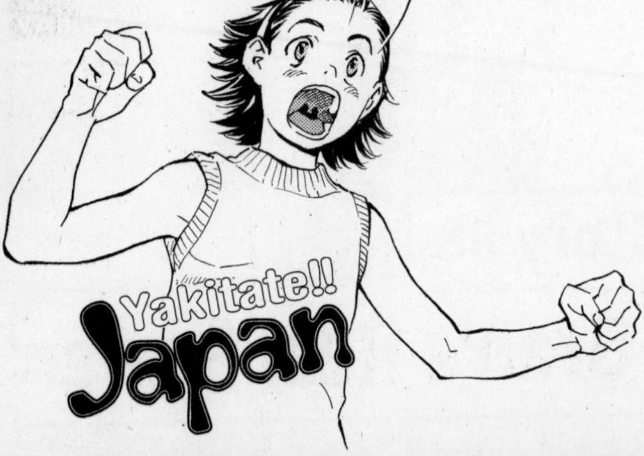
Yakitate!! Japan

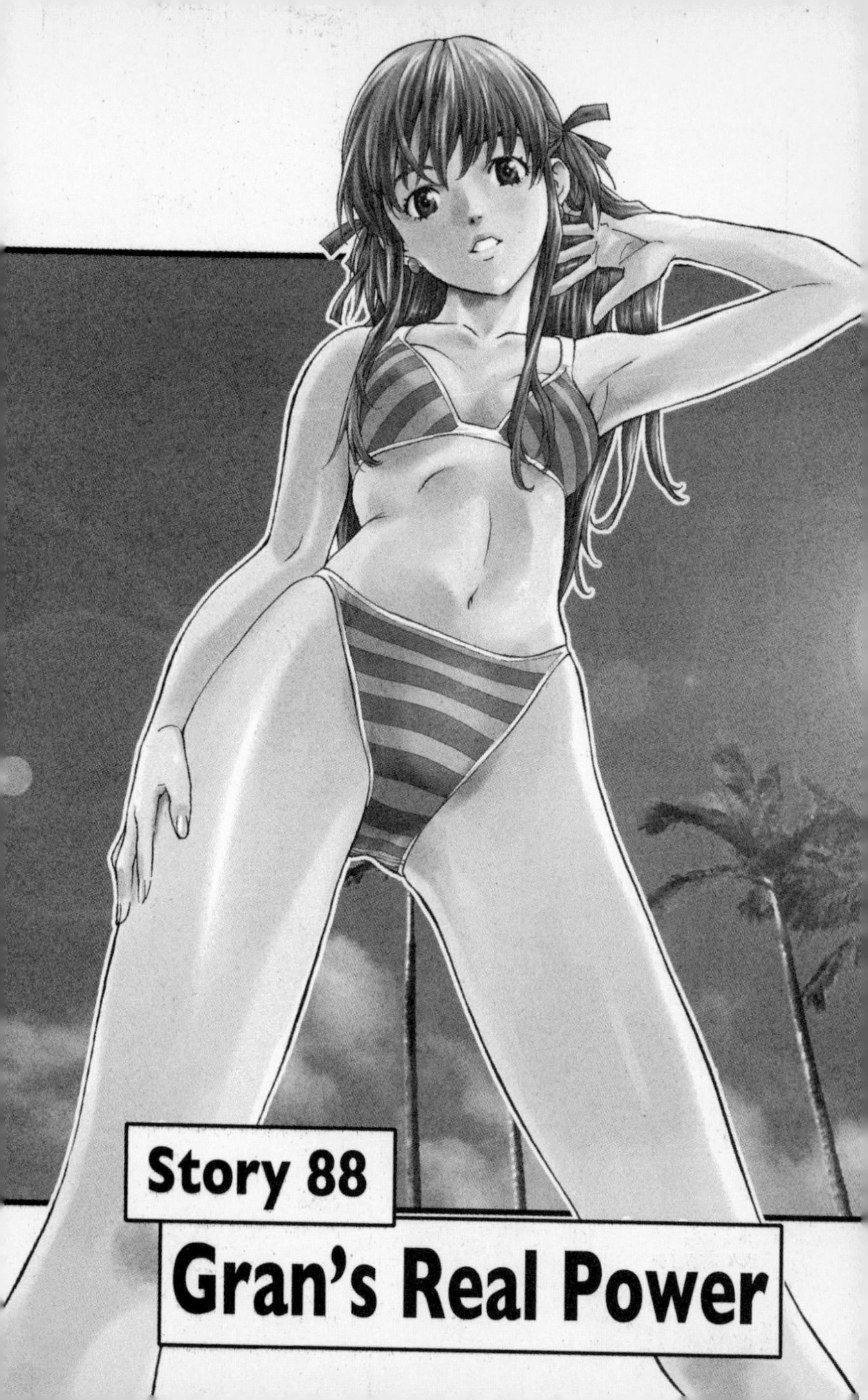
Story 88
Gran's Real Power

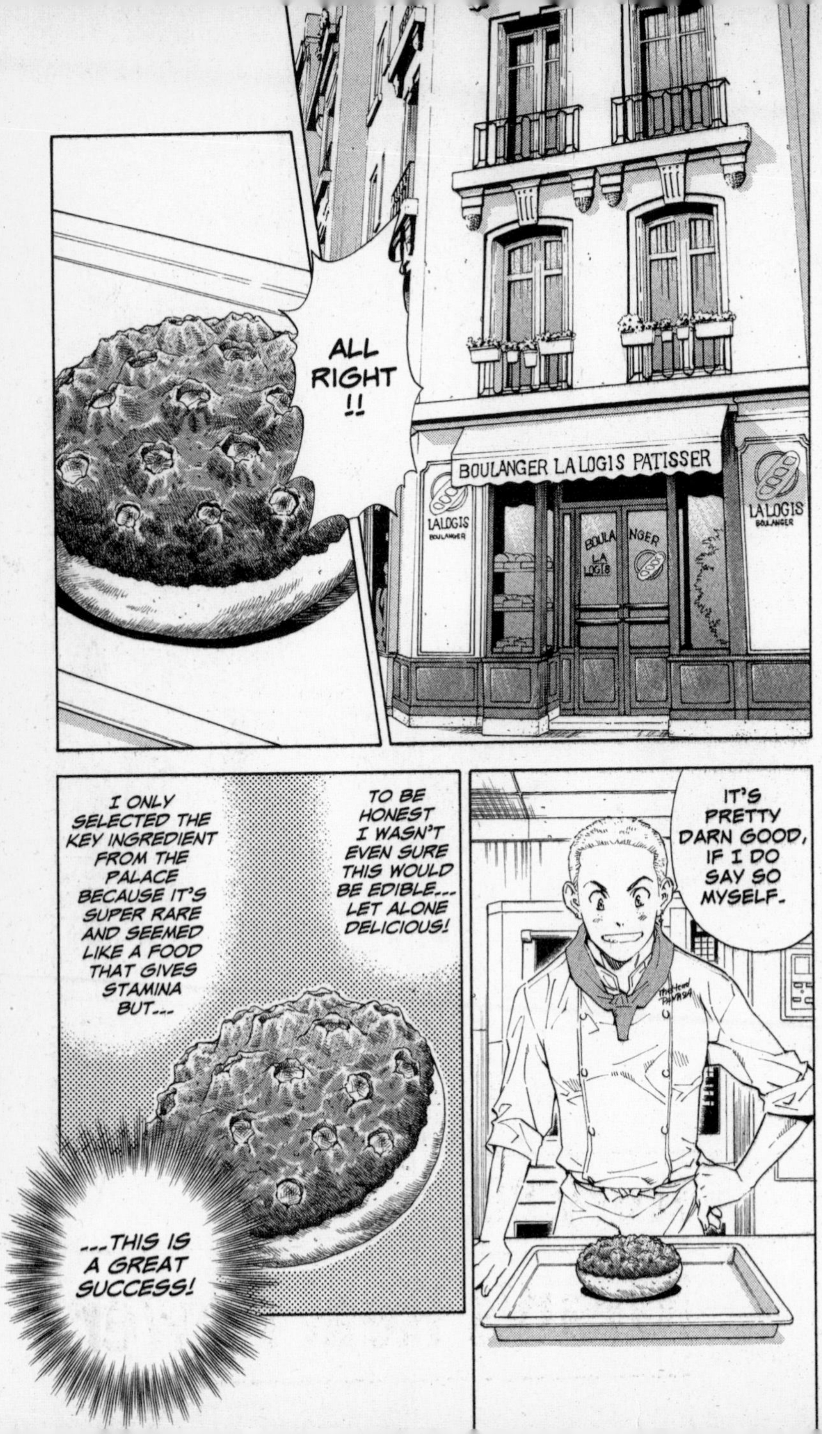
BOULANGER LALOGIS PATISSER
LALOGIS BOULANGER
BOULANGER LA LOGIS
LALOGIS BOULANGER
ALL RIGHT !!
IT'S PRETTY DARN GOOD, IF I DO SAY SO MYSELF.
TO BE HONEST I WASN'T EVEN SURE THIS WOULD BE EDIBLE... LET ALONE DELICIOUS!
I ONLY SELECTED THE KEY INGREDIENT FROM THE PALACE BECAUSE IT'S SUPER RARE AND SEEMED LIKE A FOOD THAT GIVES STAMINA BUT...
...THIS IS A GREAT SUCCESS!

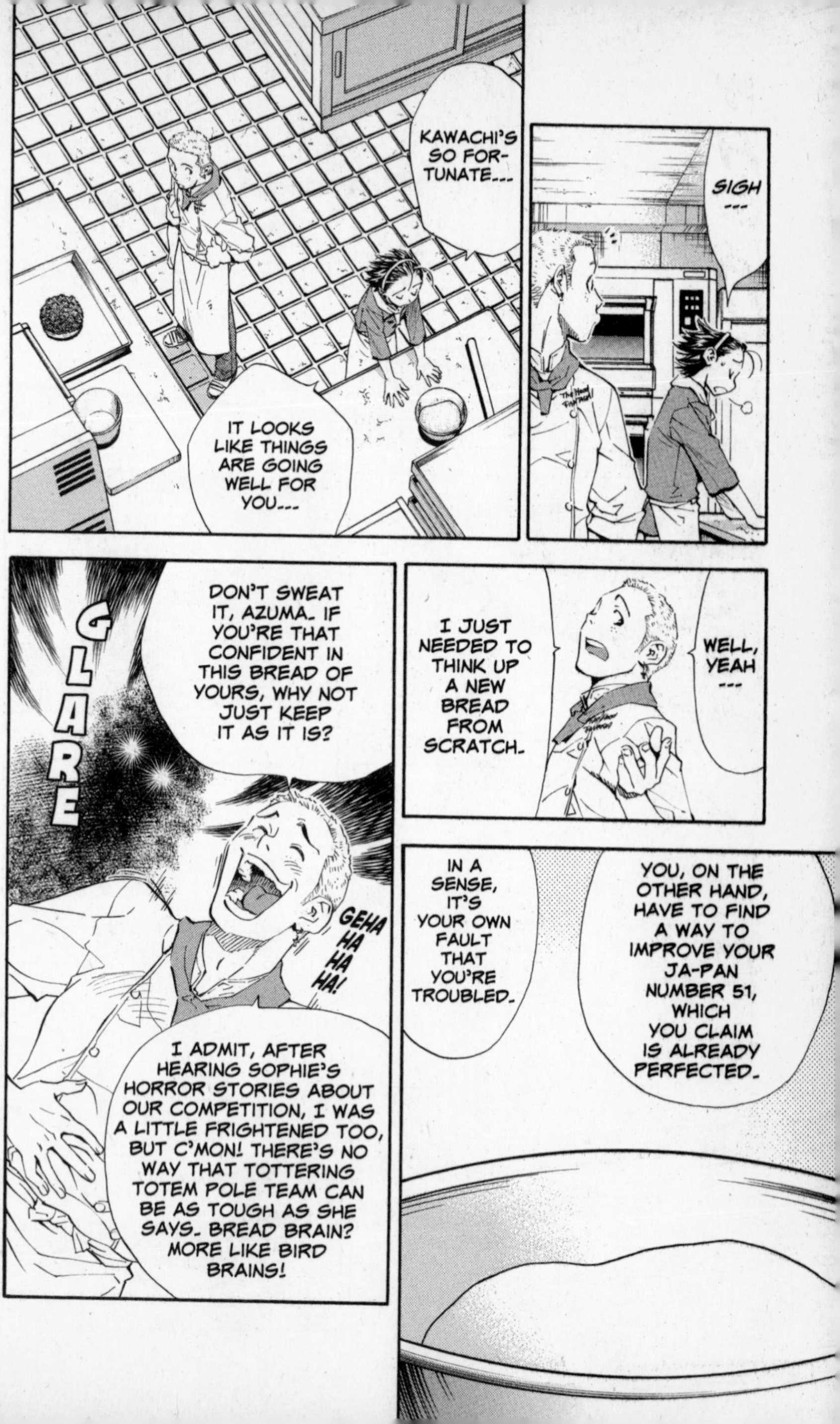
SIGH ---
KAWACHI'S SO FOR-TUNATE---
IT LOOKS LIKE THINGS ARE GOING WELL FOR YOU---
WELL, YEAH ---
I JUST NEEDED TO THINK UP A NEW BREAD FROM SCRATCH.
IN A SENSE, IT'S YOUR OWN FAULT THAT YOU'RE TROUBLED.
YOU, ON THE OTHER HAND, HAVE TO FIND A WAY TO IMPROVE YOUR JA-PAN NUMBER 51, WHICH YOU CLAIM IS ALREADY PERFECTED.
DON'T SWEAT IT, AZUMA. IF YOU'RE THAT CONFIDENT IN THIS BREAD OF YOURS, WHY NOT JUST KEEP IT AS IT IS?
GLARE
GEHA HA HA HA!
I ADMIT, AFTER HEARING SOPHIE'S HORROR STORIES ABOUT OUR COMPETITION, I WAS A LITTLE FRIGHTENED TOO, BUT C'MON! THERE'S NO WAY THAT TOTTERING TOTEM POLE TEAM CAN BE AS TOUGH AS SHE SAYS. BREAD BRAIN? MORE LIKE BIRD BRAINS!

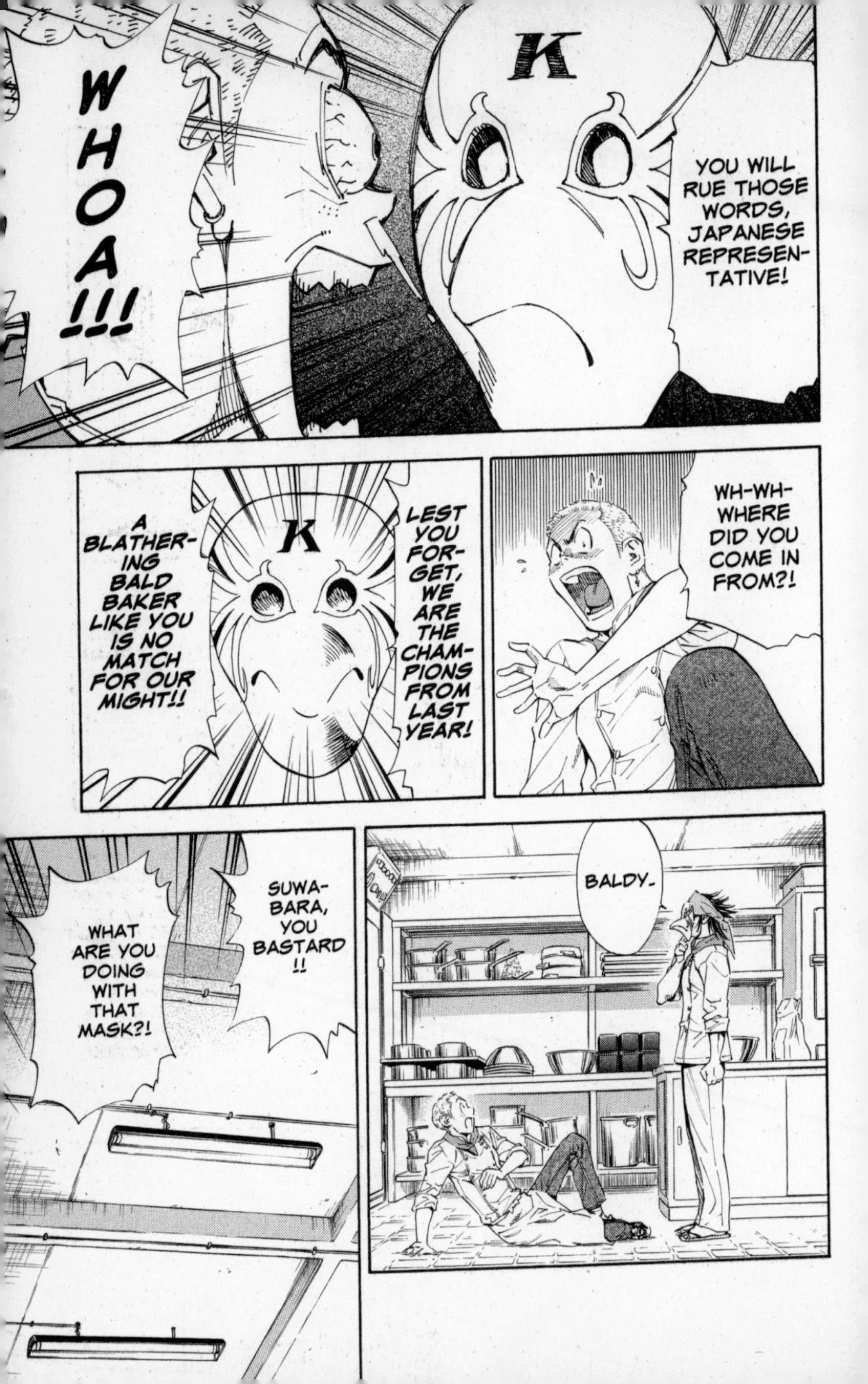
K
YOU WILL RUE THOSE WORDS, JAPANESE REPRESEN-TATIVE!
WHOA!!!
WH-WH-WHERE DID YOU COME IN FROM?!
LEST YOU FOR-GET, WE ARE THE CHAM-PIONS FROM LAST YEAR!
K
A BLATHER-ING BALD BAKER LIKE YOU IS NO MATCH FOR OUR MIGHT!!
BALDY.
SUWA-BARA, YOU BASTARD !!
WHAT ARE YOU DOING WITH THAT MASK?!

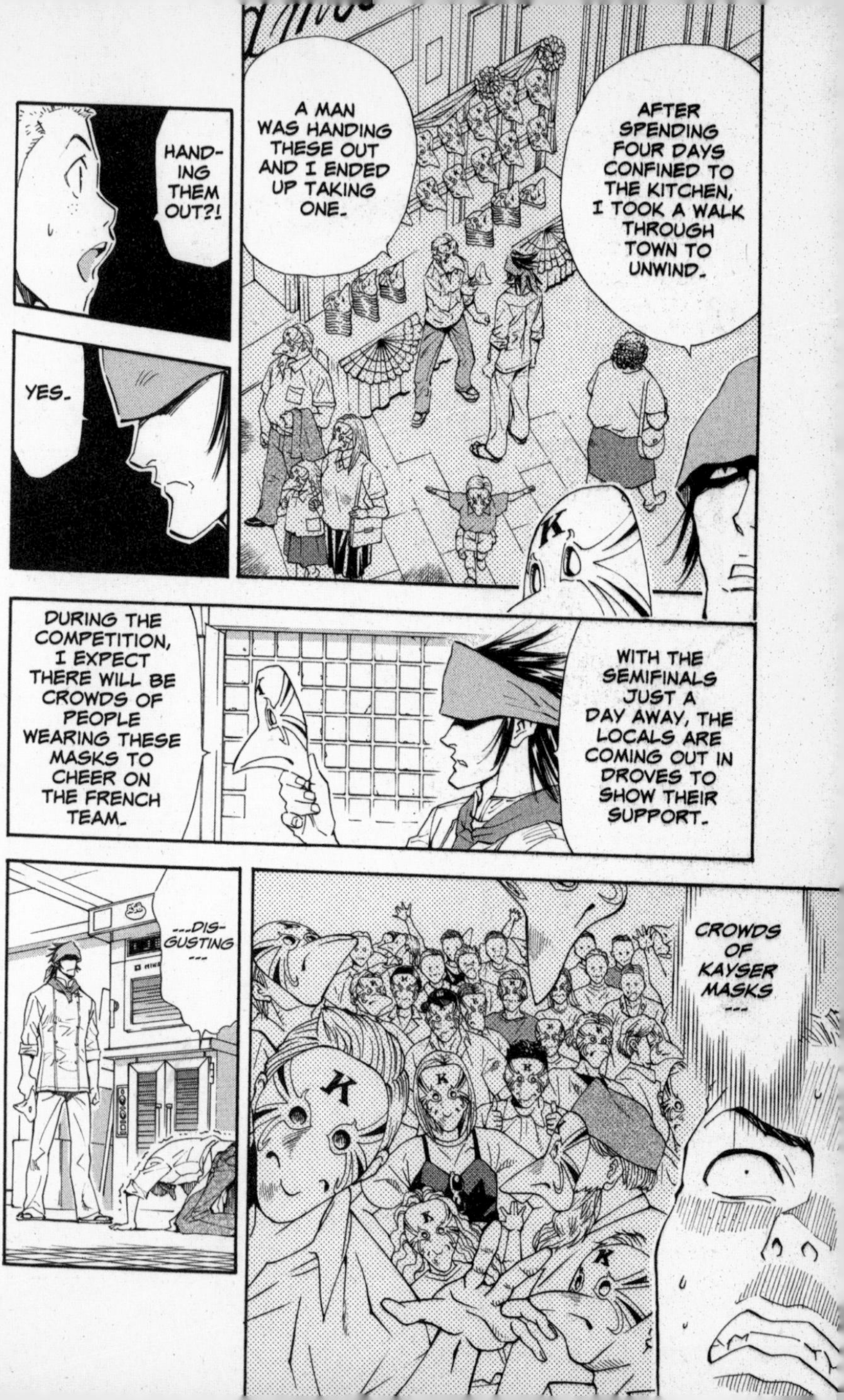
AFTER SPENDING FOUR DAYS CONFINED TO THE KITCHEN, I TOOK A WALK THROUGH TOWN TO UNWIND.
A MAN WAS HANDING THESE OUT AND I ENDED UP TAKING ONE.
HAND-ING THEM OUT?!
YES.
WITH THE SEMIFINALS JUST A DAY AWAY, THE LOCALS ARE COMING OUT IN DROVES TO SHOW THEIR SUPPORT.
DURING THE COMPETITION, I EXPECT THERE WILL BE CROWDS OF PEOPLE WEARING THESE MASKS TO CHEER ON THE FRENCH TEAM.
CROWDS OF KAYSER MASKS...
...DIS-GUSTING...

IT IS AN UNAVOIDABLE HANDICAP. THIS IS EFFECTIVELY A HOME GAME FOR THE FRENCH TEAM AND AN AWAY GAME FOR US.

WE CAN EXPECT NO MORE AUDIENCE SUPPORT THAN THE LOTTE MARINES AT A HANSHIN TIGER HOME GAME.*

*THINK PATRIOTS FANS AT THE RAIDER NATION.

YEAH...WE'VE ALREADY GOT THE ST. PIERRE OWNER'S DIRTY TRICKS TO WORRY ABOUT--THERE'S NO CHANCE OF WINNING IF WE LET THE AUDIENCE AFFECT OUR GAME.

...YEAH...

SIGH

WHAT'S THE MATTER, AZUMA? YOU LOOK DOWN.

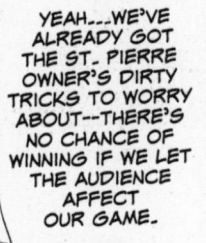

HE'S BEEN LIKE THIS ALL WEEK...

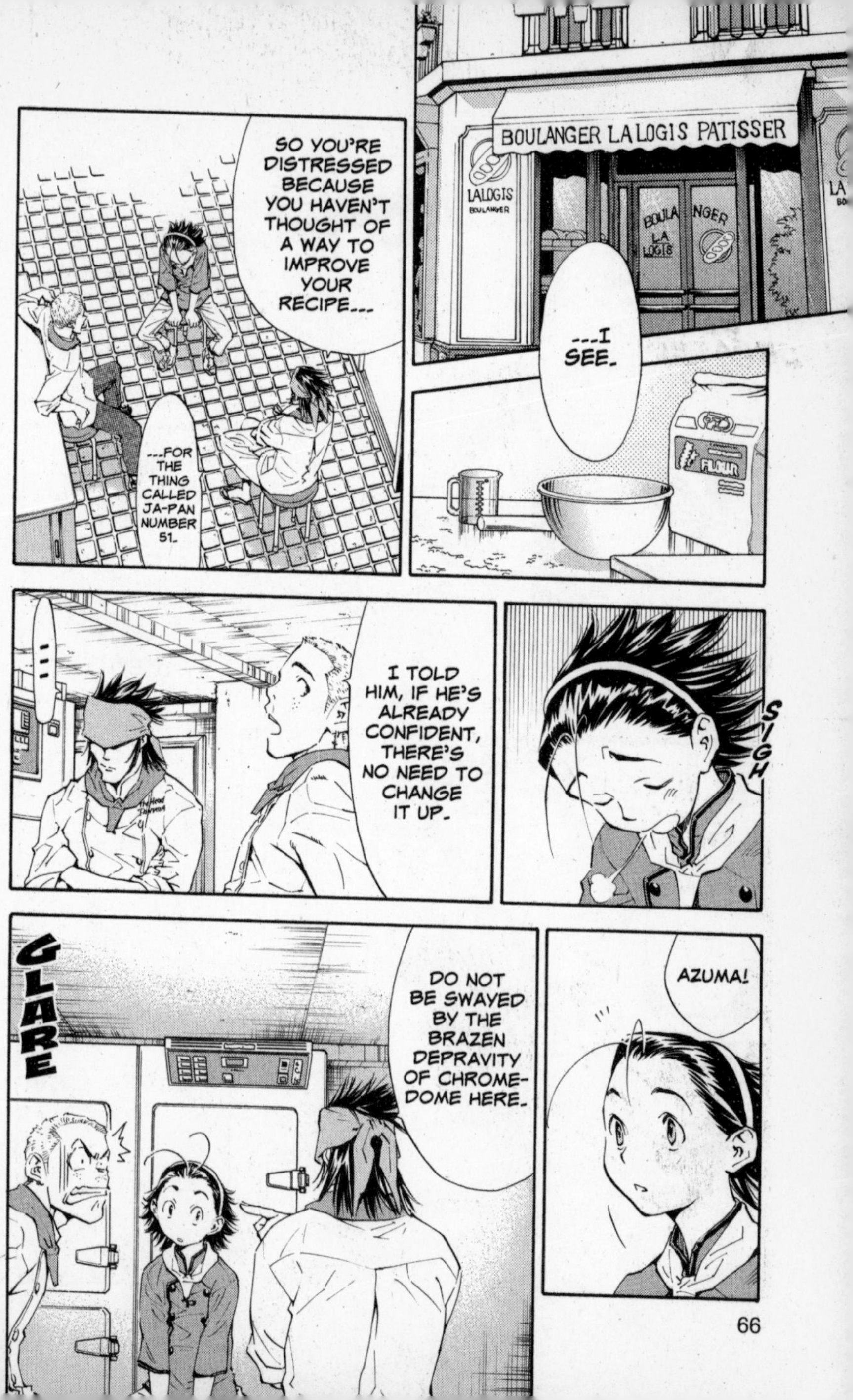
BOULANGER LALOGIS PATISSER
LALOGIS BOULANGER
BOULANGER LA LOGIS
...I SEE.
FLOUR
SO YOU'RE DISTRESSED BECAUSE YOU HAVEN'T THOUGHT OF A WAY TO IMPROVE YOUR RECIPE...
...FOR THE THING CALLED JA-PAN NUMBER 51.
SIGH
I TOLD HIM, IF HE'S ALREADY CONFIDENT, THERE'S NO NEED TO CHANGE IT UP.
...
AZUMA!
DO NOT BE SWAYED BY THE BRAZEN DEPRAVITY OF CHROME-DOME HERE.
GLARE

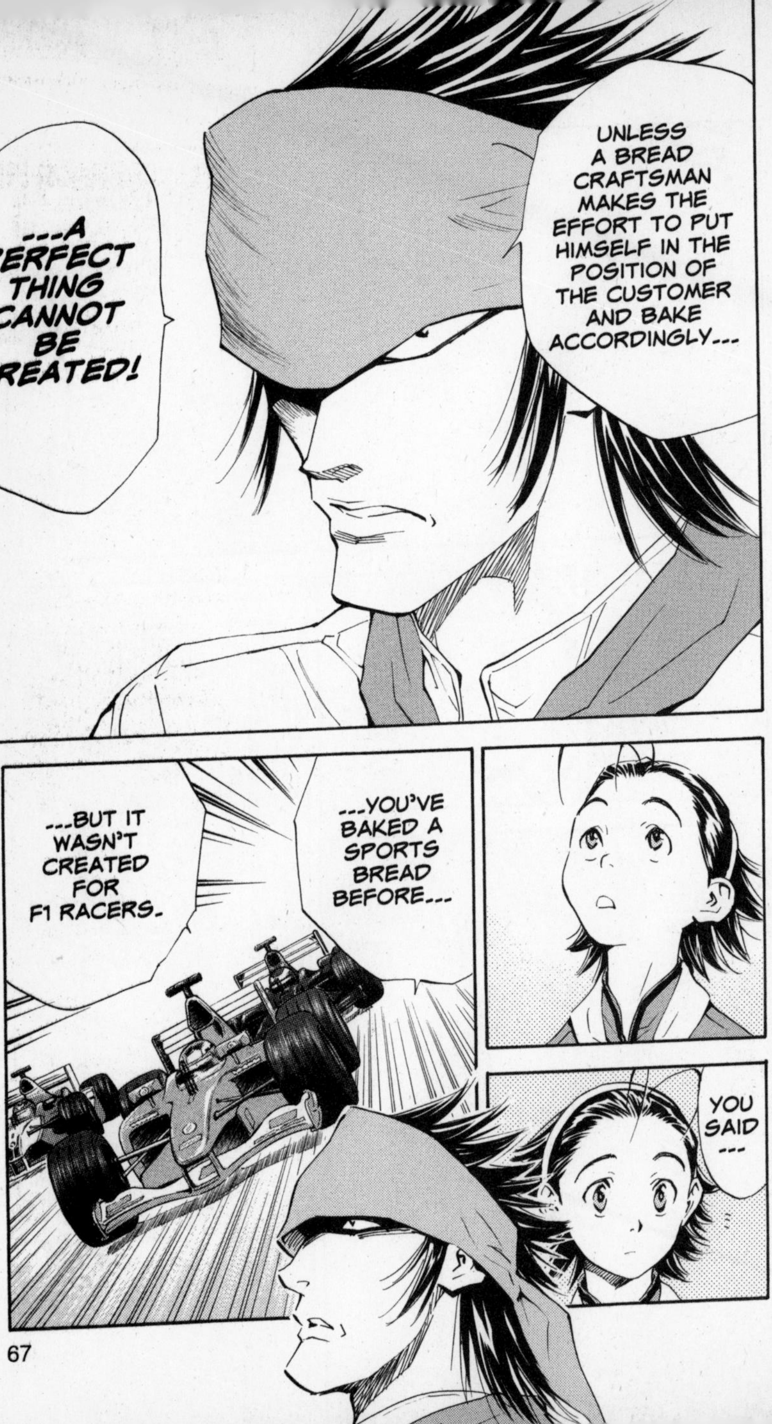
UNLESS A BREAD CRAFTSMAN MAKES THE EFFORT TO PUT HIMSELF IN THE POSITION OF THE CUSTOMER AND BAKE ACCORDINGLY...
...A PERFECT THING CANNOT BE CREATED!
YOU SAID ...
...YOU'VE BAKED A SPORTS BREAD BEFORE...
...BUT IT WASN'T CREATED FOR F1 RACERS.

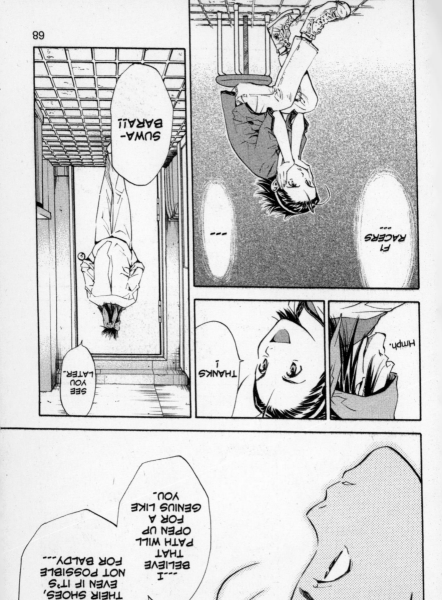

SUWA-BARAI!

F1 RACERS ---

SEE YOU LATER.

THANKS!

Hmph.

IF YOU CAN TRULY IMAGINE YOURSELF IN THEIR SHOES, EVEN IF IT'S NOT POSSIBLE FOR BALDY...

...I BELIEVE THAT PATH WILL OPEN UP FOR A GENIUS LIKE YOU.

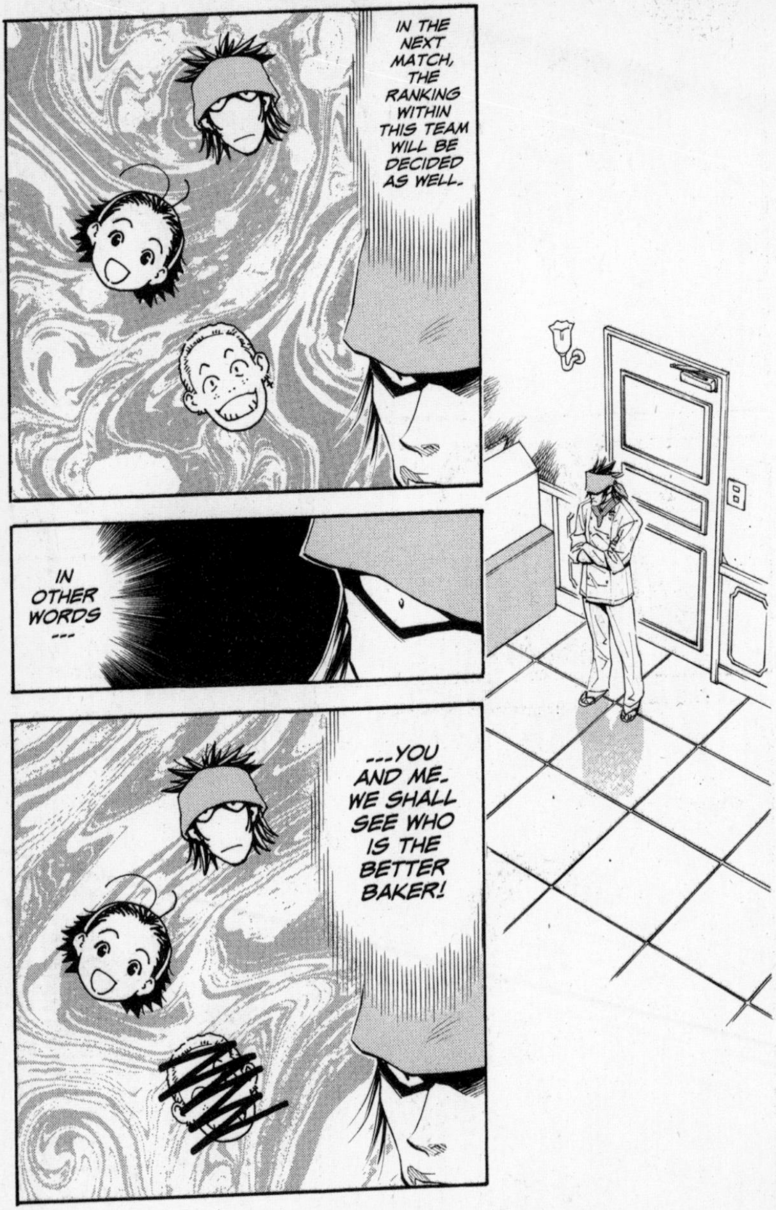
IN THE NEXT MATCH, THE RANKING WITHIN THIS TEAM WILL BE DECIDED AS WELL.
IN OTHER WORDS ---
---YOU AND ME. WE SHALL SEE WHO IS THE BETTER BAKER!

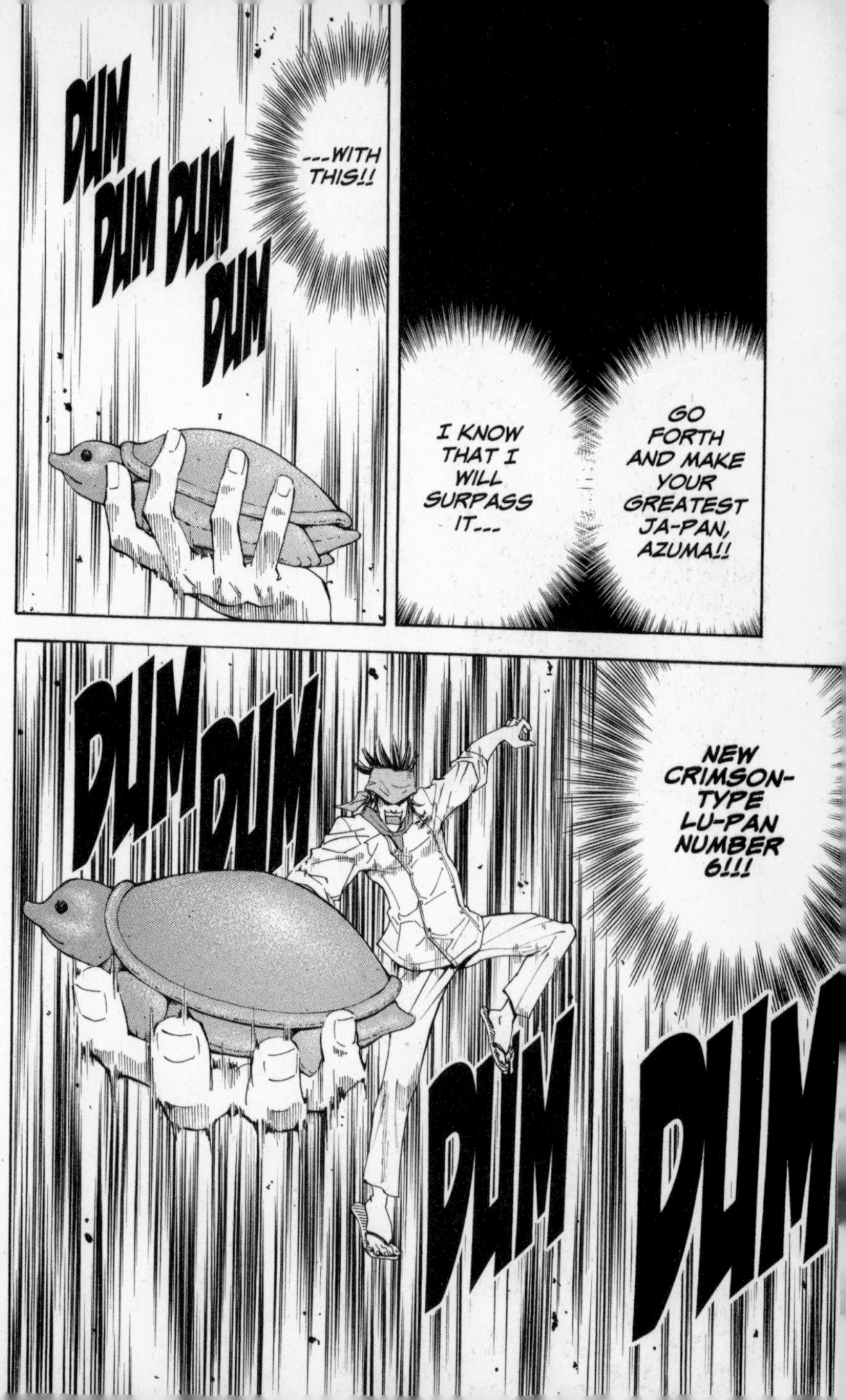
GO FORTH AND MAKE YOUR GREATEST JA-PAN, AZUMA!!
I KNOW THAT I WILL SURPASS IT---
---WITH THIS!!
DUM DUM DUM DUM DUM
NEW CRIMSON-TYPE LU-PAN NUMBER 6!!!
DUM DUM
DUM DUM

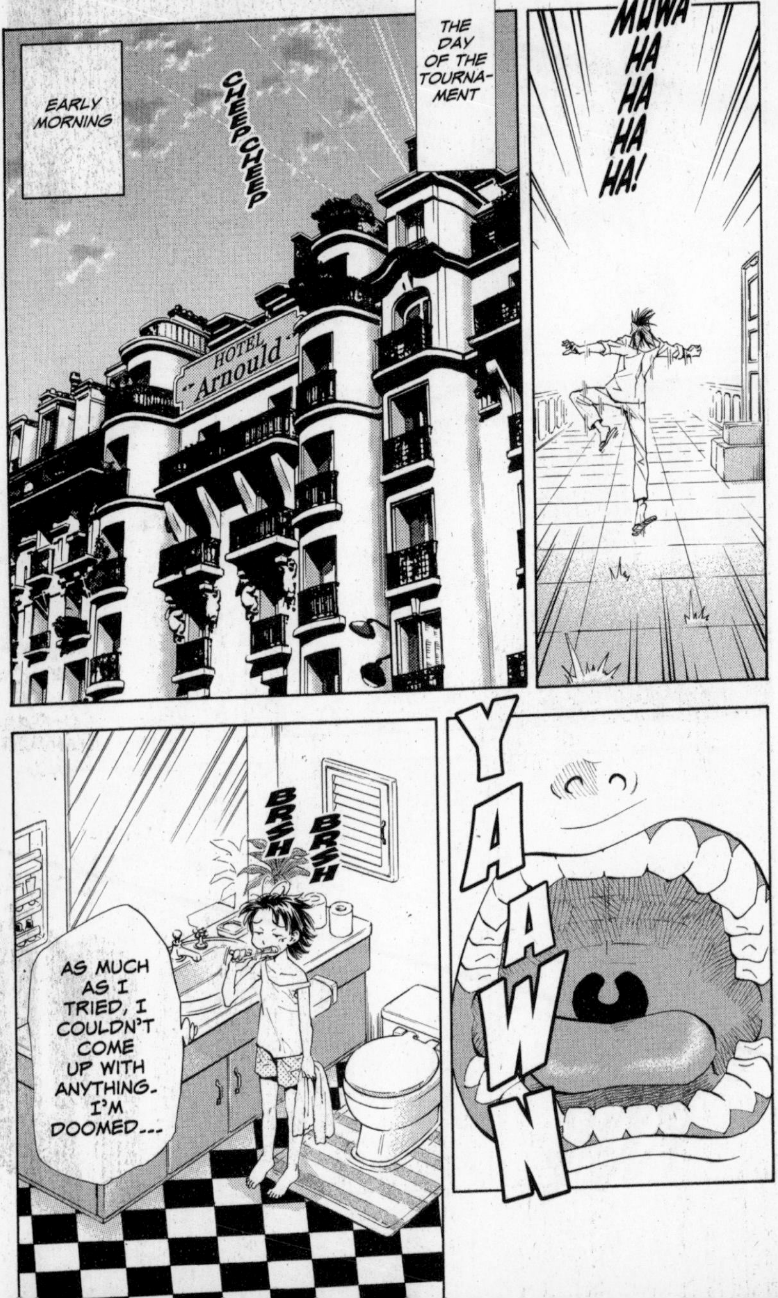
MUWA HA HA HA HA HA!
THE DAY OF THE TOURNAMENT
CHEEP CHEEP
EARLY MORNING
HOTEL Arnould
YAWN
BRSH BRSH
AS MUCH AS I TRIED, I COULDN'T COME UP WITH ANYTHING. I'M DOOMED...

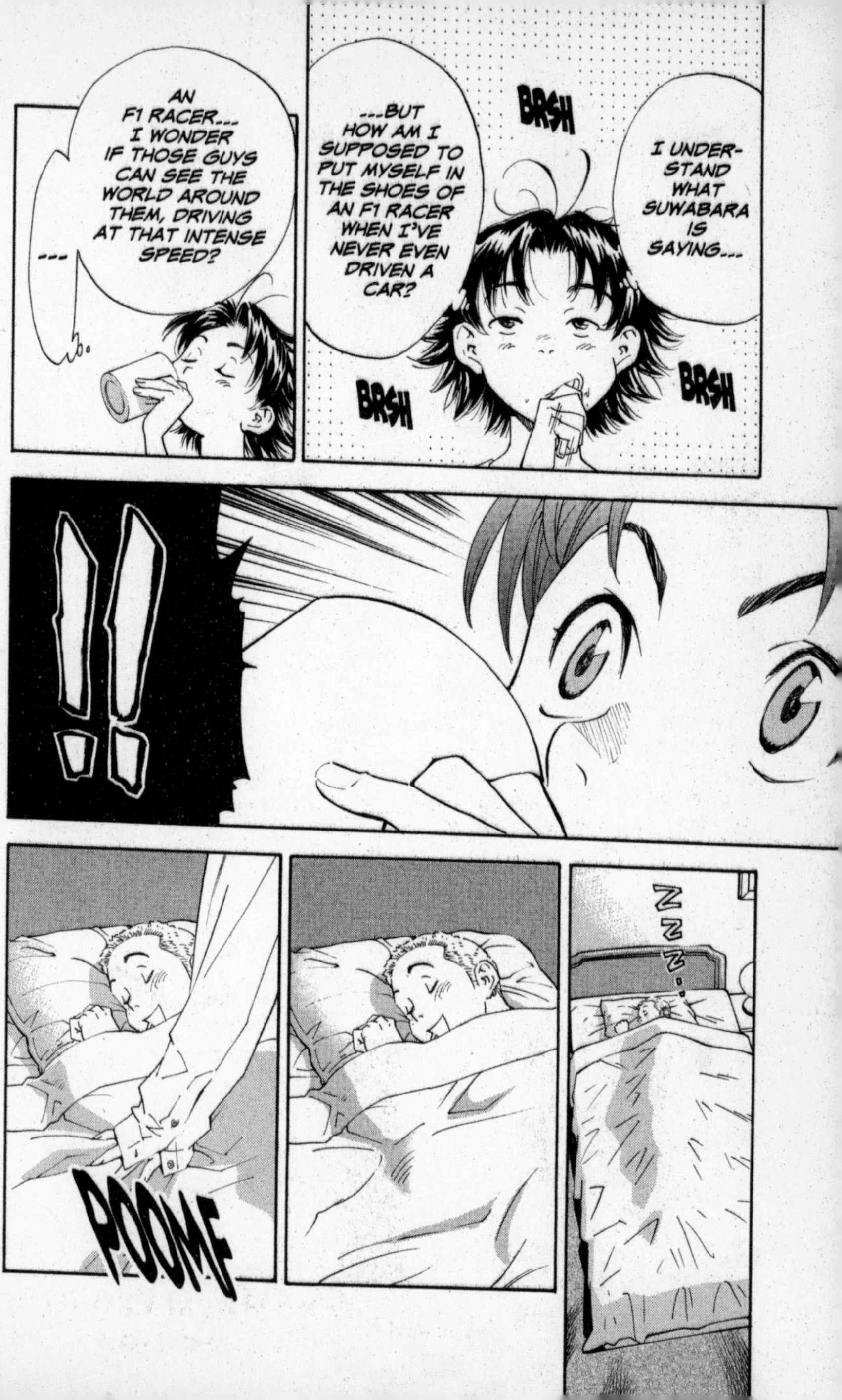
I UNDER-STAND WHAT SUWABARA IS SAYING...
BRSH
BRSH
...BUT HOW AM I SUPPOSED TO PUT MYSELF IN THE SHOES OF AN F1 RACER WHEN I'VE NEVER EVEN DRIVEN A CAR?
BRSH
AN F1 RACER... I WONDER IF THOSE GUYS CAN SEE THE WORLD AROUND THEM, DRIVING AT THAT INTENSE SPEED?
...
!!
Z Z Z...
POOMF

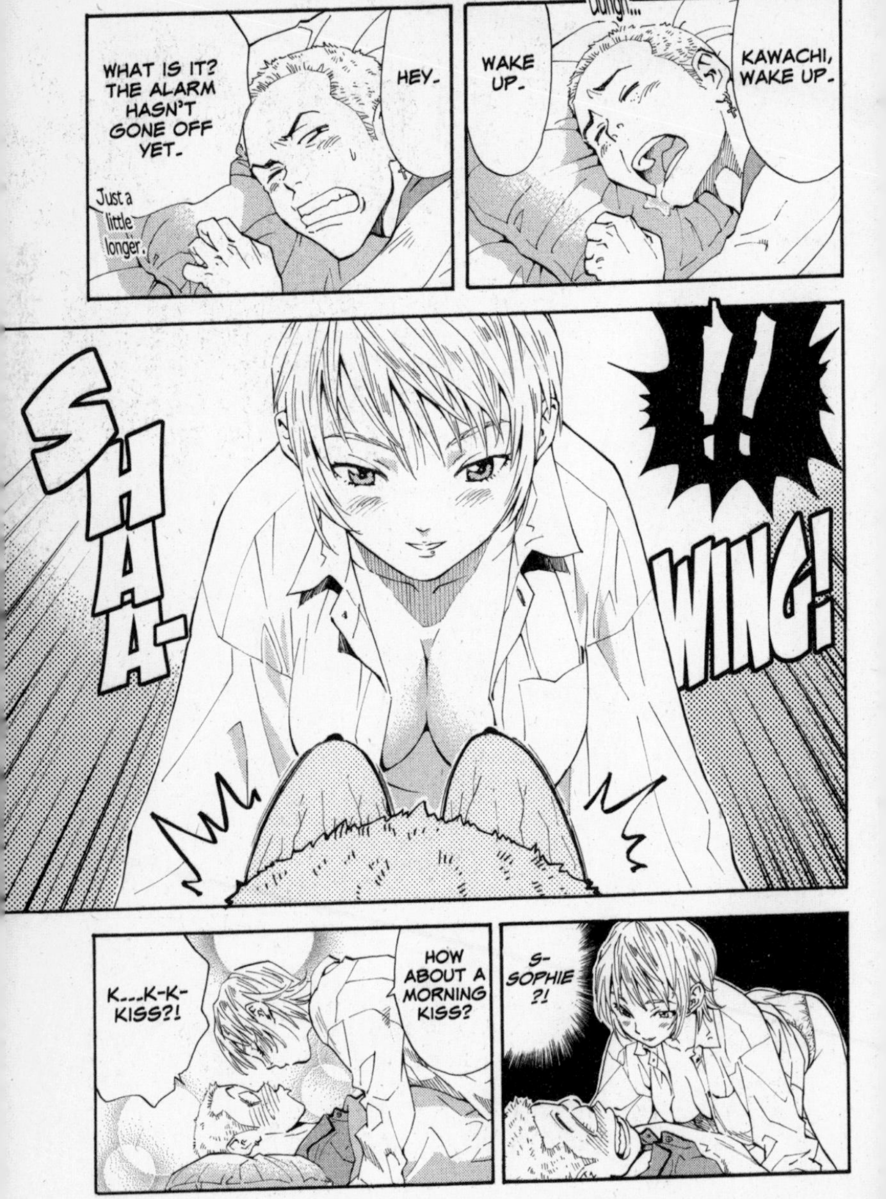
Uungh...
KAWACHI, WAKE UP.
WAKE UP.
HEY.
WHAT IS IT? THE ALARM HASN'T GONE OFF YET.
Just a little longer.
!!
WING!
SHA-A-
S-SOPHIE?!
HOW ABOUT A MORNING KISS?
K...K-K-KISS?!

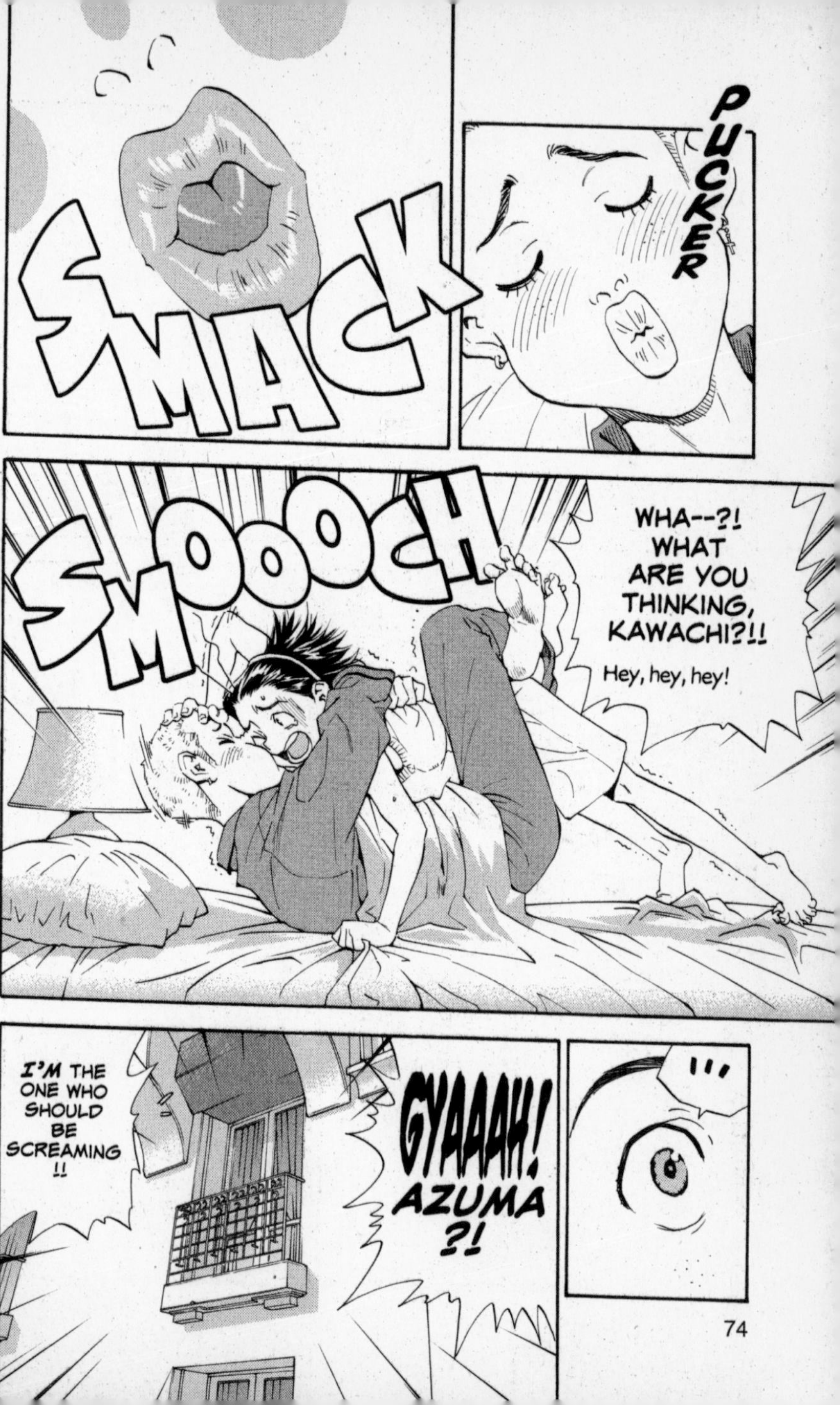
PUCKER
SMACK
SMOOOCH
WHA--?! WHAT ARE YOU THINKING, KAWACHI?!!
Hey, hey, hey!
...
GYAAAH! AZUMA ?!
I'M THE ONE WHO SHOULD BE SCREAMING !!

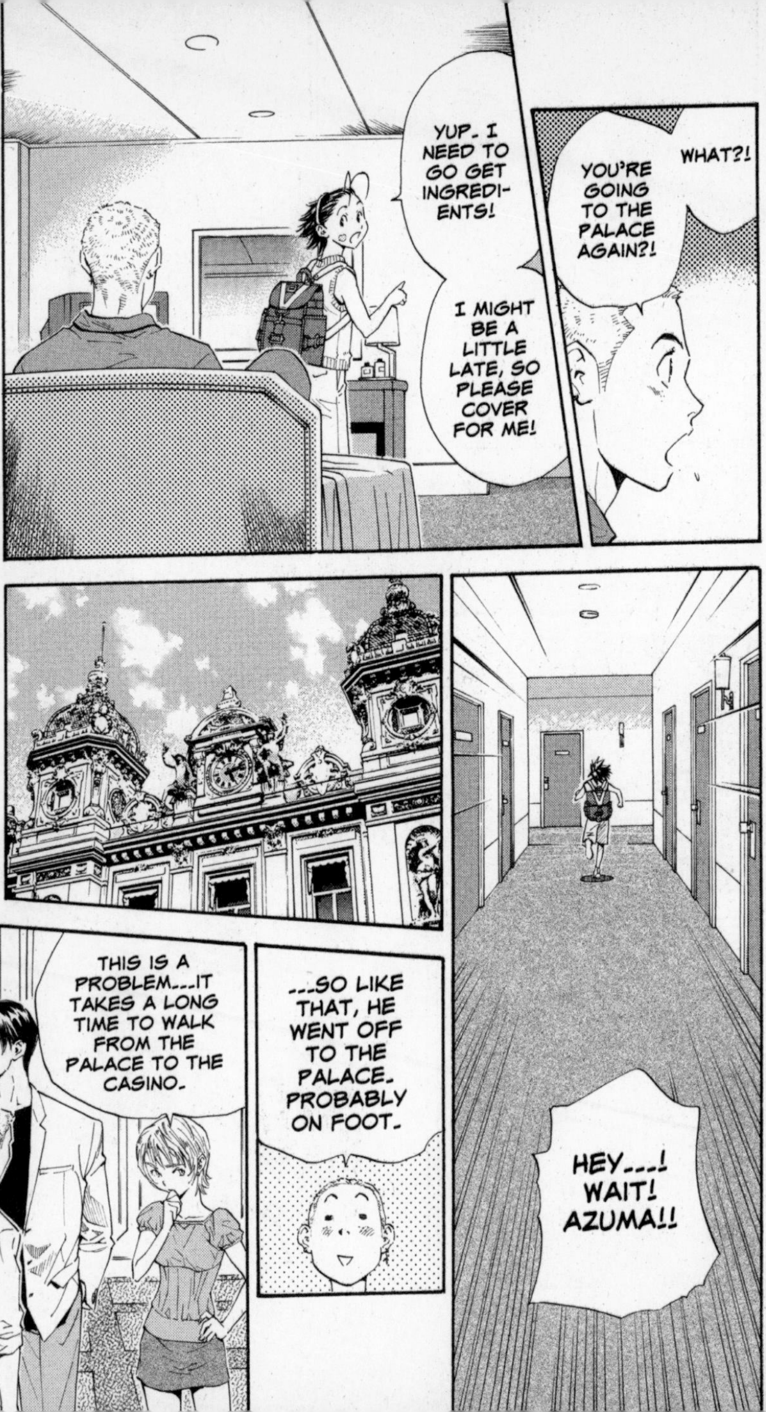
WHAT?!
YOU'RE GOING TO THE PALACE AGAIN?!
YUP. I NEED TO GO GET INGREDI-ENTS!
I MIGHT BE A LITTLE LATE, SO PLEASE COVER FOR ME!
HEY...! WAIT! AZUMA!!
...SO LIKE THAT, HE WENT OFF TO THE PALACE. PROBABLY ON FOOT.
THIS IS A PROBLEM...IT TAKES A LONG TIME TO WALK FROM THE PALACE TO THE CASINO.

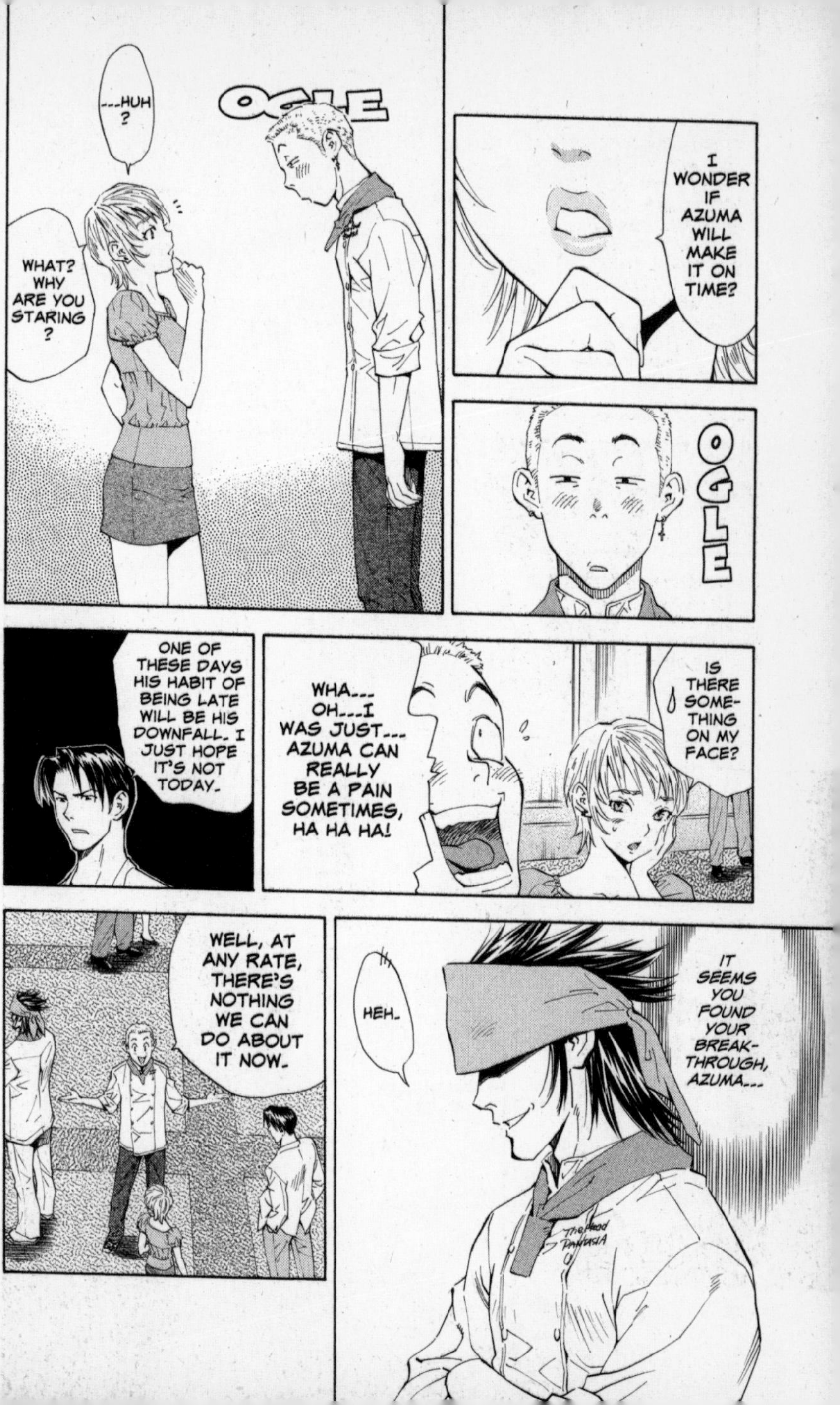
I WONDER IF AZUMA WILL MAKE IT ON TIME?
OGLE
OGLE
---HUH?
WHAT? WHY ARE YOU STARING?
IS THERE SOMETHING ON MY FACE?
WHA... OH...I WAS JUST... AZUMA CAN REALLY BE A PAIN SOMETIMES, HA HA HA!
ONE OF THESE DAYS HIS HABIT OF BEING LATE WILL BE HIS DOWNFALL. I JUST HOPE IT'S NOT TODAY.
IT SEEMS YOU FOUND YOUR BREAK-THROUGH, AZUMA...
HEH.
WELL, AT ANY RATE, THERE'S NOTHING WE CAN DO ABOUT IT NOW.

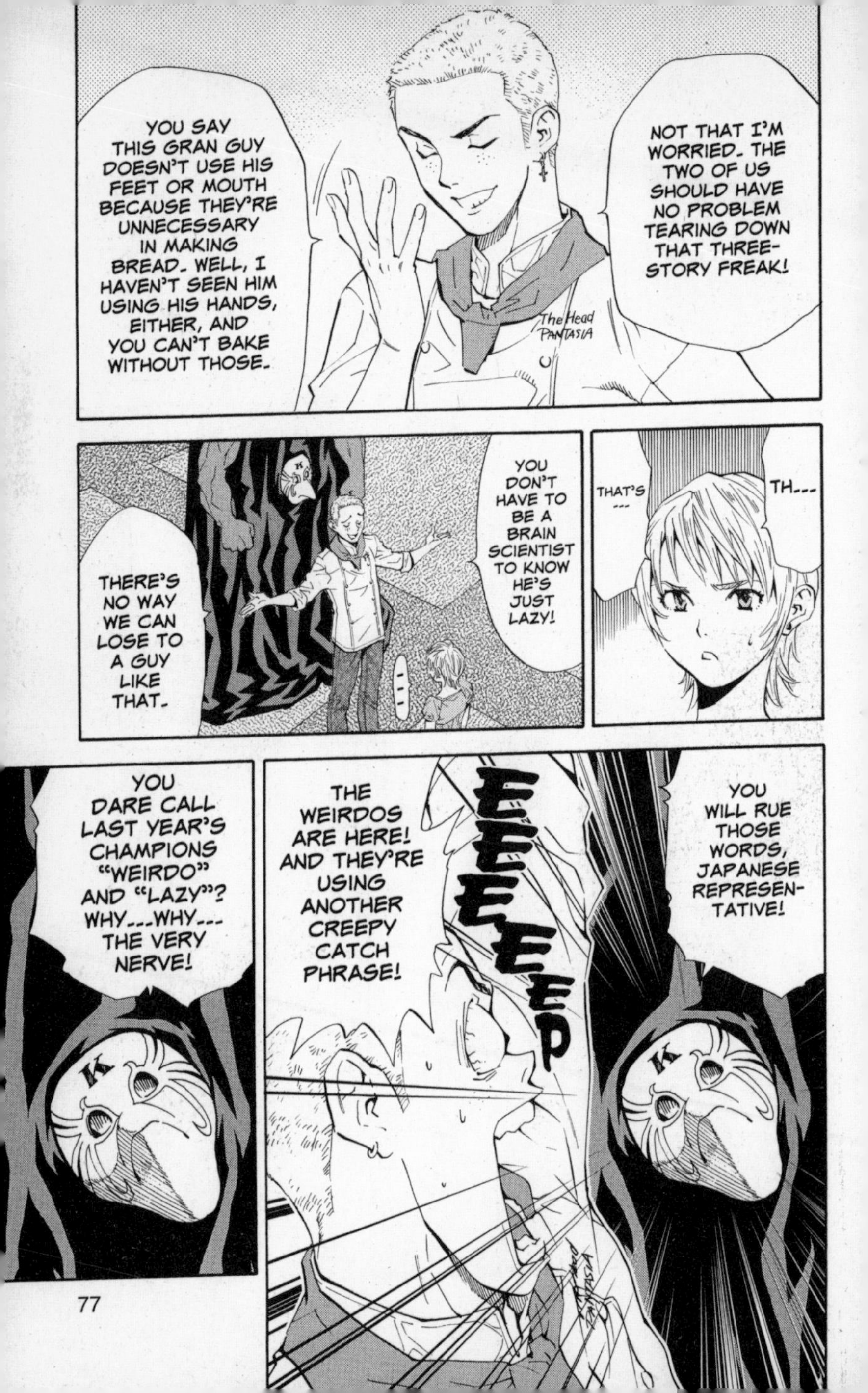
YOU SAY THIS GRAN GUY DOESN'T USE HIS FEET OR MOUTH BECAUSE THEY'RE UNNECESSARY IN MAKING BREAD. WELL, I HAVEN'T SEEN HIM USING HIS HANDS, EITHER, AND YOU CAN'T BAKE WITHOUT THOSE.
NOT THAT I'M WORRIED. THE TWO OF US SHOULD HAVE NO PROBLEM TEARING DOWN THAT THREE-STORY FREAK!
The Head PANTASIA
TH...
THAT'S ...
YOU DON'T HAVE TO BE A BRAIN SCIENTIST TO KNOW HE'S JUST LAZY!
THERE'S NO WAY WE CAN LOSE TO A GUY LIKE THAT.
...
YOU WILL RUE THOSE WORDS, JAPANESE REPRESEN-TATIVE!
EEEEEP
THE WEIRDOS ARE HERE! AND THEY'RE USING ANOTHER CREEPY CATCH PHRASE!
YOU DARE CALL LAST YEAR'S CHAMPIONS "WEIRDO" AND "LAZY"? WHY...WHY... THE VERY NERVE!

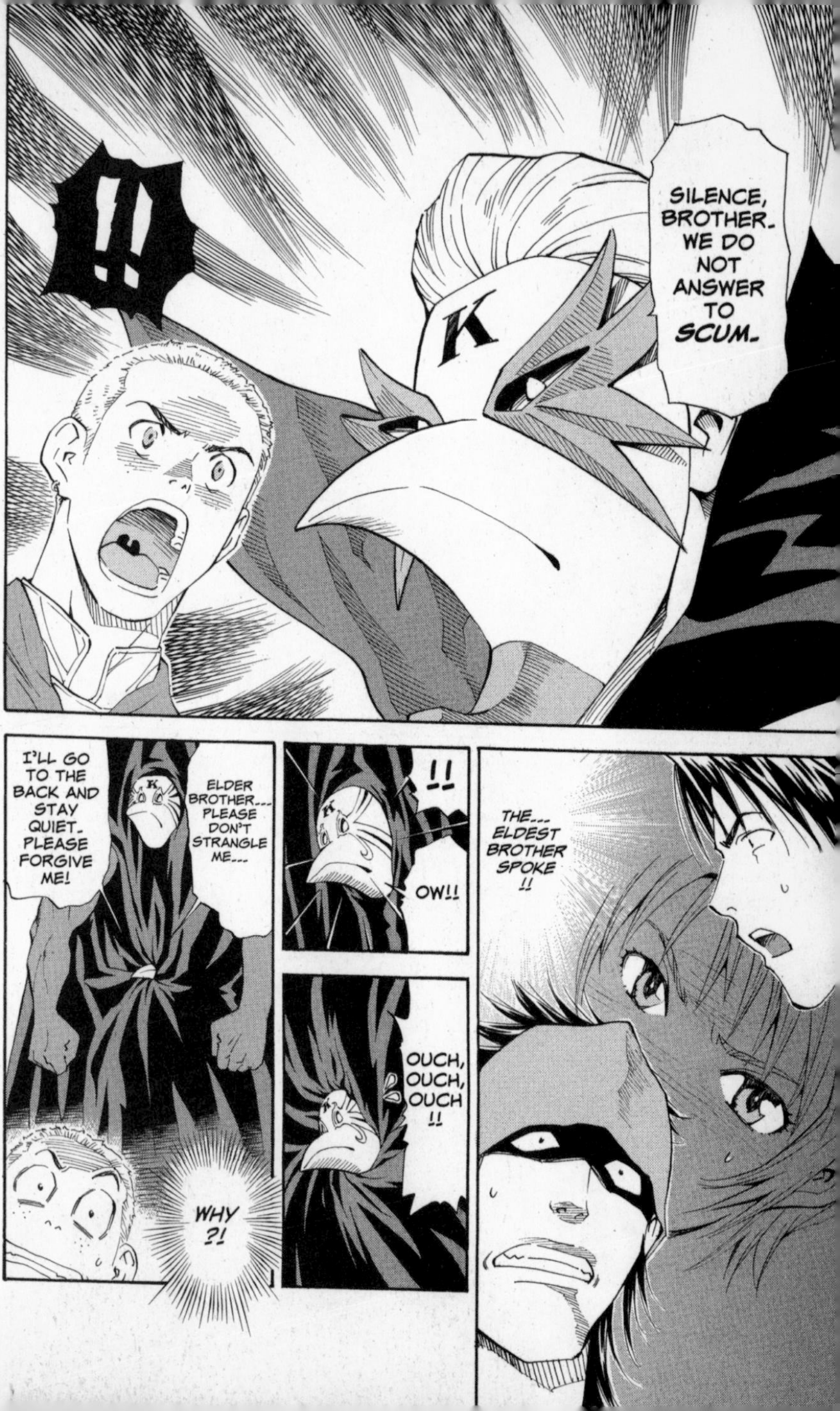
SILENCE, BROTHER. WE DO NOT ANSWER TO SCUM.
!!
THE... ELDEST BROTHER SPOKE !!
!!
OW!!
OUCH, OUCH, OUCH !!
ELDER BROTHER... PLEASE DON'T STRANGLE ME...
I'LL GO TO THE BACK AND STAY QUIET. PLEASE FORGIVE ME!
WHY ?!

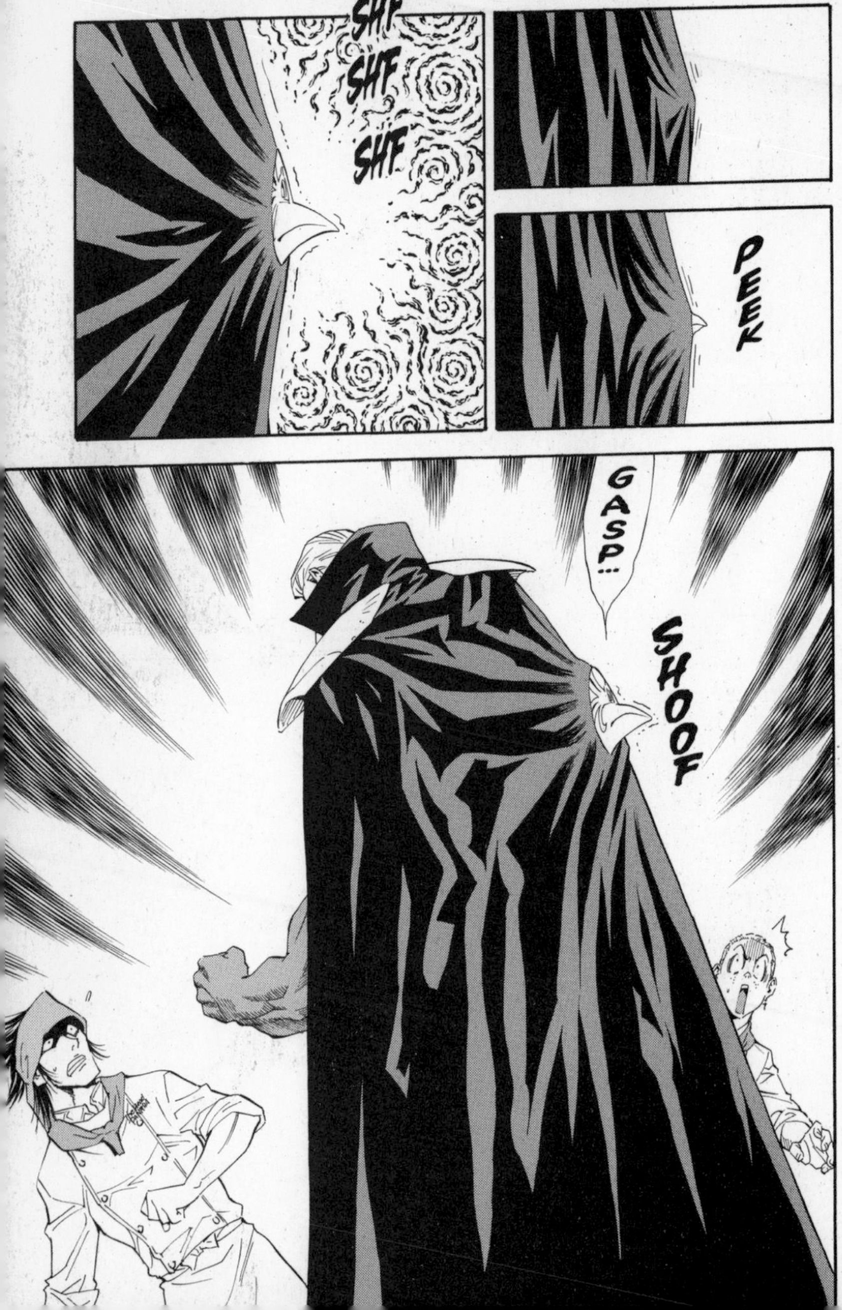
PEEK
SHF
SHF
SHF
GASP!!
SHOOF

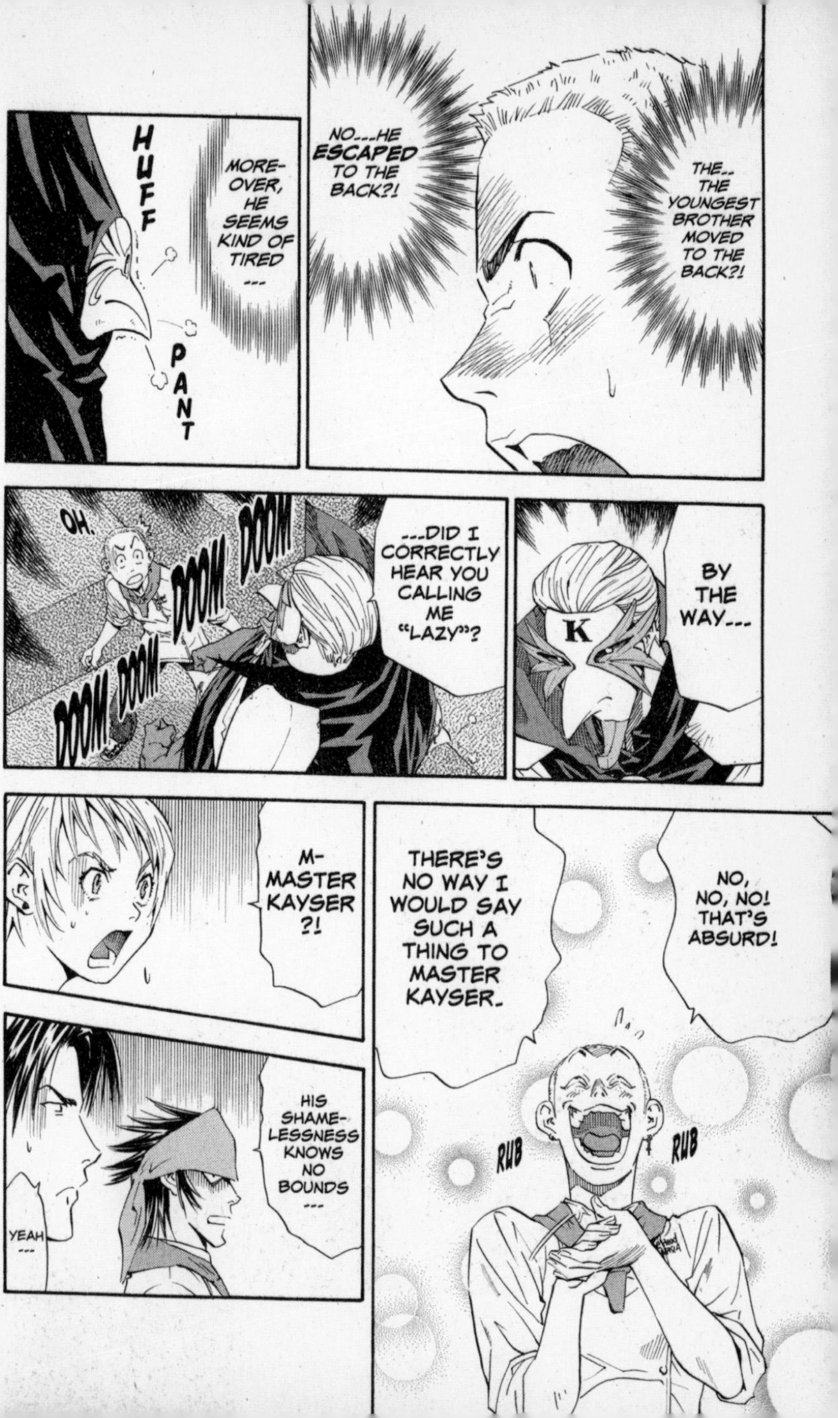
THE.. THE YOUNGEST BROTHER MOVED TO THE BACK?!
NO...HE ESCAPED TO THE BACK?!
MORE-OVER, HE SEEMS KIND OF TIRED ...
HUFF
PANT
BY THE WAY...
...DID I CORRECTLY HEAR YOU CALLING ME "LAZY"?
DOOM DOOM DOOM DOOM DOOM
OH.
NO, NO, NO! THAT'S ABSURD!
THERE'S NO WAY I WOULD SAY SUCH A THING TO MASTER KAYSER.
RUB RUB
M-MASTER KAYSER ?!
HIS SHAME-LESSNESS KNOWS NO BOUNDS ...
YEAH ...

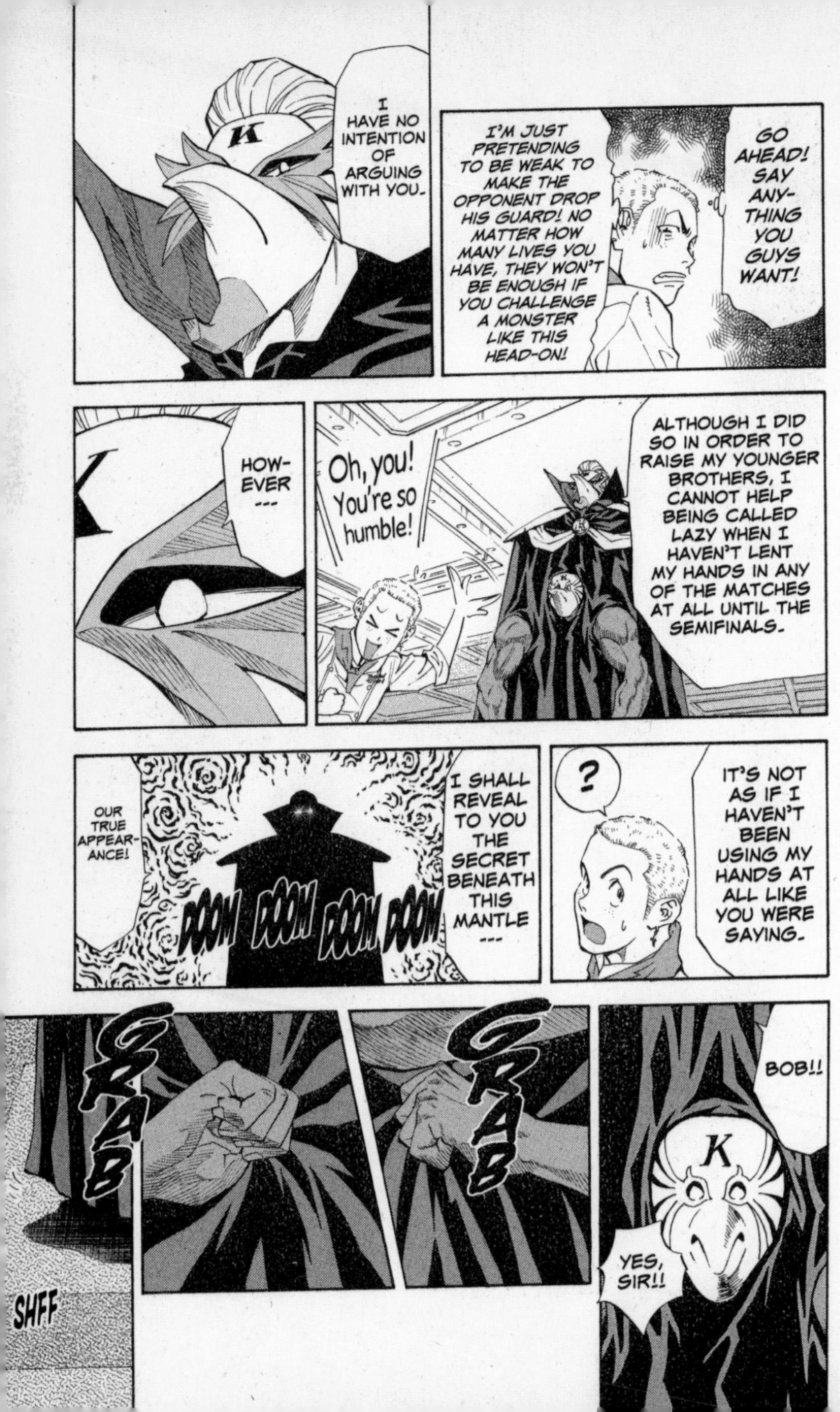
GO AHEAD! SAY ANY-THING YOU GUYS WANT!
I'M JUST PRETENDING TO BE WEAK TO MAKE THE OPPONENT DROP HIS GUARD! NO MATTER HOW MANY LIVES YOU HAVE, THEY WON'T BE ENOUGH IF YOU CHALLENGE A MONSTER LIKE THIS HEAD-ON!
I HAVE NO INTENTION OF ARGUING WITH YOU.
ALTHOUGH I DID SO IN ORDER TO RAISE MY YOUNGER BROTHERS, I CANNOT HELP BEING CALLED LAZY WHEN I HAVEN'T LENT MY HANDS IN ANY OF THE MATCHES AT ALL UNTIL THE SEMIFINALS.
Oh, you! You're so humble!
HOW-EVER ---
IT'S NOT AS IF I HAVEN'T BEEN USING MY HANDS AT ALL LIKE YOU WERE SAYING.
?
I SHALL REVEAL TO YOU THE SECRET BENEATH THIS MANTLE ---
DOOM DOOM DOOM DOOM
OUR TRUE APPEAR-ANCE!
BOB!!
YES, SIR!!
GRAB
GRAB
SHFF

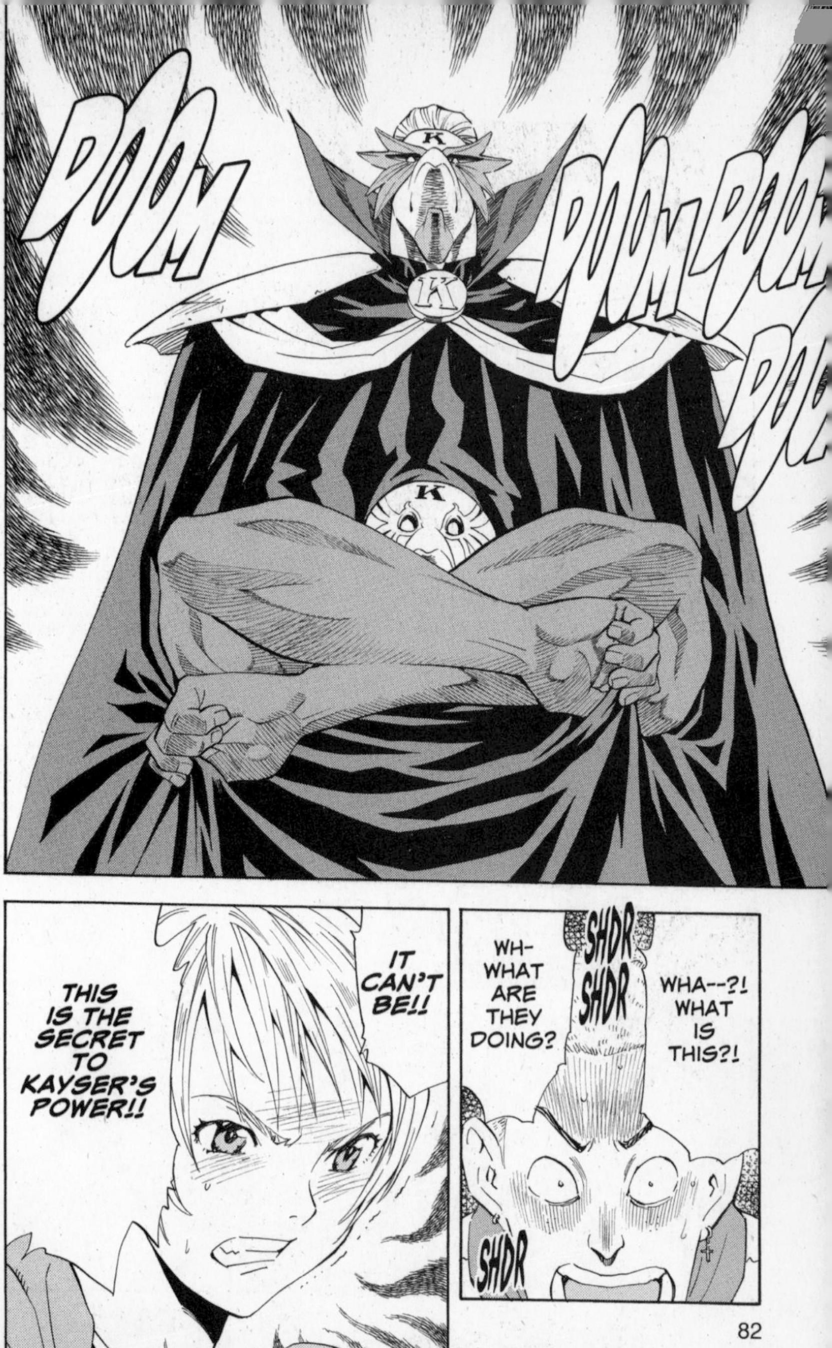
DOOM
DOOM DOOM
DOO
WHA--?! WHAT IS THIS?!
SHDR
SHDR
WH- WHAT ARE THEY DOING?
SHDR
IT CAN'T BE!!
THIS IS THE SECRET TO KAYSER'S POWER!!

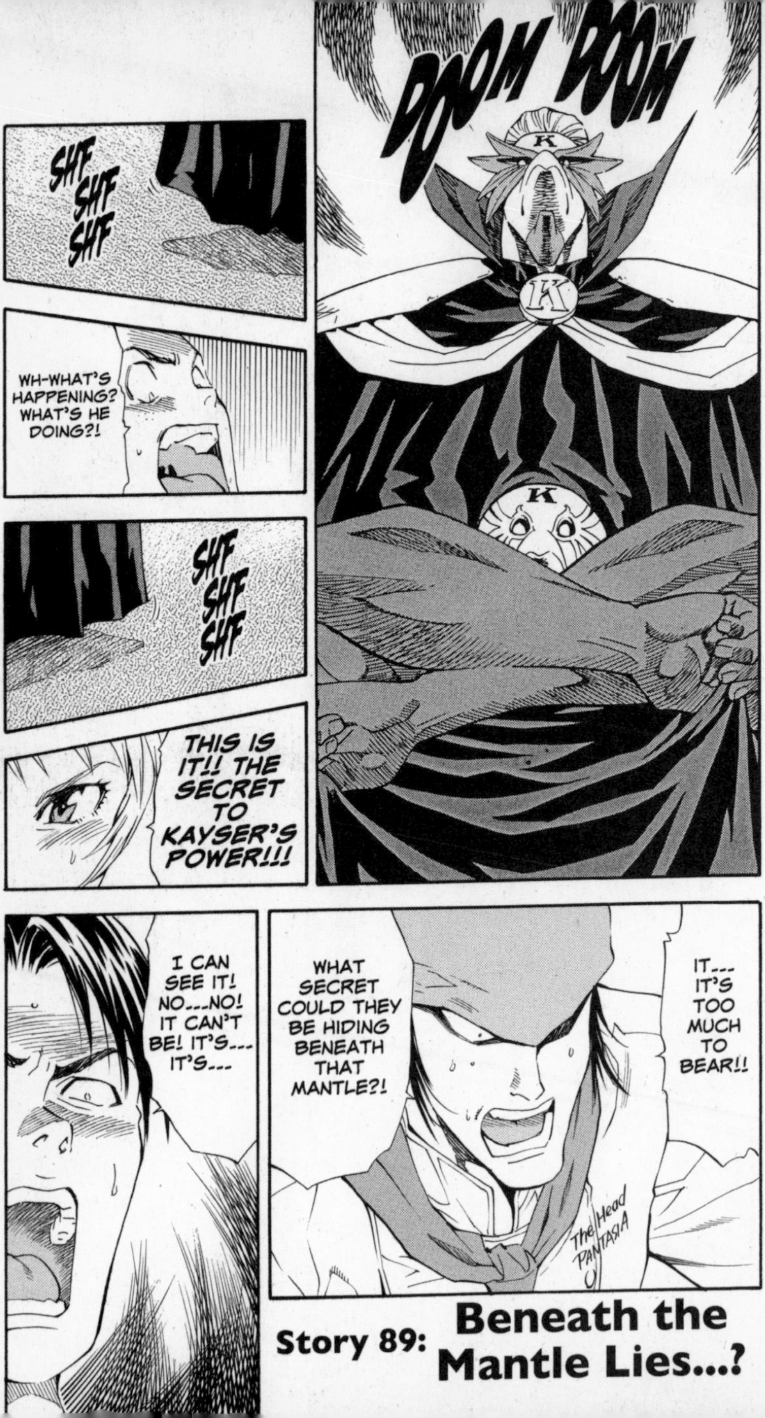
DOOM DOOM
SHF SHF SHF
WH-WHAT'S HAPPENING? WHAT'S HE DOING?!
SHF SHF SHF
THIS IS IT!! THE SECRET TO KAYSER'S POWER!!!
IT... IT'S TOO MUCH TO BEAR!!
WHAT SECRET COULD THEY BE HIDING BENEATH THAT MANTLE?!
The Head PANTASIA
I CAN SEE IT! NO...NO! IT CAN'T BE! IT'S... IT'S...

Story 89: Beneath the Mantle Lies...?

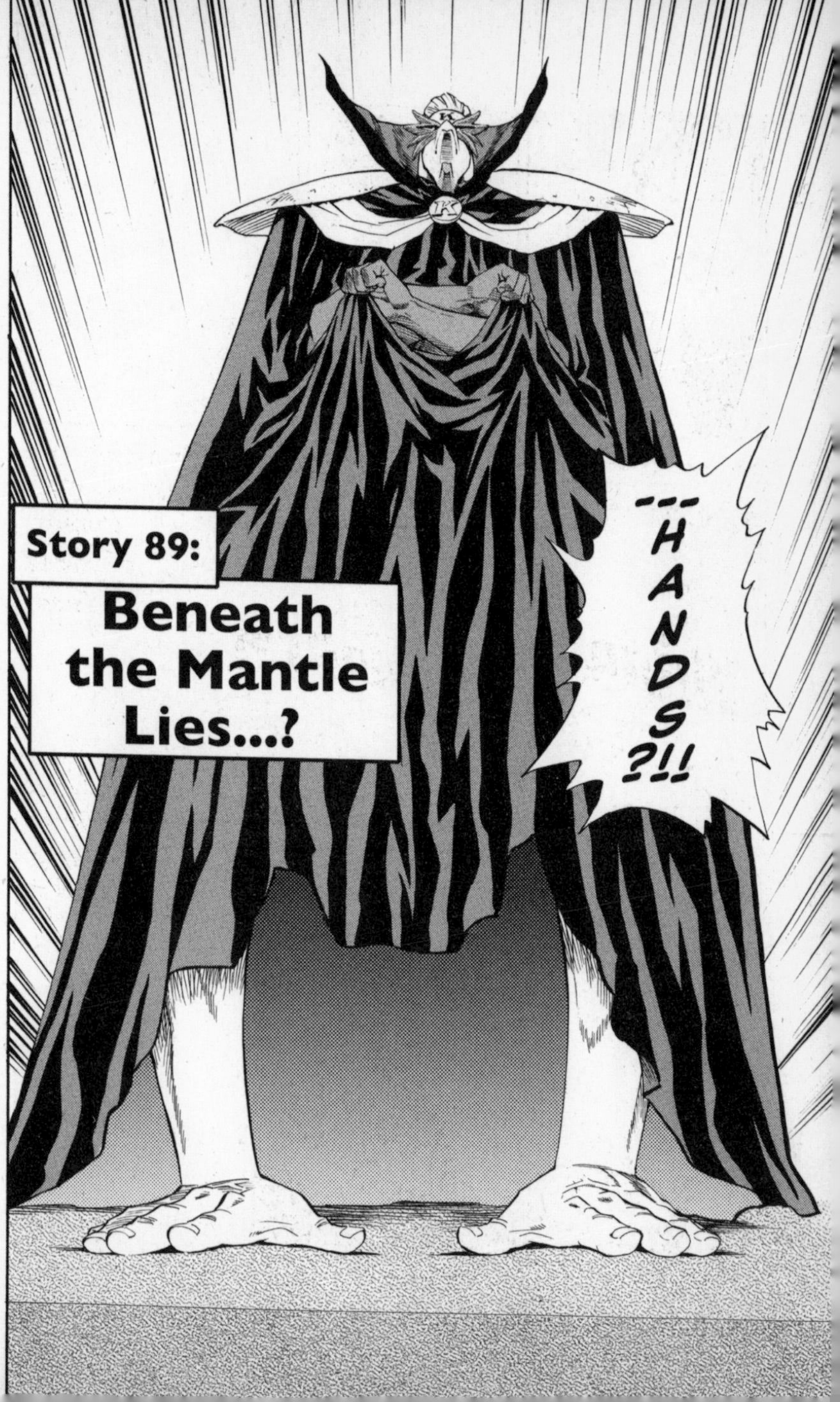
--HANDS?!!
Story 89:
Beneath the Mantle Lies...?

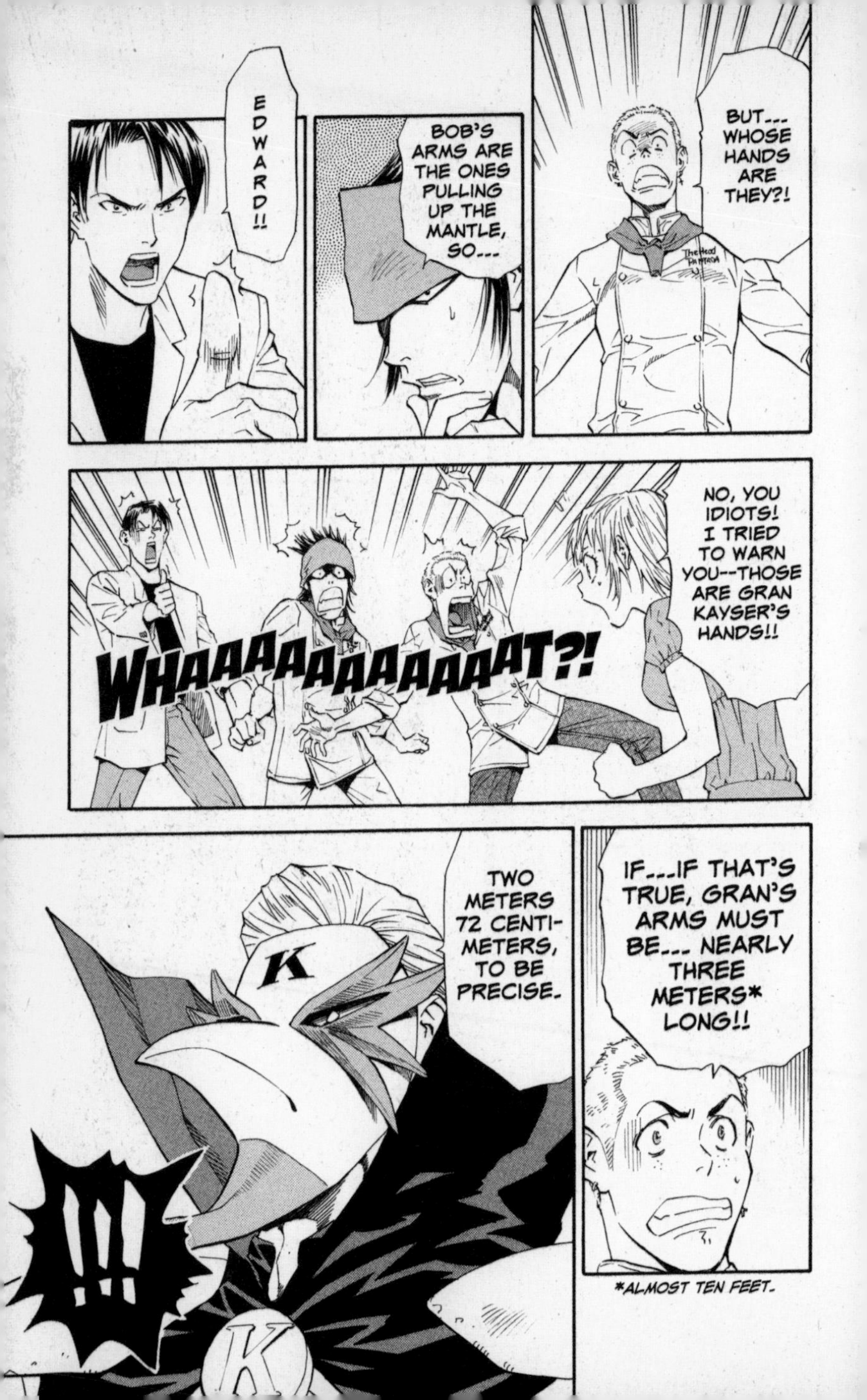
BUT... WHOSE HANDS ARE THEY?!
BOB'S ARMS ARE THE ONES PULLING UP THE MANTLE, SO...
EDWARD!!
NO, YOU IDIOTS! I TRIED TO WARN YOU--THOSE ARE GRAN KAYSER'S HANDS!!
WHAAAAAAAAAAAT?!
IF...IF THAT'S TRUE, GRAN'S ARMS MUST BE... NEARLY THREE METERS* LONG!!
TWO METERS 72 CENTI-METERS, TO BE PRECISE.
!!!

*ALMOST TEN FEET.

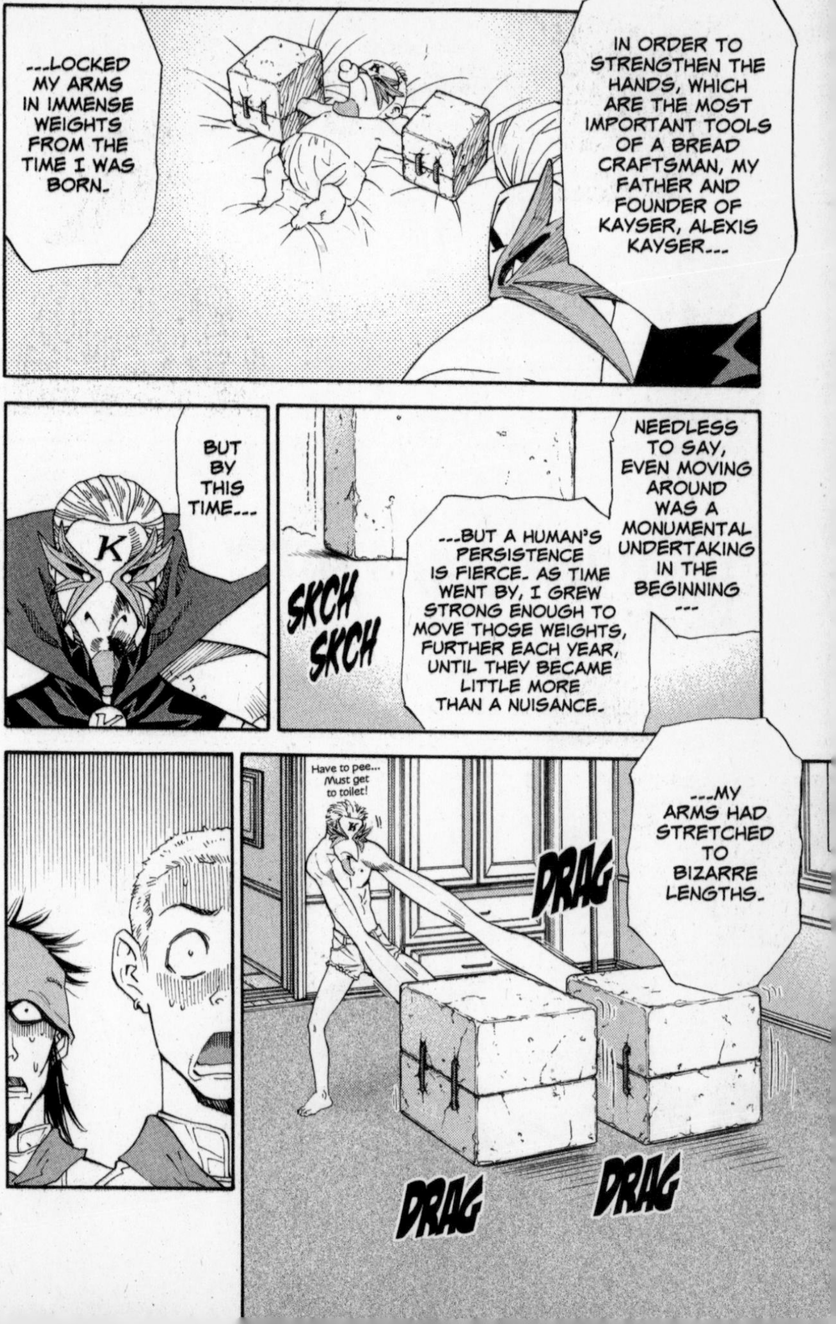
IN ORDER TO STRENGTHEN THE HANDS, WHICH ARE THE MOST IMPORTANT TOOLS OF A BREAD CRAFTSMAN, MY FATHER AND FOUNDER OF KAYSER, ALEXIS KAYSER...
...LOCKED MY ARMS IN IMMENSE WEIGHTS FROM THE TIME I WAS BORN.
NEEDLESS TO SAY, EVEN MOVING AROUND WAS A MONUMENTAL UNDERTAKING IN THE BEGINNING ---
...BUT A HUMAN'S PERSISTENCE IS FIERCE. AS TIME WENT BY, I GREW STRONG ENOUGH TO MOVE THOSE WEIGHTS, FURTHER EACH YEAR, UNTIL THEY BECAME LITTLE MORE THAN A NUISANCE.
SKCH SKCH
BUT BY THIS TIME...
...MY ARMS HAD STRETCHED TO BIZARRE LENGTHS.
Have to pee... Must get to toilet!
DRAG
DRAG
DRAG

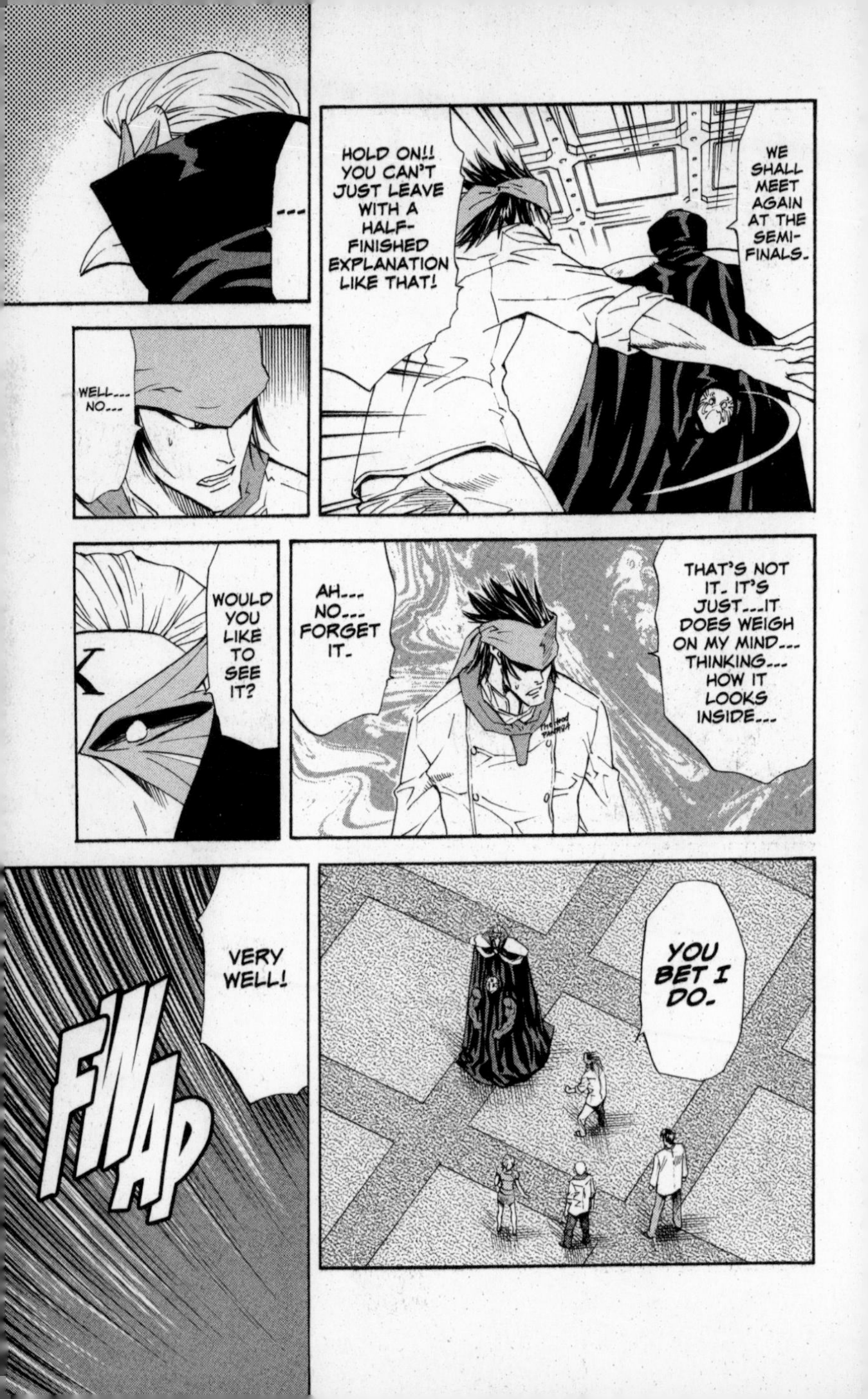
WE SHALL MEET AGAIN AT THE SEMI-FINALS.
HOLD ON!! YOU CAN'T JUST LEAVE WITH A HALF-FINISHED EXPLANATION LIKE THAT!
...
WELL... NO...
THAT'S NOT IT. IT'S JUST...IT DOES WEIGH ON MY MIND... THINKING... HOW IT LOOKS INSIDE...
AH... NO... FORGET IT.
WOULD YOU LIKE TO SEE IT?
YOU BET I DO.
VERY WELL!
FWAP

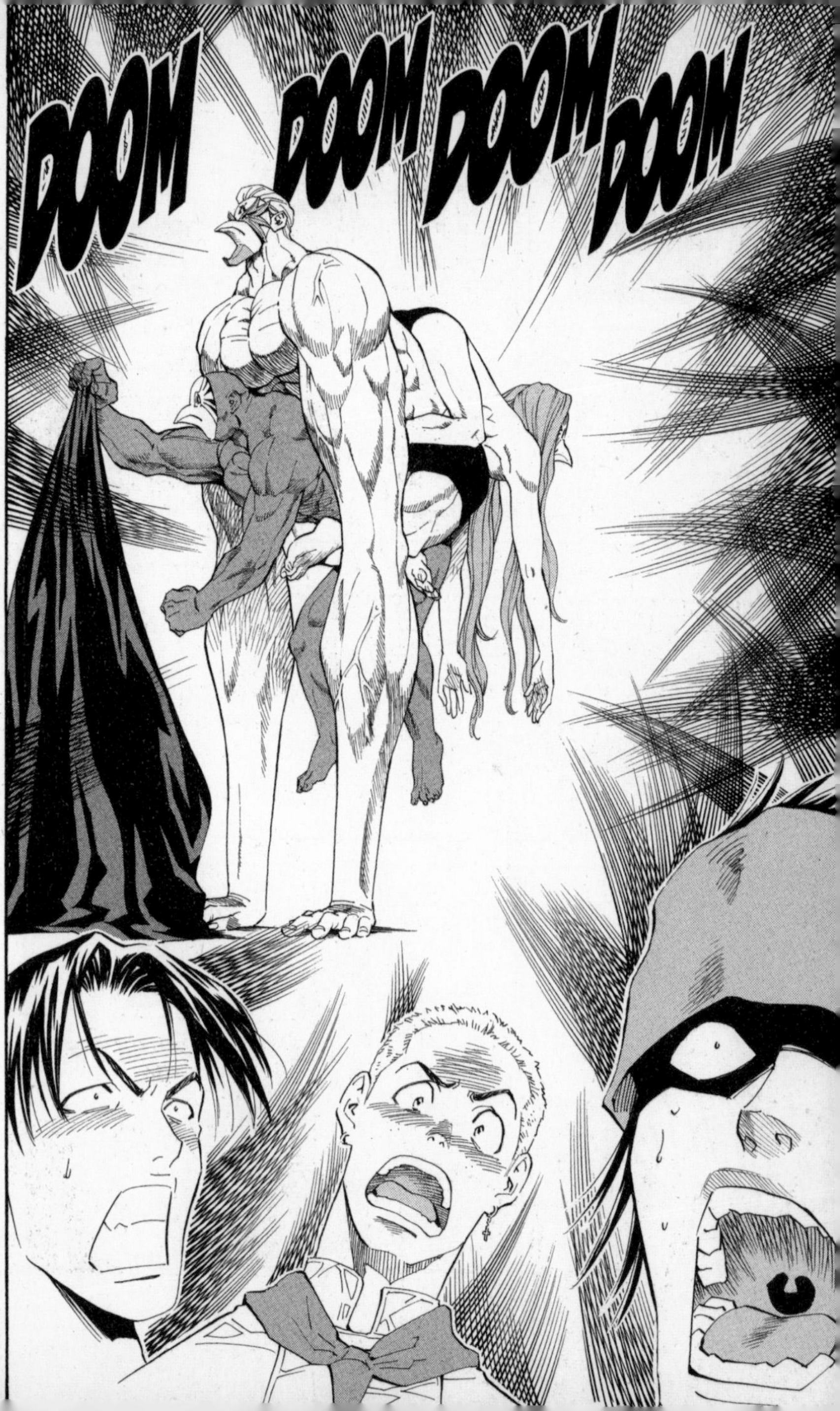
DOOM
DOOM
DOOM
DOOM

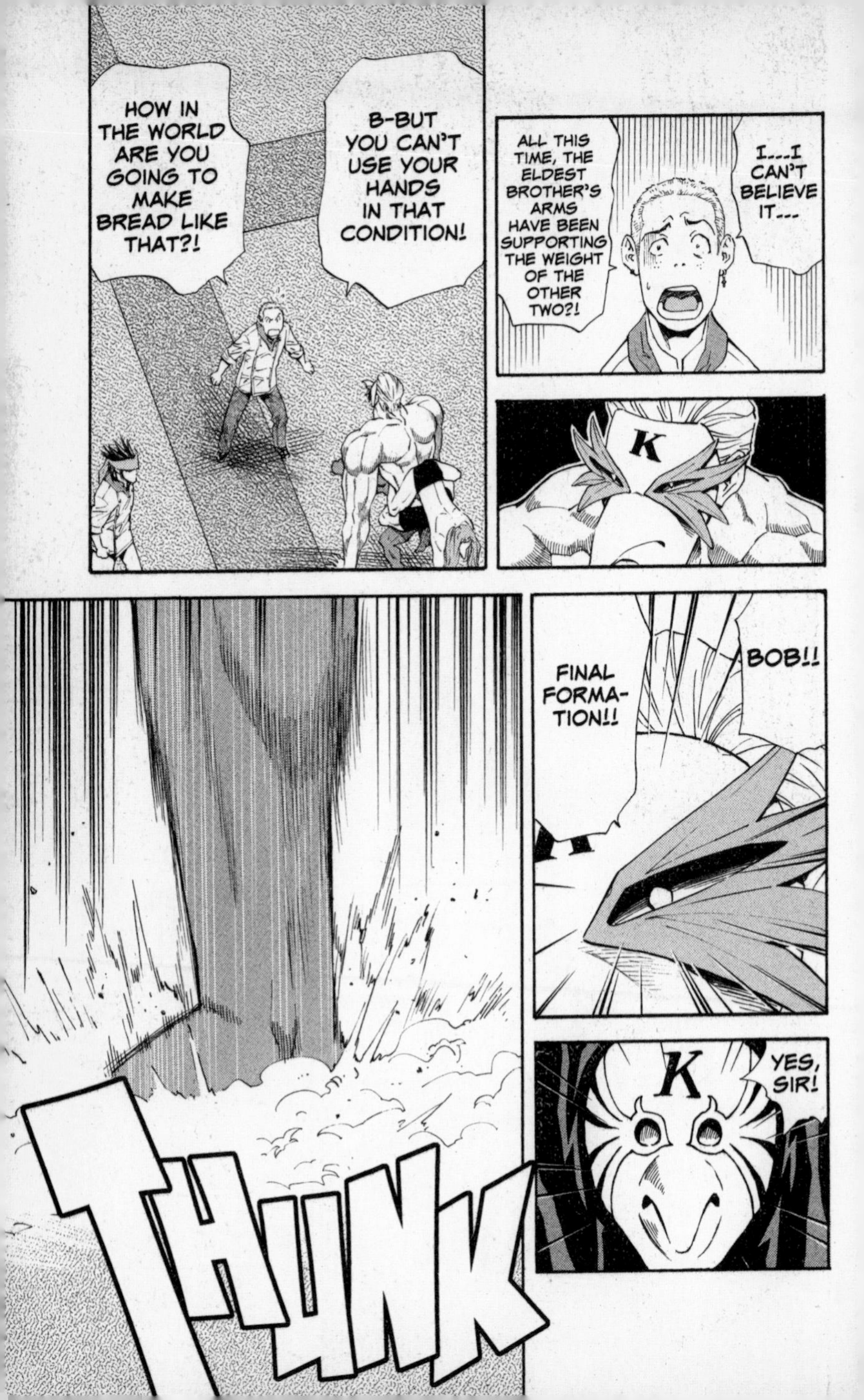
I---I CAN'T BELIEVE IT---
ALL THIS TIME, THE ELDEST BROTHER'S ARMS HAVE BEEN SUPPORTING THE WEIGHT OF THE OTHER TWO?!
B-BUT YOU CAN'T USE YOUR HANDS IN THAT CONDITION!
HOW IN THE WORLD ARE YOU GOING TO MAKE BREAD LIKE THAT?!
BOB!!
FINAL FORMA-TION!!
YES, SIR!
THUNK

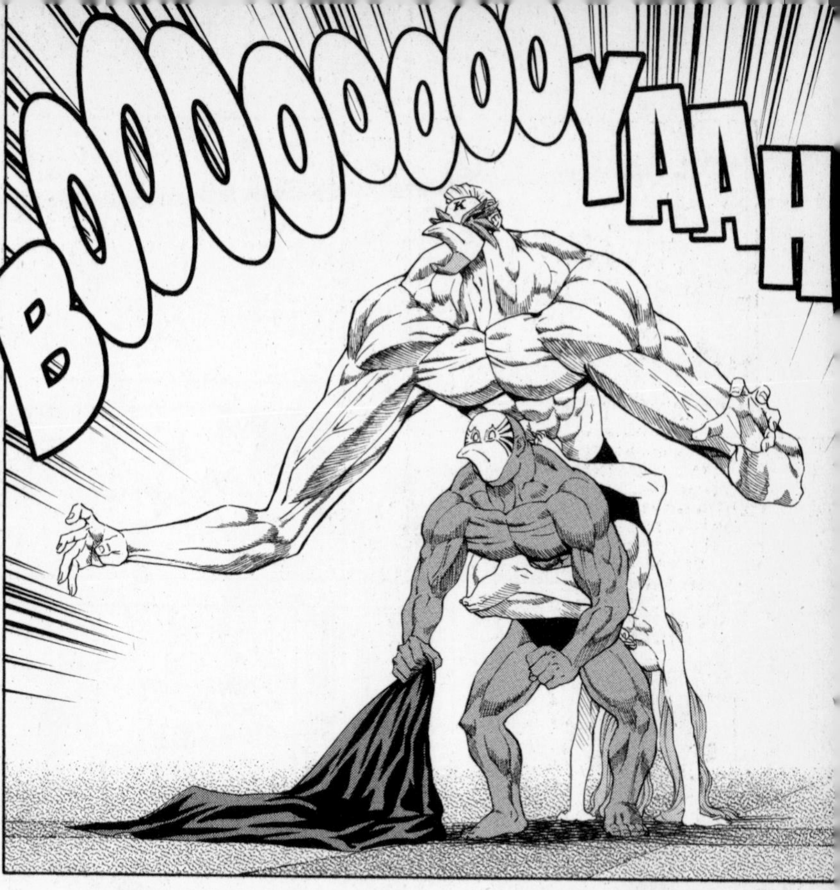
BOOOOOOOOYAAH

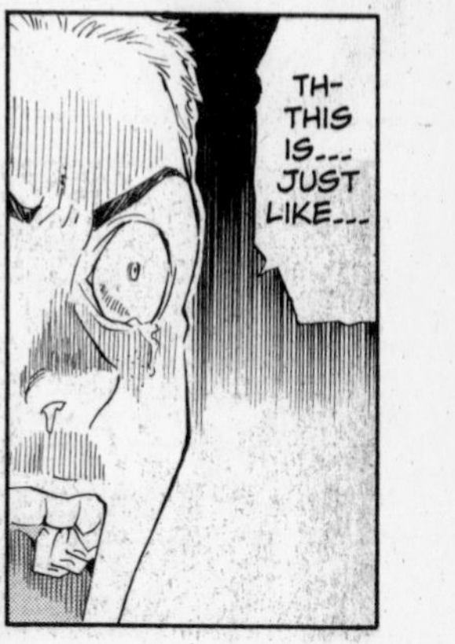
TH-THIS IS... JUST LIKE...

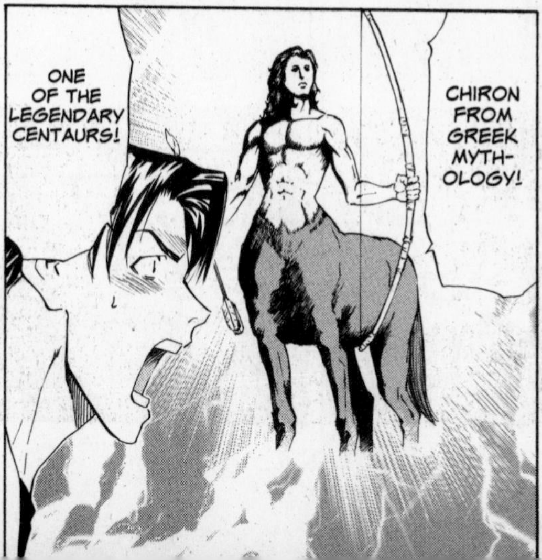
CHIRON FROM GREEK MYTH-OLOGY!
ONE OF THE LEGENDARY CENTAURS!

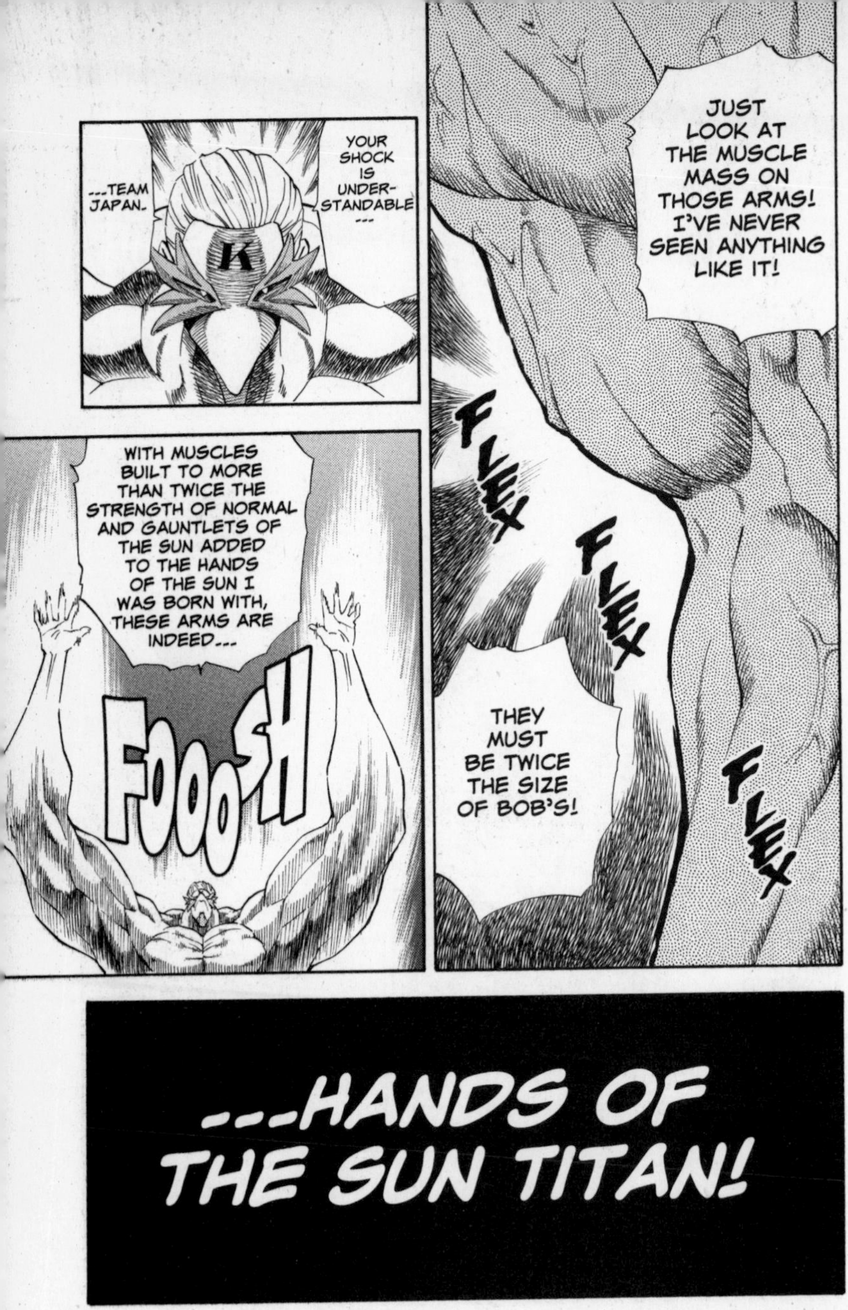
JUST LOOK AT THE MUSCLE MASS ON THOSE ARMS! I'VE NEVER SEEN ANYTHING LIKE IT!
FLEX
FLEX
FLEX
THEY MUST BE TWICE THE SIZE OF BOB'S!
YOUR SHOCK IS UNDER-STANDABLE...
...TEAM JAPAN.
WITH MUSCLES BUILT TO MORE THAN TWICE THE STRENGTH OF NORMAL AND GAUNTLETS OF THE SUN ADDED TO THE HANDS OF THE SUN I WAS BORN WITH, THESE ARMS ARE INDEED...
FOOOSH
...HANDS OF THE SUN TITAN!

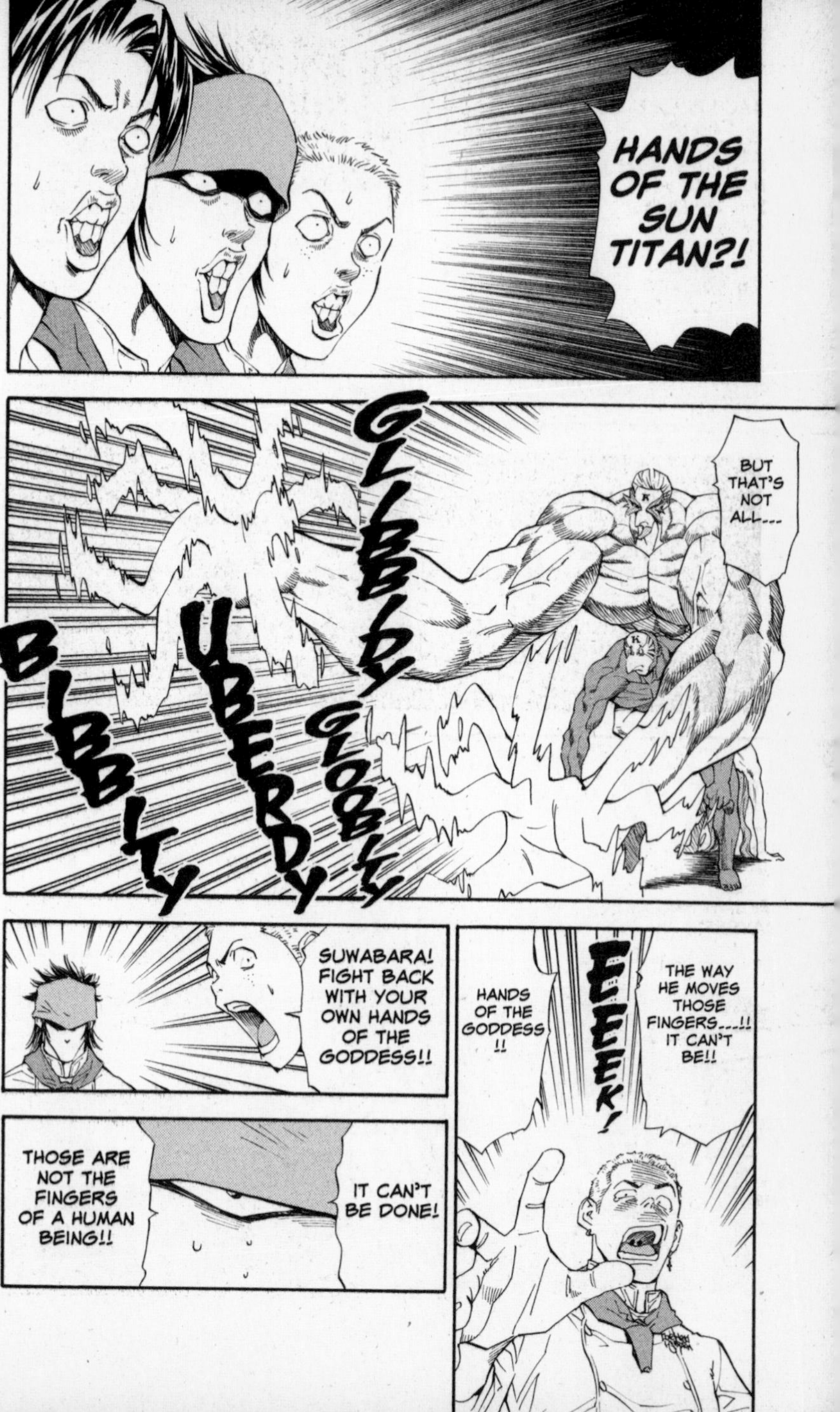
HANDS OF THE SUN TITAN?!
BUT THAT'S NOT ALL...
GLBBLY GLOBBLY
UBBERDY
BIBBLY
THE WAY HE MOVES THOSE FINGERS...!! IT CAN'T BE!!
EEEEK!
HANDS OF THE GODDESS !!
SUWABARA! FIGHT BACK WITH YOUR OWN HANDS OF THE GODDESS!!
THOSE ARE NOT THE FINGERS OF A HUMAN BEING!!
IT CAN'T BE DONE!

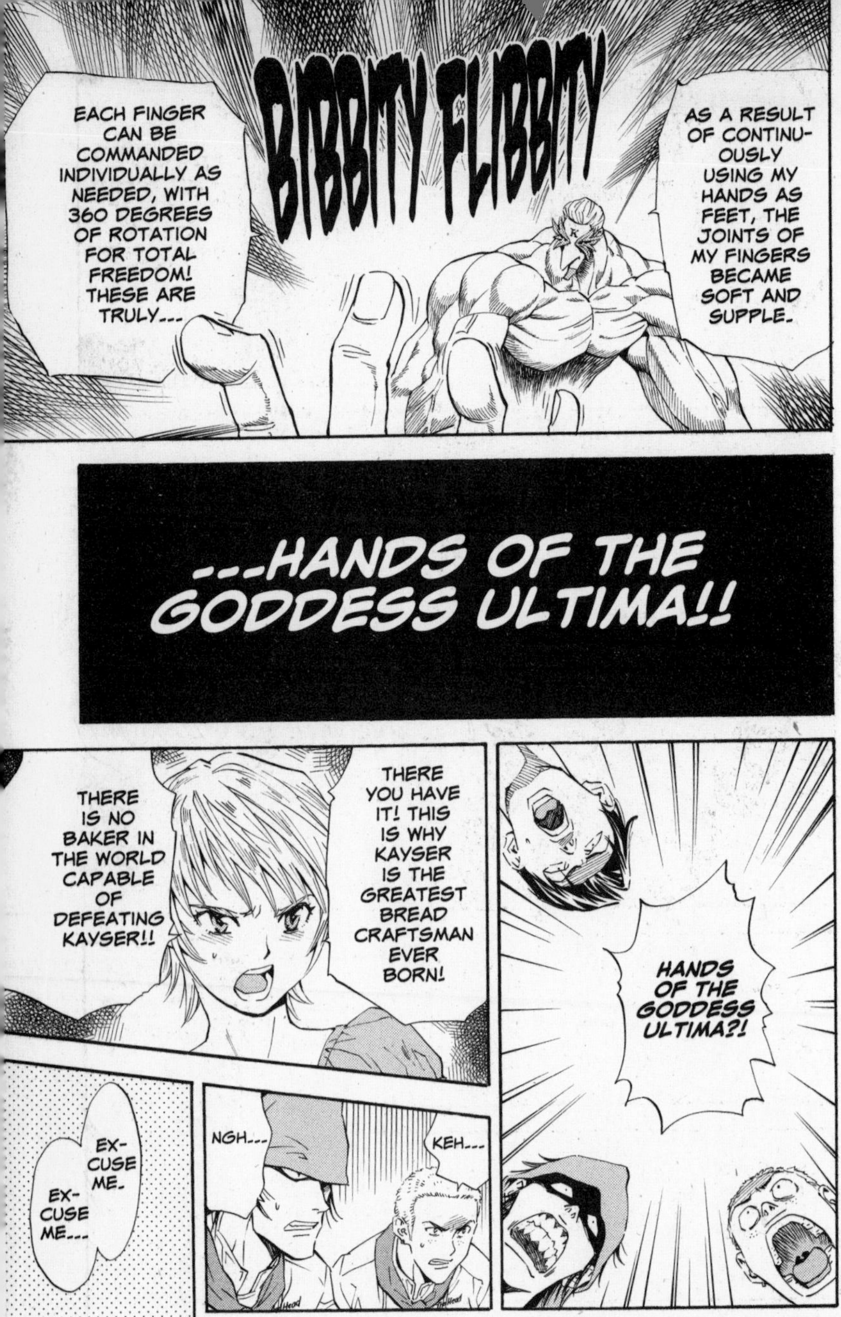
AS A RESULT OF CONTINU-OUSLY USING MY HANDS AS FEET, THE JOINTS OF MY FINGERS BECAME SOFT AND SUPPLE.
BIBBITY FLIBBITY
EACH FINGER CAN BE COMMANDED INDIVIDUALLY AS NEEDED, WITH 360 DEGREES OF ROTATION FOR TOTAL FREEDOM! THESE ARE TRULY...
...HANDS OF THE GODDESS ULTIMA!!
HANDS OF THE GODDESS ULTIMA?!
THERE YOU HAVE IT! THIS IS WHY KAYSER IS THE GREATEST BREAD CRAFTSMAN EVER BORN!
THERE IS NO BAKER IN THE WORLD CAPABLE OF DEFEATING KAYSER!!
KEH...
NGH...
EX-CUSE ME.
EX-CUSE ME...

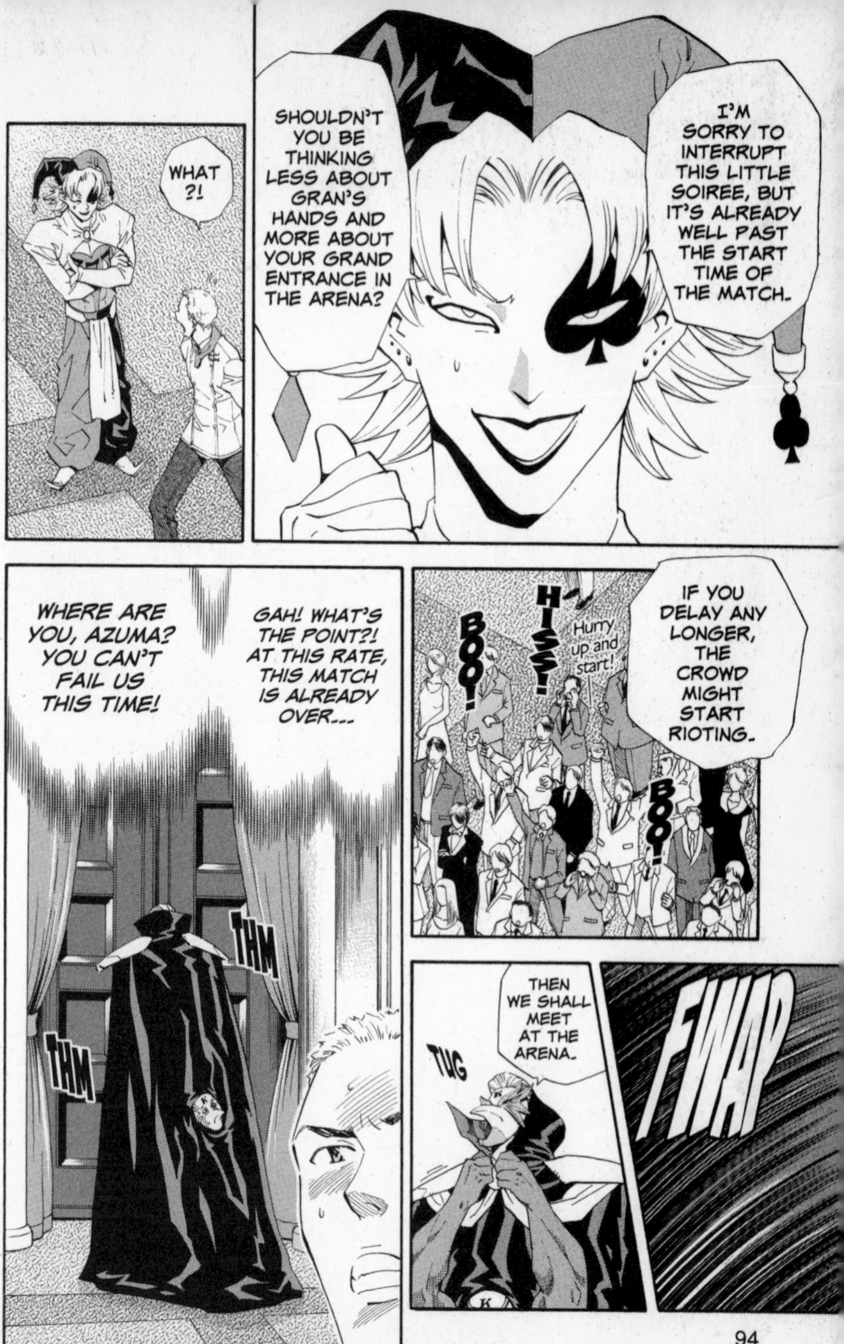
I'M SORRY TO INTERRUPT THIS LITTLE SOIREE, BUT IT'S ALREADY WELL PAST THE START TIME OF THE MATCH.
SHOULDN'T YOU BE THINKING LESS ABOUT GRAN'S HANDS AND MORE ABOUT YOUR GRAND ENTRANCE IN THE ARENA?
WHAT ?!
IF YOU DELAY ANY LONGER, THE CROWD MIGHT START RIOTING.
HISS!
Hurry up and start!
BOO!
BOO!
FWAP
THEN WE SHALL MEET AT THE ARENA.
TUG
WHERE ARE YOU, AZUMA? YOU CAN'T FAIL US THIS TIME!
GAH! WHAT'S THE POINT?! AT THIS RATE, THIS MATCH IS ALREADY OVER...
THM
THM

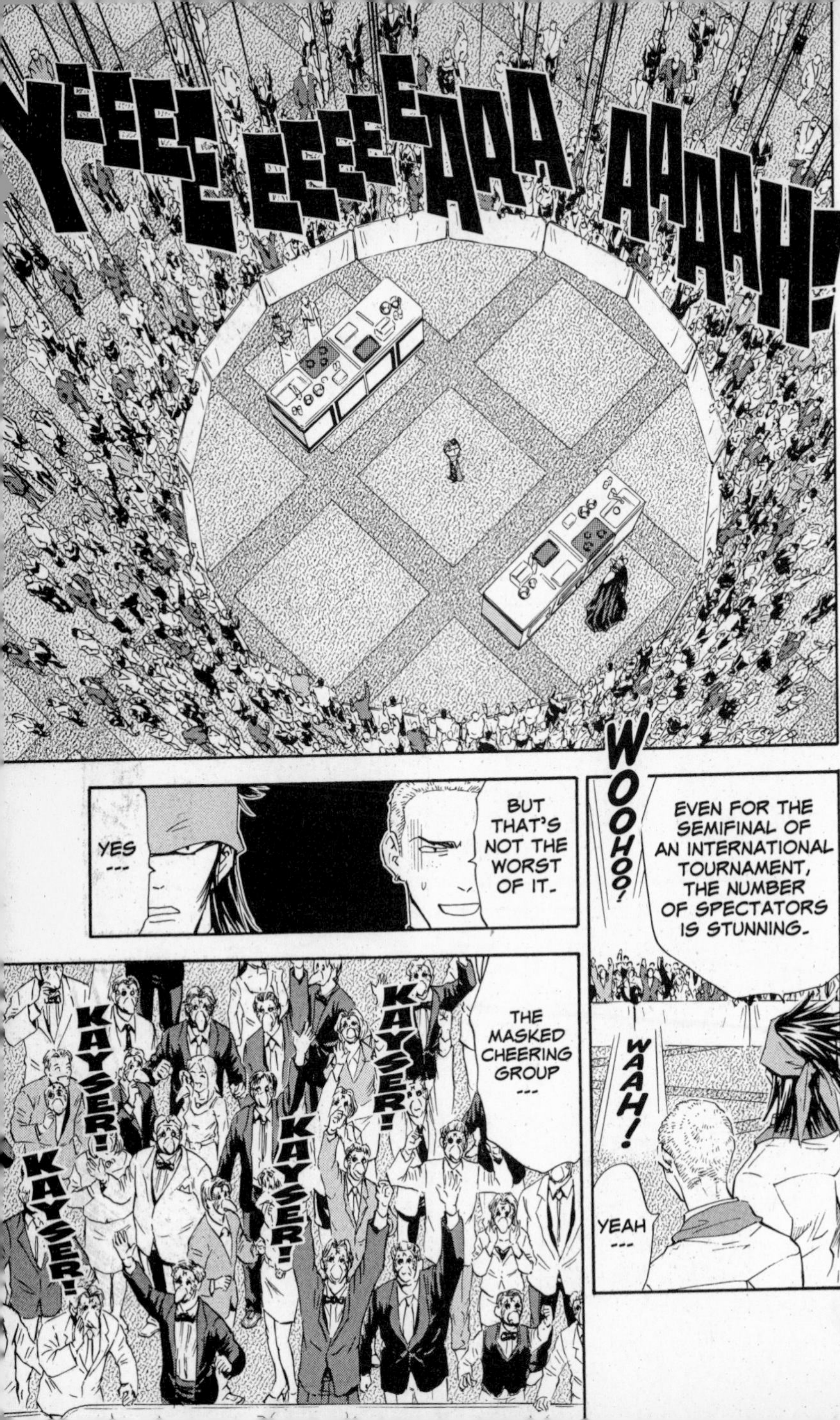
YEEEEEEEEEAAAAAAH!
WOOHOO!
EVEN FOR THE SEMIFINAL OF AN INTERNATIONAL TOURNAMENT, THE NUMBER OF SPECTATORS IS STUNNING.
WAAH!
YEAH ---
BUT THAT'S NOT THE WORST OF IT.
YES ---
THE MASKED CHEERING GROUP ---
KAYSER!
KAYSER!
KAYSER!
KAYSER!

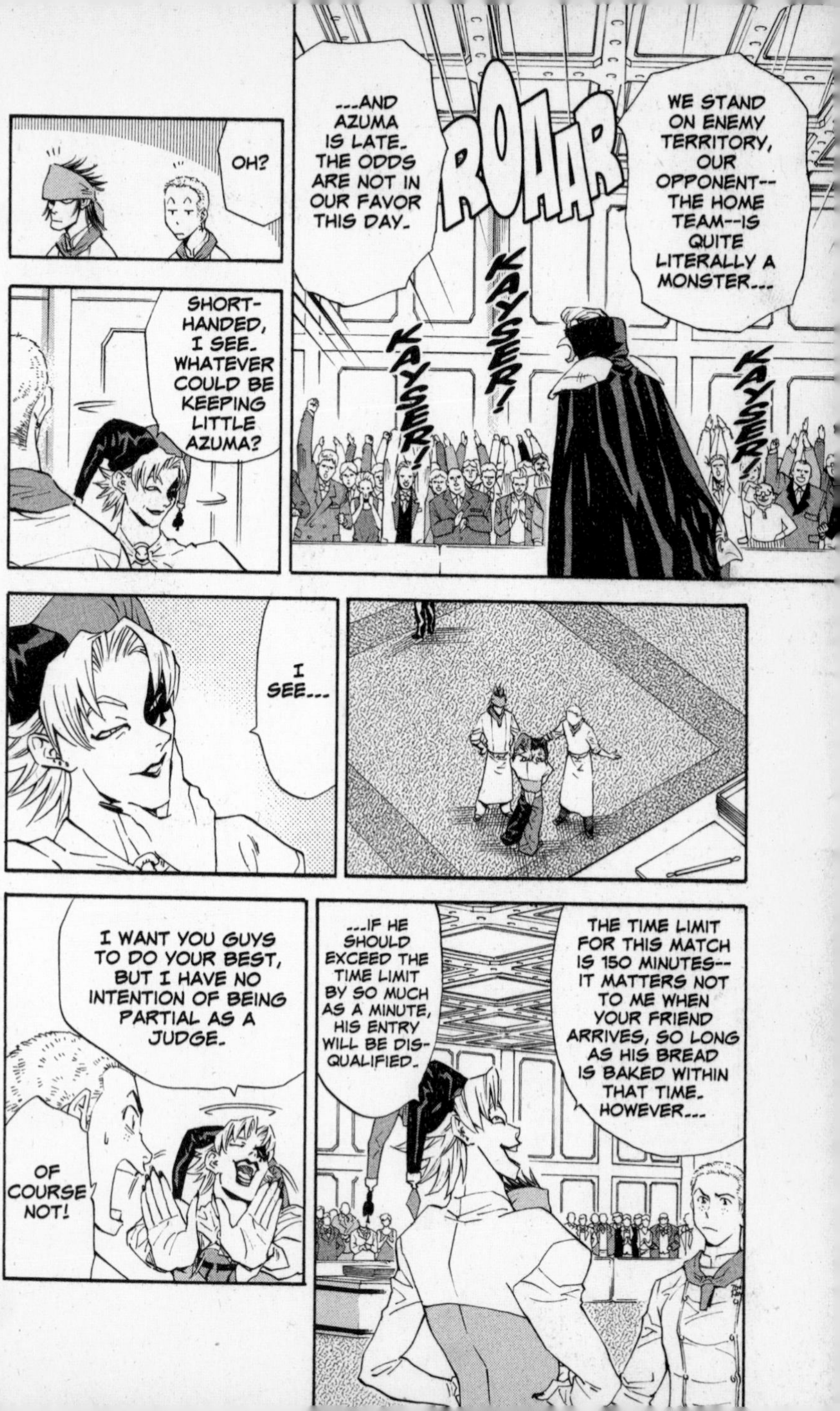
WE STAND ON ENEMY TERRITORY, OUR OPPONENT--THE HOME TEAM--IS QUITE LITERALLY A MONSTER...
ROAAR
KAYSER!
KAYSER!
KAYSER!
...AND AZUMA IS LATE. THE ODDS ARE NOT IN OUR FAVOR THIS DAY.
OH?
SHORT-HANDED, I SEE. WHATEVER COULD BE KEEPING LITTLE AZUMA?
I SEE...
THE TIME LIMIT FOR THIS MATCH IS 150 MINUTES--IT MATTERS NOT TO ME WHEN YOUR FRIEND ARRIVES, SO LONG AS HIS BREAD IS BAKED WITHIN THAT TIME. HOWEVER...
...IF HE SHOULD EXCEED THE TIME LIMIT BY SO MUCH AS A MINUTE, HIS ENTRY WILL BE DISQUALIFIED.
I WANT YOU GUYS TO DO YOUR BEST, BUT I HAVE NO INTENTION OF BEING PARTIAL AS A JUDGE.
OF COURSE NOT!

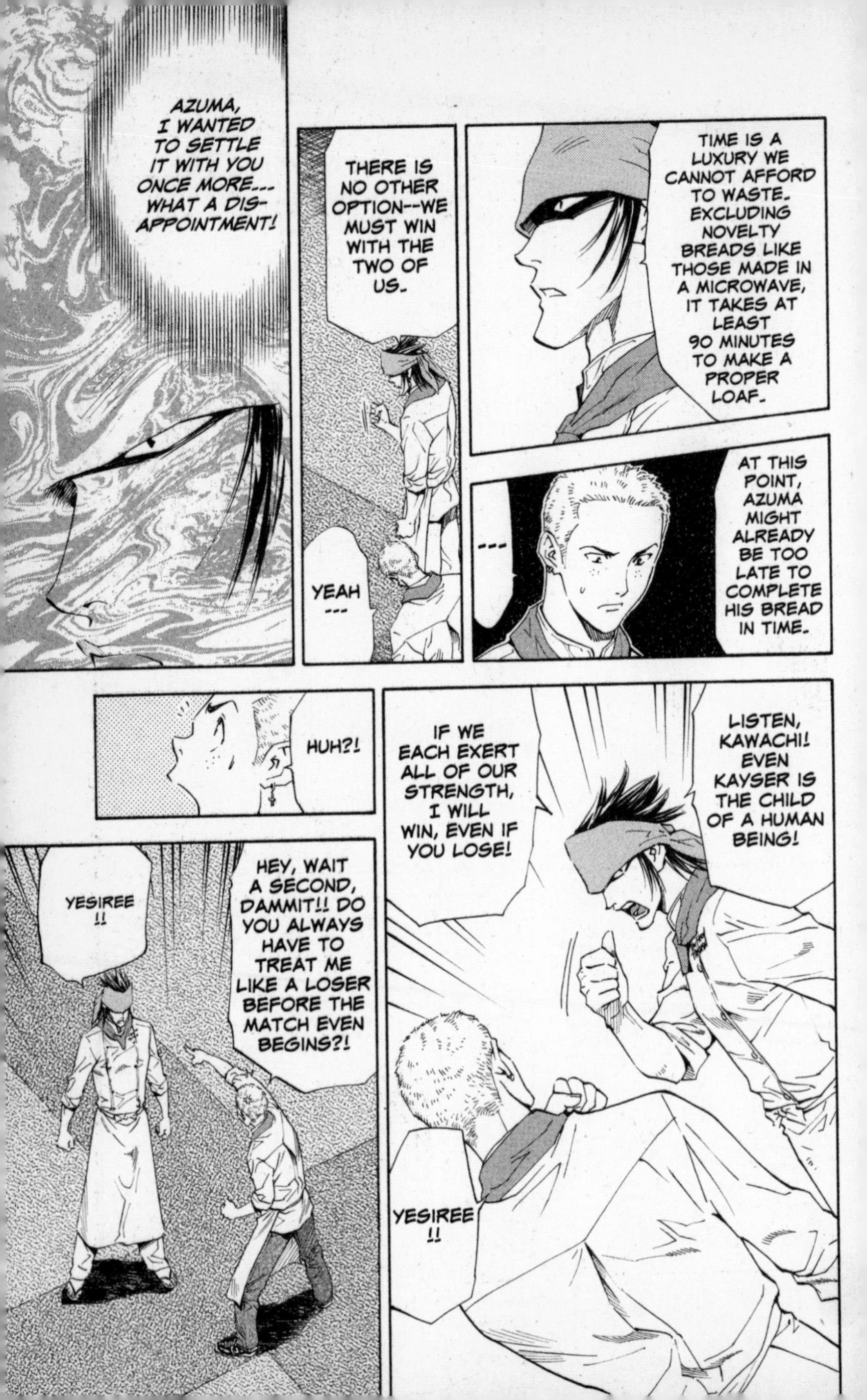
TIME IS A LUXURY WE CANNOT AFFORD TO WASTE. EXCLUDING NOVELTY BREADS LIKE THOSE MADE IN A MICROWAVE, IT TAKES AT LEAST 90 MINUTES TO MAKE A PROPER LOAF.
AT THIS POINT, AZUMA MIGHT ALREADY BE TOO LATE TO COMPLETE HIS BREAD IN TIME.

THERE IS NO OTHER OPTION--WE MUST WIN WITH THE TWO OF US.
YEAH ---
AZUMA, I WANTED TO SETTLE IT WITH YOU ONCE MORE... WHAT A DIS-APPOINTMENT!
LISTEN, KAWACHI! EVEN KAYSER IS THE CHILD OF A HUMAN BEING!
IF WE EACH EXERT ALL OF OUR STRENGTH, I WILL WIN, EVEN IF YOU LOSE!
YESIREE !!
HUH?!
HEY, WAIT A SECOND, DAMMIT!! DO YOU ALWAYS HAVE TO TREAT ME LIKE A LOSER BEFORE THE MATCH EVEN BEGINS?!
YESIREE !!

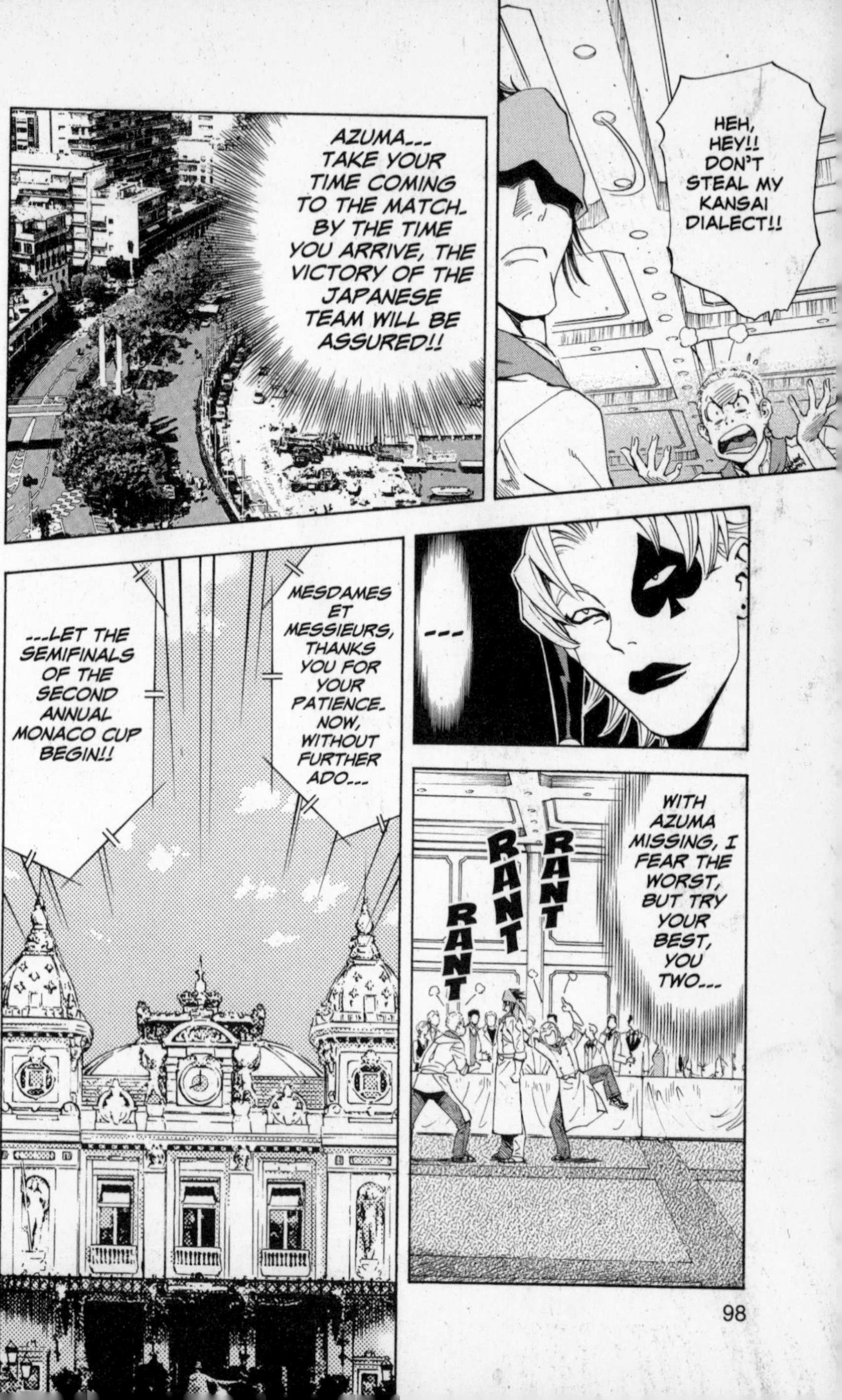
HEH, HEY!! DON'T STEAL MY KANSAI DIALECT!!
AZUMA... TAKE YOUR TIME COMING TO THE MATCH. BY THE TIME YOU ARRIVE, THE VICTORY OF THE JAPANESE TEAM WILL BE ASSURED!!
...
WITH AZUMA MISSING, I FEAR THE WORST, BUT TRY YOUR BEST, YOU TWO...
RANT
RANT
RANT
MESDAMES ET MESSIEURS, THANKS YOU FOR YOUR PATIENCE. NOW, WITHOUT FURTHER ADO...
...LET THE SEMIFINALS OF THE SECOND ANNUAL MONACO CUP BEGIN!!

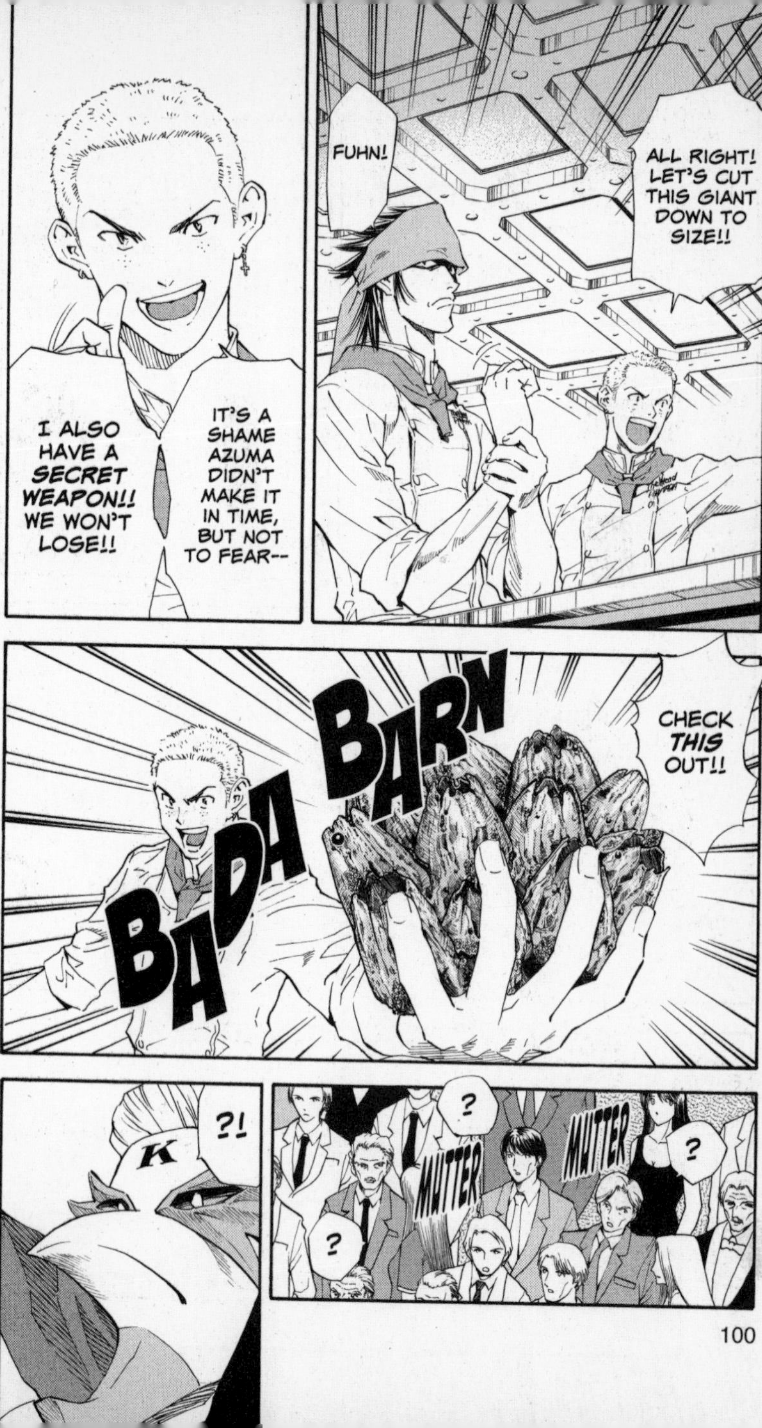
ALL RIGHT! LET'S CUT THIS GIANT DOWN TO SIZE!!
FUHN!
IT'S A SHAME AZUMA DIDN'T MAKE IT IN TIME, BUT NOT TO FEAR--
I ALSO HAVE A SECRET WEAPON!! WE WON'T LOSE!!
CHECK THIS OUT!!
BADA BARN
?
MUTTER
?
MUTTER
?
?!
K

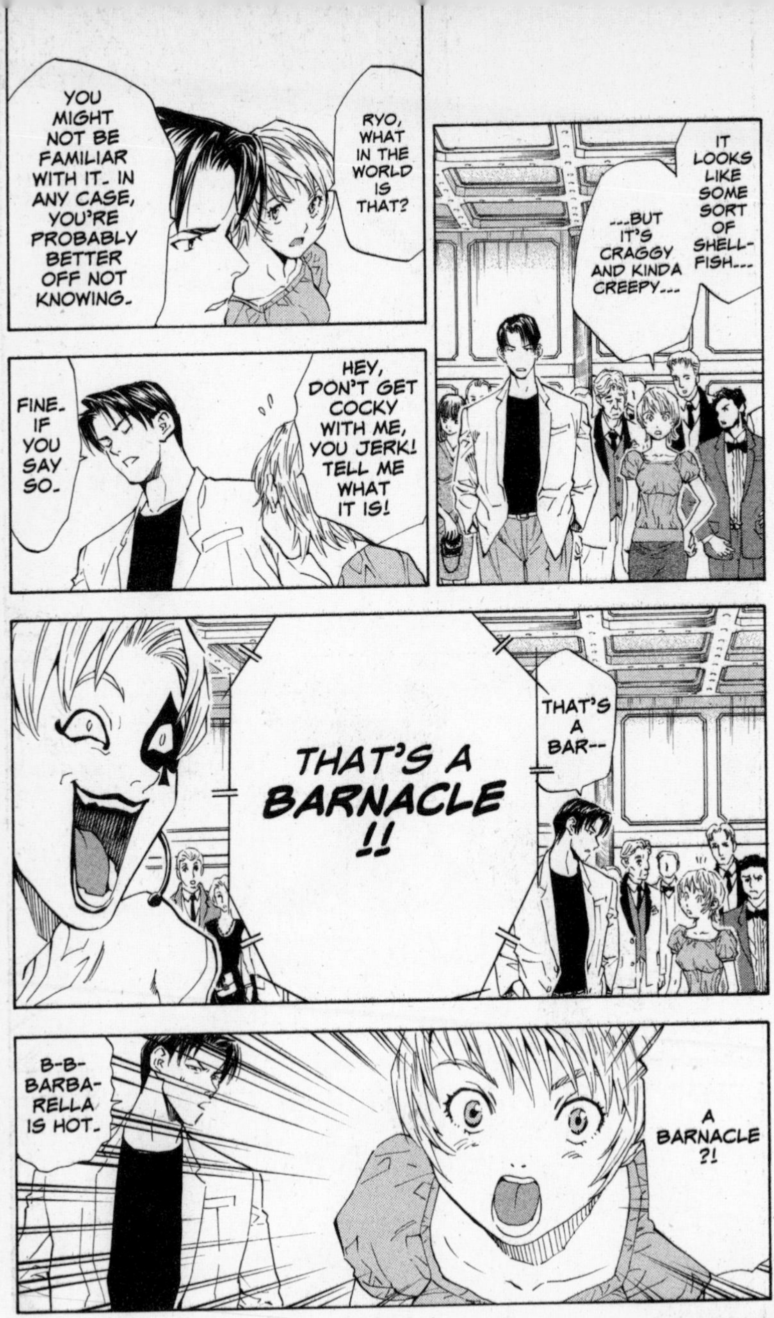

IT LOOKS LIKE SOME SORT OF SHELL-FISH...
...BUT IT'S CRAGGY AND KINDA CREEPY...
RYO, WHAT IN THE WORLD IS THAT?
YOU MIGHT NOT BE FAMILIAR WITH IT. IN ANY CASE, YOU'RE PROBABLY BETTER OFF NOT KNOWING.
HEY, DON'T GET COCKY WITH ME, YOU JERK! TELL ME WHAT IT IS!
FINE. IF YOU SAY SO.
THAT'S A BAR--
THAT'S A BARNACLE !!
A BARNACLE ?!
B-B-BARBA-RELLA IS HOT.

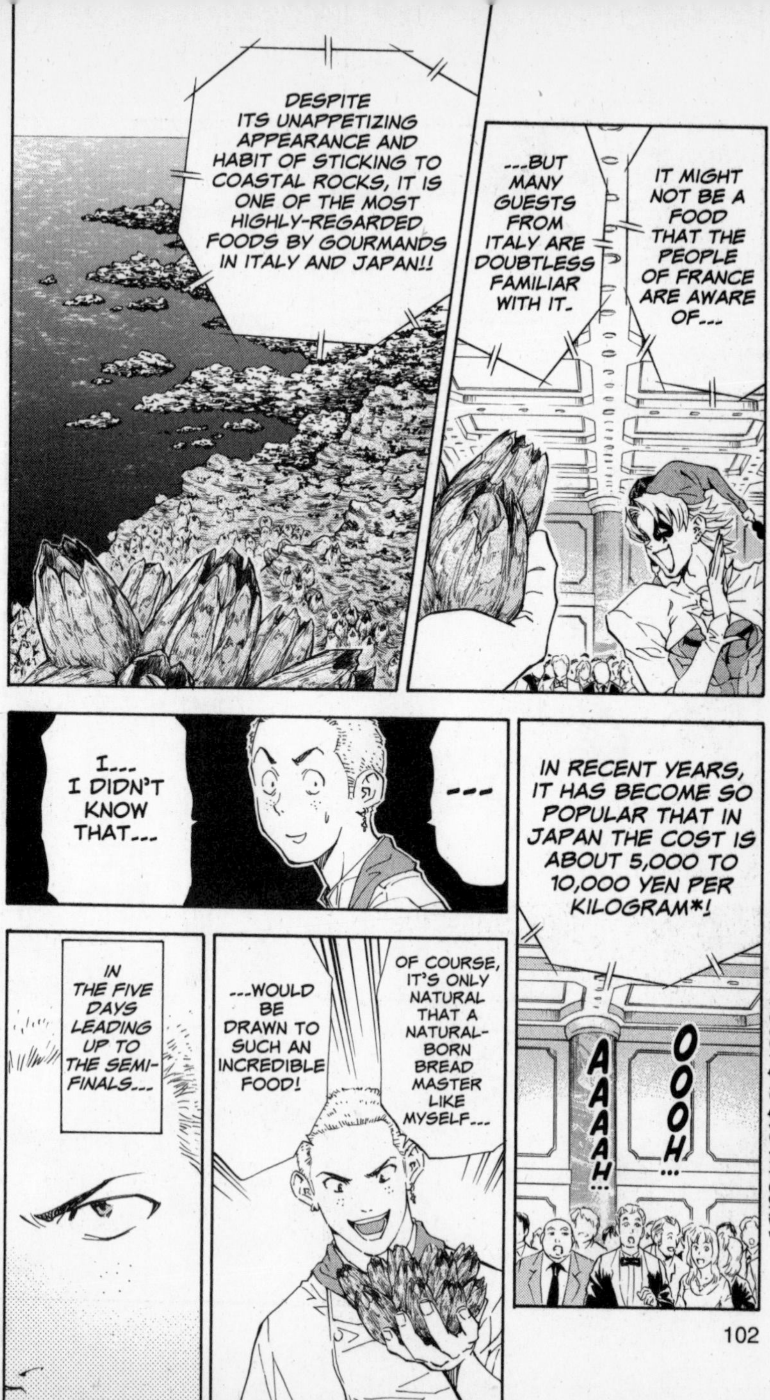

IT MIGHT NOT BE A FOOD THAT THE PEOPLE OF FRANCE ARE AWARE OF...
...BUT MANY GUESTS FROM ITALY ARE DOUBTLESS FAMILIAR WITH IT.
DESPITE ITS UNAPPETIZING APPEARANCE AND HABIT OF STICKING TO COASTAL ROCKS, IT IS ONE OF THE MOST HIGHLY-REGARDED FOODS BY GOURMANDS IN ITALY AND JAPAN!!
IN RECENT YEARS, IT HAS BECOME SO POPULAR THAT IN JAPAN THE COST IS ABOUT 5,000 TO 10,000 YEN PER KILOGRAM*!
OOOH...
AAAAH...
...
I... I DIDN'T KNOW THAT...
OF COURSE, IT'S ONLY NATURAL THAT A NATURAL-BORN BREAD MASTER LIKE MYSELF...
...WOULD BE DRAWN TO SUCH AN INCREDIBLE FOOD!
IN THE FIVE DAYS LEADING UP TO THE SEMI-FINALS...

*ABOUT $45-$90 A POUND.

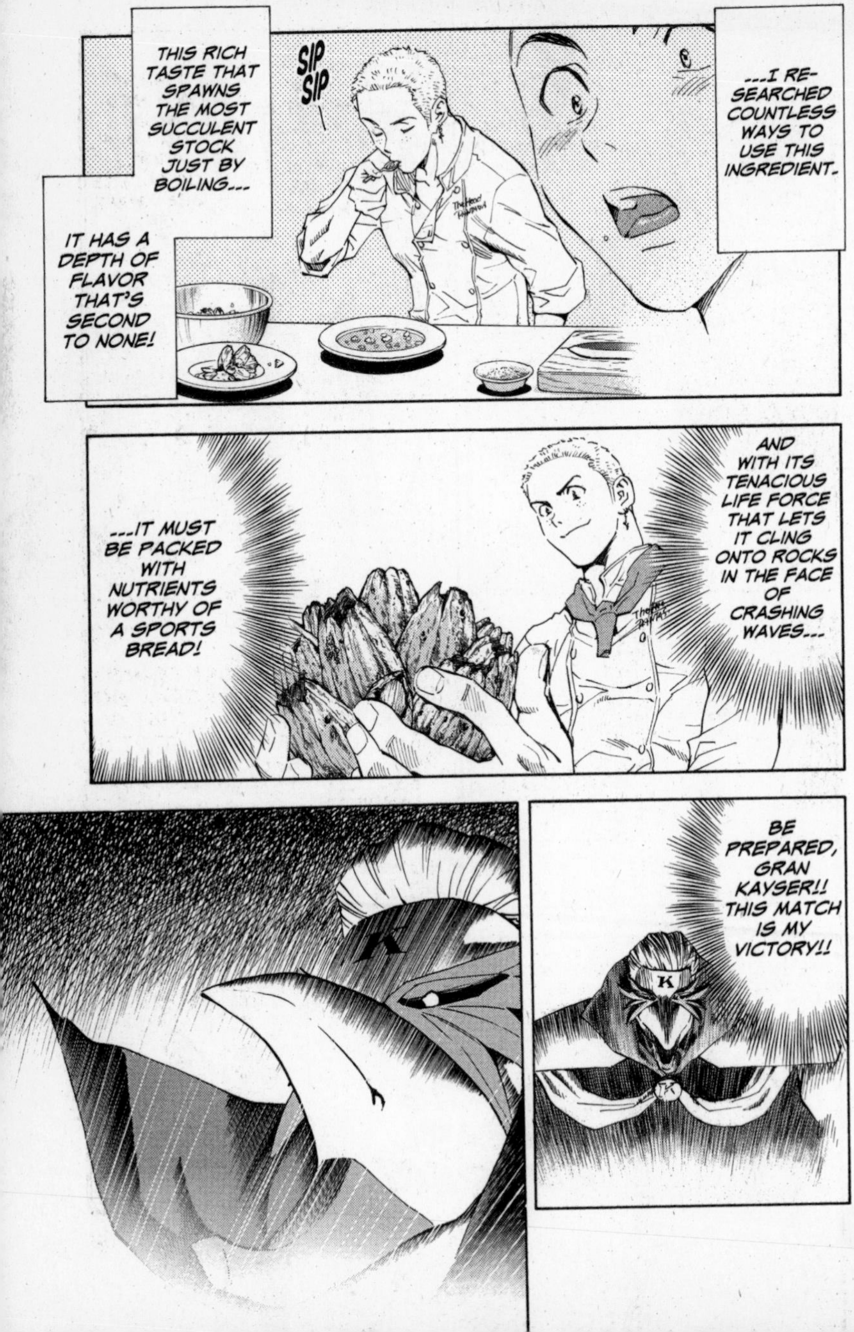

...I RE-SEARCHED COUNTLESS WAYS TO USE THIS INGREDIENT.
THIS RICH TASTE THAT SPAWNS THE MOST SUCCULENT STOCK JUST BY BOILING...
SIP SIP
IT HAS A DEPTH OF FLAVOR THAT'S SECOND TO NONE!
AND WITH ITS TENACIOUS LIFE FORCE THAT LETS IT CLING ONTO ROCKS IN THE FACE OF CRASHING WAVES...
...IT MUST BE PACKED WITH NUTRIENTS WORTHY OF A SPORTS BREAD!
BE PREPARED, GRAN KAYSER!! THIS MATCH IS MY VICTORY!!

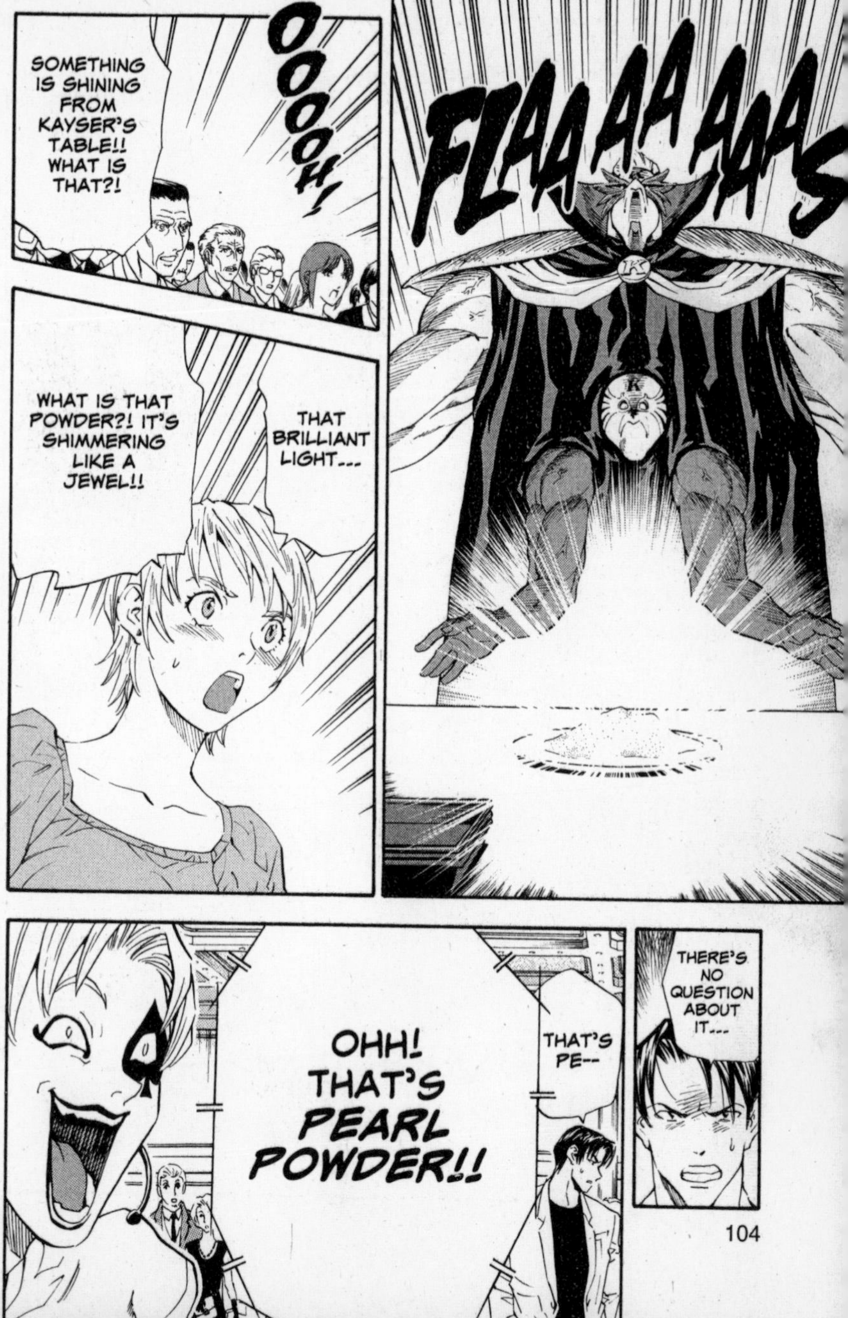
FLAAAAAAAS
OOOOOH!
SOMETHING IS SHINING FROM KAYSER'S TABLE!! WHAT IS THAT?!
THAT BRILLIANT LIGHT...
WHAT IS THAT POWDER?! IT'S SHIMMERING LIKE A JEWEL!!
THERE'S NO QUESTION ABOUT IT...
THAT'S PE--
OHH! THAT'S PEARL POWDER!!

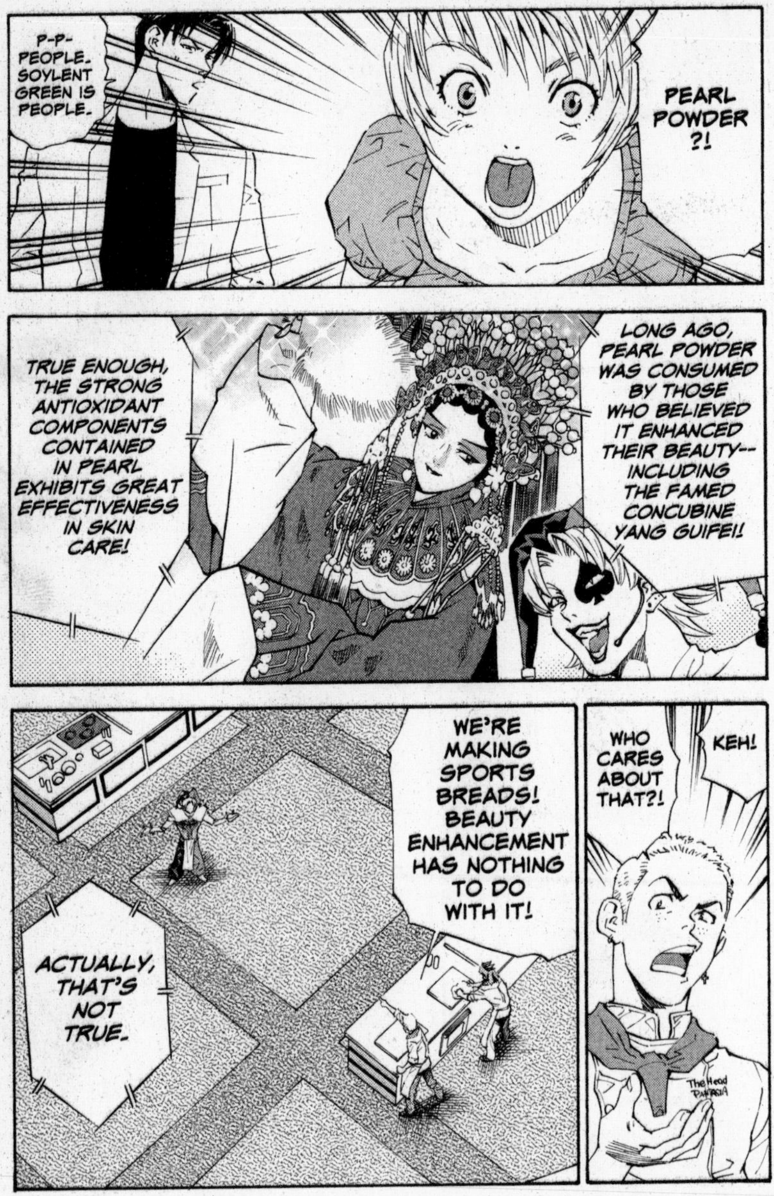
PEARL POWDER ?!
P-P-PEOPLE. SOYLENT GREEN IS PEOPLE.
LONG AGO, PEARL POWDER WAS CONSUMED BY THOSE WHO BELIEVED IT ENHANCED THEIR BEAUTY-- INCLUDING THE FAMED CONCUBINE YANG GUIFEI!
TRUE ENOUGH, THE STRONG ANTIOXIDANT COMPONENTS CONTAINED IN PEARL EXHIBITS GREAT EFFECTIVENESS IN SKIN CARE!
KEH!
WHO CARES ABOUT THAT?!
The Head PANTASIA
WE'RE MAKING SPORTS BREADS! BEAUTY ENHANCEMENT HAS NOTHING TO DO WITH IT!
ACTUALLY, THAT'S NOT TRUE.

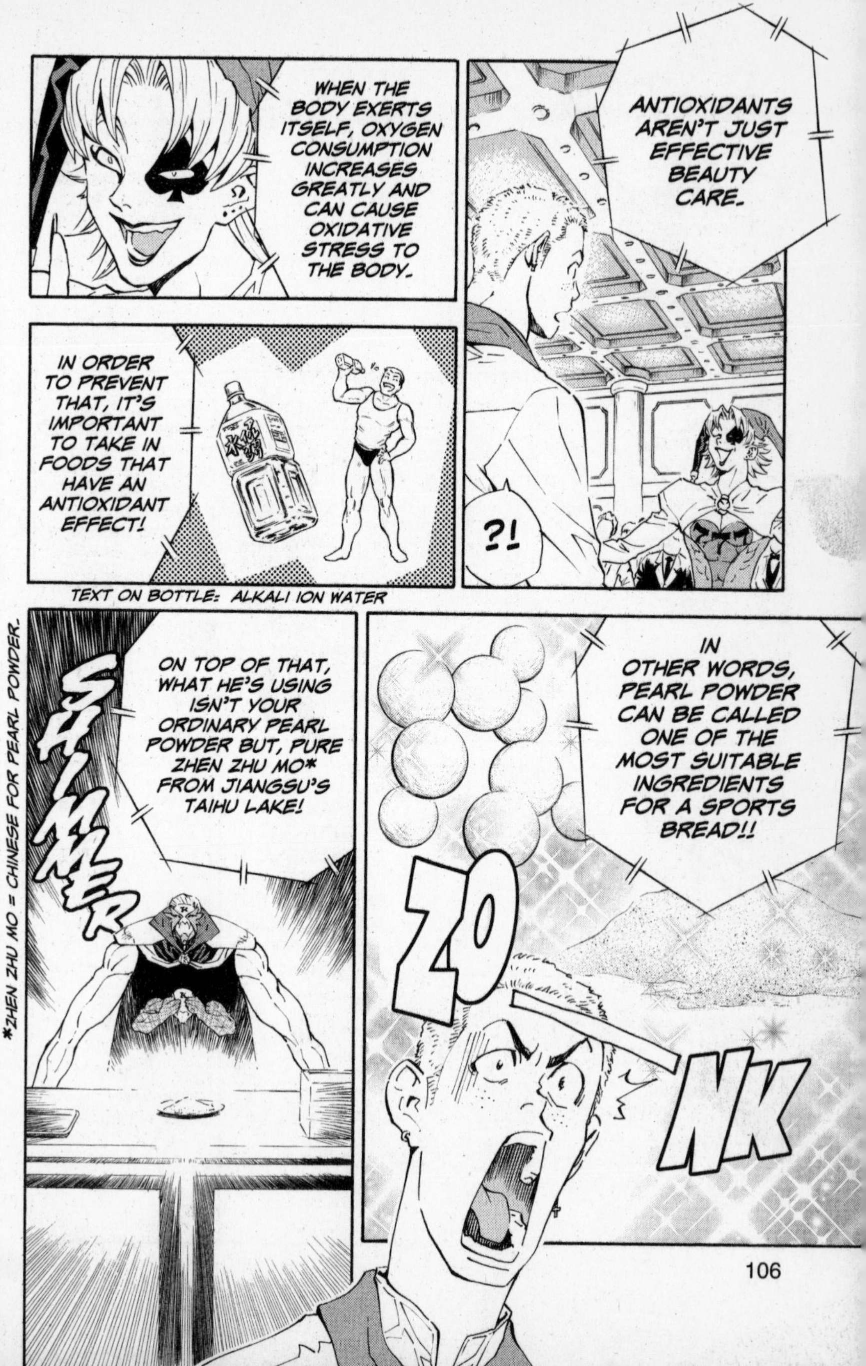
ANTIOXIDANTS AREN'T JUST EFFECTIVE BEAUTY CARE.
WHEN THE BODY EXERTS ITSELF, OXYGEN CONSUMPTION INCREASES GREATLY AND CAN CAUSE OXIDATIVE STRESS TO THE BODY.
?!
IN ORDER TO PREVENT THAT, IT'S IMPORTANT TO TAKE IN FOODS THAT HAVE AN ANTIOXIDANT EFFECT!
TEXT ON BOTTLE: ALKALI ION WATER
IN OTHER WORDS, PEARL POWDER CAN BE CALLED ONE OF THE MOST SUITABLE INGREDIENTS FOR A SPORTS BREAD!!
ZO
NK
ON TOP OF THAT, WHAT HE'S USING ISN'T YOUR ORDINARY PEARL POWDER BUT, PURE ZHEN ZHU MO* FROM JIANGSU'S TAIHU LAKE!
SHIMMER
*ZHEN ZHU MO = CHINESE FOR PEARL POWDER.

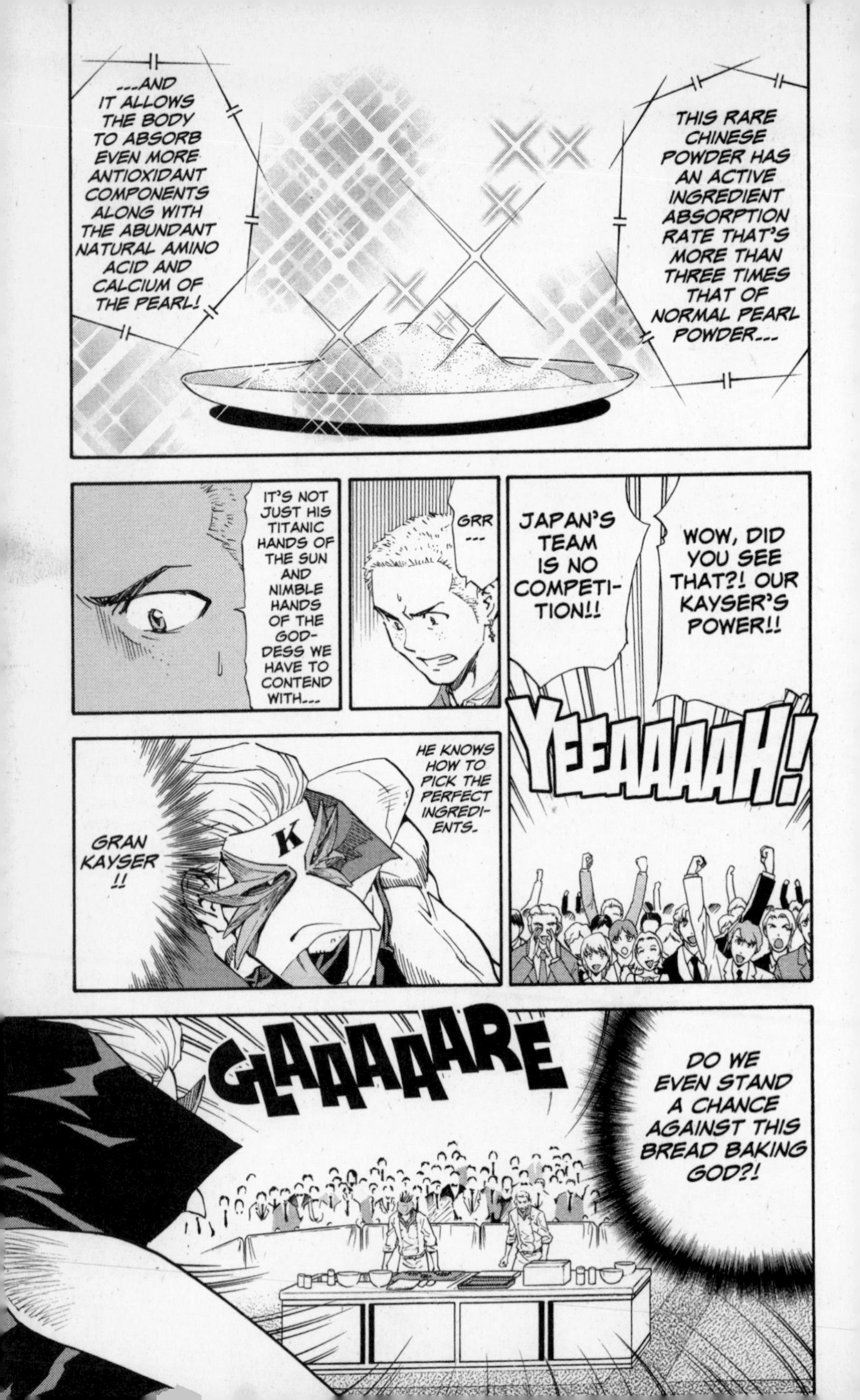
THIS RARE CHINESE POWDER HAS AN ACTIVE INGREDIENT ABSORPTION RATE THAT'S MORE THAN THREE TIMES THAT OF NORMAL PEARL POWDER...
...AND IT ALLOWS THE BODY TO ABSORB EVEN MORE ANTIOXIDANT COMPONENTS ALONG WITH THE ABUNDANT NATURAL AMINO ACID AND CALCIUM OF THE PEARL!
WOW, DID YOU SEE THAT?! OUR KAYSER'S POWER!!
JAPAN'S TEAM IS NO COMPETITION!!
YEEAAAAAH!
GRR---
IT'S NOT JUST HIS TITANIC HANDS OF THE SUN AND NIMBLE HANDS OF THE GODDESS WE HAVE TO CONTEND WITH...
HE KNOWS HOW TO PICK THE PERFECT INGREDIENTS.
GRAN KAYSER!!
DO WE EVEN STAND A CHANCE AGAINST THIS BREAD BAKING GOD?!
GLAAAAARE

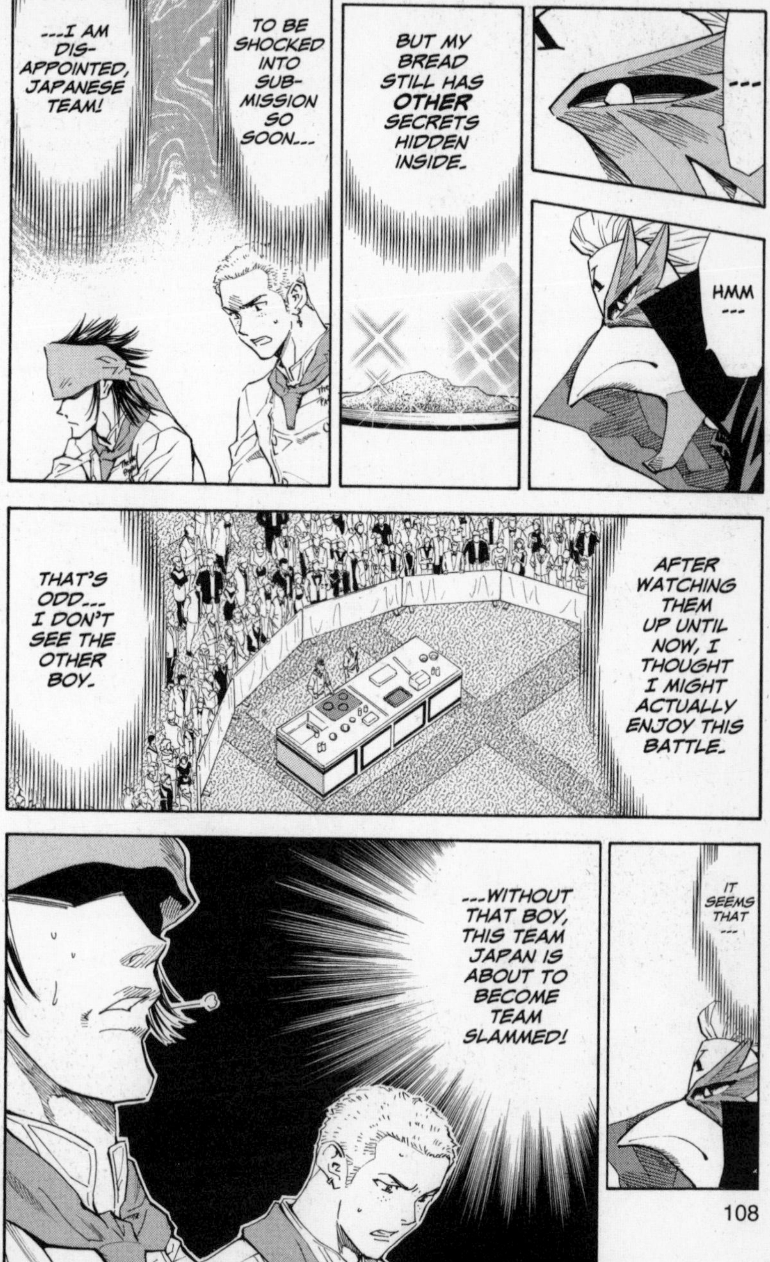

HMM ---
BUT MY BREAD STILL HAS **OTHER** SECRETS HIDDEN INSIDE.
---I AM DIS-APPOINTED, JAPANESE TEAM!
TO BE SHOCKED INTO SUB-MISSION SO SOON...
AFTER WATCHING THEM UP UNTIL NOW, I THOUGHT I MIGHT ACTUALLY ENJOY THIS BATTLE.
THAT'S ODD... I DON'T SEE THE OTHER BOY.
IT SEEMS THAT ---
---WITHOUT THAT BOY, THIS TEAM JAPAN IS ABOUT TO BECOME TEAM SLAMMED!

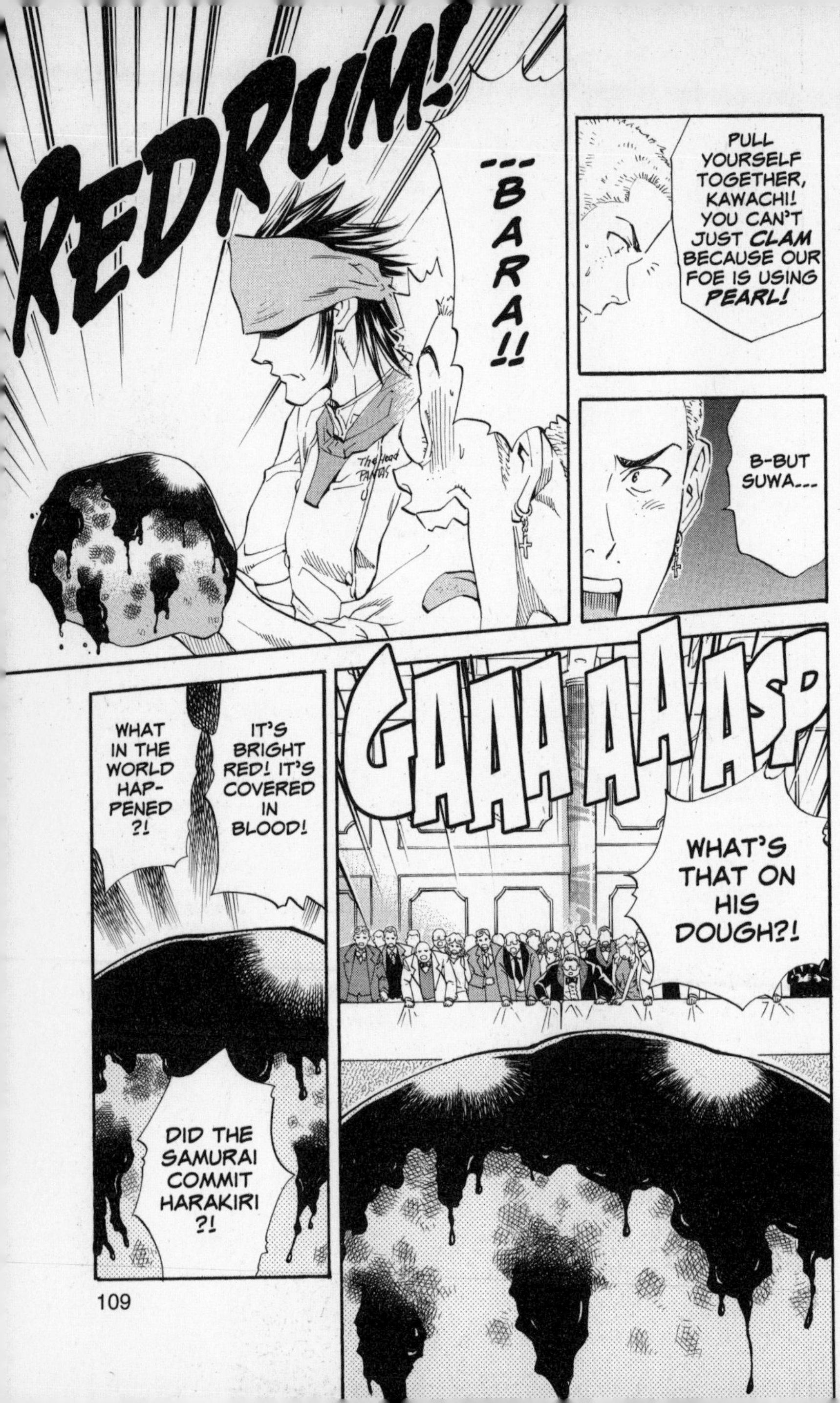
PULL YOURSELF TOGETHER, KAWACHI! YOU CAN'T JUST *CLAM* BECAUSE OUR FOE IS USING *PEARL!*
B-BUT SUWA...
...BARA!!
REDRUM!
The Head PANTAS
GAAAAAASP
WHAT'S THAT ON HIS DOUGH?!
IT'S BRIGHT RED! IT'S COVERED IN BLOOD!
WHAT IN THE WORLD HAP-PENED ?!
DID THE SAMURAI COMMIT HARAKIRI ?!

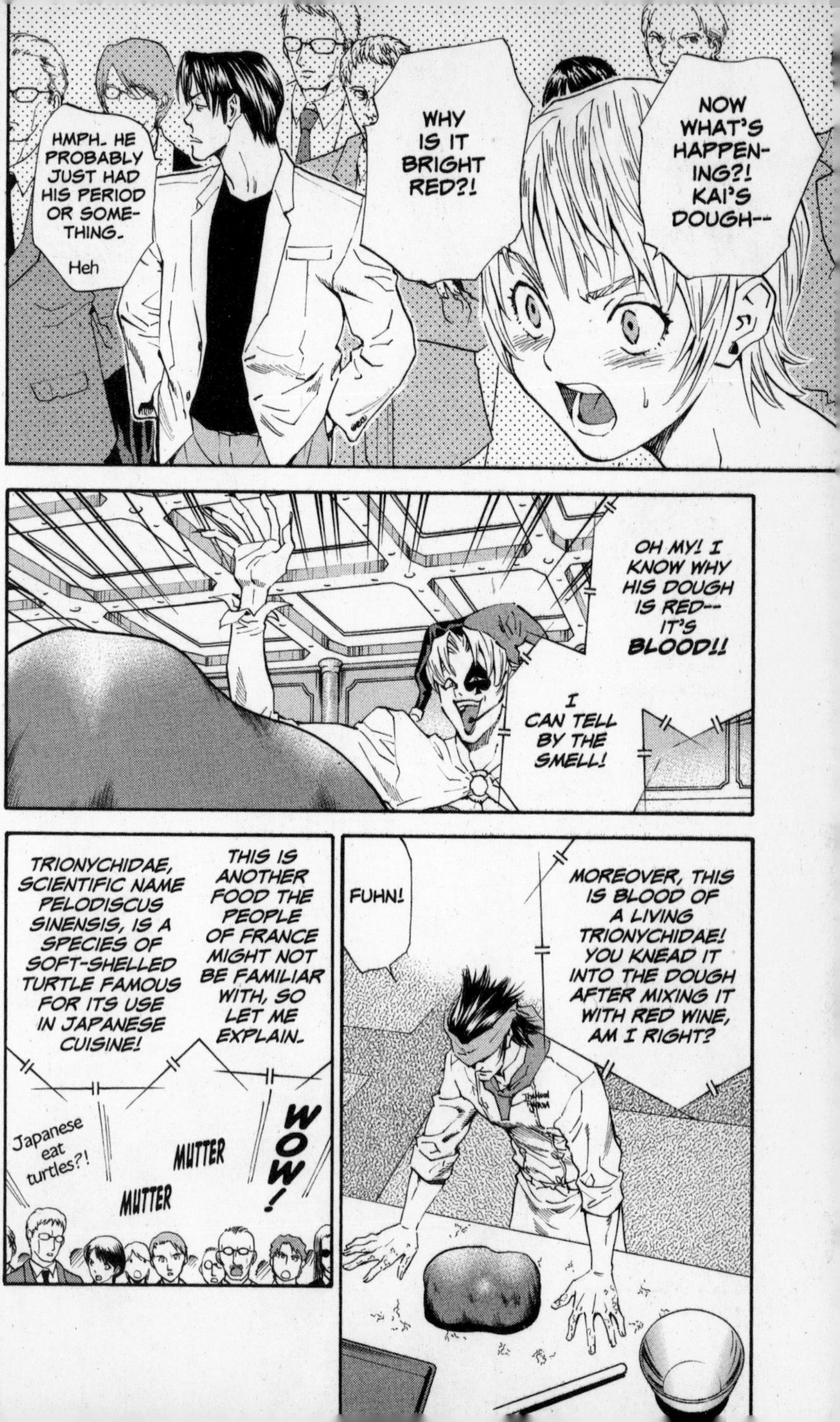
NOW WHAT'S HAPPEN-ING?! KAI'S DOUGH--
WHY IS IT BRIGHT RED?!
HMPH. HE PROBABLY JUST HAD HIS PERIOD OR SOME-THING.
Heh
OH MY! I KNOW WHY HIS DOUGH IS RED-- IT'S BLOOD!!
I CAN TELL BY THE SMELL!
MOREOVER, THIS IS BLOOD OF A LIVING TRIONYCHIDAE! YOU KNEAD IT INTO THE DOUGH AFTER MIXING IT WITH RED WINE, AM I RIGHT?
FUHN!
THIS IS ANOTHER FOOD THE PEOPLE OF FRANCE MIGHT NOT BE FAMILIAR WITH, SO LET ME EXPLAIN.
TRIONYCHIDAE, SCIENTIFIC NAME PELODISCUS SINENSIS, IS A SPECIES OF SOFT-SHELLED TURTLE FAMOUS FOR ITS USE IN JAPANESE CUISINE!
WOW!
MUTTER
MUTTER
Japanese eat turtles?!

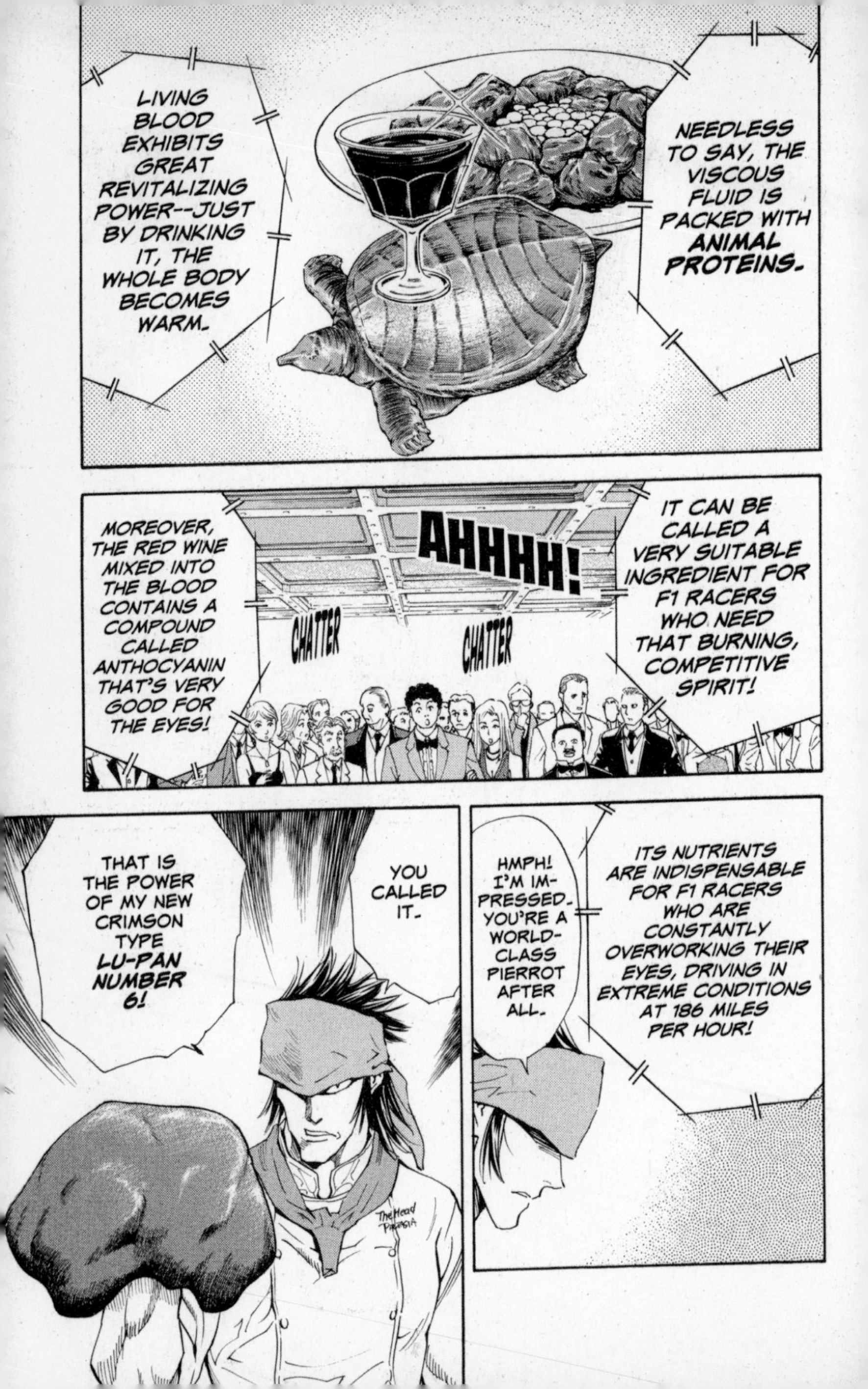
NEEDLESS TO SAY, THE VISCOUS FLUID IS PACKED WITH **ANIMAL PROTEINS.**
LIVING BLOOD EXHIBITS GREAT REVITALIZING POWER--JUST BY DRINKING IT, THE WHOLE BODY BECOMES WARM.
IT CAN BE CALLED A VERY SUITABLE INGREDIENT FOR F1 RACERS WHO NEED THAT BURNING, COMPETITIVE SPIRIT!
AHHHH!
CHATTER
CHATTER
MOREOVER, THE RED WINE MIXED INTO THE BLOOD CONTAINS A COMPOUND CALLED ANTHOCYANIN THAT'S VERY GOOD FOR THE EYES!
ITS NUTRIENTS ARE INDISPENSABLE FOR F1 RACERS WHO ARE CONSTANTLY OVERWORKING THEIR EYES, DRIVING IN EXTREME CONDITIONS AT 186 MILES PER HOUR!
HMPH! I'M IM-PRESSED. YOU'RE A WORLD-CLASS PIERROT AFTER ALL.
YOU CALLED IT.
THAT IS THE POWER OF MY NEW CRIMSON TYPE **LU-PAN NUMBER 6!**

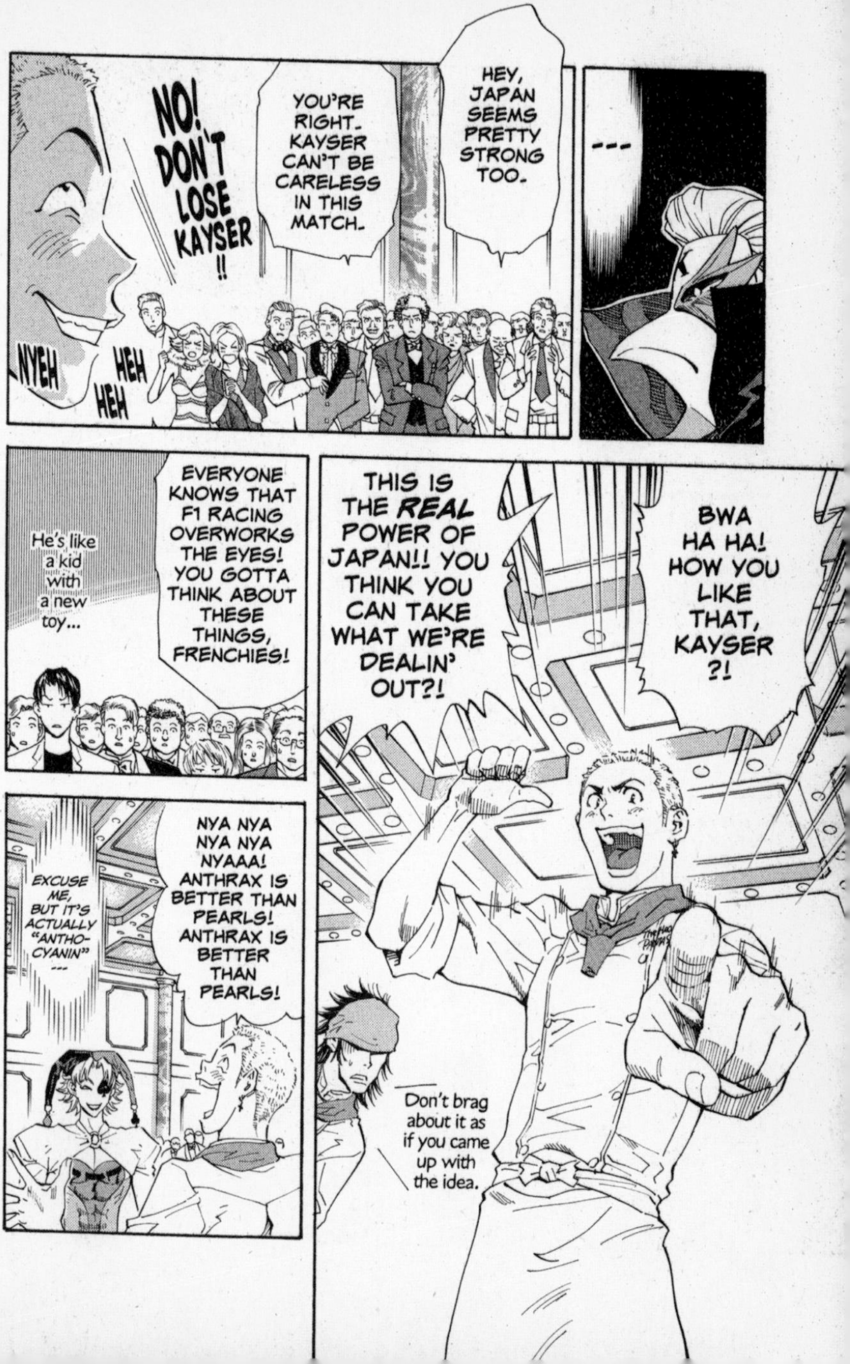
...
HEY, JAPAN SEEMS PRETTY STRONG TOO.
YOU'RE RIGHT. KAYSER CAN'T BE CARELESS IN THIS MATCH.
NO! DON'T LOSE KAYSER!!
NYEH HEH HEH
BWA HA HA! HOW YOU LIKE THAT, KAYSER?!
THIS IS THE REAL POWER OF JAPAN!! YOU THINK YOU CAN TAKE WHAT WE'RE DEALIN' OUT?!
Don't brag about it as if you came up with the idea.
EVERYONE KNOWS THAT F1 RACING OVERWORKS THE EYES! YOU GOTTA THINK ABOUT THESE THINGS, FRENCHIES!
He's like a kid with a new toy...
NYA NYA NYA NYA NYAAA! ANTHRAX IS BETTER THAN PEARLS! ANTHRAX IS BETTER THAN PEARLS!
EXCUSE ME, BUT IT'S ACTUALLY "ANTHOCYANIN"...

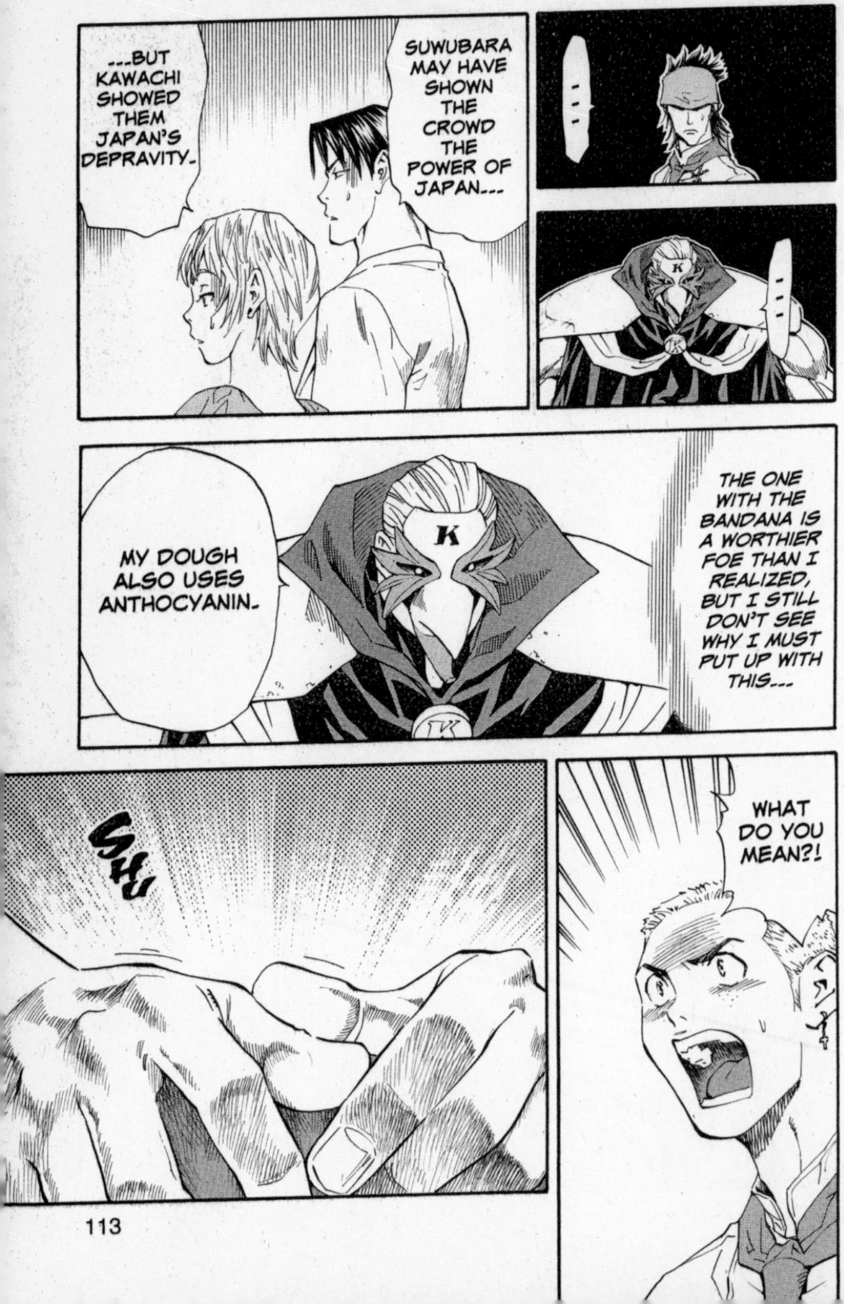
...
...
SUWUBARA MAY HAVE SHOWN THE CROWD THE POWER OF JAPAN...
...BUT KAWACHI SHOWED THEM JAPAN'S DEPRAVITY.
THE ONE WITH THE BANDANA IS A WORTHIER FOE THAN I REALIZED, BUT I STILL DON'T SEE WHY I MUST PUT UP WITH THIS...
MY DOUGH ALSO USES ANTHOCYANIN.
WHAT DO YOU MEAN?!
SHU

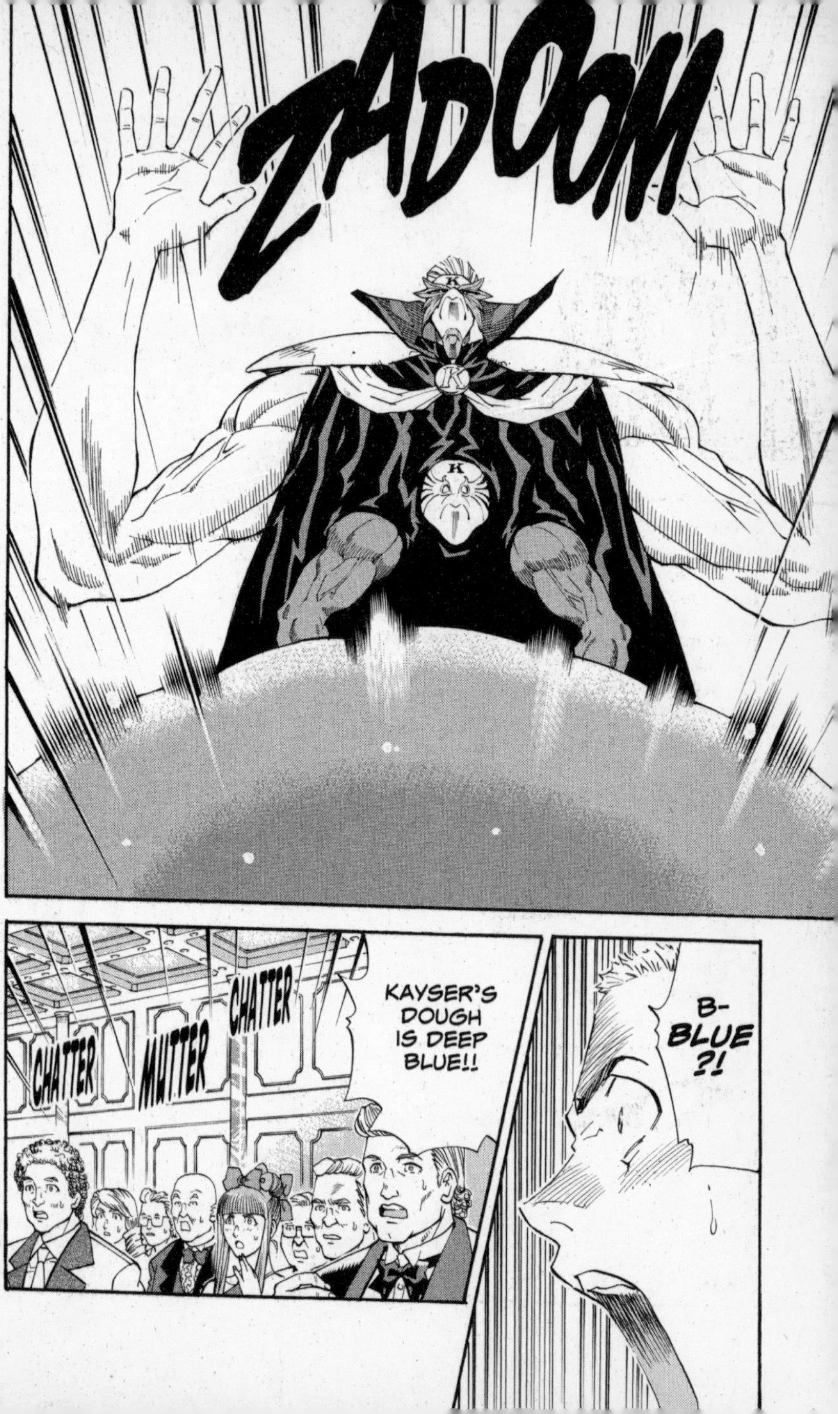
ZADOOM
B-BLUE?!
KAYSER'S DOUGH IS DEEP BLUE!!
CHATTER
MUTTER
CHATTER

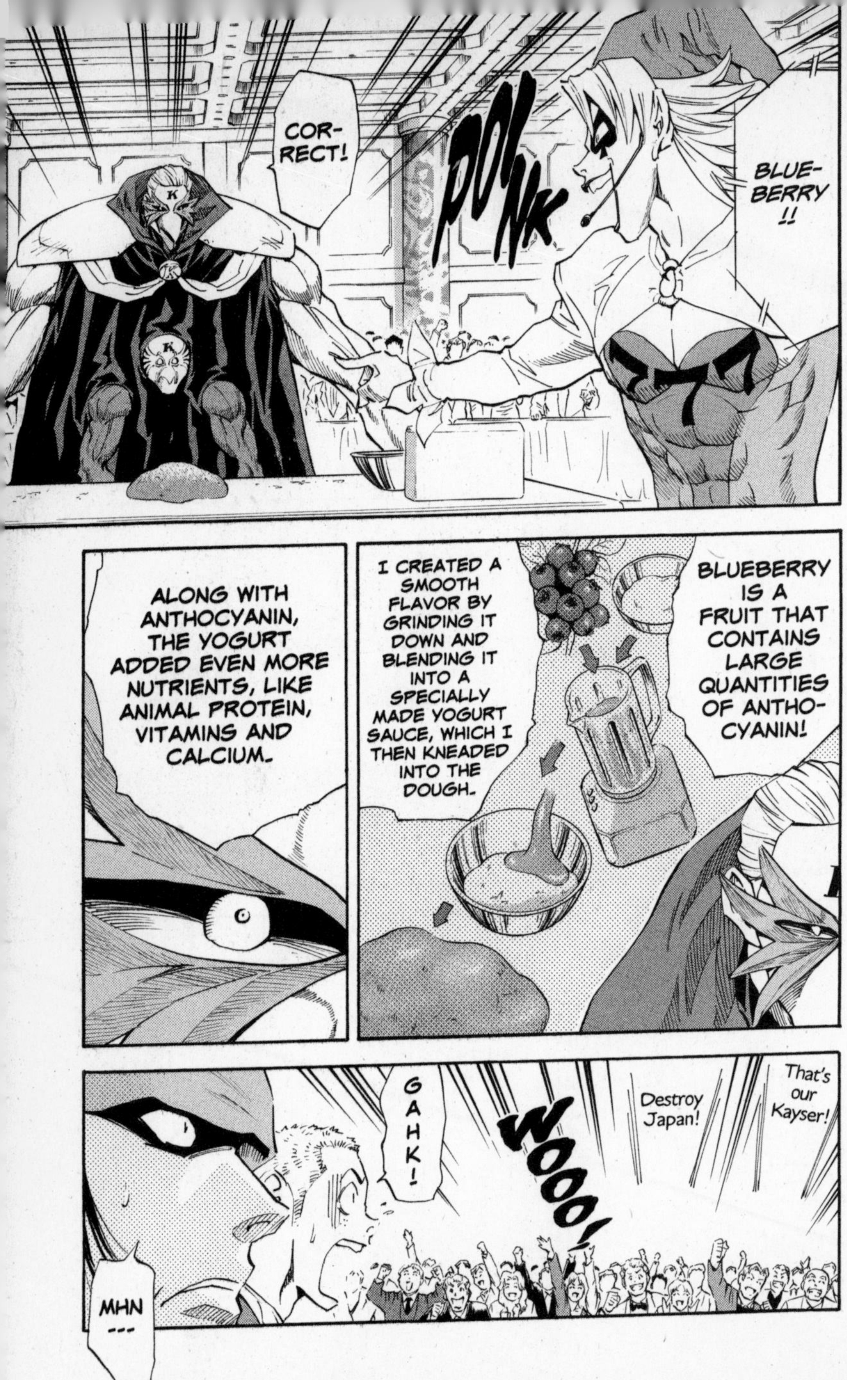
BLUE-BERRY!!
PONK
COR-RECT!
BLUEBERRY IS A FRUIT THAT CONTAINS LARGE QUANTITIES OF ANTHO-CYANIN!
I CREATED A SMOOTH FLAVOR BY GRINDING IT DOWN AND BLENDING IT INTO A SPECIALLY MADE YOGURT SAUCE, WHICH I THEN KNEADED INTO THE DOUGH.
ALONG WITH ANTHOCYANIN, THE YOGURT ADDED EVEN MORE NUTRIENTS, LIKE ANIMAL PROTEIN, VITAMINS AND CALCIUM.
That's our Kayser!
Destroy Japan!
WOOO!
GAHK!
MHN ---

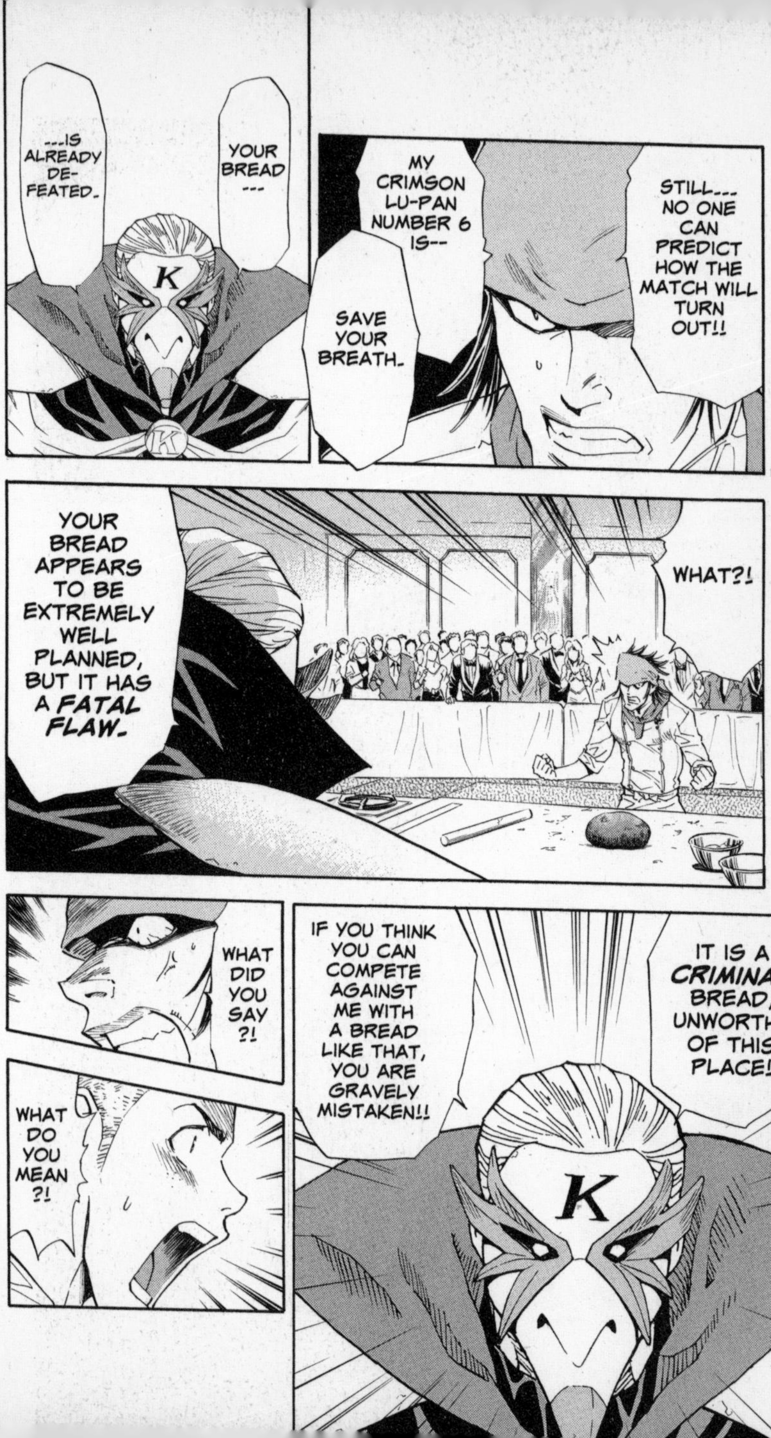
STILL... NO ONE CAN PREDICT HOW THE MATCH WILL TURN OUT!!
MY CRIMSON LU-PAN NUMBER 6 IS--
SAVE YOUR BREATH.
YOUR BREAD ---
---IS ALREADY DE-FEATED.
WHAT?!
YOUR BREAD APPEARS TO BE EXTREMELY WELL PLANNED, BUT IT HAS A *FATAL FLAW.*
IT IS A *CRIMINAL* BREAD, UNWORTHY OF THIS PLACE!
IF YOU THINK YOU CAN COMPETE AGAINST ME WITH A BREAD LIKE THAT, YOU ARE GRAVELY MISTAKEN!!
WHAT DID YOU SAY ?!
WHAT DO YOU MEAN ?!

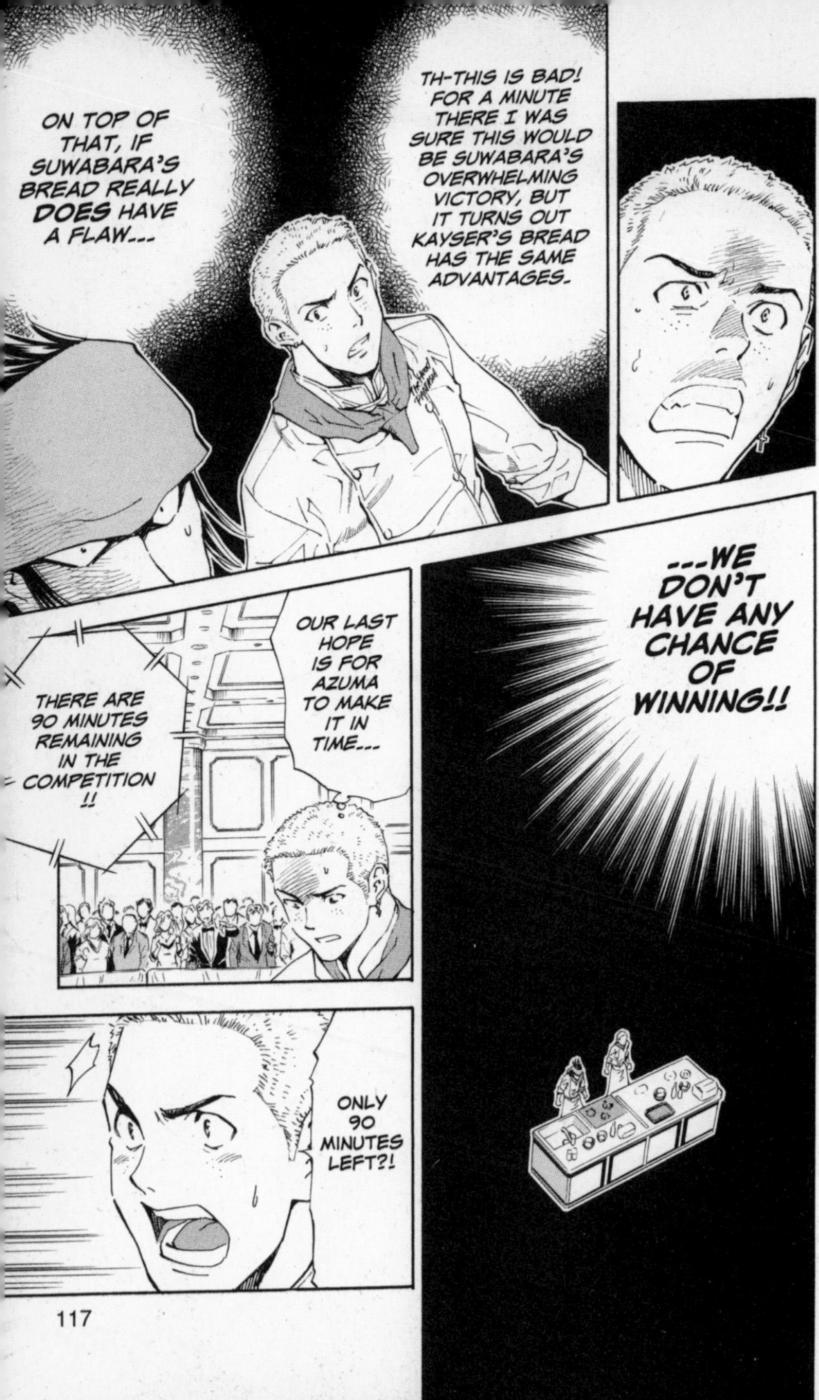

TH-THIS IS BAD! FOR A MINUTE THERE I WAS SURE THIS WOULD BE SUWABARA'S OVERWHELMING VICTORY, BUT IT TURNS OUT KAYSER'S BREAD HAS THE SAME ADVANTAGES.
ON TOP OF THAT, IF SUWABARA'S BREAD REALLY DOES HAVE A FLAW...
...WE DON'T HAVE ANY CHANCE OF WINNING!!
OUR LAST HOPE IS FOR AZUMA TO MAKE IT IN TIME...
THERE ARE 90 MINUTES REMAINING IN THE COMPETITION !!
ONLY 90 MINUTES LEFT?!

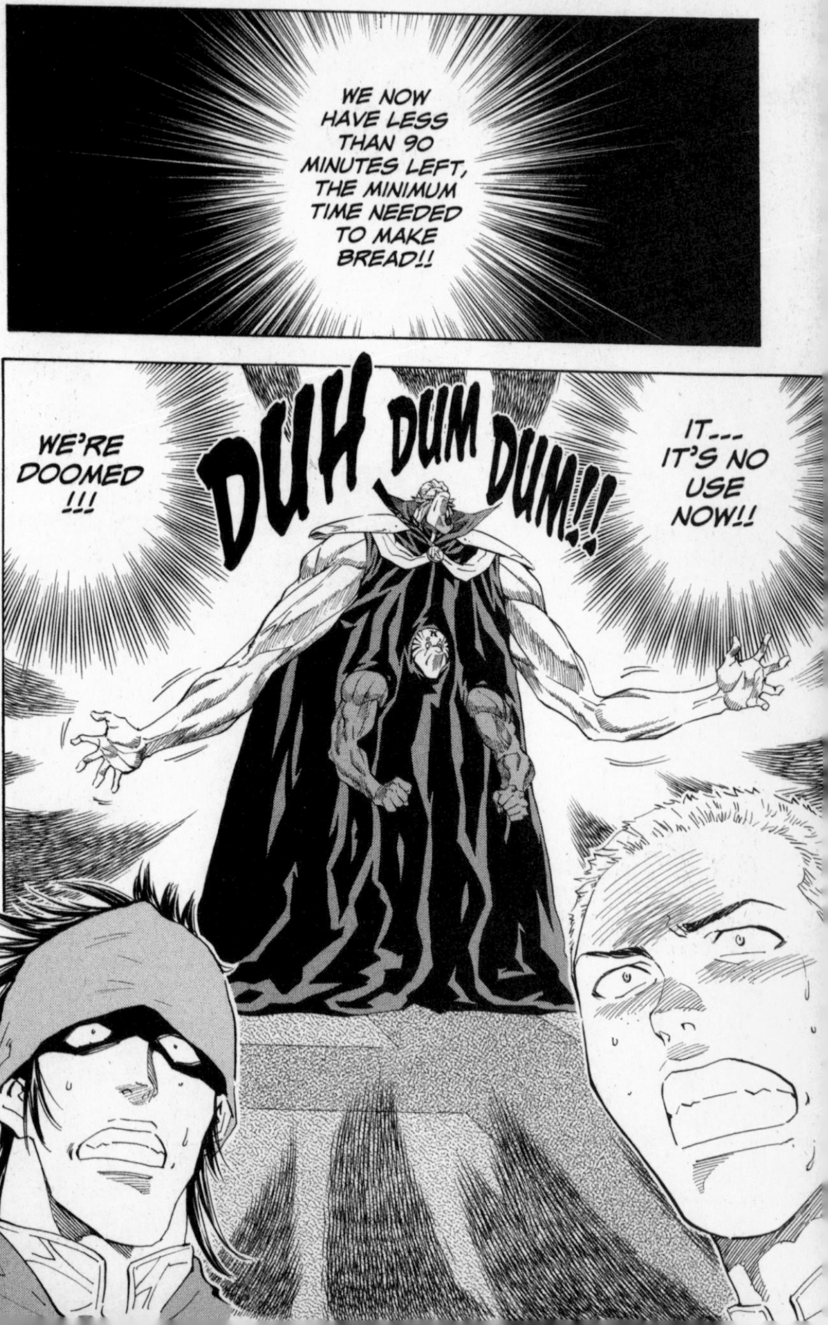
WE NOW HAVE LESS THAN 90 MINUTES LEFT, THE MINIMUM TIME NEEDED TO MAKE BREAD!!
IT... IT'S NO USE NOW!!
DUH DUM DUM!!
WE'RE DOOMED !!!

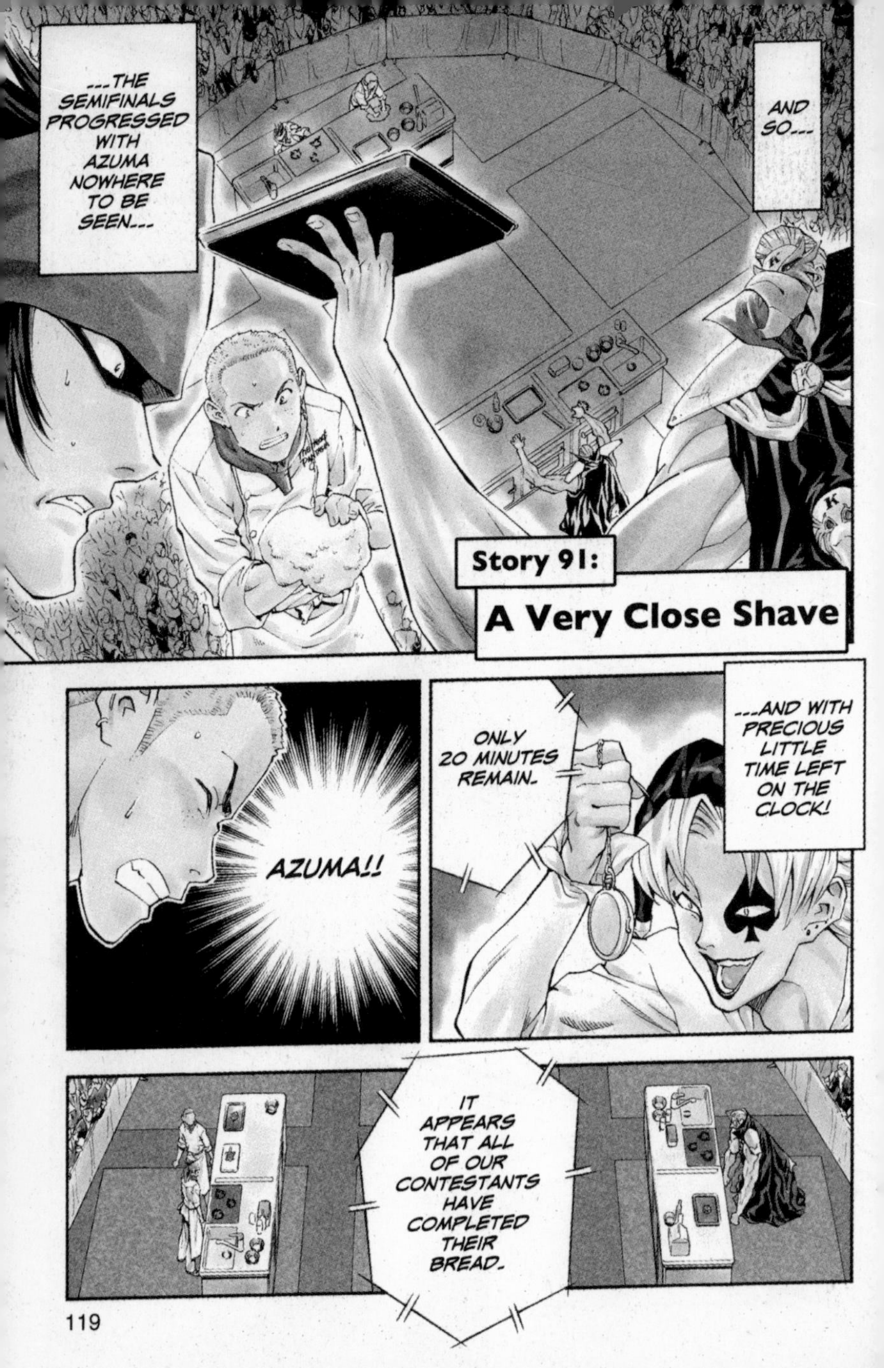
AND SO...
...THE SEMIFINALS PROGRESSED WITH AZUMA NOWHERE TO BE SEEN...
Story 91:
A Very Close Shave
...AND WITH PRECIOUS LITTLE TIME LEFT ON THE CLOCK!
ONLY 20 MINUTES REMAIN.
AZUMA!!
IT APPEARS THAT ALL OF OUR CONTESTANTS HAVE COMPLETED THEIR BREAD.

SUWA-BARA'S RED BREAD...
The Head PANTANA
KAYSER'S BLUE BREAD...
I CAN'T TELL WHO'LL WIN JUST BY APPEAR-ANCES...
...BUT KAYSER WAS SAYING HOW SUWA-BARA'S BREAD HAS A "FATAL FLAW."
IF THAT'S TRUE...
IF THAT'S TRUE...

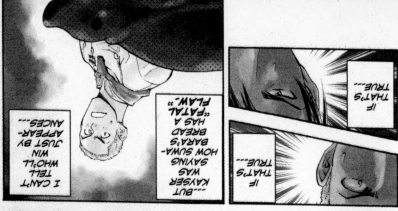

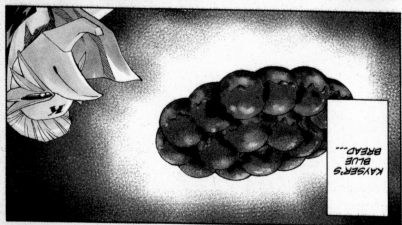

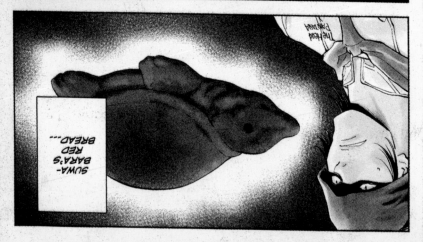

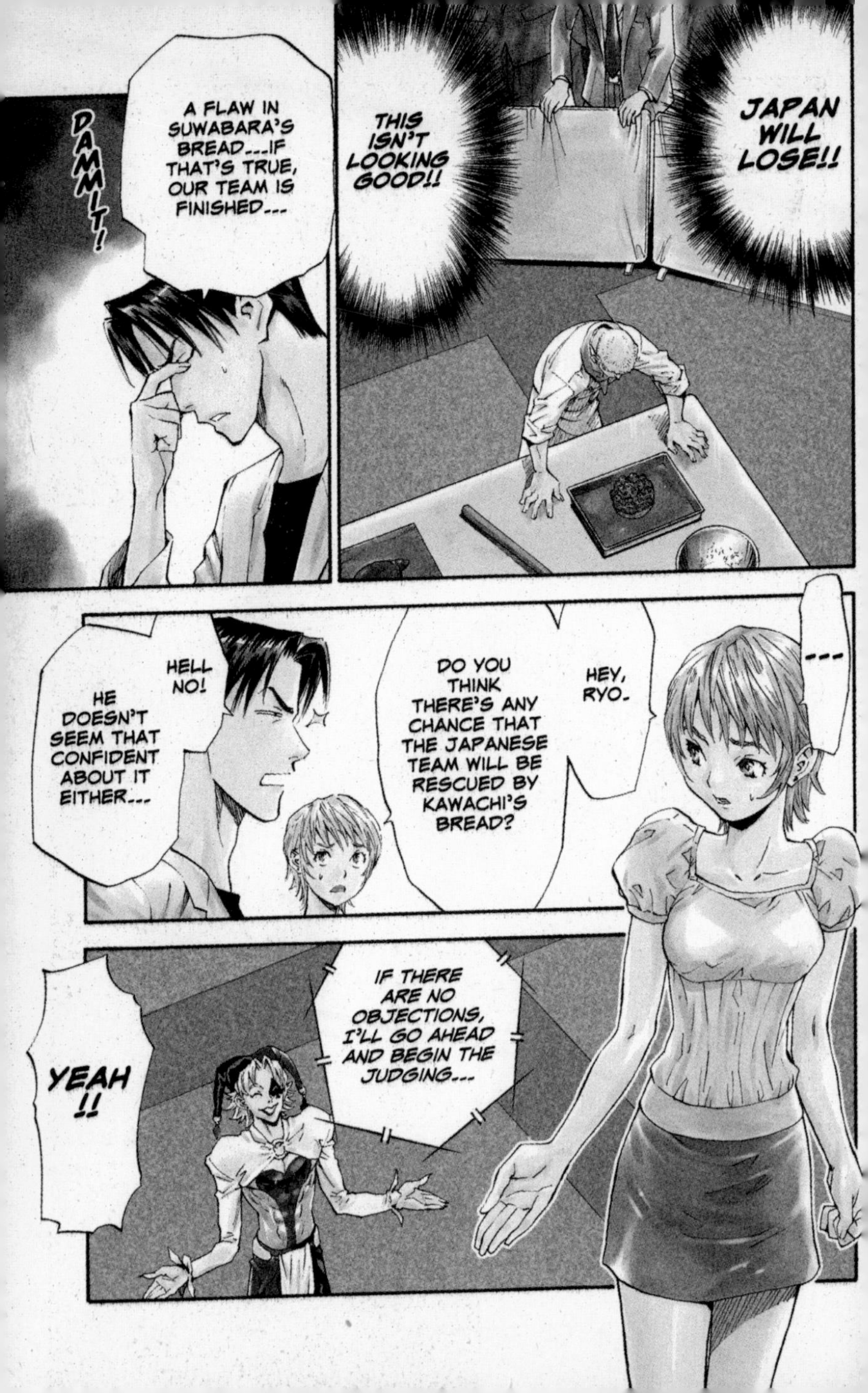
JAPAN WILL LOSE!!
THIS ISN'T LOOKING GOOD!!
A FLAW IN SUWABARA'S BREAD...IF THAT'S TRUE, OUR TEAM IS FINISHED...
DAMMIT!
...
HEY, RYO.
DO YOU THINK THERE'S ANY CHANCE THAT THE JAPANESE TEAM WILL BE RESCUED BY KAWACHI'S BREAD?
HELL NO!
HE DOESN'T SEEM THAT CONFIDENT ABOUT IT EITHER...
IF THERE ARE NO OBJECTIONS, I'LL GO AHEAD AND BEGIN THE JUDGING...
YEAH!!

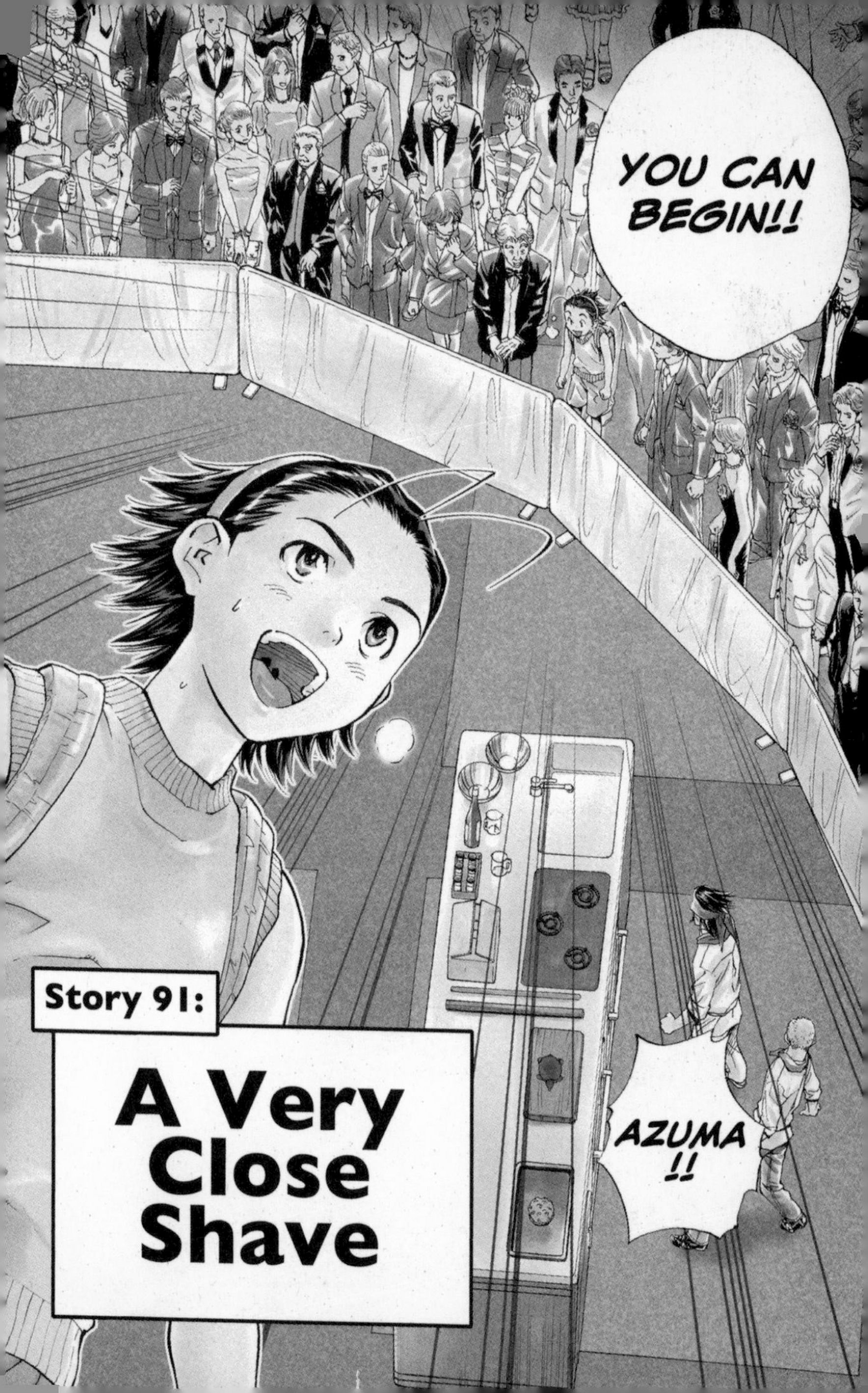
YOU CAN BEGIN!!
Story 91:
A Very Close Shave
AZUMA !!

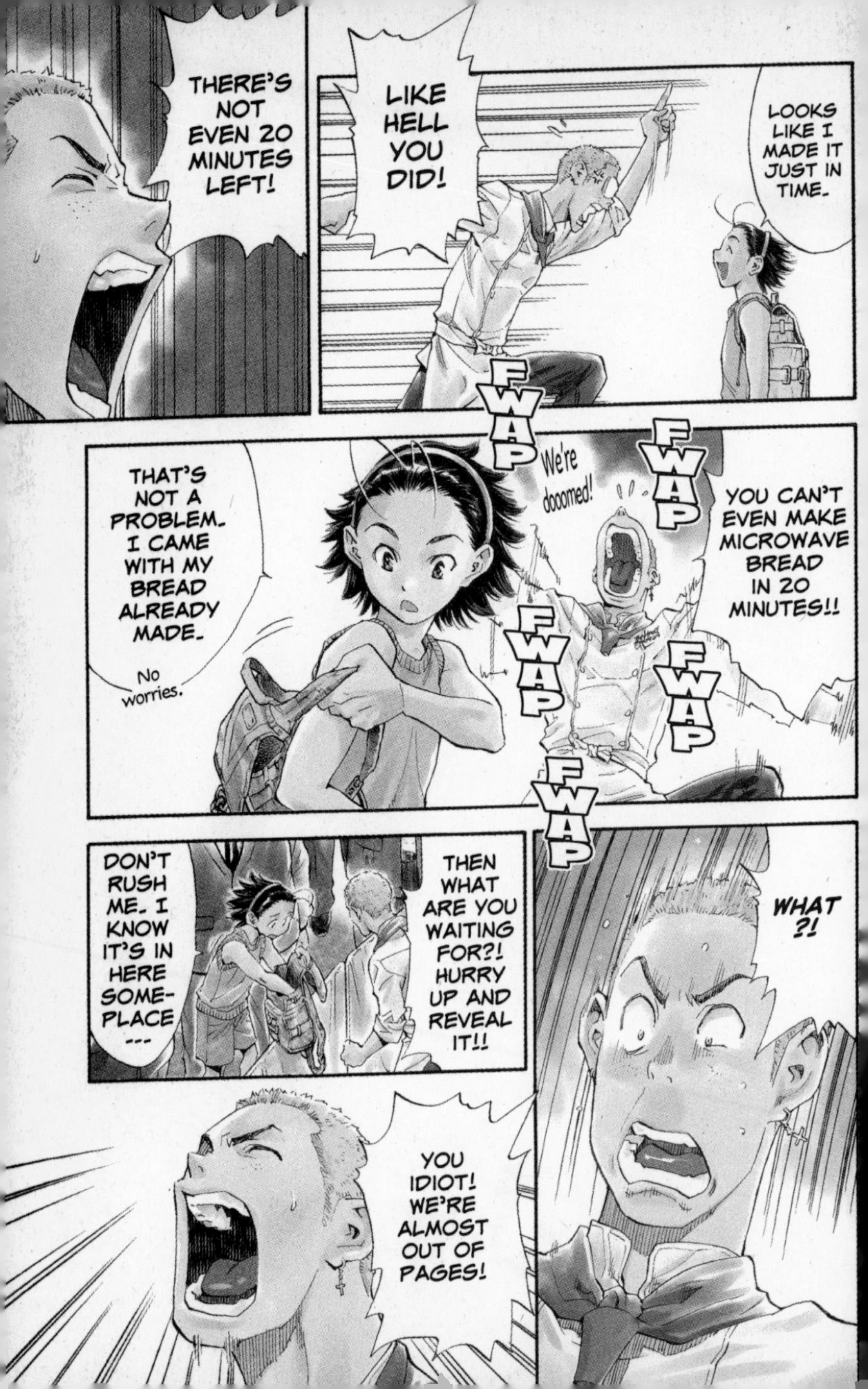
LOOKS LIKE I MADE IT JUST IN TIME.
LIKE HELL YOU DID!
THERE'S NOT EVEN 20 MINUTES LEFT!
YOU CAN'T EVEN MAKE MICROWAVE BREAD IN 20 MINUTES!!
We're dooomed!
FWAP
FWAP
FWAP
FWAP
FWAP
THAT'S NOT A PROBLEM. I CAME WITH MY BREAD ALREADY MADE.
No worries.
WHAT?!
THEN WHAT ARE YOU WAITING FOR?! HURRY UP AND REVEAL IT!!
DON'T RUSH ME. I KNOW IT'S IN HERE SOME-PLACE...
YOU IDIOT! WE'RE ALMOST OUT OF PAGES!

Yakitate!! Japan

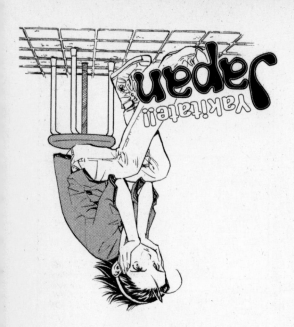

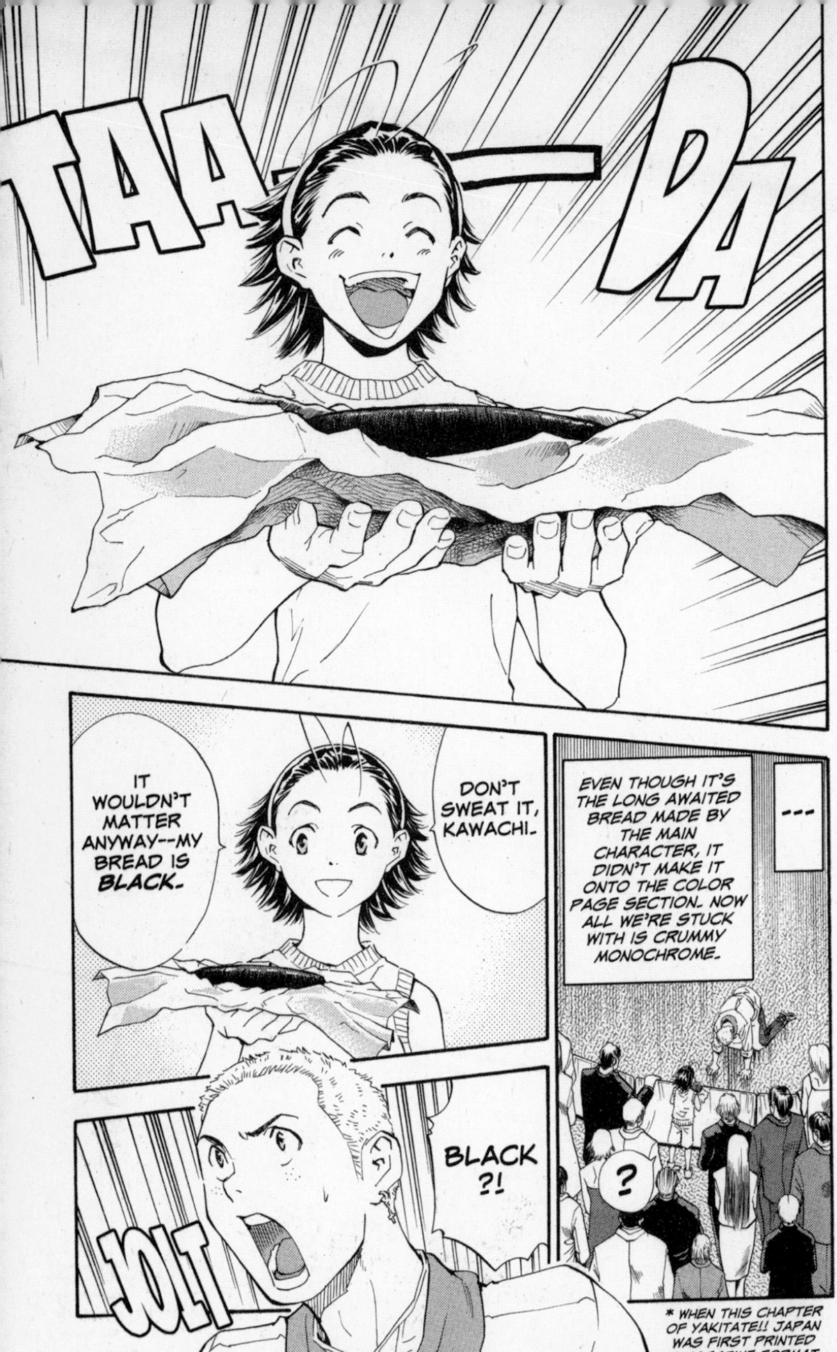
TAA—DA

EVEN THOUGH IT'S THE LONG AWAITED BREAD MADE BY THE MAIN CHARACTER, IT DIDN'T MAKE IT ONTO THE COLOR PAGE SECTION. NOW ALL WE'RE STUCK WITH IS CRUMMY MONOCHROME.
?
DON'T SWEAT IT, KAWACHI.
IT WOULDN'T MATTER ANYWAY--MY BREAD IS BLACK.
BLACK ?!
JOLT

* WHEN THIS CHAPTER OF YAKITATE!! JAPAN WAS FIRST PRINTED IN MAGAZINE FORMAT, THE FIRST FIVE PAGES WERE IN COLOR.

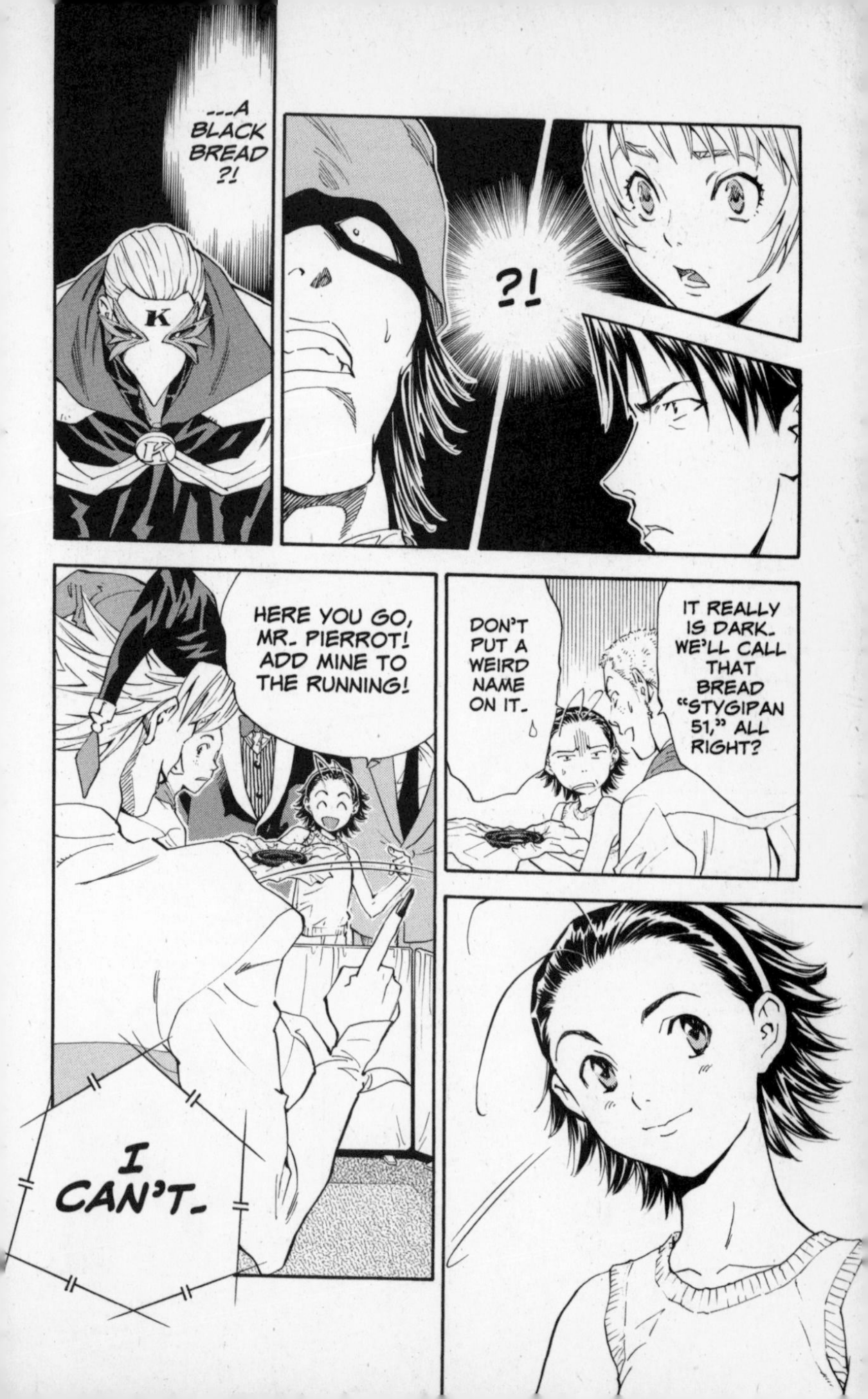
?!
...A BLACK BREAD?!
IT REALLY IS DARK. WE'LL CALL THAT BREAD "STYGIPAN 51," ALL RIGHT?
DON'T PUT A WEIRD NAME ON IT.
HERE YOU GO, MR. PIERROT! ADD MINE TO THE RUNNING!
I CAN'T.

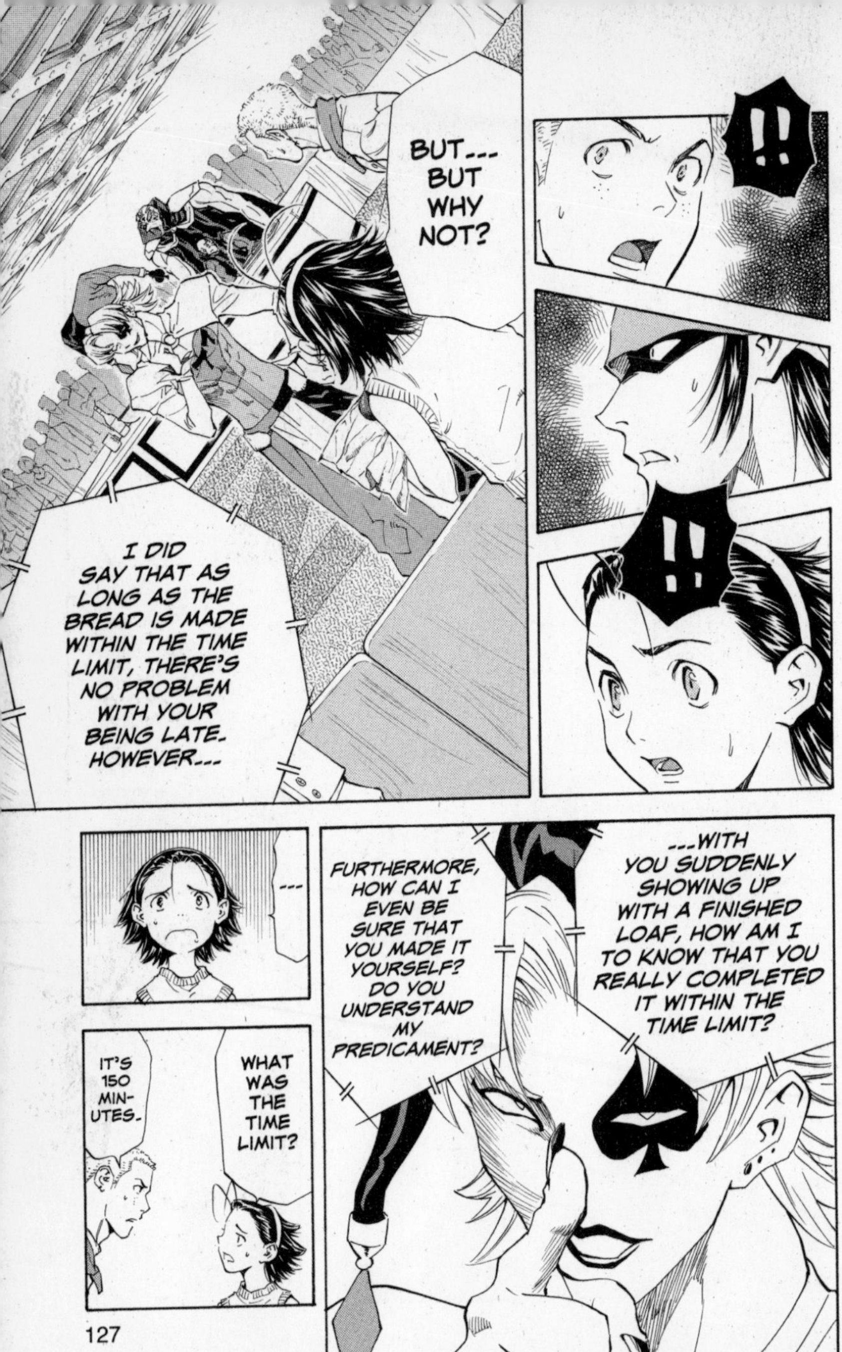
!!
!!
BUT... BUT WHY NOT?
I DID SAY THAT AS LONG AS THE BREAD IS MADE WITHIN THE TIME LIMIT, THERE'S NO PROBLEM WITH YOUR BEING LATE. HOWEVER...
...WITH YOU SUDDENLY SHOWING UP WITH A FINISHED LOAF, HOW AM I TO KNOW THAT YOU REALLY COMPLETED IT WITHIN THE TIME LIMIT?
FURTHERMORE, HOW CAN I EVEN BE SURE THAT YOU MADE IT YOURSELF? DO YOU UNDERSTAND MY PREDICAMENT?
...
WHAT WAS THE TIME LIMIT?
IT'S 150 MIN-UTES.

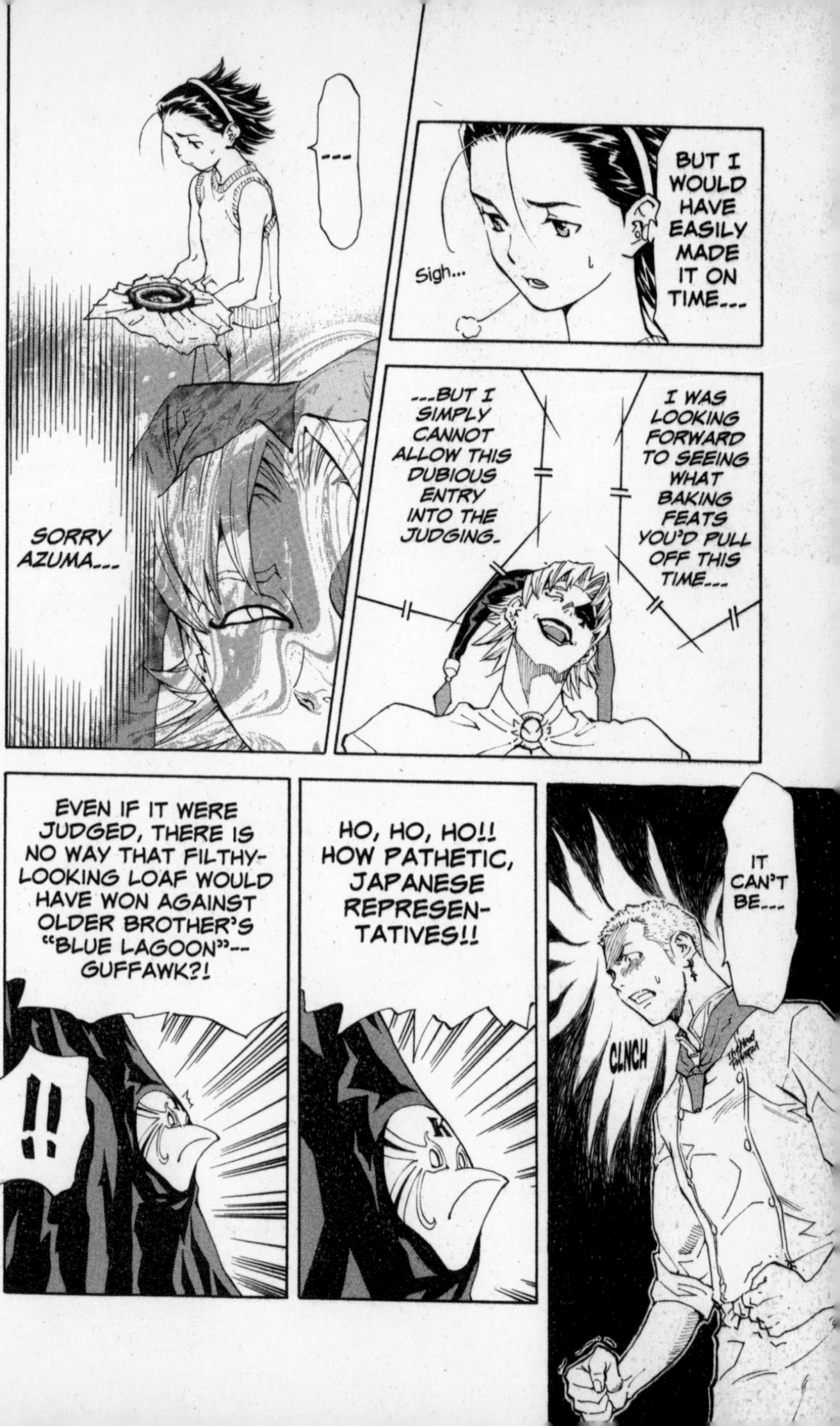
BUT I WOULD HAVE EASILY MADE IT ON TIME...
Sigh...
I WAS LOOKING FORWARD TO SEEING WHAT BAKING FEATS YOU'D PULL OFF THIS TIME...
...BUT I SIMPLY CANNOT ALLOW THIS DUBIOUS ENTRY INTO THE JUDGING.
...
SORRY AZUMA...
IT CAN'T BE...
CLINCH
HO, HO, HO!! HOW PATHETIC, JAPANESE REPRESEN-TATIVES!!
EVEN IF IT WERE JUDGED, THERE IS NO WAY THAT FILTHY-LOOKING LOAF WOULD HAVE WON AGAINST OLDER BROTHER'S "BLUE LAGOON"-- GUFFAWK?!
!!

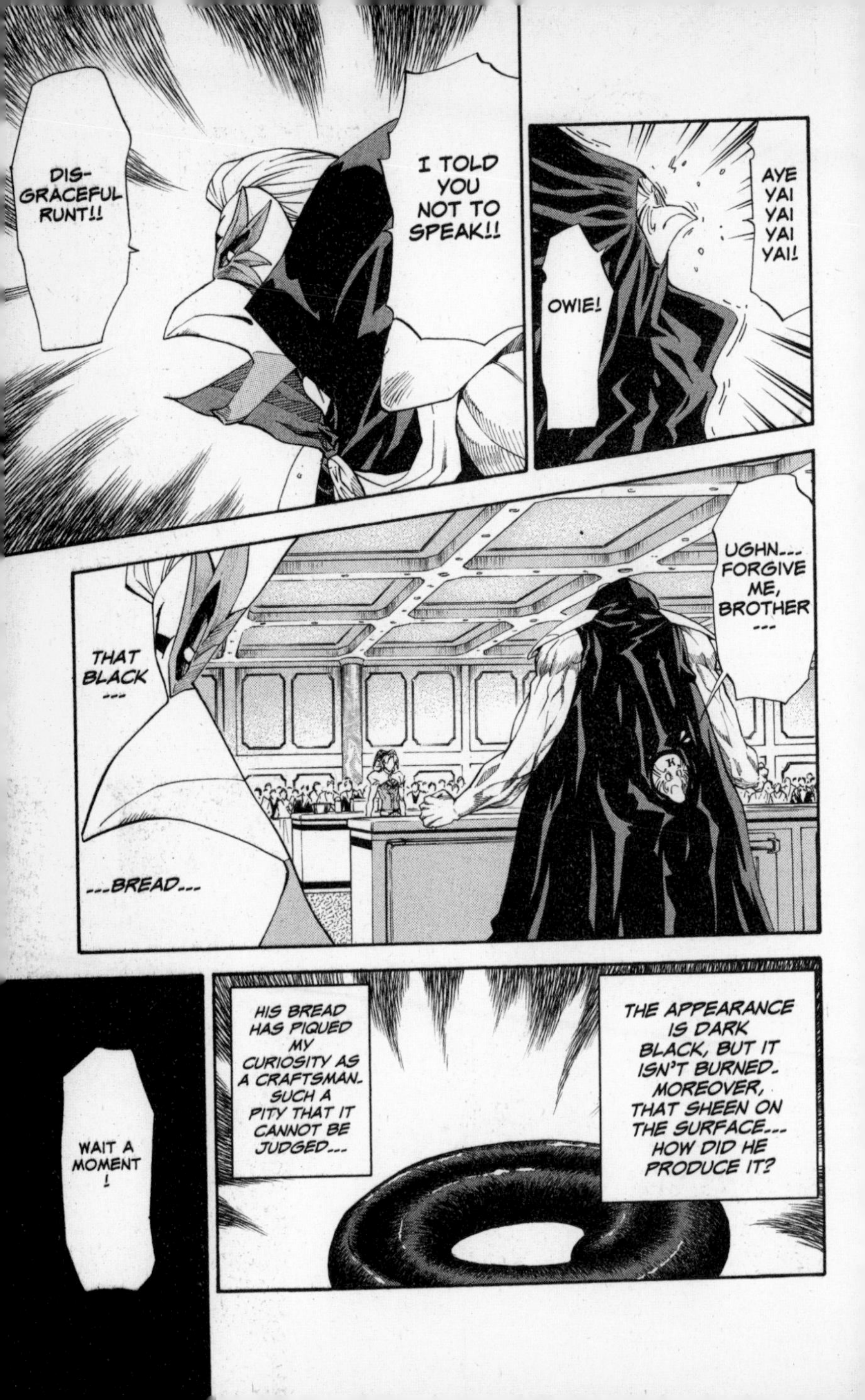
AYE YAI YAI YAI YAI!
OWIE!
I TOLD YOU NOT TO SPEAK!!
DIS-GRACEFUL RUNT!!
UGHN... FORGIVE ME, BROTHER...
THAT BLACK...
...BREAD...
THE APPEARANCE IS DARK BLACK, BUT IT ISN'T BURNED. MOREOVER, THAT SHEEN ON THE SURFACE... HOW DID HE PRODUCE IT?
HIS BREAD HAS PIQUED MY CURIOSITY AS A CRAFTSMAN. SUCH A PITY THAT IT CANNOT BE JUDGED...
WAIT A MOMENT!

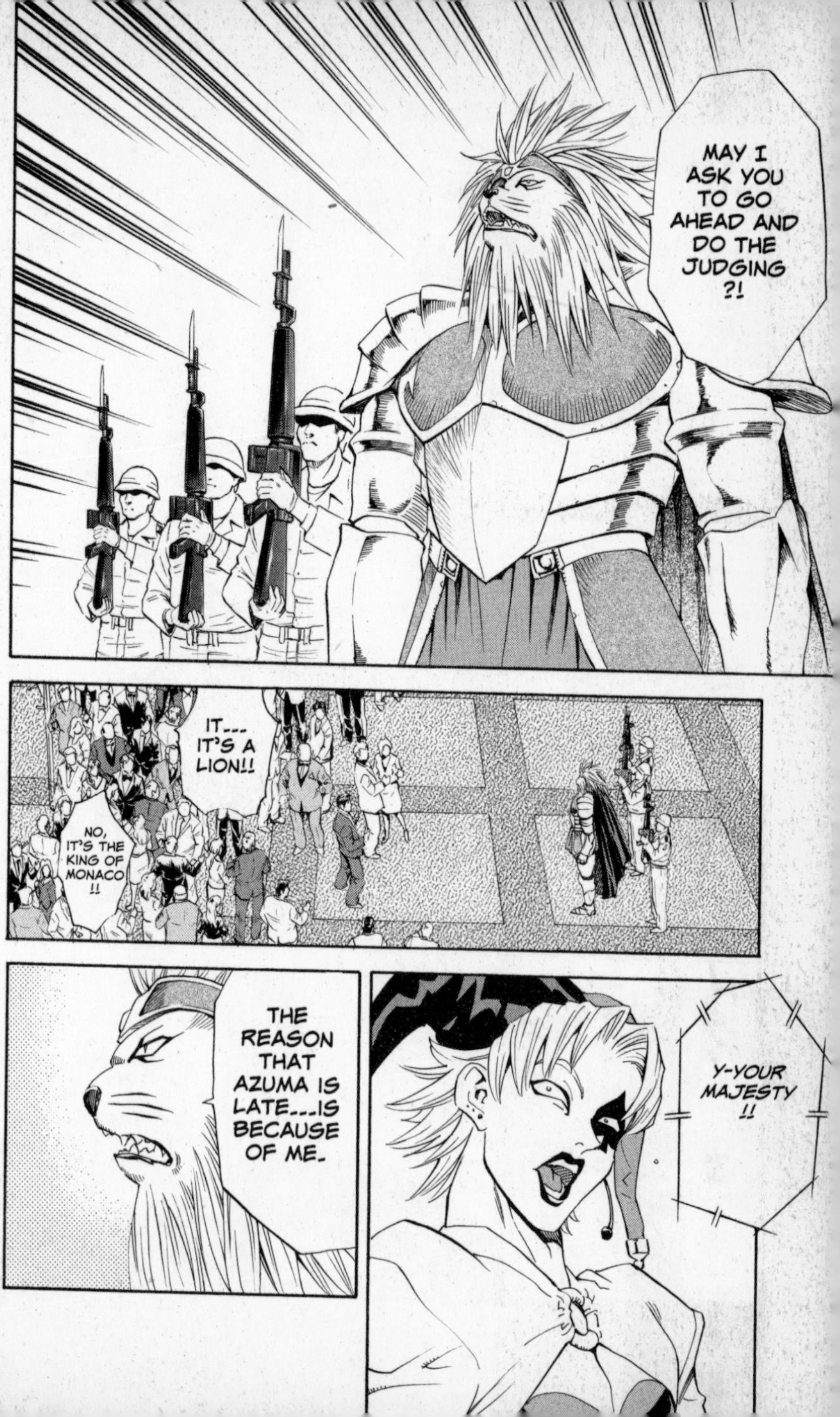
MAY I ASK YOU TO GO AHEAD AND DO THE JUDGING ?!
IT... IT'S A LION!!
NO, IT'S THE KING OF MONACO !!
Y-YOUR MAJESTY !!
THE REASON THAT AZUMA IS LATE...IS BECAUSE OF ME.

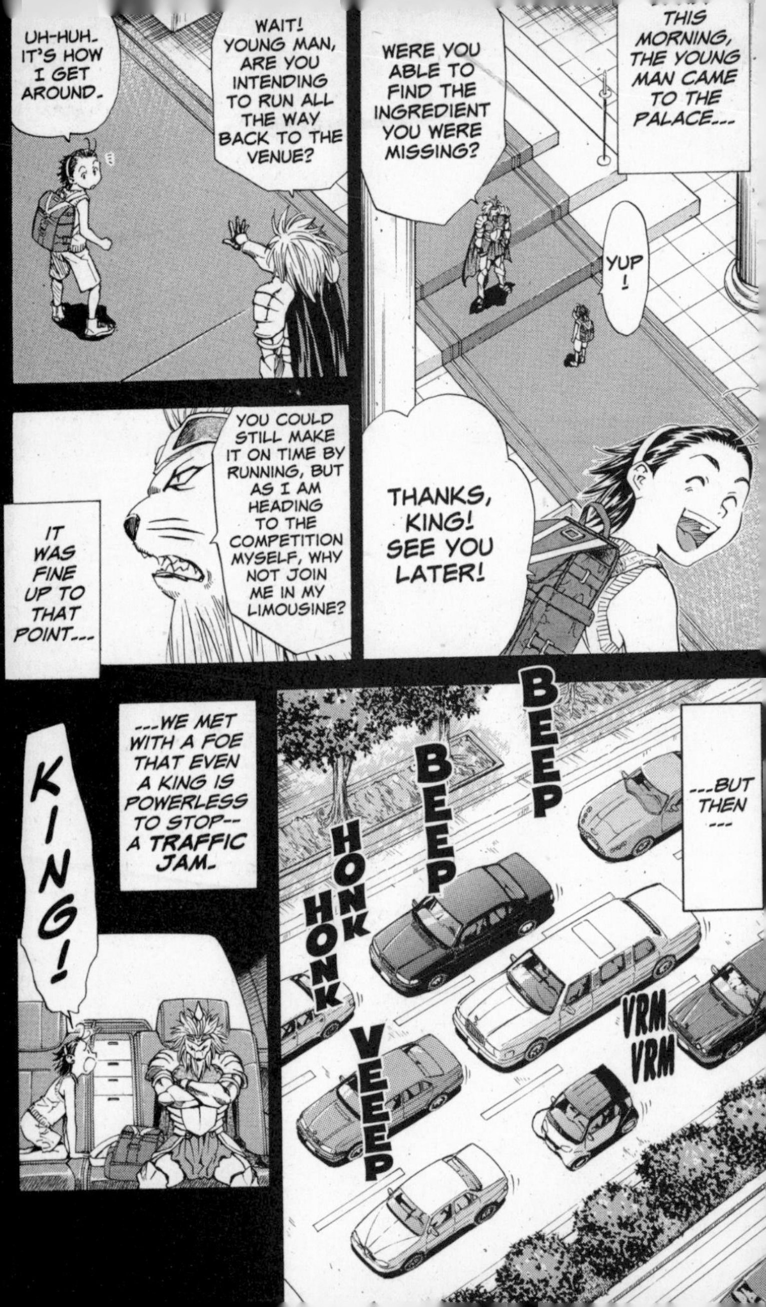
THIS MORNING, THE YOUNG MAN CAME TO THE PALACE...
WERE YOU ABLE TO FIND THE INGREDIENT YOU WERE MISSING?
YUP!
WAIT! YOUNG MAN, ARE YOU INTENDING TO RUN ALL THE WAY BACK TO THE VENUE?
UH-HUH. IT'S HOW I GET AROUND.
THANKS, KING! SEE YOU LATER!
YOU COULD STILL MAKE IT ON TIME BY RUNNING, BUT AS I AM HEADING TO THE COMPETITION MYSELF, WHY NOT JOIN ME IN MY LIMOUSINE?
IT WAS FINE UP TO THAT POINT...
...BUT THEN...
BEEP
BEEP
HONK HONK
VRM VRM
VEEEP
...WE MET WITH A FOE THAT EVEN A KING IS POWERLESS TO STOP-- A TRAFFIC JAM.
KING!

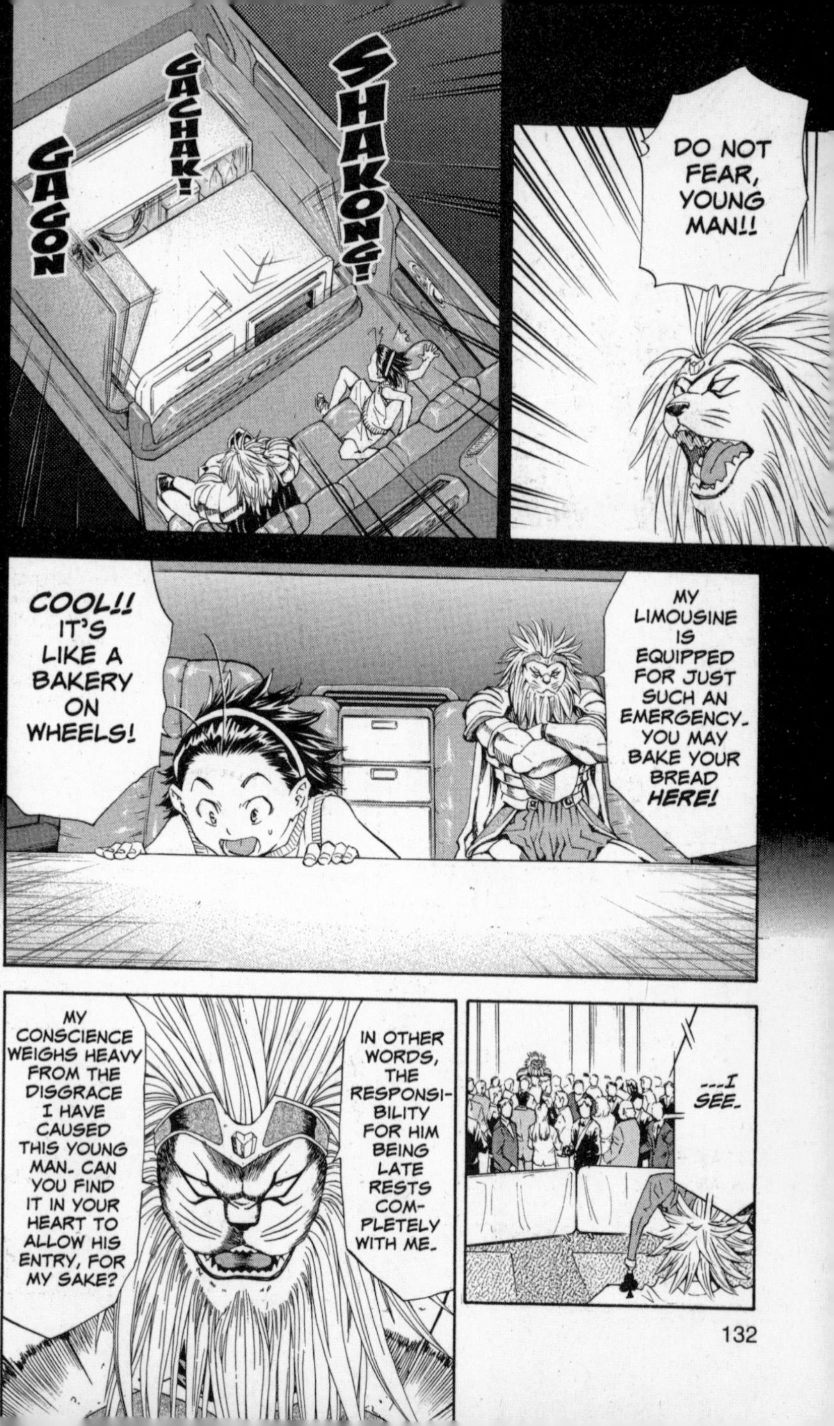
DO NOT FEAR, YOUNG MAN!!
SHAKONG!
GACHAK!
GAGON
MY LIMOUSINE IS EQUIPPED FOR JUST SUCH AN EMERGENCY. YOU MAY BAKE YOUR BREAD HERE!
COOL!! IT'S LIKE A BAKERY ON WHEELS!
---I SEE.
IN OTHER WORDS, THE RESPONSIBILITY FOR HIM BEING LATE RESTS COMPLETELY WITH ME.
MY CONSCIENCE WEIGHS HEAVY FROM THE DISGRACE I HAVE CAUSED THIS YOUNG MAN. CAN YOU FIND IT IN YOUR HEART TO ALLOW HIS ENTRY, FOR MY SAKE?

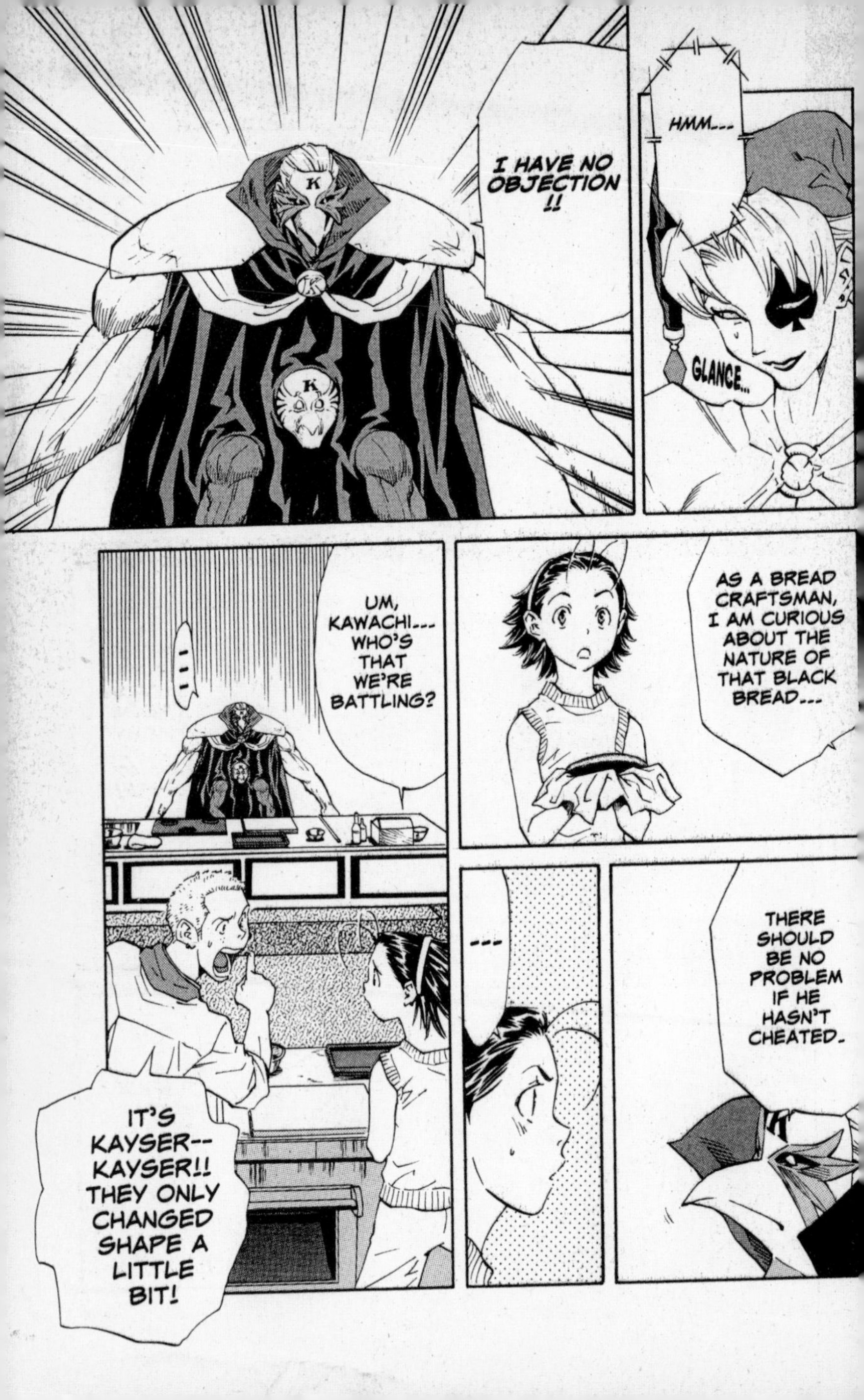
HMM...
GLANCE...
I HAVE NO OBJECTION !!
AS A BREAD CRAFTSMAN, I AM CURIOUS ABOUT THE NATURE OF THAT BLACK BREAD...
THERE SHOULD BE NO PROBLEM IF HE HASN'T CHEATED.
...
UM, KAWACHI... WHO'S THAT WE'RE BATTLING?
...
IT'S KAYSER-- KAYSER!! THEY ONLY CHANGED SHAPE A LITTLE BIT!

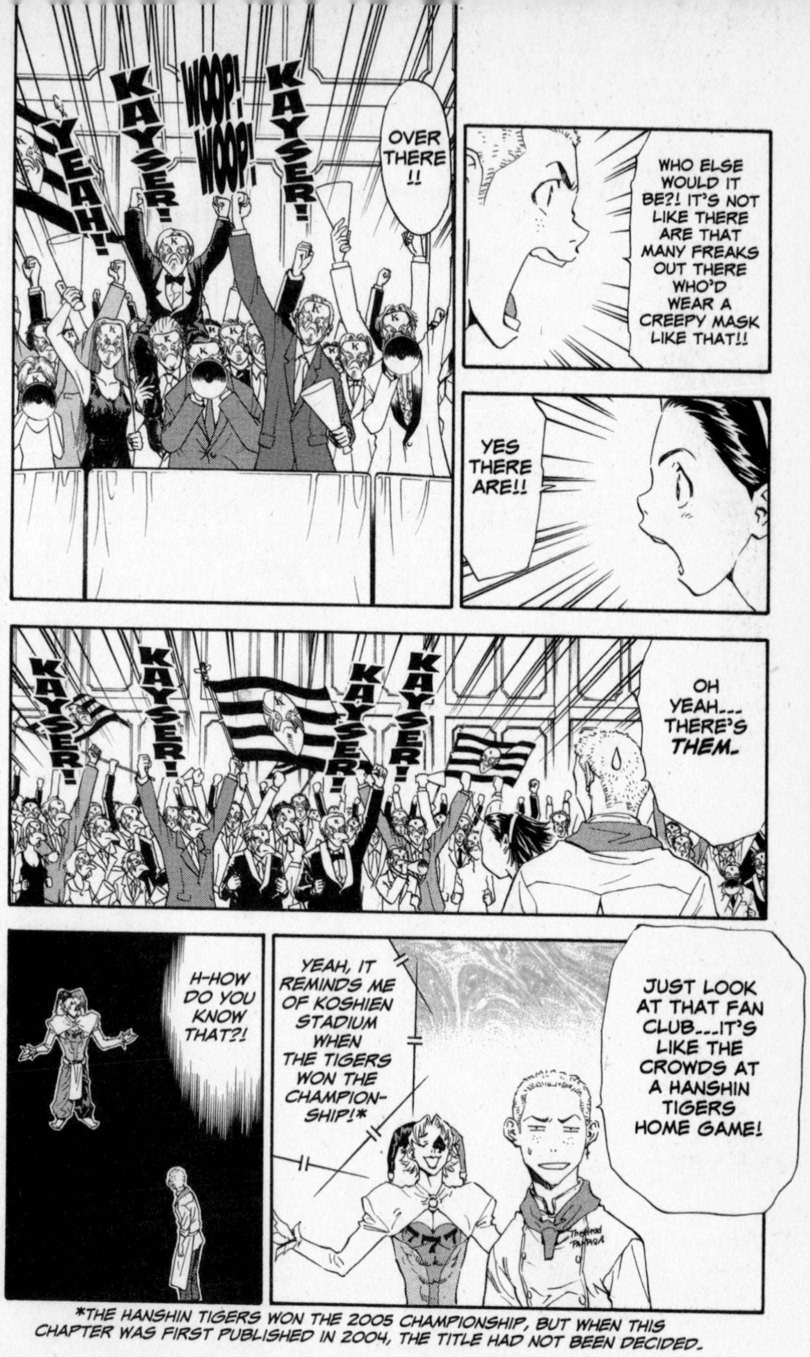
WHO ELSE WOULD IT BE?! IT'S NOT LIKE THERE ARE THAT MANY FREAKS OUT THERE WHO'D WEAR A CREEPY MASK LIKE THAT!!
OVER THERE !!
KAYSER!
WOOP! WOOP!
KAYSER!
YEAH!
YES THERE ARE!!
OH YEAH... THERE'S THEM.
KAYSER!
KAYSER!
KAYSER!
KAYSER!
JUST LOOK AT THAT FAN CLUB...IT'S LIKE THE CROWDS AT A HANSHIN TIGERS HOME GAME!
YEAH, IT REMINDS ME OF KOSHIEN STADIUM WHEN THE TIGERS WON THE CHAMPION-SHIP!*
H-HOW DO YOU KNOW THAT?!

*THE HANSHIN TIGERS WON THE 2005 CHAMPIONSHIP, BUT WHEN THIS CHAPTER WAS FIRST PUBLISHED IN 2004, THE TITLE HAD NOT BEEN DECIDED.

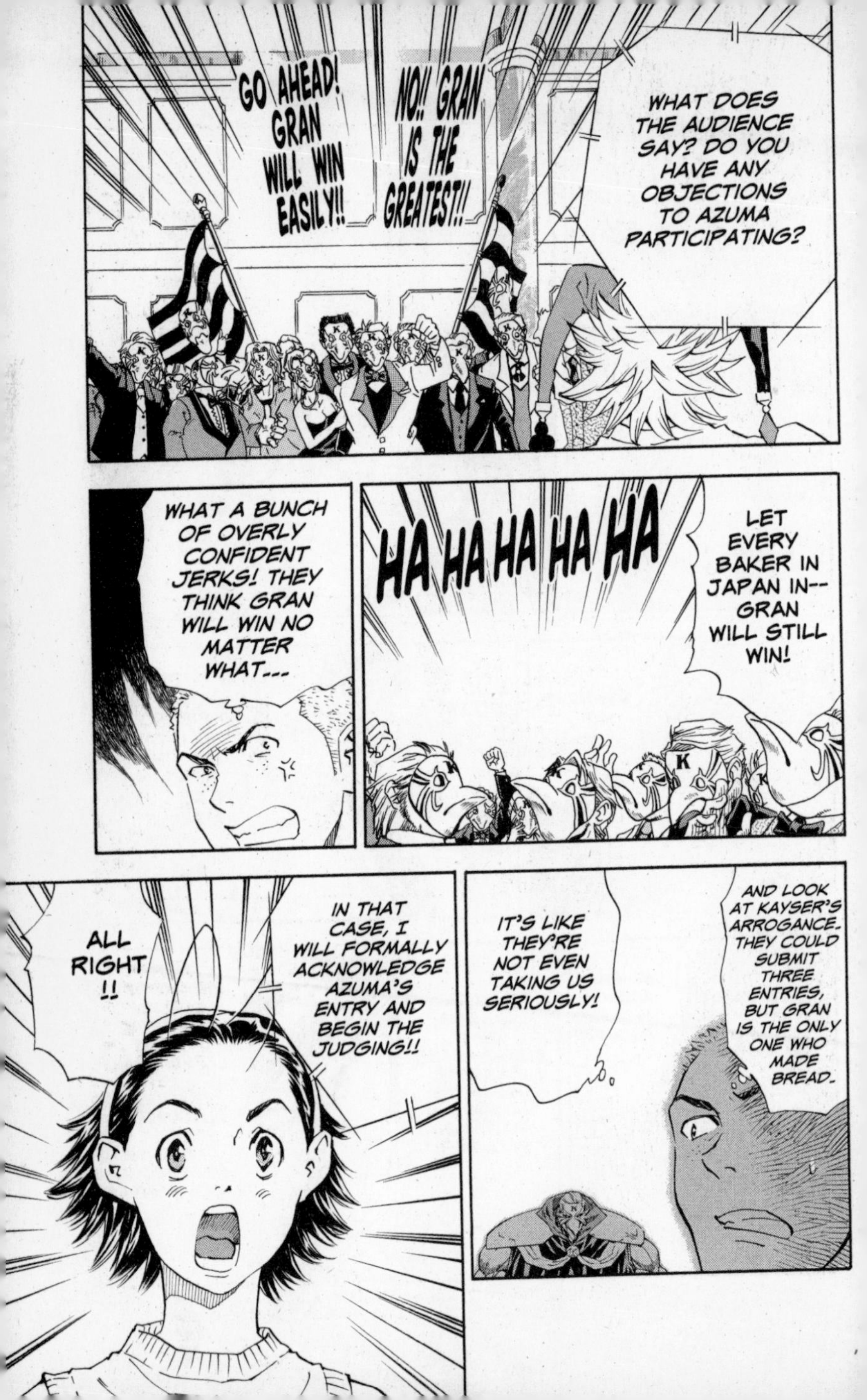
WHAT DOES THE AUDIENCE SAY? DO YOU HAVE ANY OBJECTIONS TO AZUMA PARTICIPATING?
NO!! GRAN IS THE GREATEST!!
GO AHEAD! GRAN WILL WIN EASILY!!
LET EVERY BAKER IN JAPAN IN-- GRAN WILL STILL WIN!
HA HA HA HA HA
WHAT A BUNCH OF OVERLY CONFIDENT JERKS! THEY THINK GRAN WILL WIN NO MATTER WHAT...
AND LOOK AT KAYSER'S ARROGANCE. THEY COULD SUBMIT THREE ENTRIES, BUT GRAN IS THE ONLY ONE WHO MADE BREAD.
IT'S LIKE THEY'RE NOT EVEN TAKING US SERIOUSLY!
IN THAT CASE, I WILL FORMALLY ACKNOWLEDGE AZUMA'S ENTRY AND BEGIN THE JUDGING!!
ALL RIGHT !!

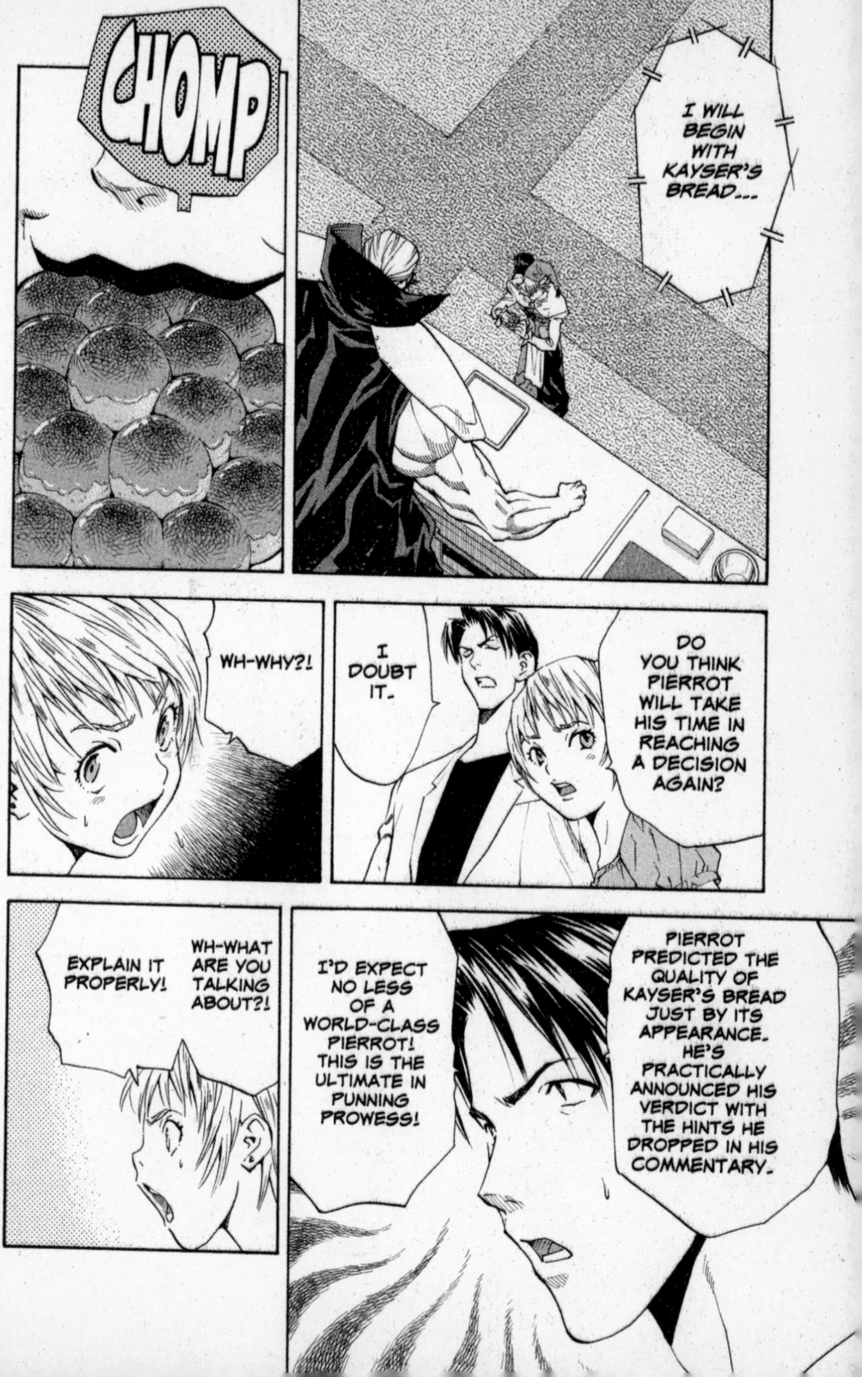
I WILL BEGIN WITH KAYSER'S BREAD...
CHOMP
DO YOU THINK PIERROT WILL TAKE HIS TIME IN REACHING A DECISION AGAIN?
I DOUBT IT.
WH-WHY?!
PIERROT PREDICTED THE QUALITY OF KAYSER'S BREAD JUST BY ITS APPEARANCE. HE'S PRACTICALLY ANNOUNCED HIS VERDICT WITH THE HINTS HE DROPPED IN HIS COMMENTARY.
I'D EXPECT NO LESS OF A WORLD-CLASS PIERROT! THIS IS THE ULTIMATE IN PUNNING PROWESS!
WH-WHAT ARE YOU TALKING ABOUT?!
EXPLAIN IT PROPERLY!

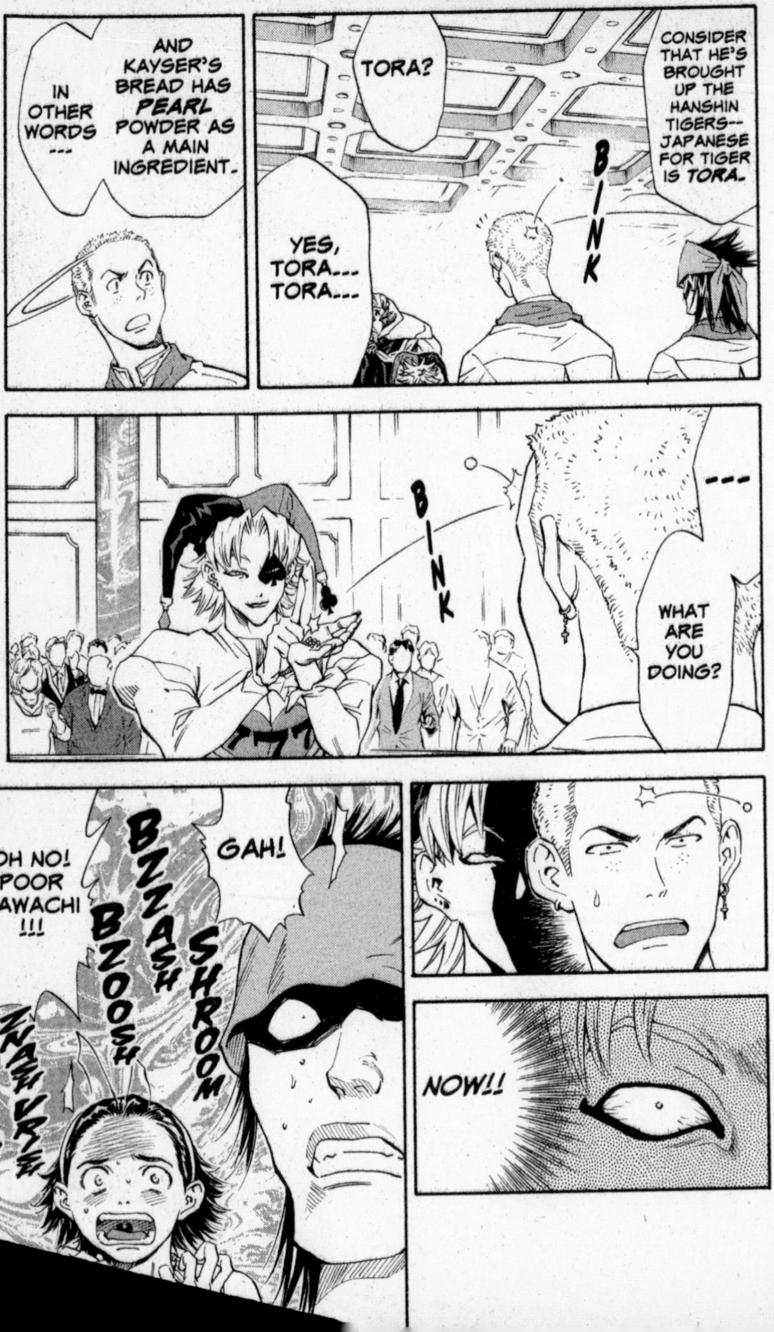
CONSIDER THAT HE'S BROUGHT UP THE HANSHIN TIGERS--JAPANESE FOR TIGER IS TORA.
BINK
TORA?
YES, TORA... TORA...
AND KAYSER'S BREAD HAS PEARL POWDER AS A MAIN INGREDIENT.
IN OTHER WORDS ...
...
WHAT ARE YOU DOING?
BINK
NOW!!
GAH!
OH NO! POOR KAWACHI !!!
BZZASH
BZOOSH
SHROOM
ZNASH VRSH
BROOSH

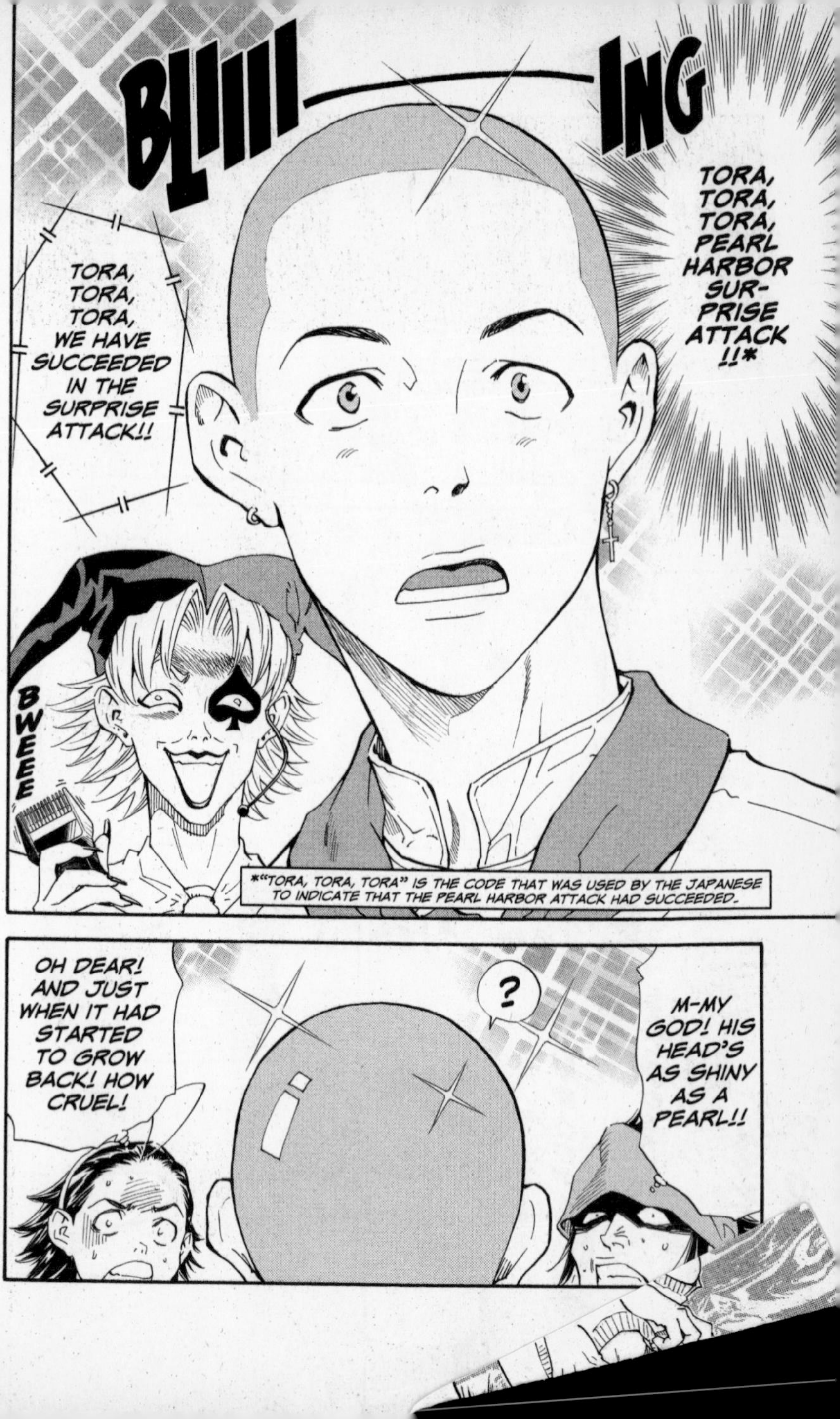
BLIIIII—ING
TORA, TORA, TORA, PEARL HARBOR SUR-PRISE ATTACK !!*
TORA, TORA, TORA, WE HAVE SUCCEEDED IN THE SURPRISE ATTACK!!
BWEEE
*"TORA, TORA, TORA" IS THE CODE THAT WAS USED BY THE JAPANESE TO INDICATE THAT THE PEARL HARBOR ATTACK HAD SUCCEEDED.
M-MY GOD! HIS HEAD'S AS SHINY AS A PEARL!!
?
OH DEAR! AND JUST WHEN IT HAD STARTED TO GROW BACK! HOW CRUEL!

TORA, TORA, TORA!

Story 92: Bald Jokes Never Get Old!

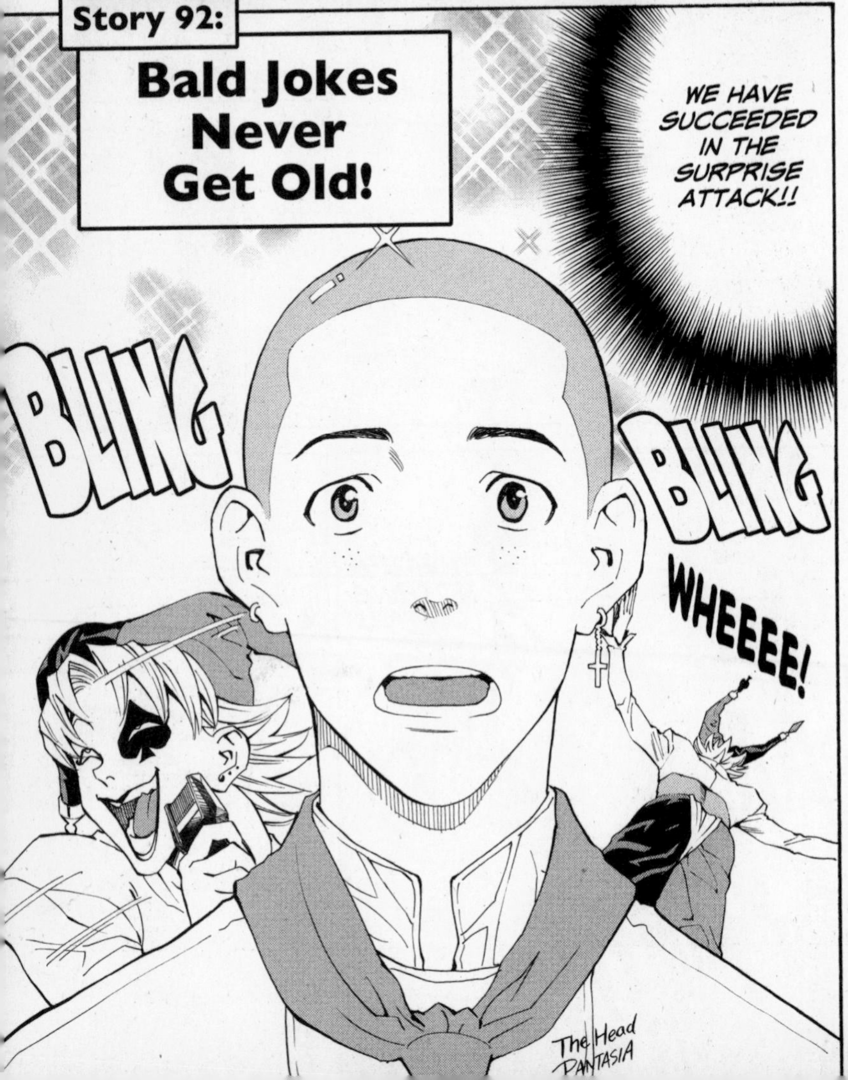
WE HAVE SUCCEEDED IN THE SURPRISE ATTACK!!
BLING
BLING
WHEEEEE!
The Head PANTASIA

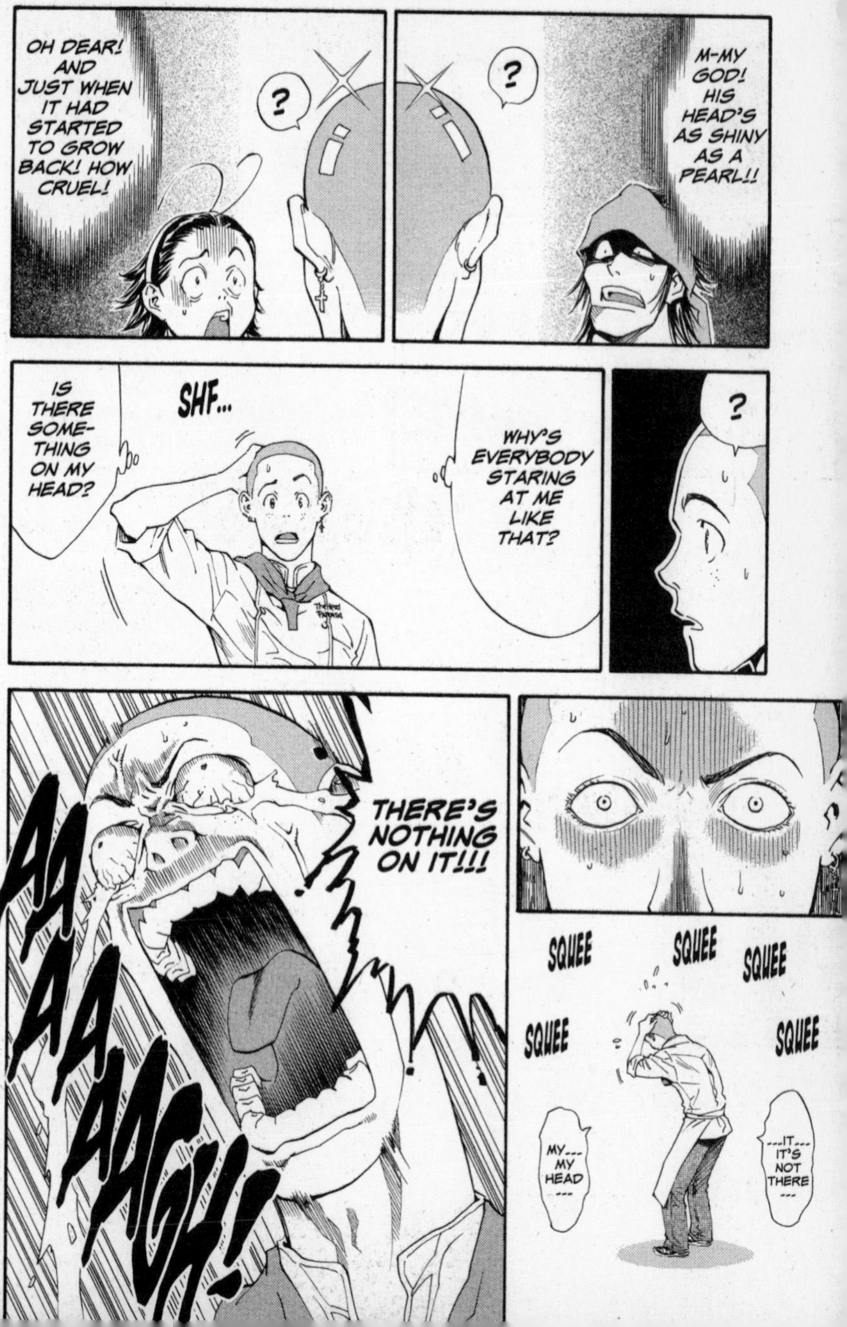
M-MY GOD! HIS HEAD'S AS SHINY AS A PEARL!!
?
?
OH DEAR! AND JUST WHEN IT HAD STARTED TO GROW BACK! HOW CRUEL!
?
WHY'S EVERYBODY STARING AT ME LIKE THAT?
SHF...
IS THERE SOME-THING ON MY HEAD?
SQUEE
SQUEE
SQUEE
SQUEE
SQUEE
...IT... IT'S NOT THERE...
MY... MY HEAD...
THERE'S NOTHING ON IT!!!
AAAAAAAGH!!

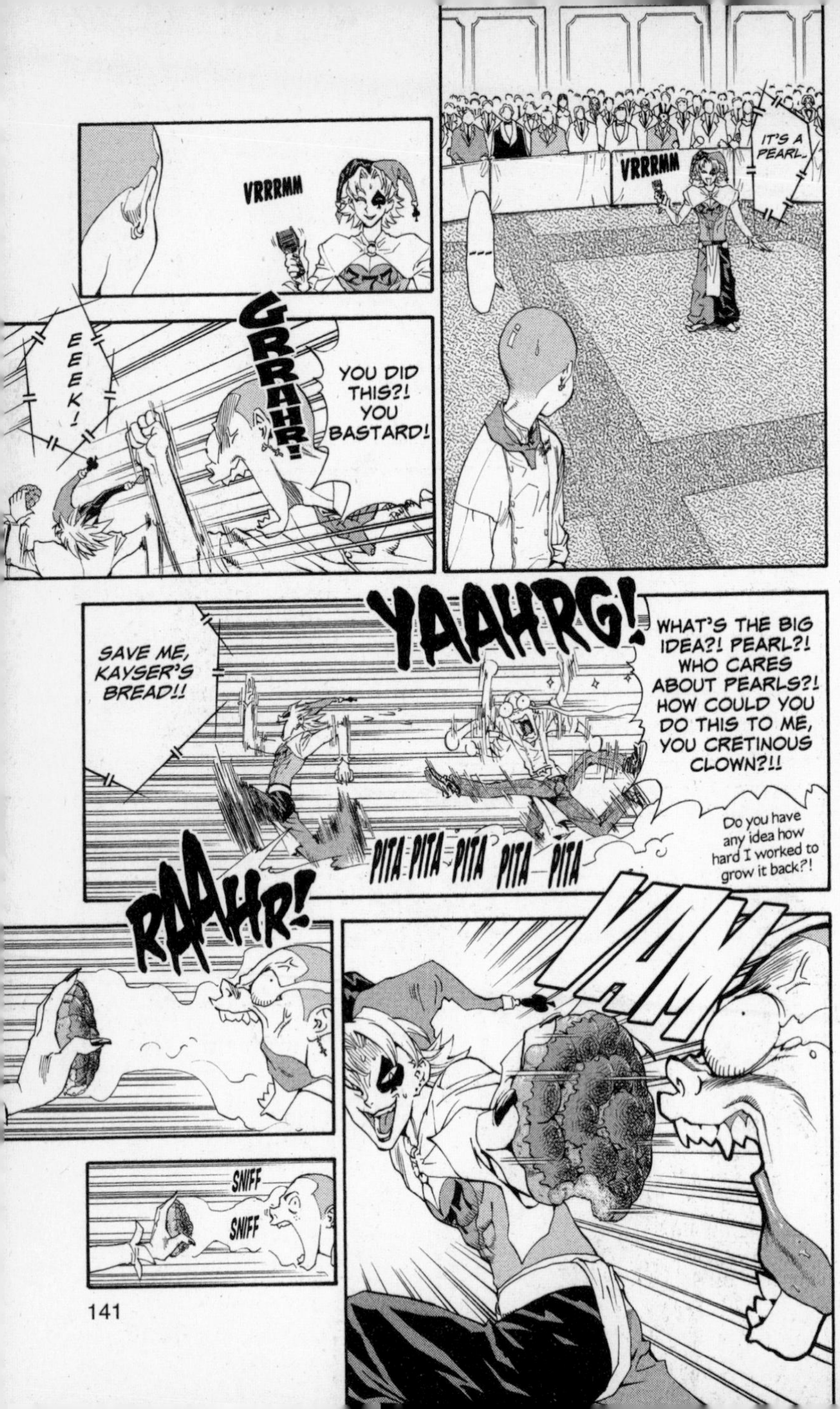
IT'S A PEARL...
VRRRMM
...
VRRRMM
GRRAHR!
YOU DID THIS?! YOU BASTARD!
EEEK!
WHAT'S THE BIG IDEA?! PEARL?! WHO CARES ABOUT PEARLS?! HOW COULD YOU DO THIS TO ME, YOU CRETINOUS CLOWN?!!
Do you have any idea how hard I worked to grow it back?!
YAAHRG!
SAVE ME, KAYSER'S BREAD!!
PITA PITA PITA PITA PITA
YAM
RAAHR!
SNIFF
SNIFF

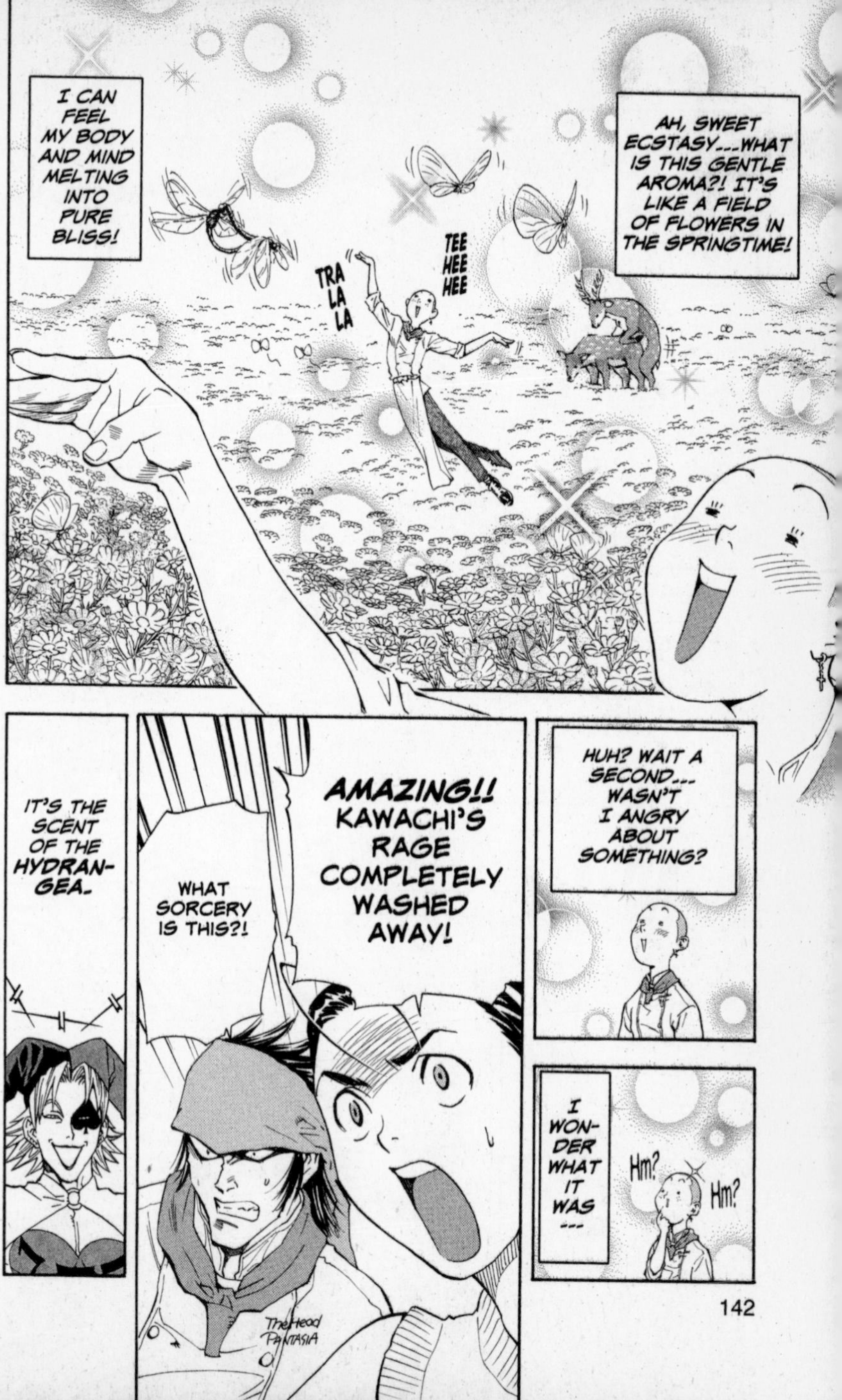
AH, SWEET ECSTASY...WHAT IS THIS GENTLE AROMA?! IT'S LIKE A FIELD OF FLOWERS IN THE SPRINGTIME!
TEE HEE HEE
TRA LA LA
I CAN FEEL MY BODY AND MIND MELTING INTO PURE BLISS!
HUH? WAIT A SECOND... WASN'T I ANGRY ABOUT SOMETHING?
I WONDER WHAT IT WAS...
Hm?
Hm?
AMAZING!! KAWACHI'S RAGE COMPLETELY WASHED AWAY!
WHAT SORCERY IS THIS?!
The Head PANTASIA
IT'S THE SCENT OF THE HYDRANGEA.

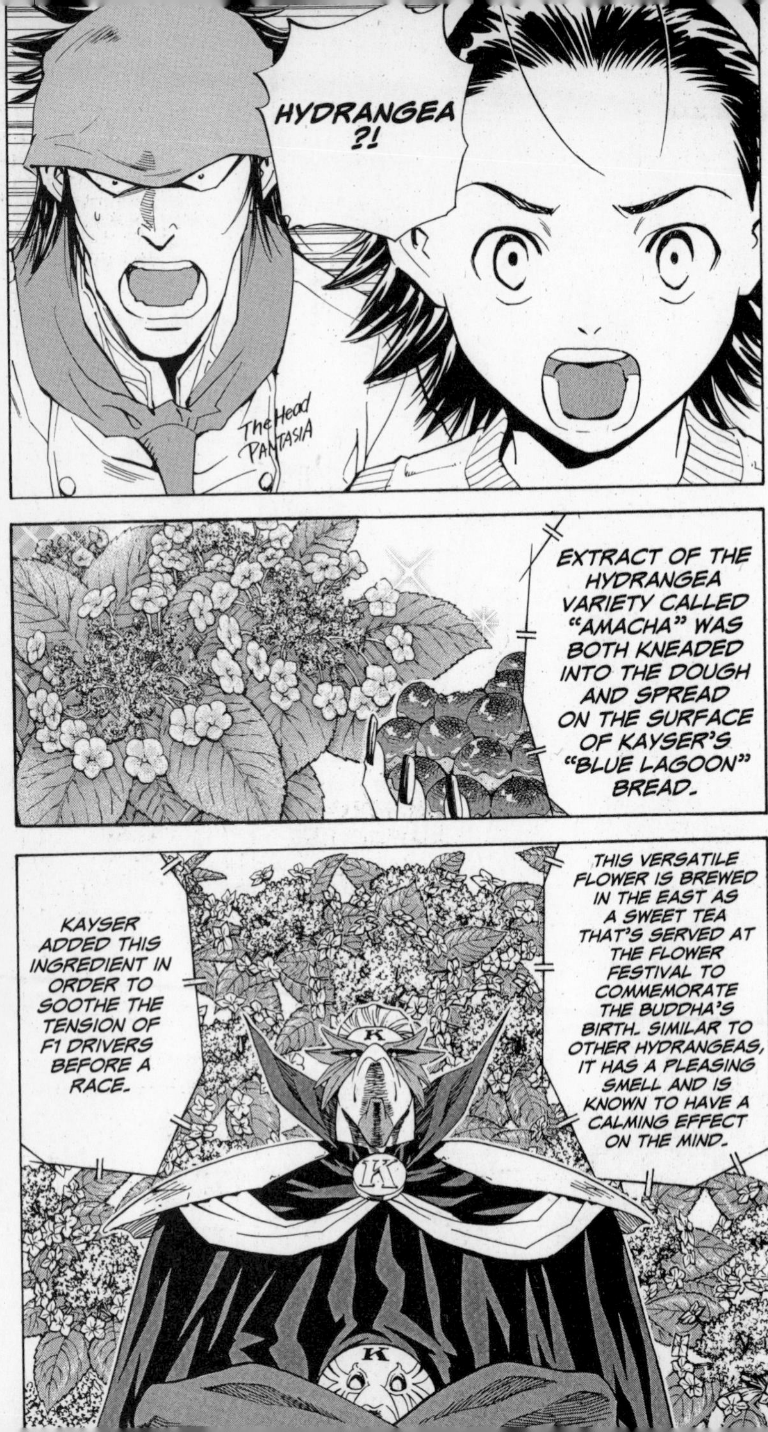
HYDRANGEA ?!
The Head PANTASIA
EXTRACT OF THE HYDRANGEA VARIETY CALLED "AMACHA" WAS BOTH KNEADED INTO THE DOUGH AND SPREAD ON THE SURFACE OF KAYSER'S "BLUE LAGOON" BREAD.
THIS VERSATILE FLOWER IS BREWED IN THE EAST AS A SWEET TEA THAT'S SERVED AT THE FLOWER FESTIVAL TO COMMEMORATE THE BUDDHA'S BIRTH. SIMILAR TO OTHER HYDRANGEAS, IT HAS A PLEASING SMELL AND IS KNOWN TO HAVE A CALMING EFFECT ON THE MIND.
KAYSER ADDED THIS INGREDIENT IN ORDER TO SOOTHE THE TENSION OF F1 DRIVERS BEFORE A RACE.

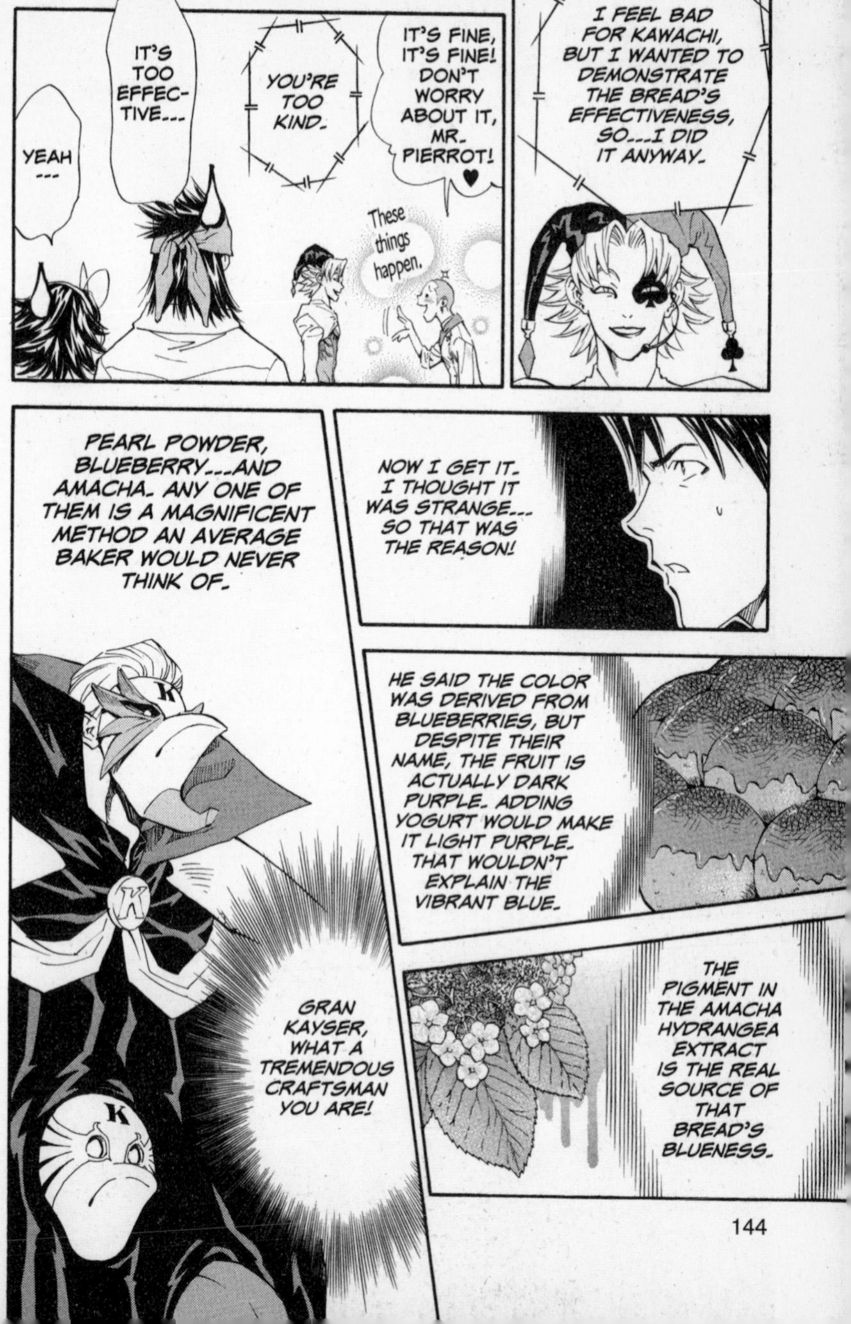
I FEEL BAD FOR KAWACHI, BUT I WANTED TO DEMONSTRATE THE BREAD'S EFFECTIVENESS, SO...I DID IT ANYWAY.
IT'S FINE, IT'S FINE! DON'T WORRY ABOUT IT, MR. PIERROT! ♥
These things happen.
YOU'RE TOO KIND.
IT'S TOO EFFEC-TIVE...
YEAH ...
NOW I GET IT. I THOUGHT IT WAS STRANGE... SO THAT WAS THE REASON!
PEARL POWDER, BLUEBERRY...AND AMACHA. ANY ONE OF THEM IS A MAGNIFICENT METHOD AN AVERAGE BAKER WOULD NEVER THINK OF.
HE SAID THE COLOR WAS DERIVED FROM BLUEBERRIES, BUT DESPITE THEIR NAME, THE FRUIT IS ACTUALLY DARK PURPLE. ADDING YOGURT WOULD MAKE IT LIGHT PURPLE. THAT WOULDN'T EXPLAIN THE VIBRANT BLUE.
THE PIGMENT IN THE AMACHA HYDRANGEA EXTRACT IS THE REAL SOURCE OF THAT BREAD'S BLUENESS.
GRAN KAYSER, WHAT A TREMENDOUS CRAFTSMAN YOU ARE!

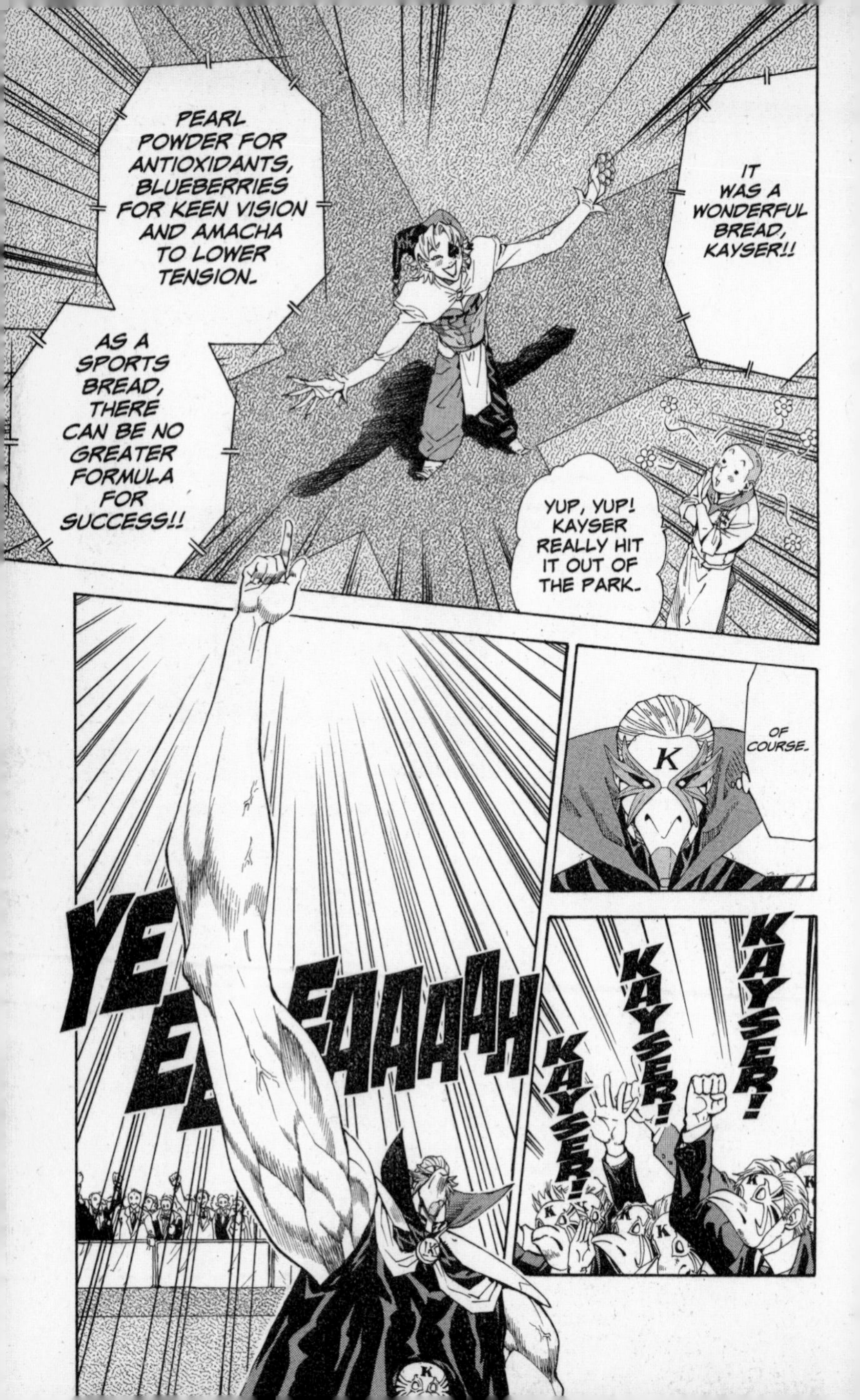
IT WAS A WONDERFUL BREAD, KAYSER!!
PEARL POWDER FOR ANTIOXIDANTS, BLUEBERRIES FOR KEEN VISION AND AMACHA TO LOWER TENSION.
AS A SPORTS BREAD, THERE CAN BE NO GREATER FORMULA FOR SUCCESS!!
YUP, YUP! KAYSER REALLY HIT IT OUT OF THE PARK.
OF COURSE.
KAYSER!
KAYSER!
KAYSER!
YEEEAAAAH

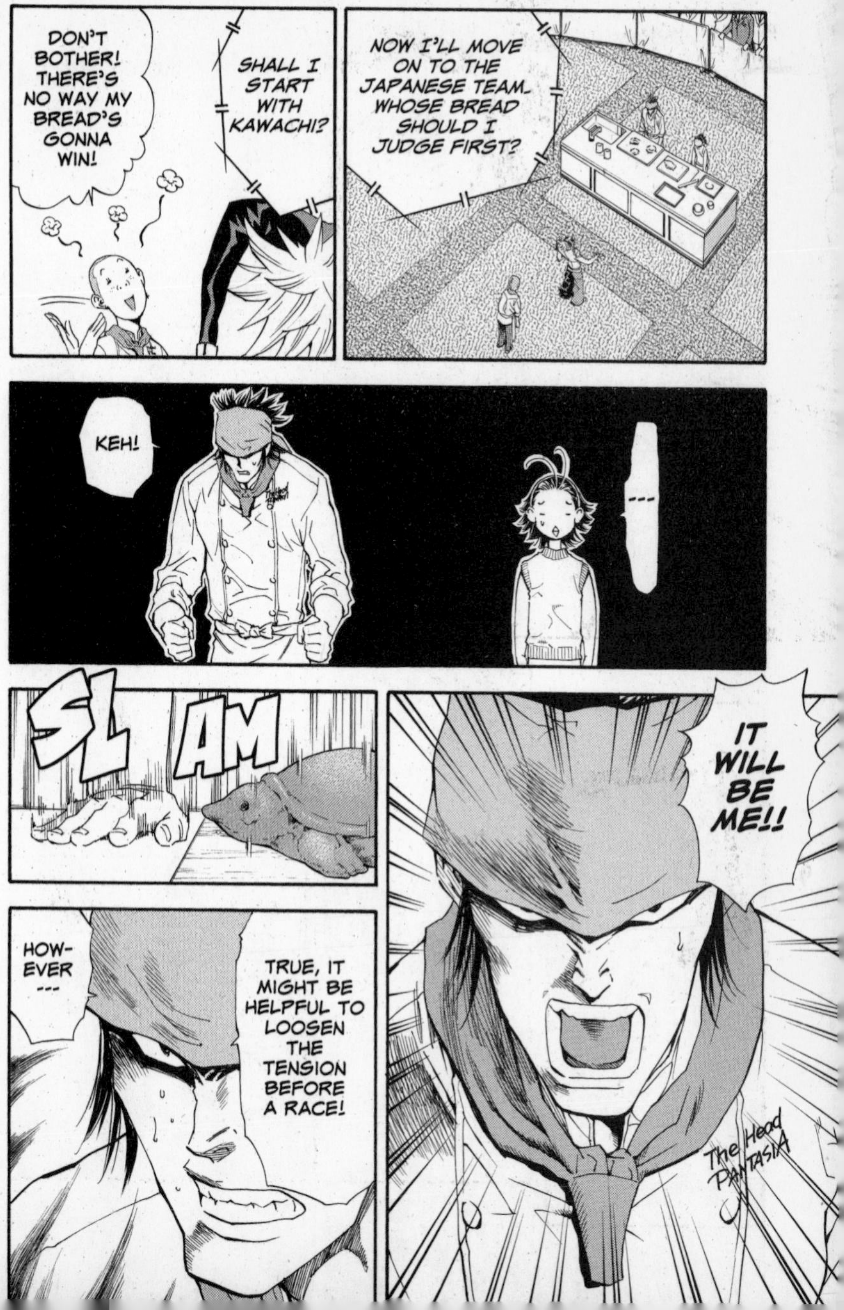
NOW I'LL MOVE ON TO THE JAPANESE TEAM. WHOSE BREAD SHOULD I JUDGE FIRST?
SHALL I START WITH KAWACHI?
DON'T BOTHER! THERE'S NO WAY MY BREAD'S GONNA WIN!

KEH!
IT WILL BE ME!!
The Head PANTASIA
SL AM
TRUE, IT MIGHT BE HELPFUL TO LOOSEN THE TENSION BEFORE A RACE!
HOW-EVER ---

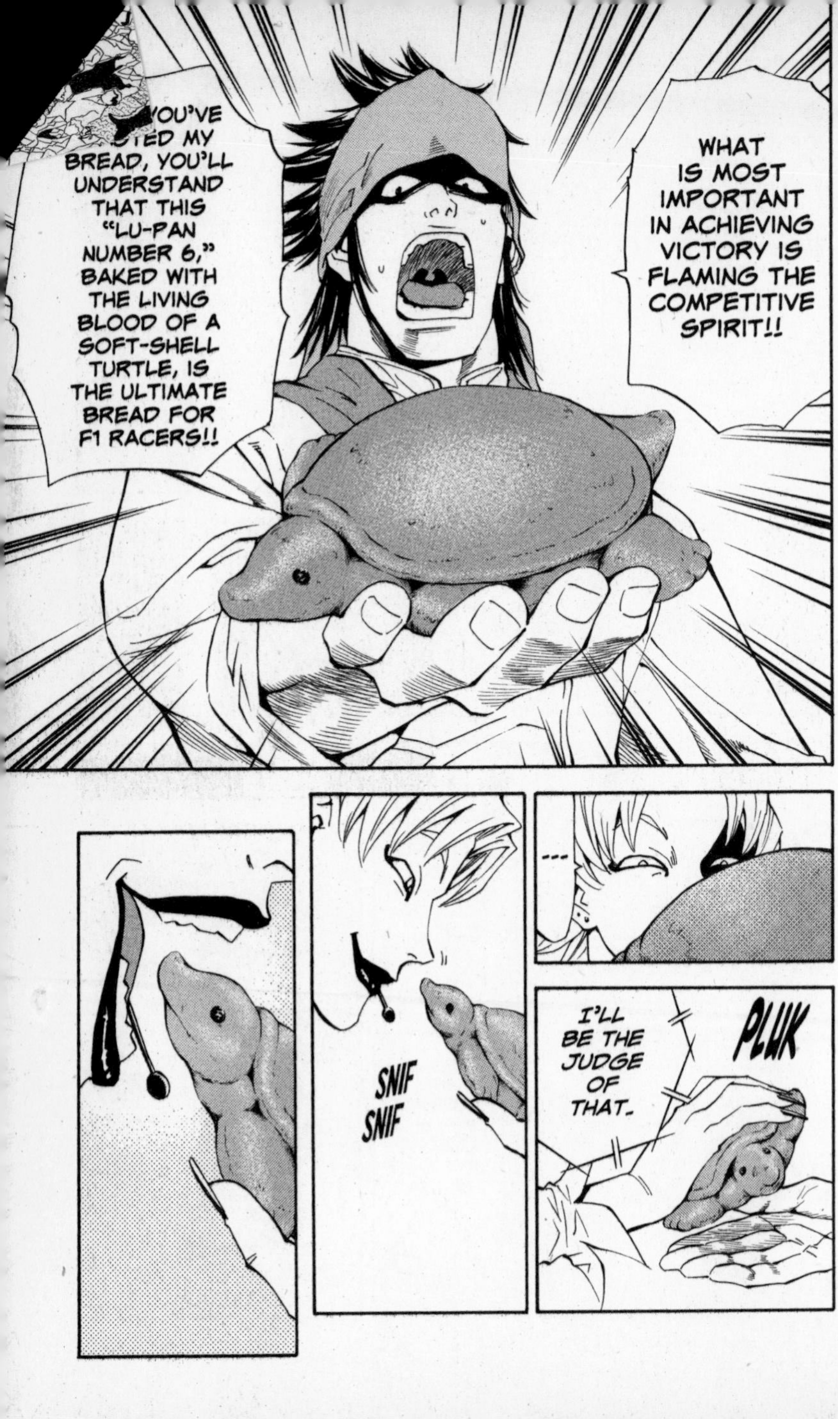
WHAT IS MOST IMPORTANT IN ACHIEVING VICTORY IS FLAMING THE COMPETITIVE SPIRIT!!
OU'VE TED MY BREAD, YOU'LL UNDERSTAND THAT THIS "LU-PAN NUMBER 6," BAKED WITH THE LIVING BLOOD OF A SOFT-SHELL TURTLE, IS THE ULTIMATE BREAD FOR F1 RACERS!!
...
PLUK
I'LL BE THE JUDGE OF THAT.
SNIF SNIF

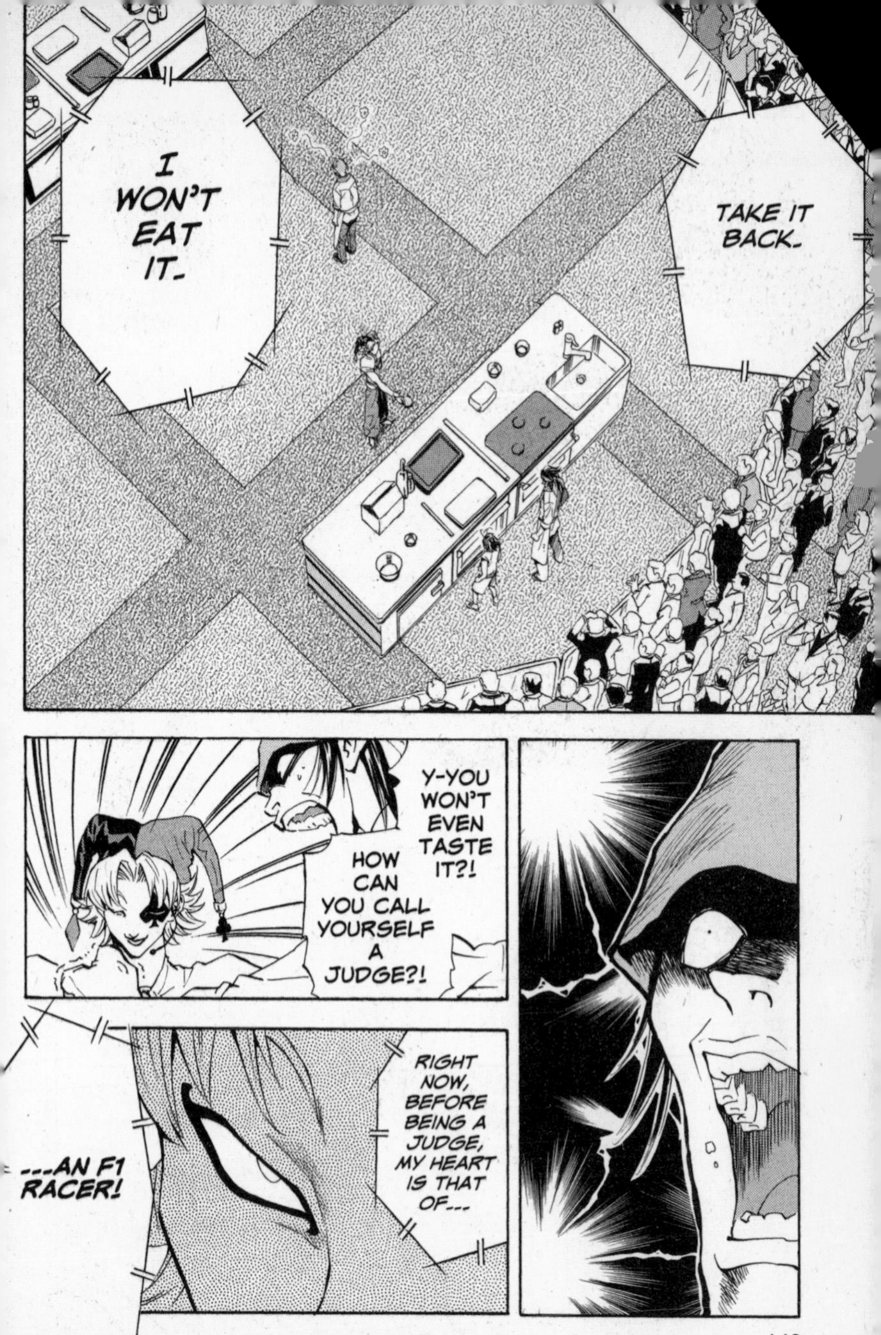
TAKE IT BACK.
I WON'T EAT IT.
Y-YOU WON'T EVEN TASTE IT?!
HOW CAN YOU CALL YOURSELF A JUDGE?!
RIGHT NOW, BEFORE BEING A JUDGE, MY HEART IS THAT OF---
---AN F1 RACER!

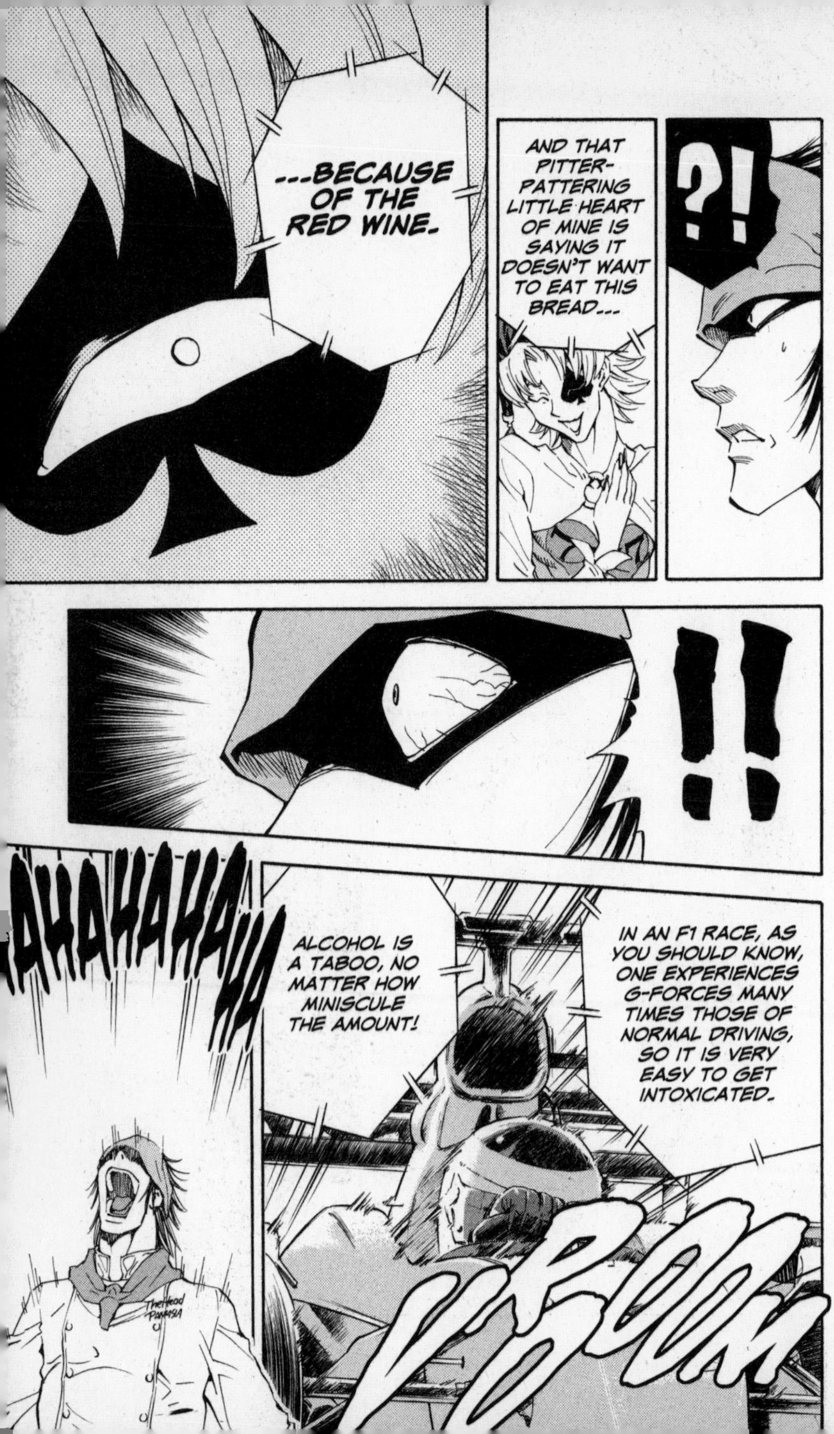
?!
AND THAT PITTER-PATTERING LITTLE HEART OF MINE IS SAYING IT DOESN'T WANT TO EAT THIS BREAD...
---BECAUSE OF THE RED WINE.
!!
IN AN F1 RACE, AS YOU SHOULD KNOW, ONE EXPERIENCES G-FORCES MANY TIMES THOSE OF NORMAL DRIVING, SO IT IS VERY EASY TO GET INTOXICATED.
VROOM
ALCOHOL IS A TABOO, NO MATTER HOW MINISCULE THE AMOUNT!
AHAHAHAHA

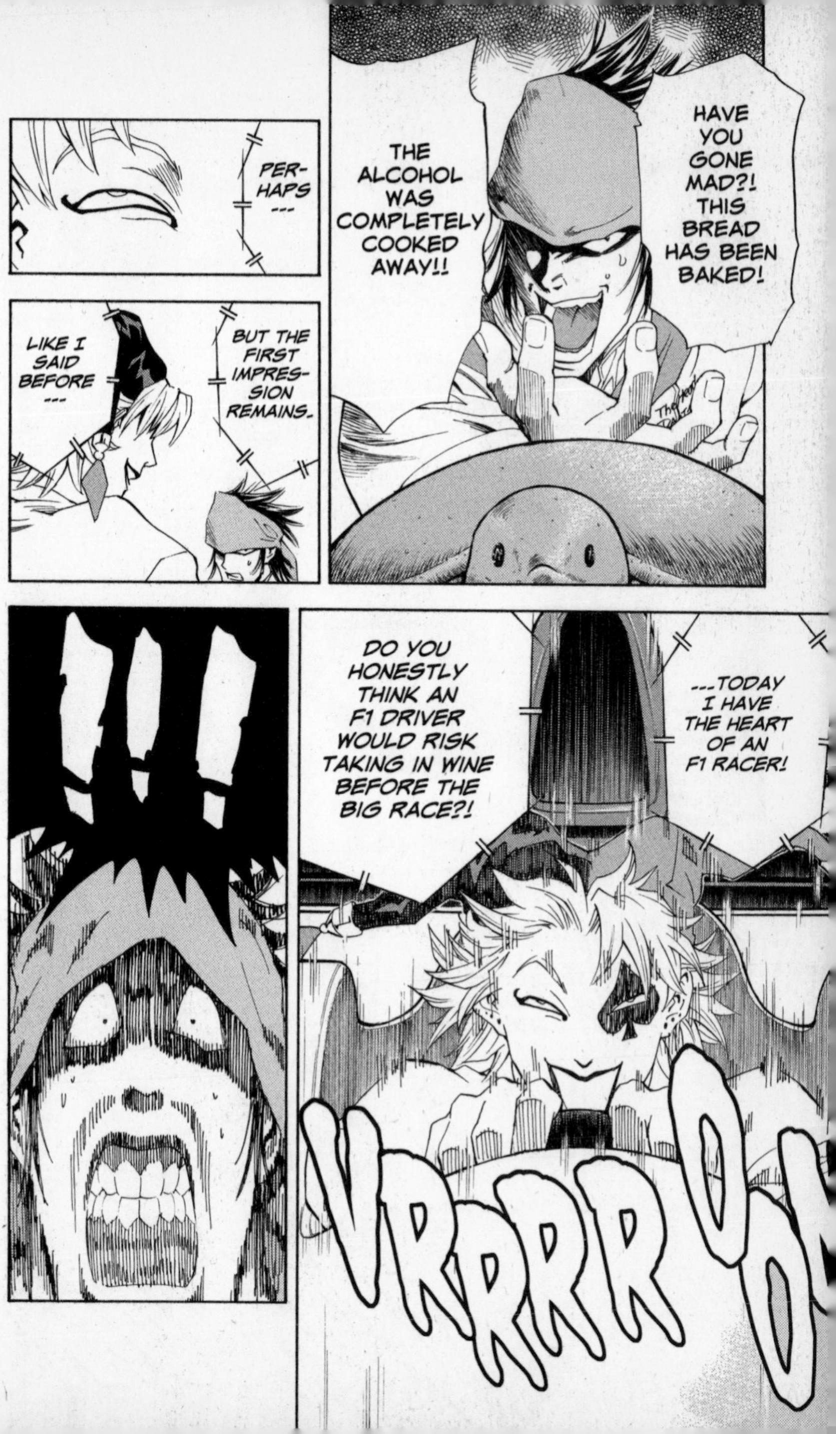
HAVE YOU GONE MAD?! THIS BREAD HAS BEEN BAKED!
THE ALCOHOL WAS COMPLETELY COOKED AWAY!!
PER-HAPS ---
BUT THE FIRST IMPRES-SION REMAINS.
LIKE I SAID BEFORE ---
---TODAY I HAVE THE HEART OF AN F1 RACER!
DO YOU HONESTLY THINK AN F1 DRIVER WOULD RISK TAKING IN WINE BEFORE THE BIG RACE?!
VRRRROO

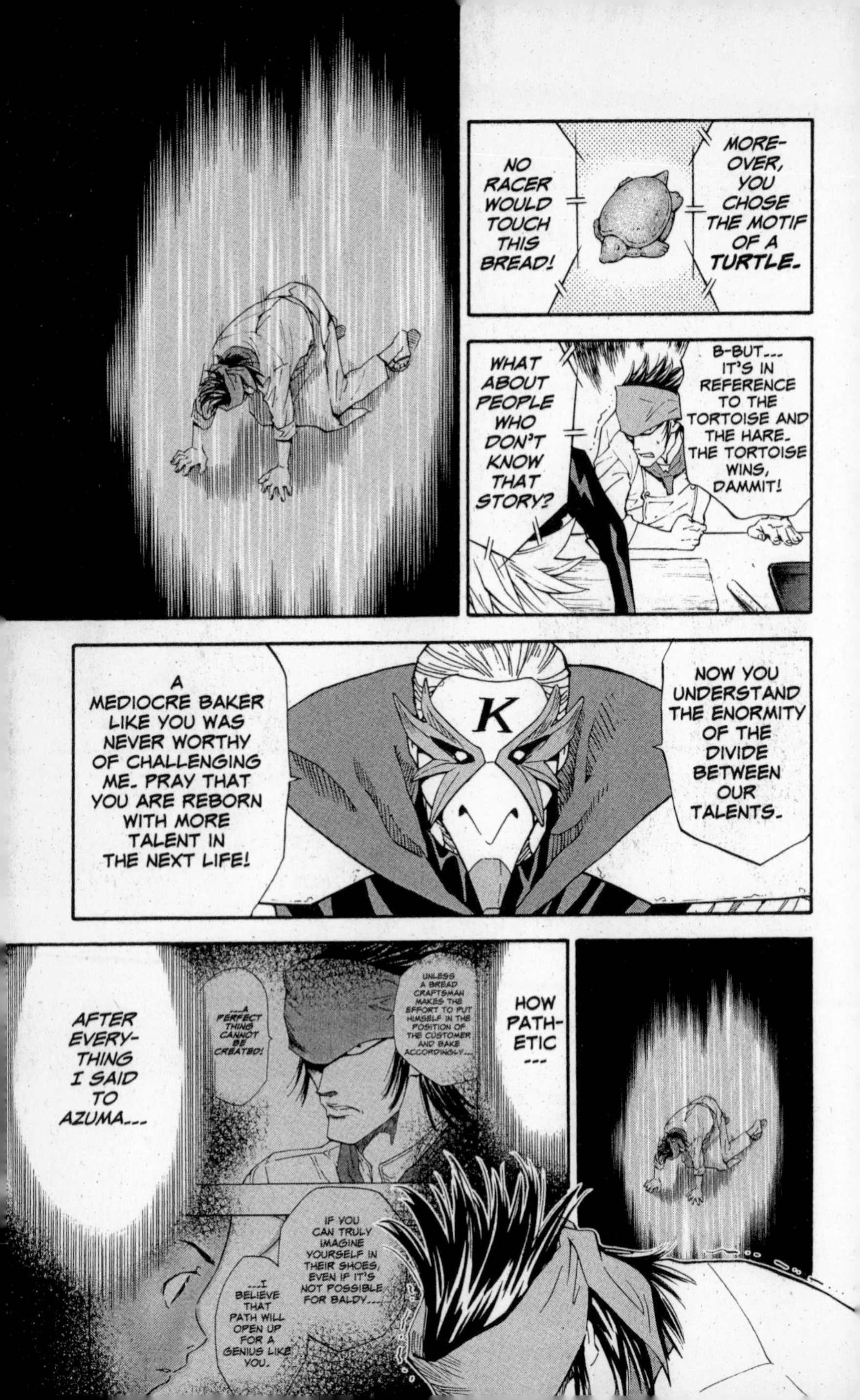
MORE-OVER, YOU CHOSE THE MOTIF OF A TURTLE.
NO RACER WOULD TOUCH THIS BREAD!
B-BUT... IT'S IN REFERENCE TO THE TORTOISE AND THE HARE. THE TORTOISE WINS, DAMMIT!
WHAT ABOUT PEOPLE WHO DON'T KNOW THAT STORY?
NOW YOU UNDERSTAND THE ENORMITY OF THE DIVIDE BETWEEN OUR TALENTS.
A MEDIOCRE BAKER LIKE YOU WAS NEVER WORTHY OF CHALLENGING ME. PRAY THAT YOU ARE REBORN WITH MORE TALENT IN THE NEXT LIFE!
HOW PATH-ETIC...
UNLESS A BREAD CRAFTSMAN MAKES THE EFFORT TO PUT HIMSELF IN THE POSITION OF THE CUSTOMER AND BAKE ACCORDINGLY...
...A PERFECT THING CANNOT BE CREATED!
AFTER EVERY-THING I SAID TO AZUMA...
IF YOU CAN TRULY IMAGINE YOURSELF IN THEIR SHOES, EVEN IF IT'S NOT POSSIBLE FOR BALDY...
...I BELIEVE THAT PATH WILL OPEN UP FOR A GENIUS LIKE YOU.

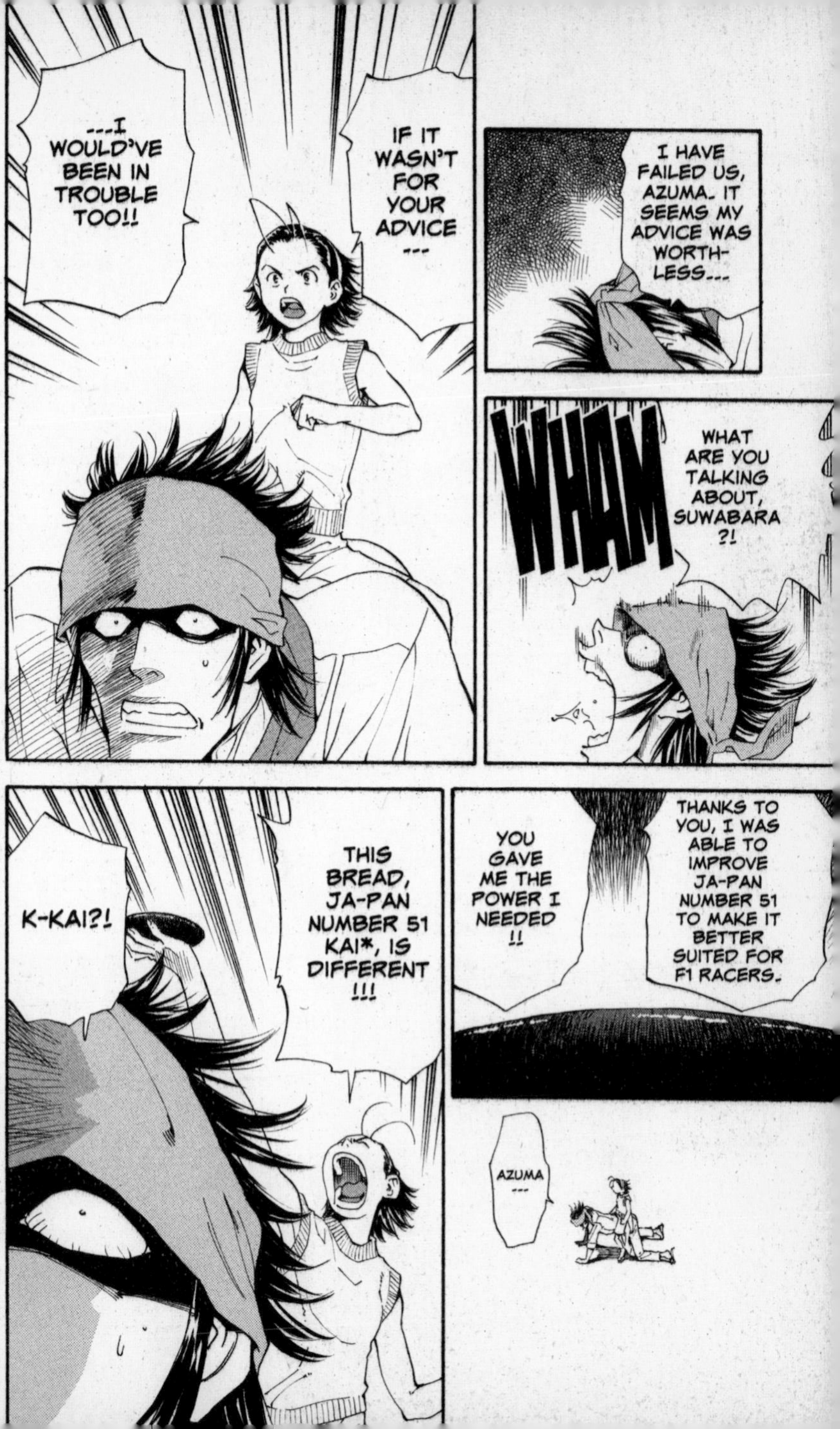
I HAVE FAILED US, AZUMA. IT SEEMS MY ADVICE WAS WORTH-LESS...
WHAT ARE YOU TALKING ABOUT, SUWABARA ?!
WHAM
IF IT WASN'T FOR YOUR ADVICE ---
---I WOULD'VE BEEN IN TROUBLE TOO!!
THANKS TO YOU, I WAS ABLE TO IMPROVE JA-PAN NUMBER 51 TO MAKE IT BETTER SUITED FOR F1 RACERS.
YOU GAVE ME THE POWER I NEEDED !!
AZUMA ---
THIS BREAD, JA-PAN NUMBER 51 KAI*, IS DIFFERENT !!!
K-KAI?!

*"KAI" IS USED TO DENOTE NEW-AND-IMPROVED STATUS. IT IS ALSO A PUN ON SUWABARA'S FIRST NAME.

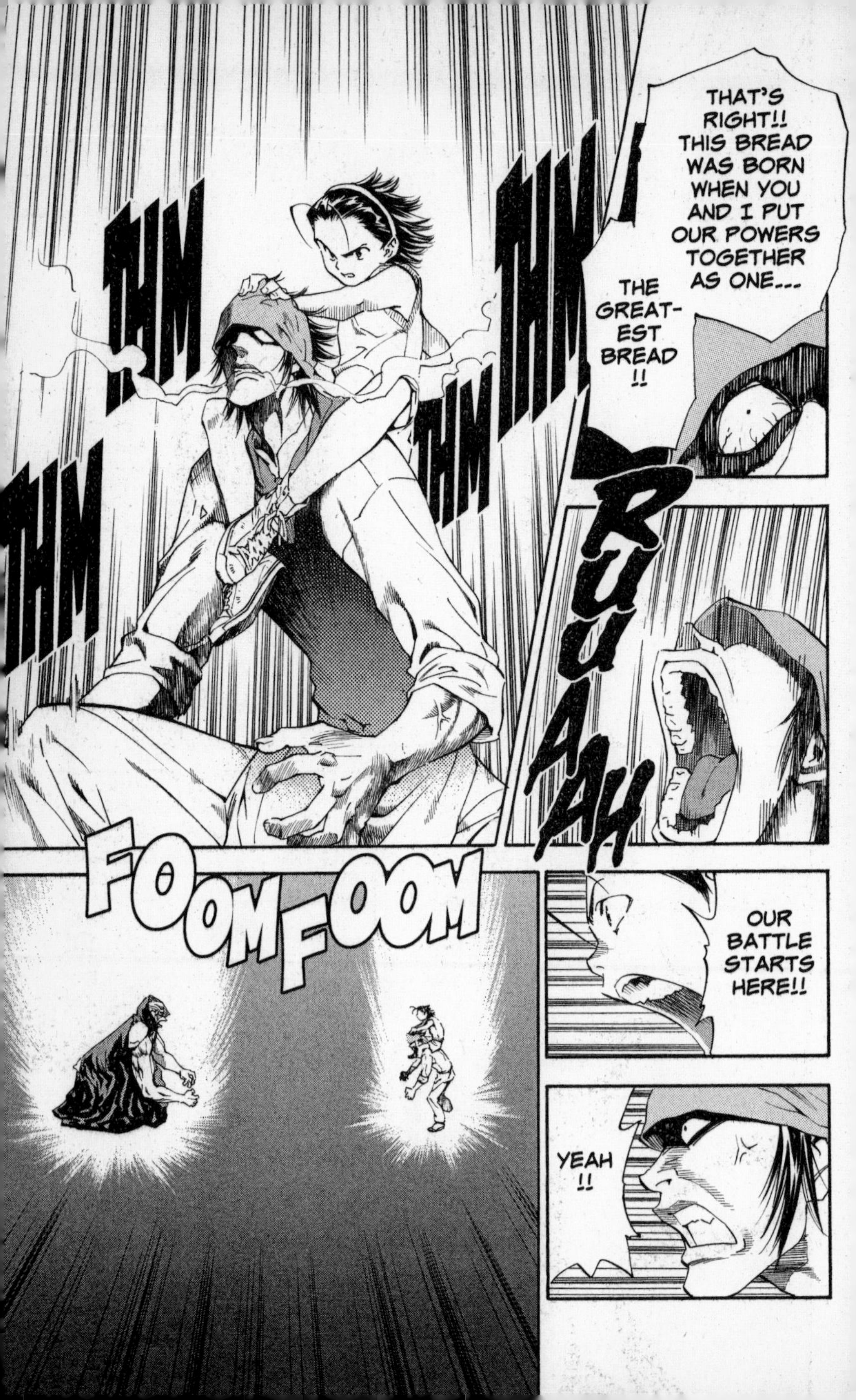
THAT'S RIGHT!! THIS BREAD WAS BORN WHEN YOU AND I PUT OUR POWERS TOGETHER AS ONE...
THE GREAT-EST BREAD !!
BUUAAH
THM THM THM THM
THM THM
OUR BATTLE STARTS HERE!!
YEAH !!
FOOM FOOM

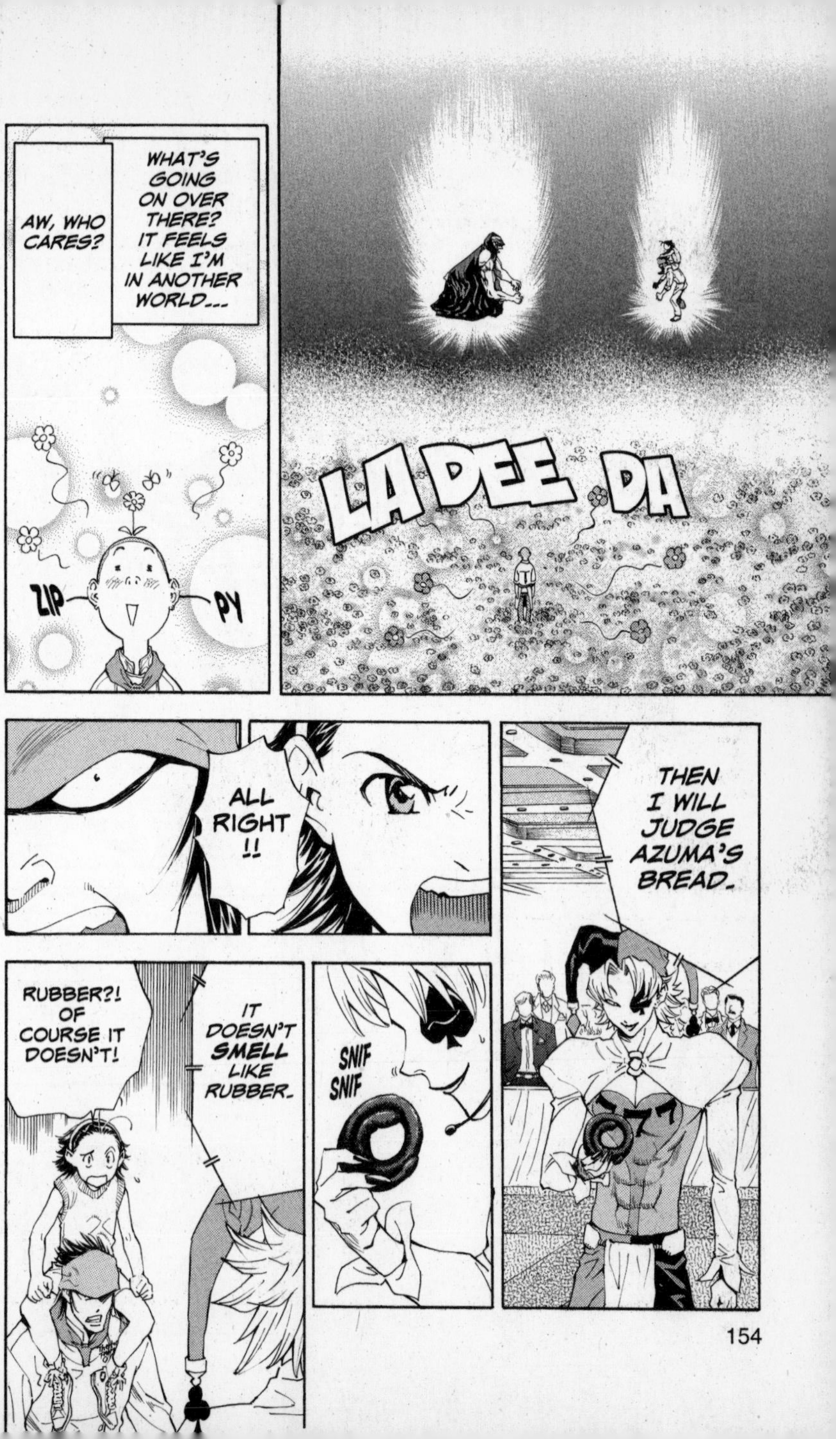
LA DEE DA
WHAT'S GOING ON OVER THERE? IT FEELS LIKE I'M IN ANOTHER WORLD...
AW, WHO CARES?
ZIP
PY
THEN I WILL JUDGE AZUMA'S BREAD.
ALL RIGHT !!
SNIF SNIF
IT DOESN'T SMELL LIKE RUBBER.
RUBBER?! OF COURSE IT DOESN'T!

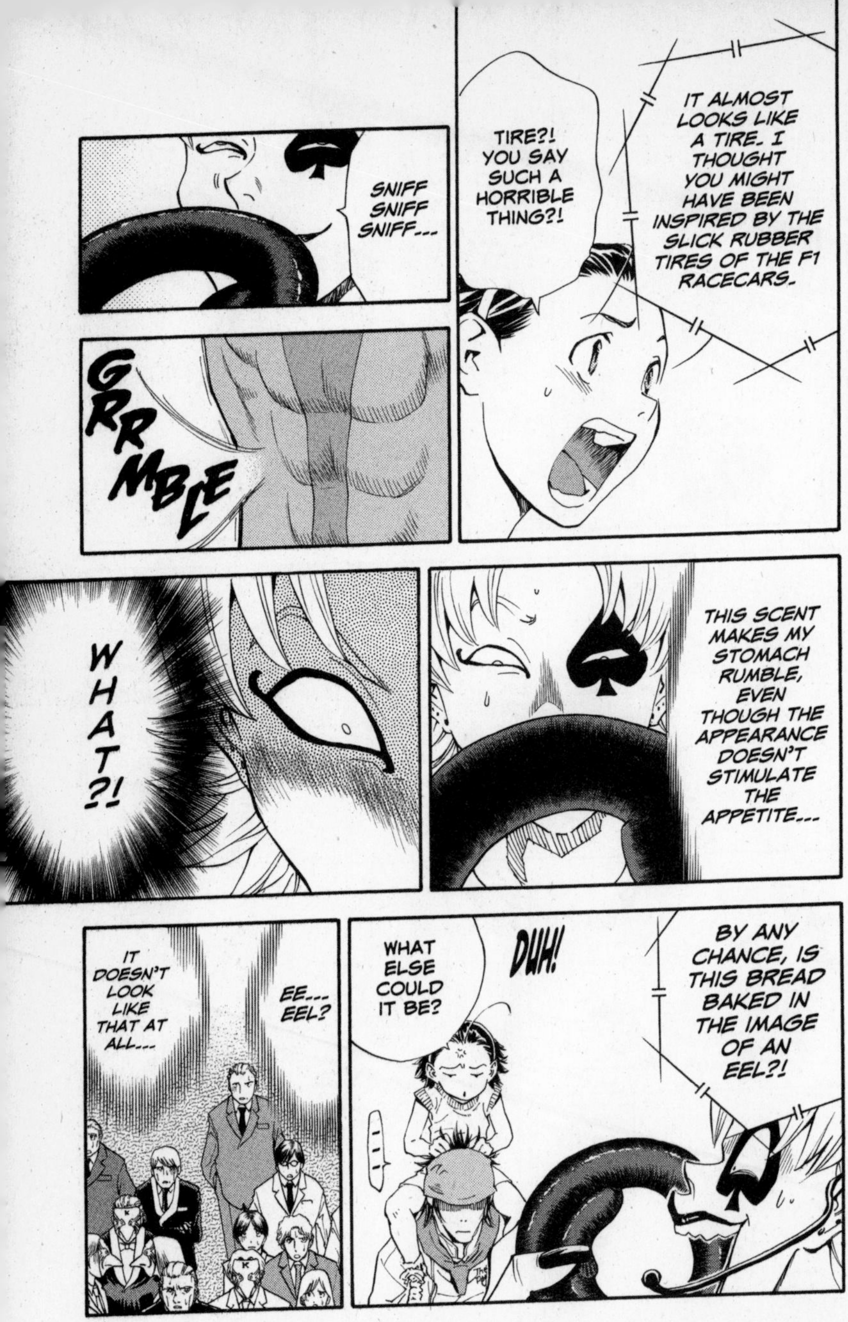
IT ALMOST LOOKS LIKE A TIRE. I THOUGHT YOU MIGHT HAVE BEEN INSPIRED BY THE SLICK RUBBER TIRES OF THE F1 RACECARS.
TIRE?! YOU SAY SUCH A HORRIBLE THING?!
SNIFF SNIFF SNIFF...
GRRMBLE
THIS SCENT MAKES MY STOMACH RUMBLE, EVEN THOUGH THE APPEARANCE DOESN'T STIMULATE THE APPETITE...
WHAT?!
BY ANY CHANCE, IS THIS BREAD BAKED IN THE IMAGE OF AN EEL?!
DUH!
WHAT ELSE COULD IT BE?
...
EE... EEL?
IT DOESN'T LOOK LIKE THAT AT ALL...

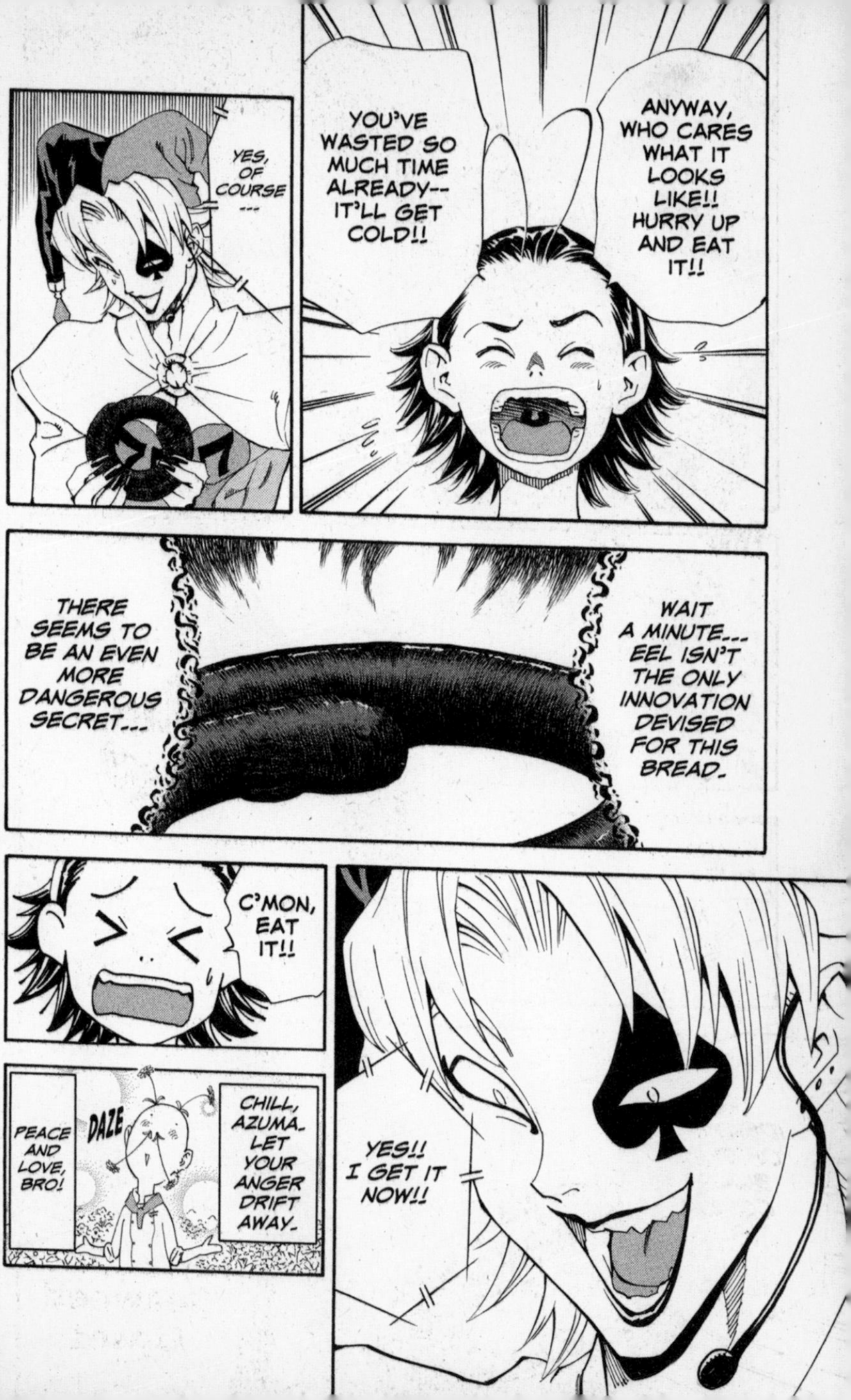
ANYWAY, WHO CARES WHAT IT LOOKS LIKE!! HURRY UP AND EAT IT!!
YOU'VE WASTED SO MUCH TIME ALREADY-- IT'LL GET COLD!!
YES, OF COURSE ---
WAIT A MINUTE... EEL ISN'T THE ONLY INNOVATION DEVISED FOR THIS BREAD.
THERE SEEMS TO BE AN EVEN MORE DANGEROUS SECRET...
YES!! I GET IT NOW!!
C'MON, EAT IT!!
CHILL, AZUMA. LET YOUR ANGER DRIFT AWAY.
DAZE
PEACE AND LOVE, BRO!

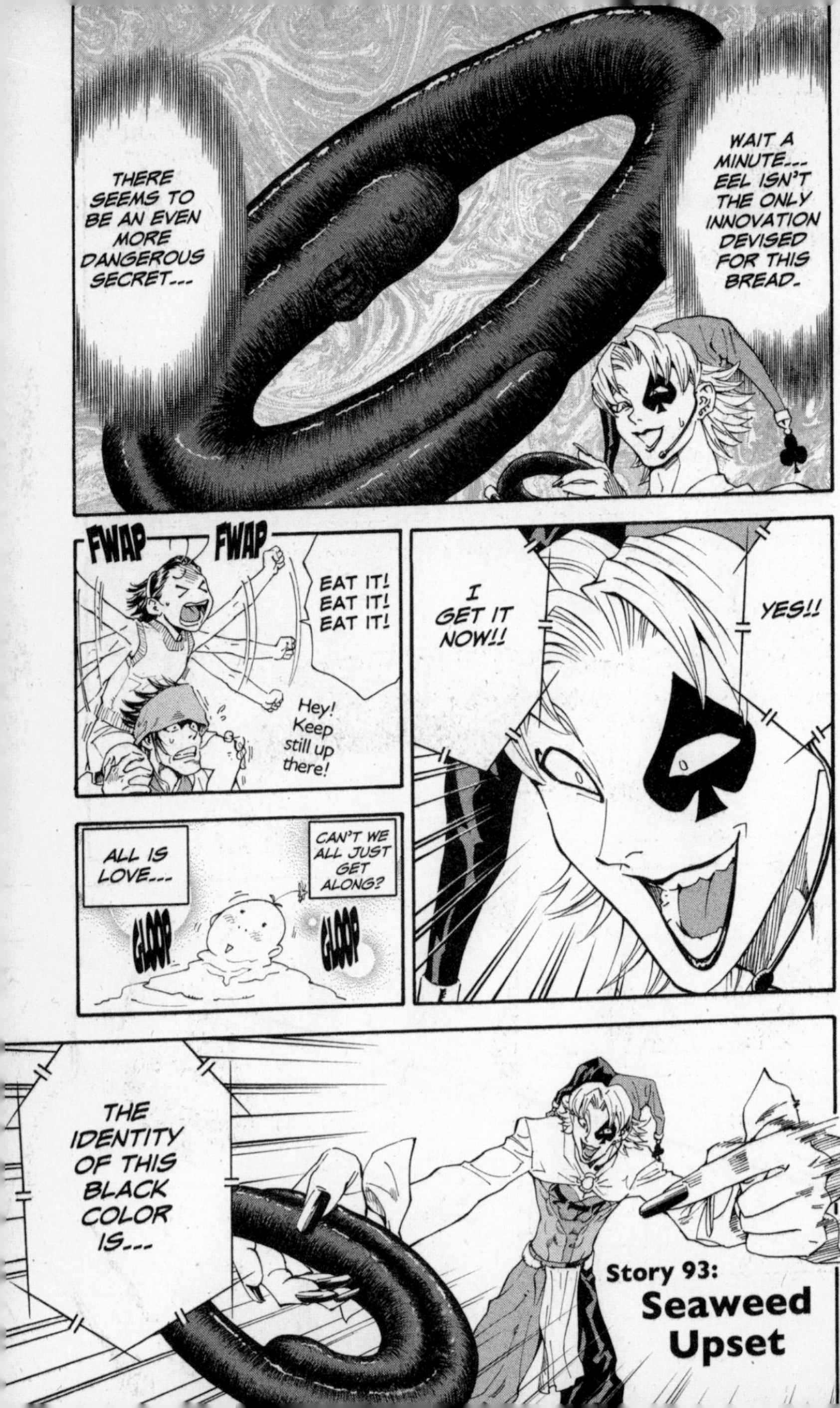
WAIT A MINUTE... EEL ISN'T THE ONLY INNOVATION DEVISED FOR THIS BREAD.
THERE SEEMS TO BE AN EVEN MORE DANGEROUS SECRET...
YES!!
I GET IT NOW!!
FWAP
FWAP
EAT IT! EAT IT! EAT IT!
Hey! Keep still up there!
CAN'T WE ALL JUST GET ALONG?
ALL IS LOVE...
GLOOP
GLOOP
THE IDENTITY OF THIS BLACK COLOR IS...
Story 93:
Seaweed Upset

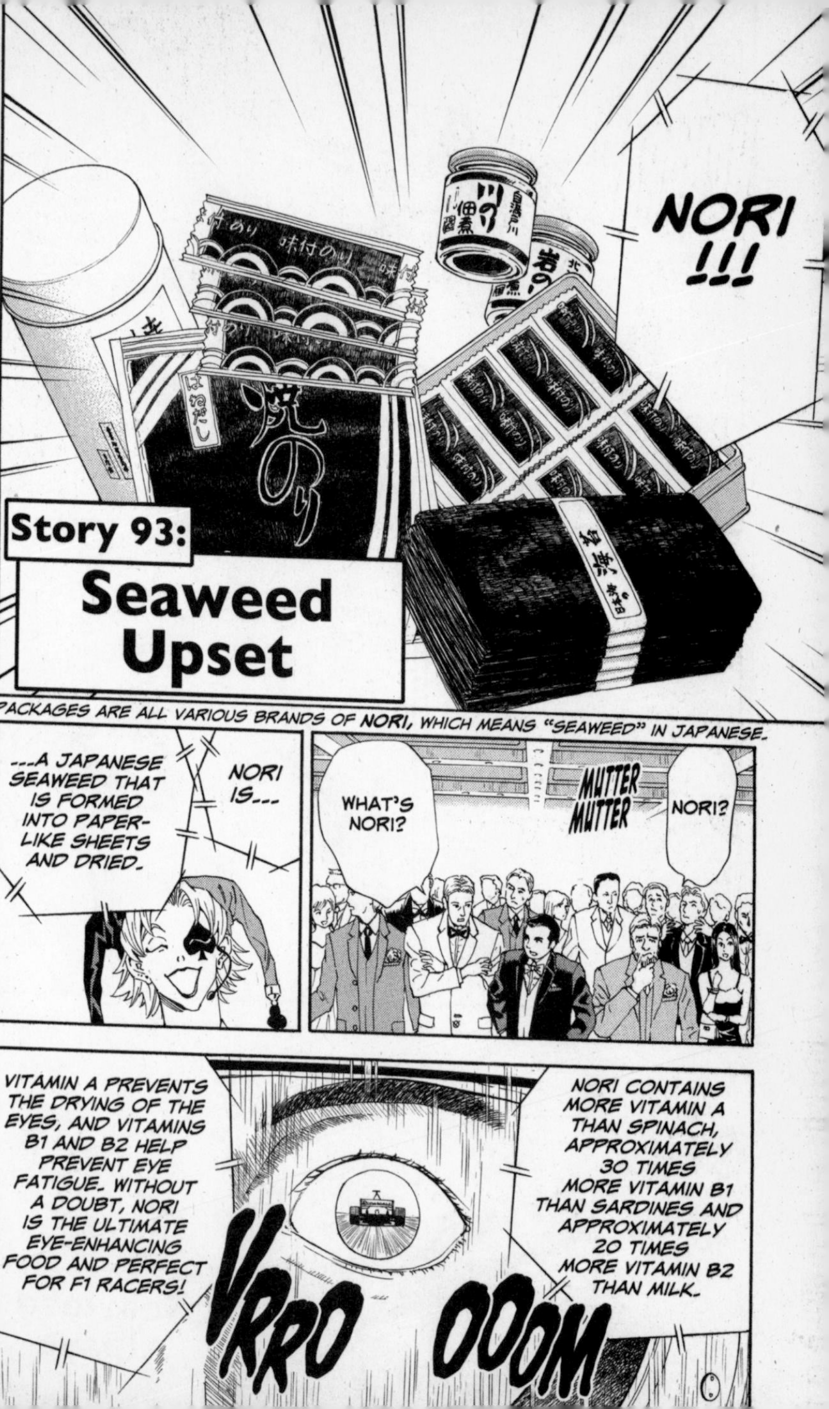
NORI !!!
Story 93:
Seaweed Upset
PACKAGES ARE ALL VARIOUS BRANDS OF NORI, WHICH MEANS "SEAWEED" IN JAPANESE.
NORI?
MUTTER MUTTER
WHAT'S NORI?
NORI IS...
...A JAPANESE SEAWEED THAT IS FORMED INTO PAPER-LIKE SHEETS AND DRIED.
NORI CONTAINS MORE VITAMIN A THAN SPINACH, APPROXIMATELY 30 TIMES MORE VITAMIN B1 THAN SARDINES AND APPROXIMATELY 20 TIMES MORE VITAMIN B2 THAN MILK.
VITAMIN A PREVENTS THE DRYING OF THE EYES, AND VITAMINS B1 AND B2 HELP PREVENT EYE FATIGUE. WITHOUT A DOUBT, NORI IS THE ULTIMATE EYE-ENHANCING FOOD AND PERFECT FOR F1 RACERS!
VRRO OOOM

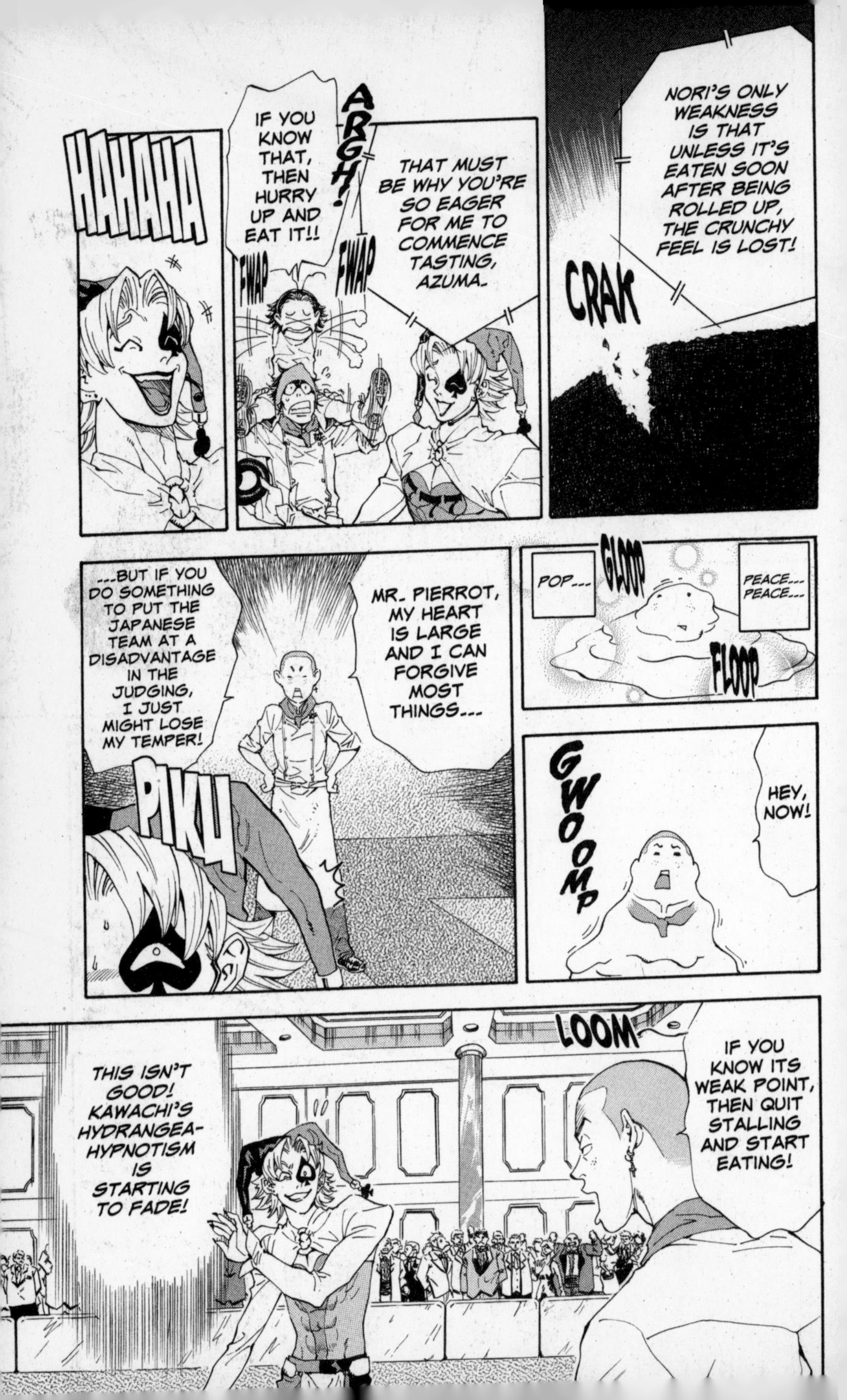
NORI'S ONLY WEAKNESS IS THAT UNLESS IT'S EATEN SOON AFTER BEING ROLLED UP, THE CRUNCHY FEEL IS LOST!
CRAK
THAT MUST BE WHY YOU'RE SO EAGER FOR ME TO COMMENCE TASTING, AZUMA.
ARGH!
FWAP
FWAP
IF YOU KNOW THAT, THEN HURRY UP AND EAT IT!!
HAHAHA
PEACE... PEACE...
GLOOP
POP...
FLOOP
HEY, NOW!
GWOOOMP
MR. PIERROT, MY HEART IS LARGE AND I CAN FORGIVE MOST THINGS...
...BUT IF YOU DO SOMETHING TO PUT THE JAPANESE TEAM AT A DISADVANTAGE IN THE JUDGING, I JUST MIGHT LOSE MY TEMPER!
PIKU
IF YOU KNOW ITS WEAK POINT, THEN QUIT STALLING AND START EATING!
LOOM
THIS ISN'T GOOD! KAWACHI'S HYDRANGEA-HYPNOTISM IS STARTING TO FADE!

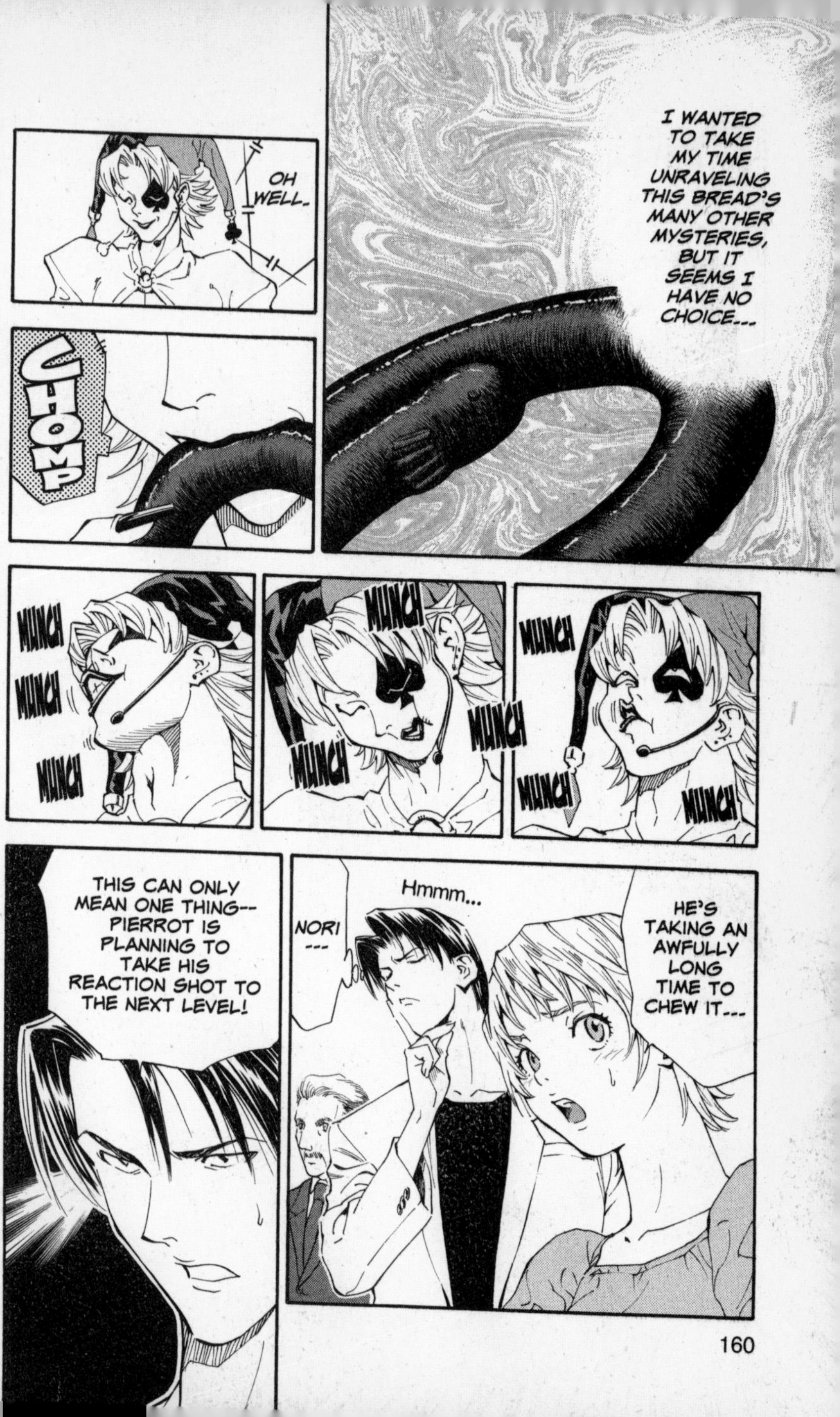
I WANTED TO TAKE MY TIME UNRAVELING THIS BREAD'S MANY OTHER MYSTERIES, BUT IT SEEMS I HAVE NO CHOICE...
OH WELL...
CHOMP
MUNCH
MUNCH
MUNCH
MUNCH
MUNCH
MUNCH
MUNCH
MUNCH
HE'S TAKING AN AWFULLY LONG TIME TO CHEW IT...
Hmmm...
NORI---
THIS CAN ONLY MEAN ONE THING--PIERROT IS PLANNING TO TAKE HIS REACTION SHOT TO THE NEXT LEVEL!

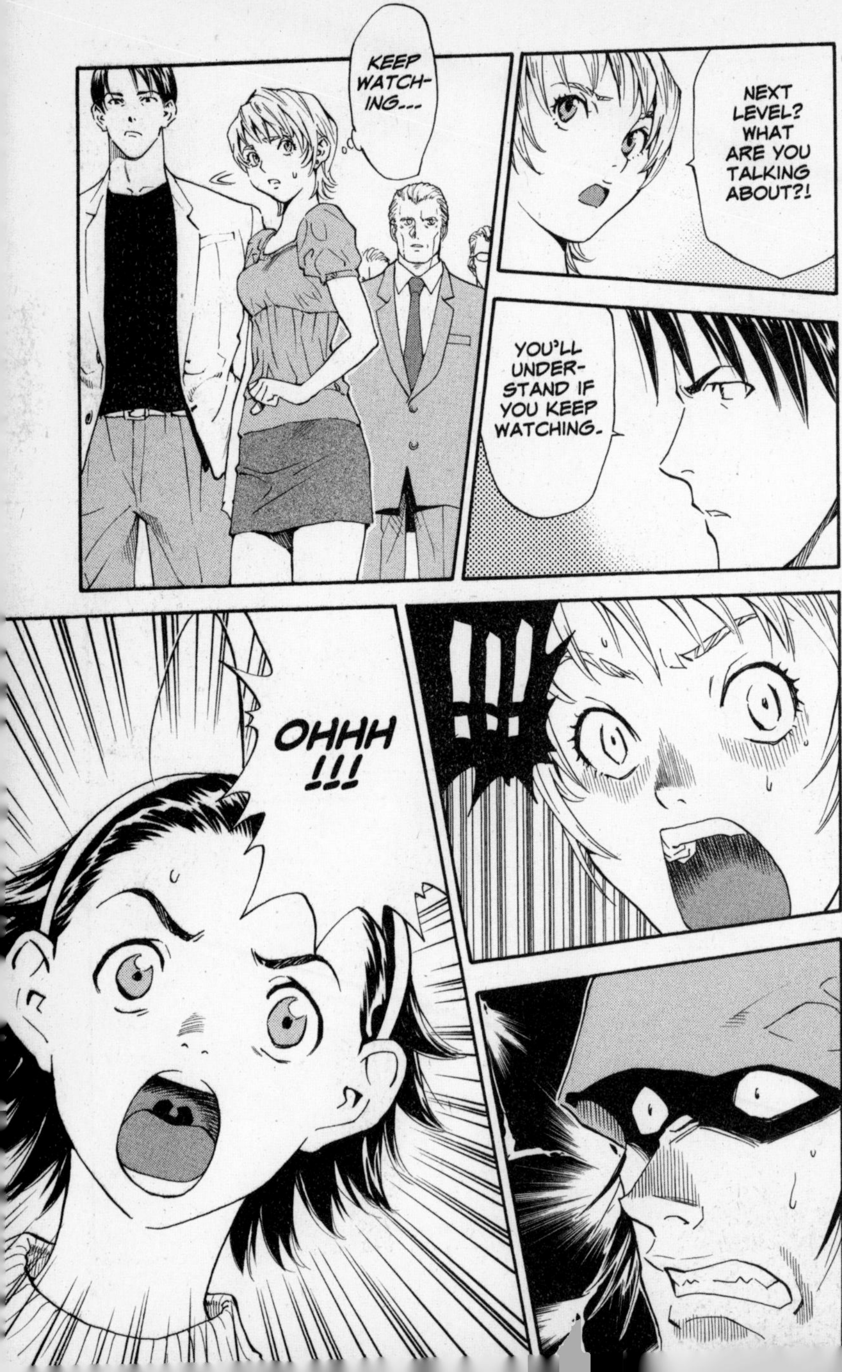
NEXT LEVEL? WHAT ARE YOU TALKING ABOUT?!
YOU'LL UNDER-STAND IF YOU KEEP WATCHING.
KEEP WATCH-ING...
!!!
OHHH !!!

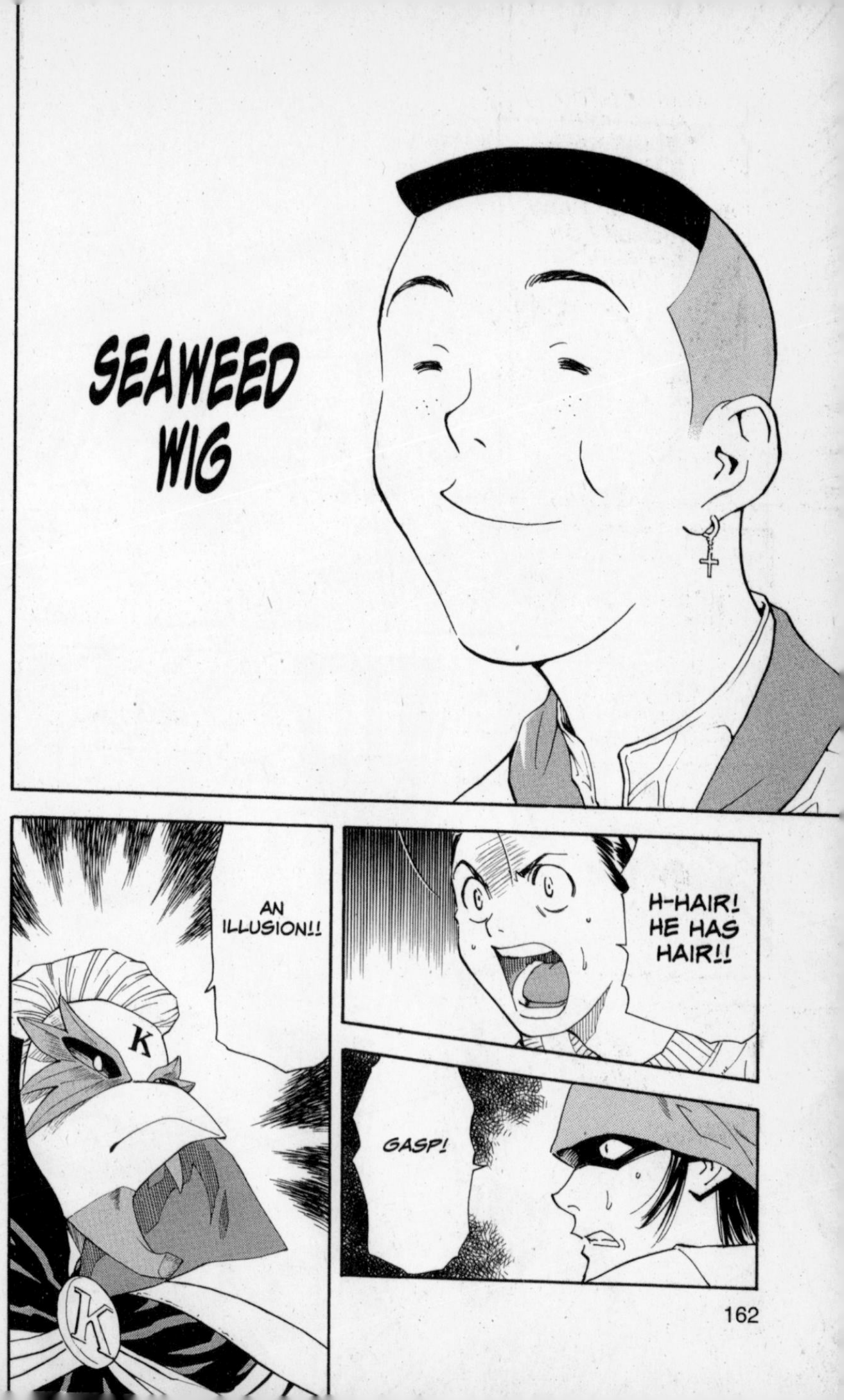
SEAWEED WIG
H-HAIR! HE HAS HAIR!!
GASP!
AN ILLUSION!!

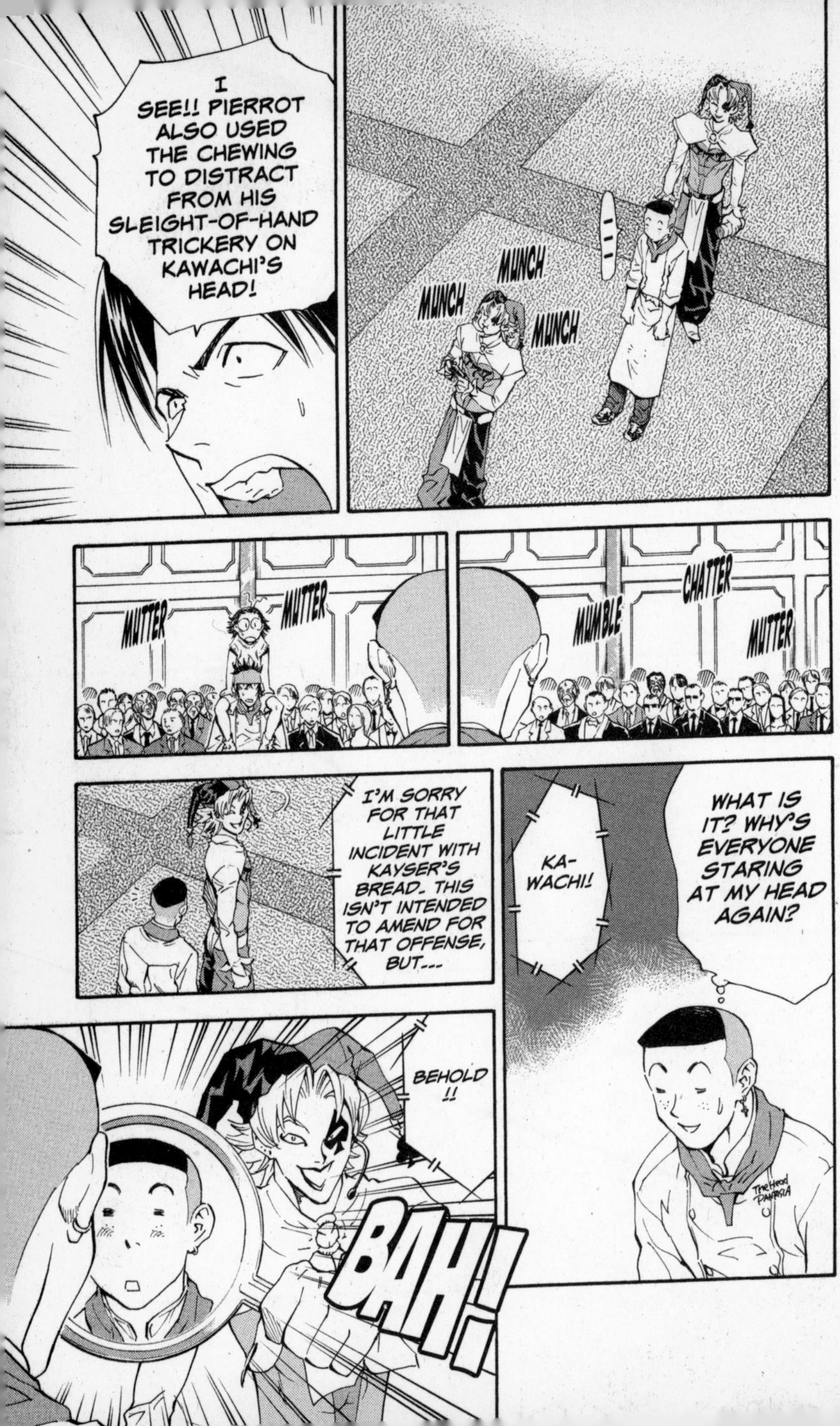

MUNCH
MUNCH
MUNCH
...
I SEE!! PIERROT ALSO USED THE CHEWING TO DISTRACT FROM HIS SLEIGHT-OF-HAND TRICKERY ON KAWACHI'S HEAD!
MUTTER
CHATTER
MUMBLE
MUTTER
MUTTER
WHAT IS IT? WHY'S EVERYONE STARING AT MY HEAD AGAIN?
KA-WACHI!
The Head PANRGIA
I'M SORRY FOR THAT LITTLE INCIDENT WITH KAYSER'S BREAD. THIS ISN'T INTENDED TO AMEND FOR THAT OFFENSE, BUT...
BEHOLD !!
BAH!

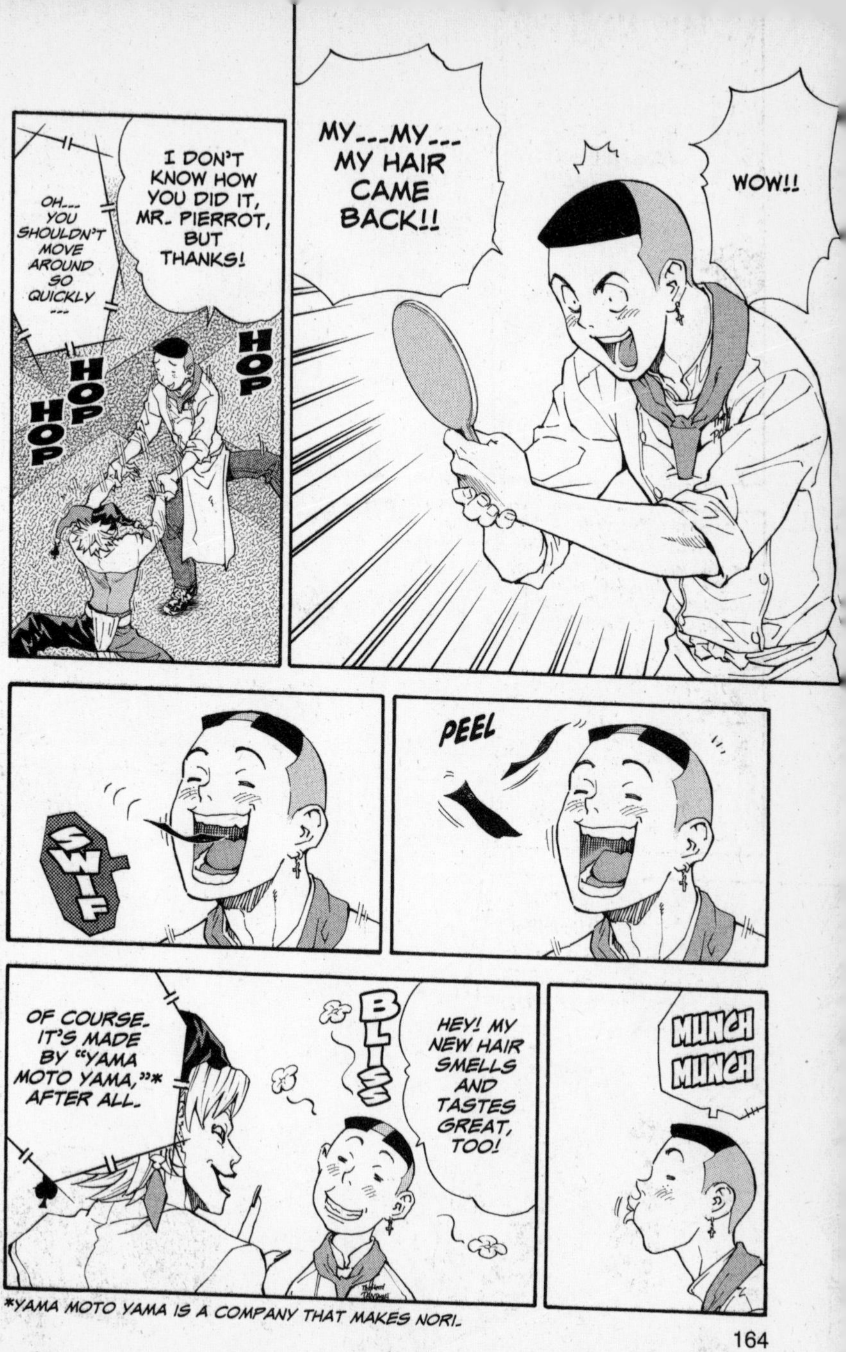
WOW!!
MY...MY... MY HAIR CAME BACK!!
I DON'T KNOW HOW YOU DID IT, MR. PIERROT, BUT THANKS!
OH... YOU SHOULDN'T MOVE AROUND SO QUICKLY ...
HOP
HOP
HOP
PEEL
SWIF
MUNCH MUNCH
HEY! MY NEW HAIR SMELLS AND TASTES GREAT, TOO!
BLISS
OF COURSE. IT'S MADE BY "YAMA MOTO YAMA,"* AFTER ALL.

*YAMA MOTO YAMA IS A COMPANY THAT MAKES NORI.

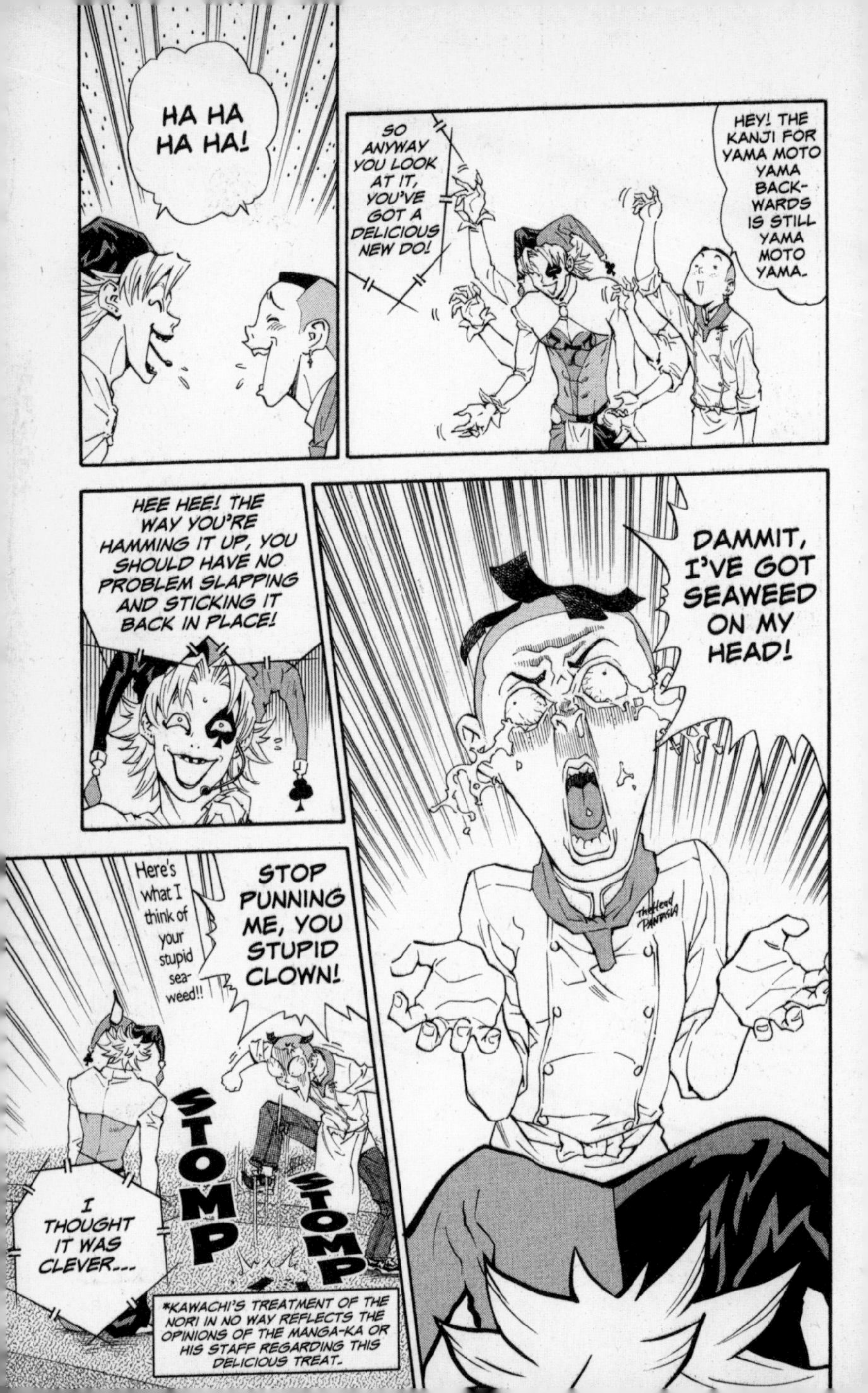
HEY! THE KANJI FOR YAMA MOTO YAMA BACKWARDS IS STILL YAMA MOTO YAMA.
SO ANYWAY YOU LOOK AT IT, YOU'VE GOT A DELICIOUS NEW DO!
HA HA HA HA!
DAMMIT, I'VE GOT SEAWEED ON MY HEAD!
HEE HEE! THE WAY YOU'RE HAMMING IT UP, YOU SHOULD HAVE NO PROBLEM SLAPPING AND STICKING IT BACK IN PLACE!
STOP PUNNING ME, YOU STUPID CLOWN!
Here's what I think of your stupid seaweed!!
STOMP
STOMP
I THOUGHT IT WAS CLEVER...
*KAWACHI'S TREATMENT OF THE NORI IN NO WAY REFLECTS THE OPINIONS OF THE MANGA-KA OR HIS STAFF REGARDING THIS DELICIOUS TREAT.

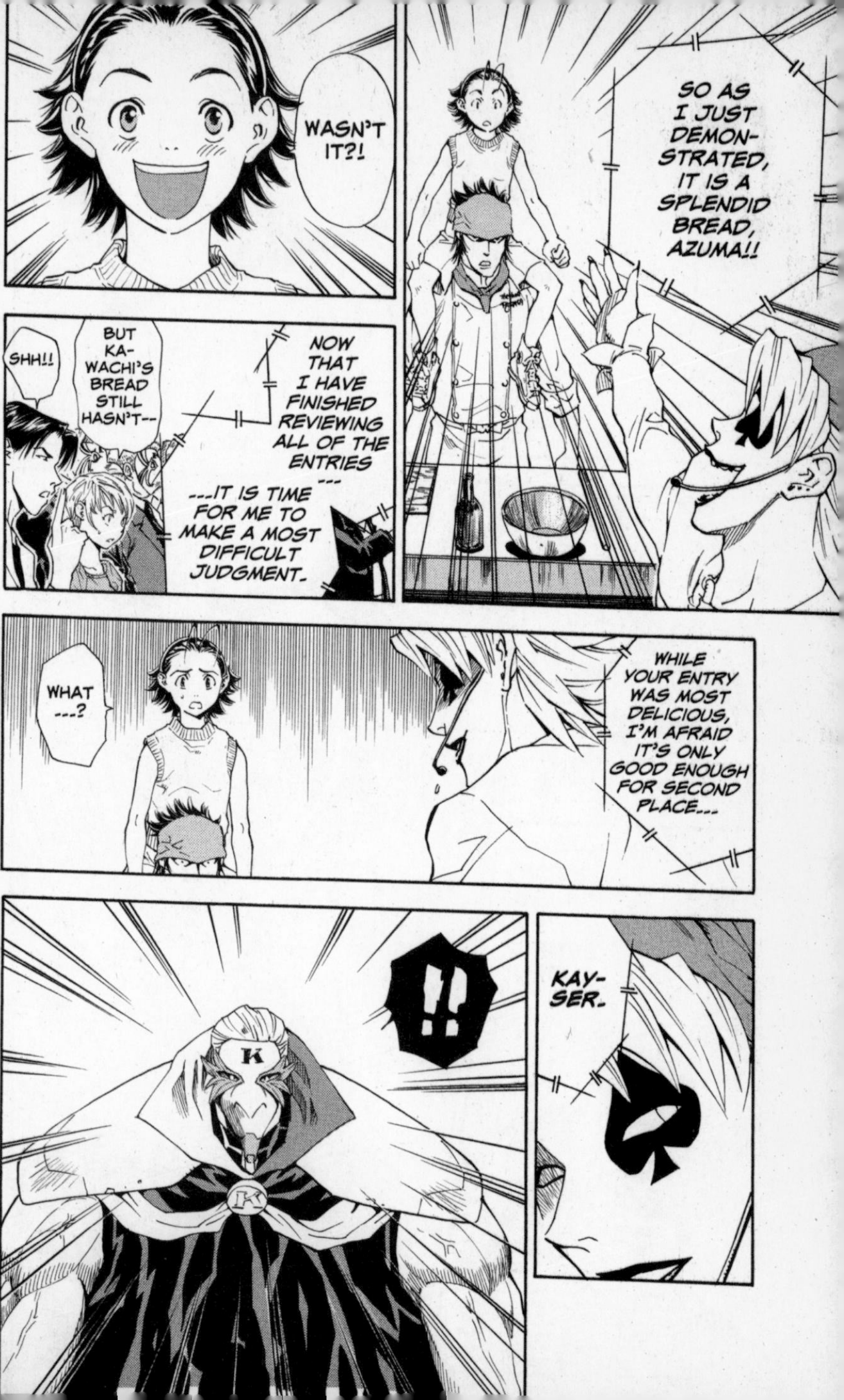
SO AS I JUST DEMON-STRATED, IT IS A SPLENDID BREAD, AZUMA!!
WASN'T IT?!
NOW THAT I HAVE FINISHED REVIEWING ALL OF THE ENTRIES ---
---IT IS TIME FOR ME TO MAKE A MOST DIFFICULT JUDGMENT.
BUT KA-WACHI'S BREAD STILL HASN'T--
SHH!!
WHILE YOUR ENTRY WAS MOST DELICIOUS, I'M AFRAID IT'S ONLY GOOD ENOUGH FOR SECOND PLACE...
WHAT ---?
KAY-SER.
!?

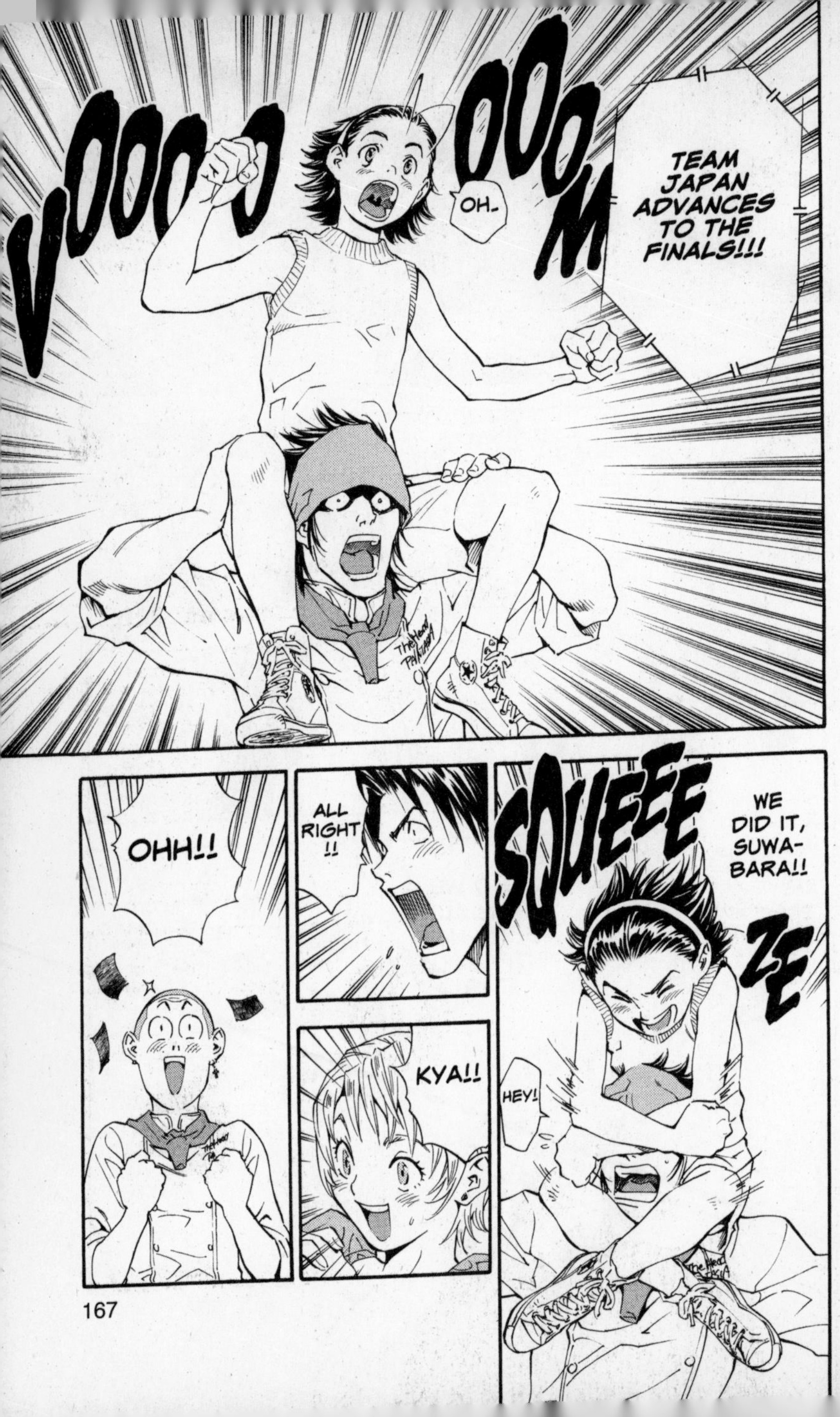
TEAM JAPAN ADVANCES TO THE FINALS!!!
VOOOO OOOOM
OH-
WE DID IT, SUWA-BARA!!
SQUEEEZE
HEY!
ALL RIGHT !!
KYA!!
OHH!!

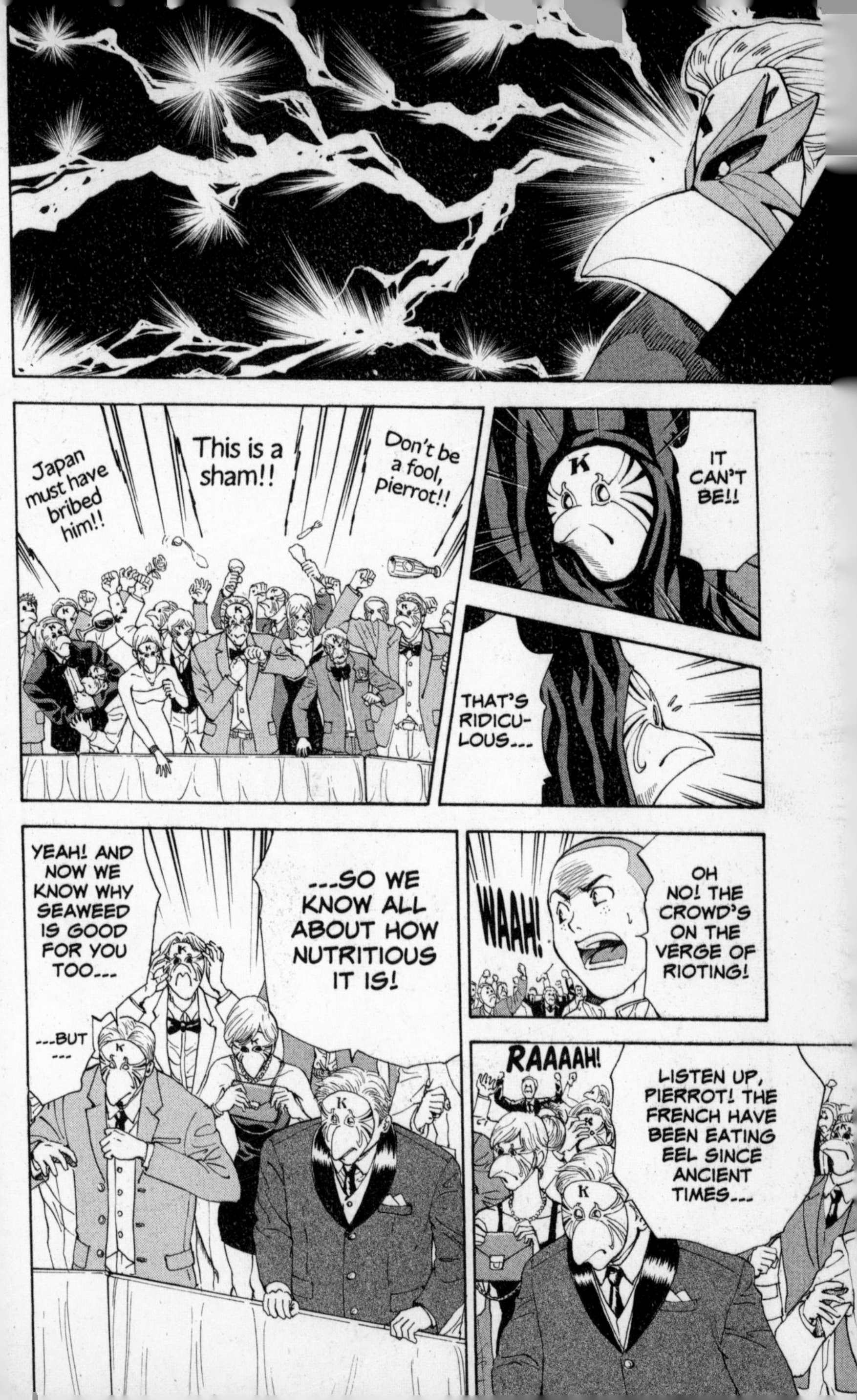
IT CAN'T BE!!
THAT'S RIDICULOUS...
Don't be a fool, pierrot!!
This is a sham!!
Japan must have bribed him!!
WAAH!
OH NO! THE CROWD'S ON THE VERGE OF RIOTING!
RAAAAH!
LISTEN UP, PIERROT! THE FRENCH HAVE BEEN EATING EEL SINCE ANCIENT TIMES...
...SO WE KNOW ALL ABOUT HOW NUTRITIOUS IT IS!
YEAH! AND NOW WE KNOW WHY SEAWEED IS GOOD FOR YOU TOO...
...BUT ...

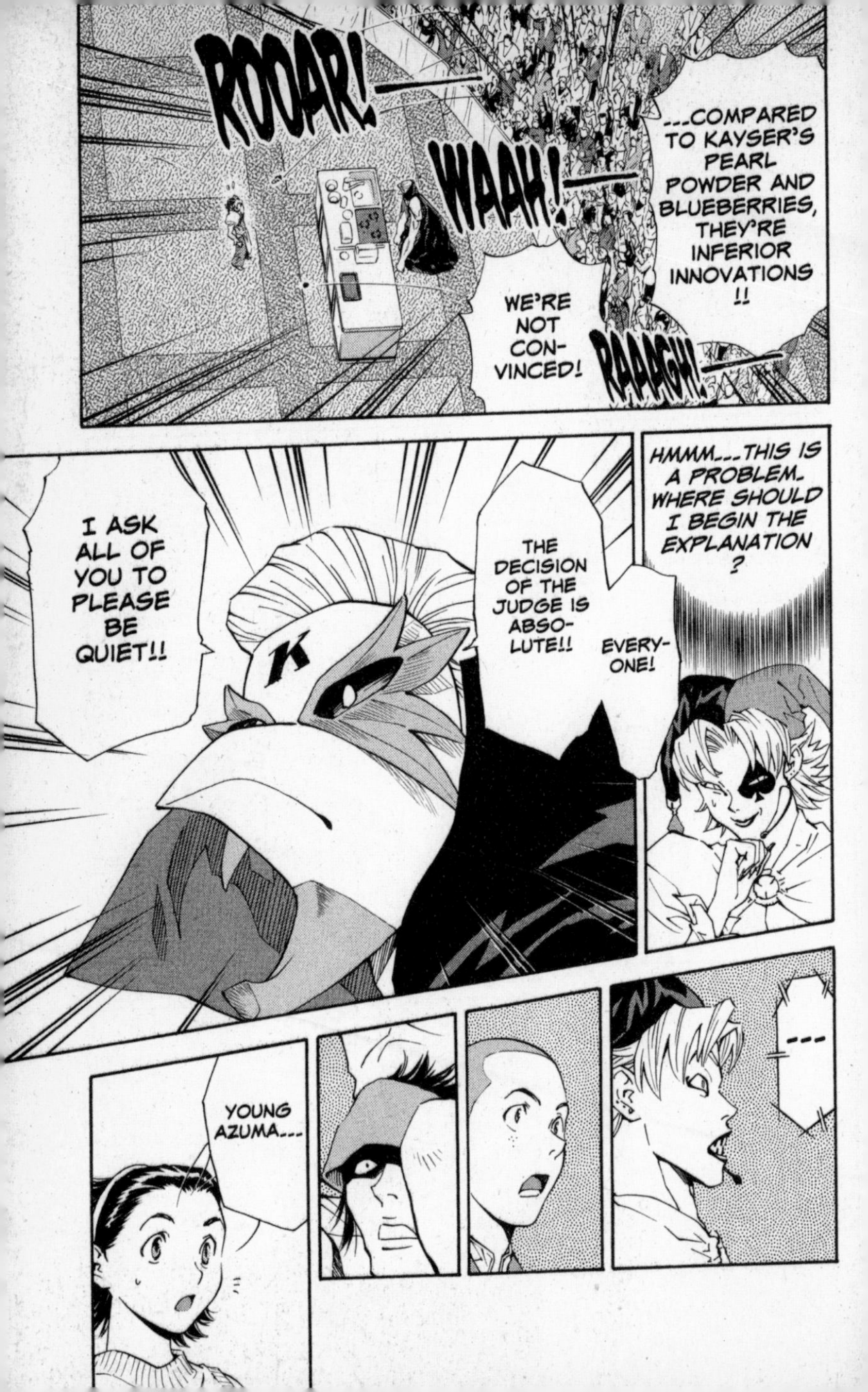
...COMPARED TO KAYSER'S PEARL POWDER AND BLUEBERRIES, THEY'RE INFERIOR INNOVATIONS !!
ROOAR!
WAAH!
RAAAGH!
WE'RE NOT CON-VINCED!
HMMM...THIS IS A PROBLEM. WHERE SHOULD I BEGIN THE EXPLANATION ?
EVERY-ONE!
THE DECISION OF THE JUDGE IS ABSO-LUTE!!
I ASK ALL OF YOU TO PLEASE BE QUIET!!
...
YOUNG AZUMA...

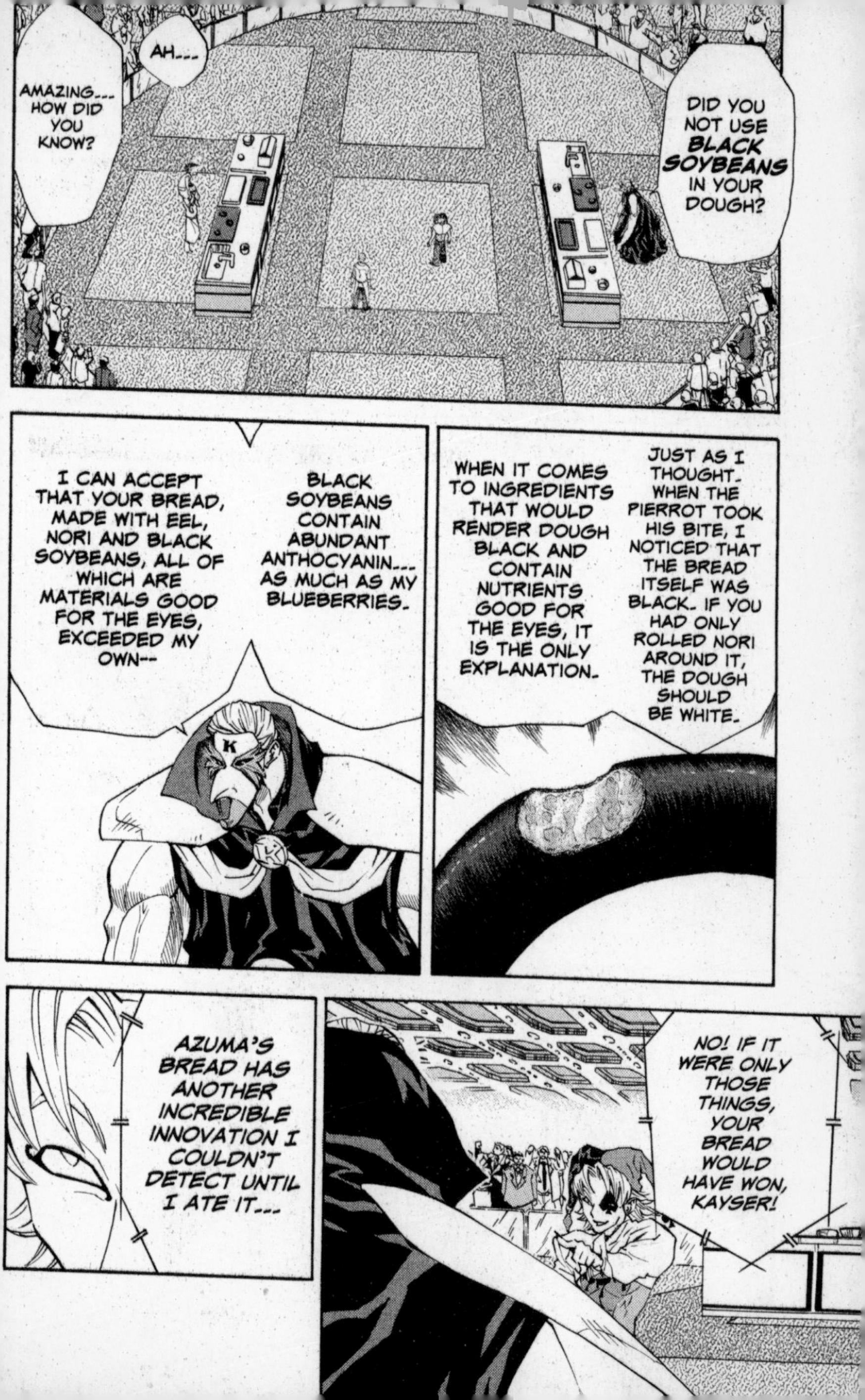
DID YOU NOT USE BLACK SOYBEANS IN YOUR DOUGH?
AH...
AMAZING... HOW DID YOU KNOW?
JUST AS I THOUGHT. WHEN THE PIERROT TOOK HIS BITE, I NOTICED THAT THE BREAD ITSELF WAS BLACK. IF YOU HAD ONLY ROLLED NORI AROUND IT, THE DOUGH SHOULD BE WHITE.
WHEN IT COMES TO INGREDIENTS THAT WOULD RENDER DOUGH BLACK AND CONTAIN NUTRIENTS GOOD FOR THE EYES, IT IS THE ONLY EXPLANATION.
BLACK SOYBEANS CONTAIN ABUNDANT ANTHOCYANIN... AS MUCH AS MY BLUEBERRIES.
I CAN ACCEPT THAT YOUR BREAD, MADE WITH EEL, NORI AND BLACK SOYBEANS, ALL OF WHICH ARE MATERIALS GOOD FOR THE EYES, EXCEEDED MY OWN--
NO! IF IT WERE ONLY THOSE THINGS, YOUR BREAD WOULD HAVE WON, KAYSER!
AZUMA'S BREAD HAS ANOTHER INCREDIBLE INNOVATION I COULDN'T DETECT UNTIL I ATE IT...

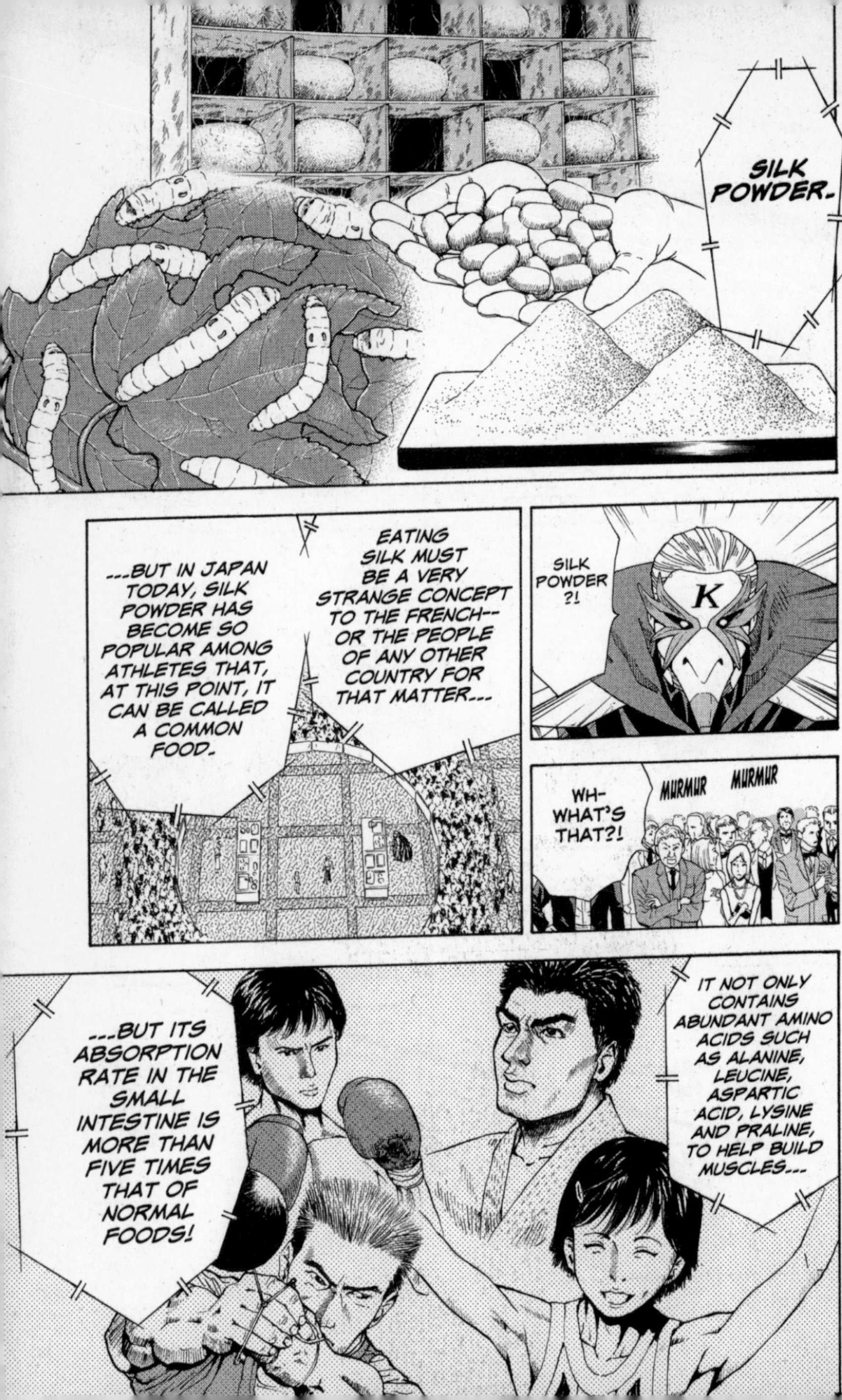
SILK POWDER.
SILK POWDER ?!
WH- WHAT'S THAT?!
MURMUR
MURMUR
EATING SILK MUST BE A VERY STRANGE CONCEPT TO THE FRENCH-- OR THE PEOPLE OF ANY OTHER COUNTRY FOR THAT MATTER...
...BUT IN JAPAN TODAY, SILK POWDER HAS BECOME SO POPULAR AMONG ATHLETES THAT, AT THIS POINT, IT CAN BE CALLED A COMMON FOOD.
IT NOT ONLY CONTAINS ABUNDANT AMINO ACIDS SUCH AS ALANINE, LEUCINE, ASPARTIC ACID, LYSINE AND PRALINE, TO HELP BUILD MUSCLES...
...BUT ITS ABSORPTION RATE IN THE SMALL INTESTINE IS MORE THAN FIVE TIMES THAT OF NORMAL FOODS!

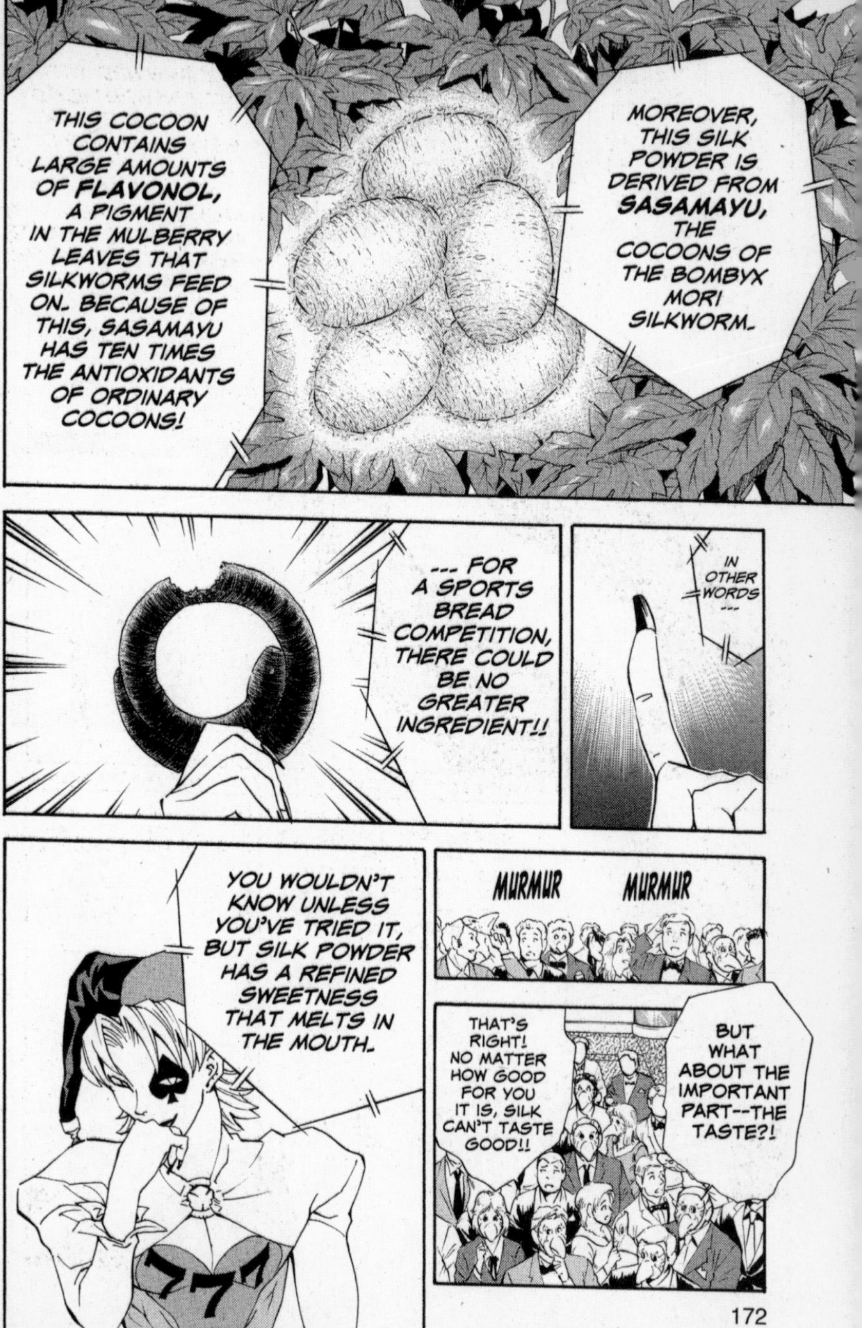
MOREOVER, THIS SILK POWDER IS DERIVED FROM SASAMAYU, THE COCOONS OF THE BOMBYX MORI SILKWORM.
THIS COCOON CONTAINS LARGE AMOUNTS OF FLAVONOL, A PIGMENT IN THE MULBERRY LEAVES THAT SILKWORMS FEED ON. BECAUSE OF THIS, SASAMAYU HAS TEN TIMES THE ANTIOXIDANTS OF ORDINARY COCOONS!
IN OTHER WORDS---
--- FOR A SPORTS BREAD COMPETITION, THERE COULD BE NO GREATER INGREDIENT!!
MURMUR
MURMUR
BUT WHAT ABOUT THE IMPORTANT PART--THE TASTE?!
THAT'S RIGHT! NO MATTER HOW GOOD FOR YOU IT IS, SILK CAN'T TASTE GOOD!!
YOU WOULDN'T KNOW UNLESS YOU'VE TRIED IT, BUT SILK POWDER HAS A REFINED SWEETNESS THAT MELTS IN THE MOUTH.

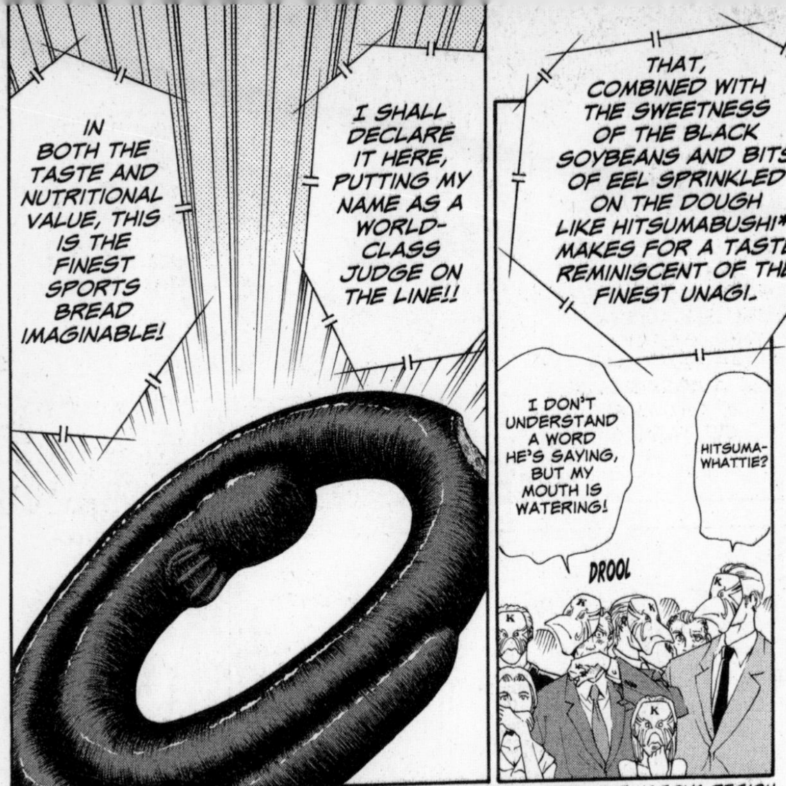
THAT, COMBINED WITH THE SWEETNESS OF THE BLACK SOYBEANS AND BITS OF EEL SPRINKLED ON THE DOUGH LIKE HITSUMABUSHI*, MAKES FOR A TASTE REMINISCENT OF THE FINEST UNAGI.
HITSUMA-WHATTIE?
I DON'T UNDERSTAND A WORD HE'S SAYING, BUT MY MOUTH IS WATERING!
DROOL
I SHALL DECLARE IT HERE, PUTTING MY NAME AS A WORLD-CLASS JUDGE ON THE LINE!!
IN BOTH THE TASTE AND NUTRITIONAL VALUE, THIS IS THE FINEST SPORTS BREAD IMAGINABLE!

*HITSUMABUSHI IS A BARBEQUED EEL ON RICE DISH FROM THE NAGOYA REGION.

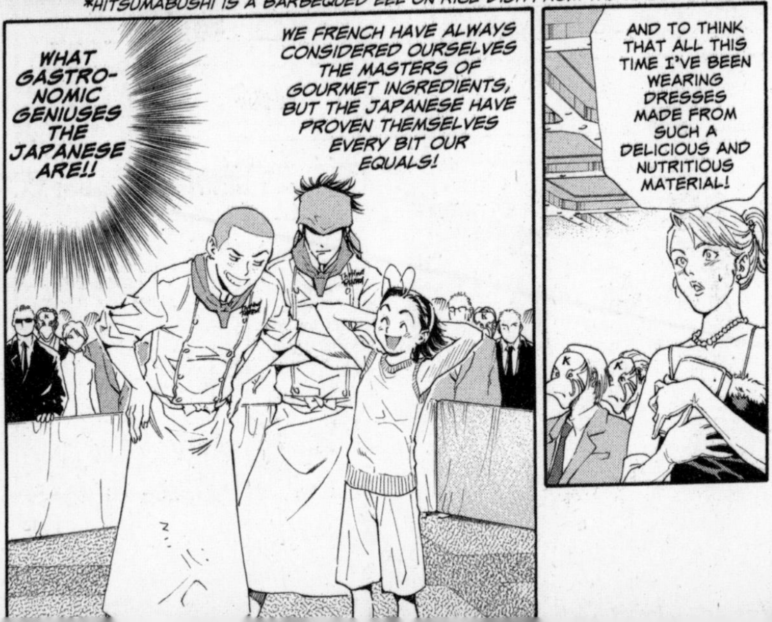
AND TO THINK THAT ALL THIS TIME I'VE BEEN WEARING DRESSES MADE FROM SUCH A DELICIOUS AND NUTRITIOUS MATERIAL!
WE FRENCH HAVE ALWAYS CONSIDERED OURSELVES THE MASTERS OF GOURMET INGREDIENTS, BUT THE JAPANESE HAVE PROVEN THEMSELVES EVERY BIT OUR EQUALS!
WHAT GASTRONOMIC GENIUSES THE JAPANESE ARE!!

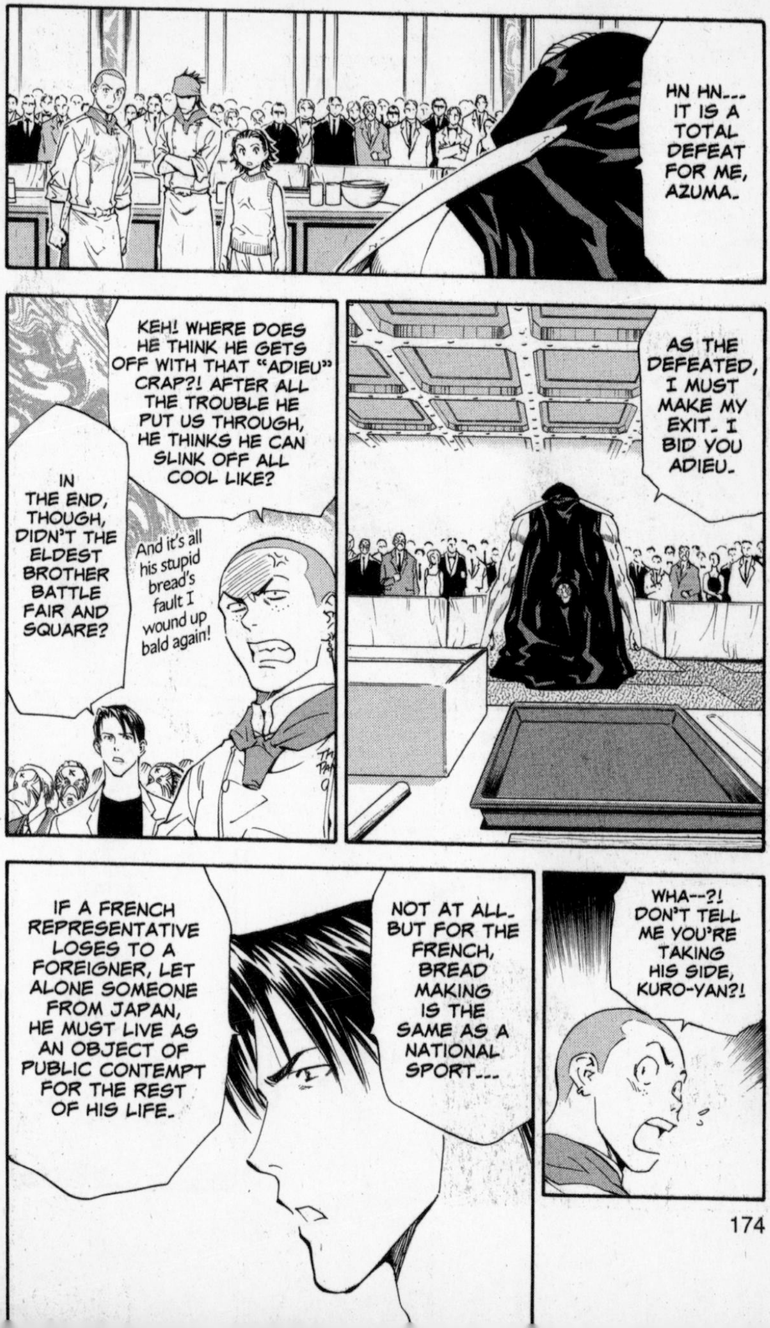
HN HN... IT IS A TOTAL DEFEAT FOR ME, AZUMA.
AS THE DEFEATED, I MUST MAKE MY EXIT. I BID YOU ADIEU.
KEH! WHERE DOES HE THINK HE GETS OFF WITH THAT "ADIEU" CRAP?! AFTER ALL THE TROUBLE HE PUT US THROUGH, HE THINKS HE CAN SLINK OFF ALL COOL LIKE?
And it's all his stupid bread's fault I wound up bald again!
IN THE END, THOUGH, DIDN'T THE ELDEST BROTHER BATTLE FAIR AND SQUARE?
WHA--?! DON'T TELL ME YOU'RE TAKING HIS SIDE, KURO-YAN?!
NOT AT ALL. BUT FOR THE FRENCH, BREAD MAKING IS THE SAME AS A NATIONAL SPORT...
IF A FRENCH REPRESENTATIVE LOSES TO A FOREIGNER, LET ALONE SOMEONE FROM JAPAN, HE MUST LIVE AS AN OBJECT OF PUBLIC CONTEMPT FOR THE REST OF HIS LIFE.

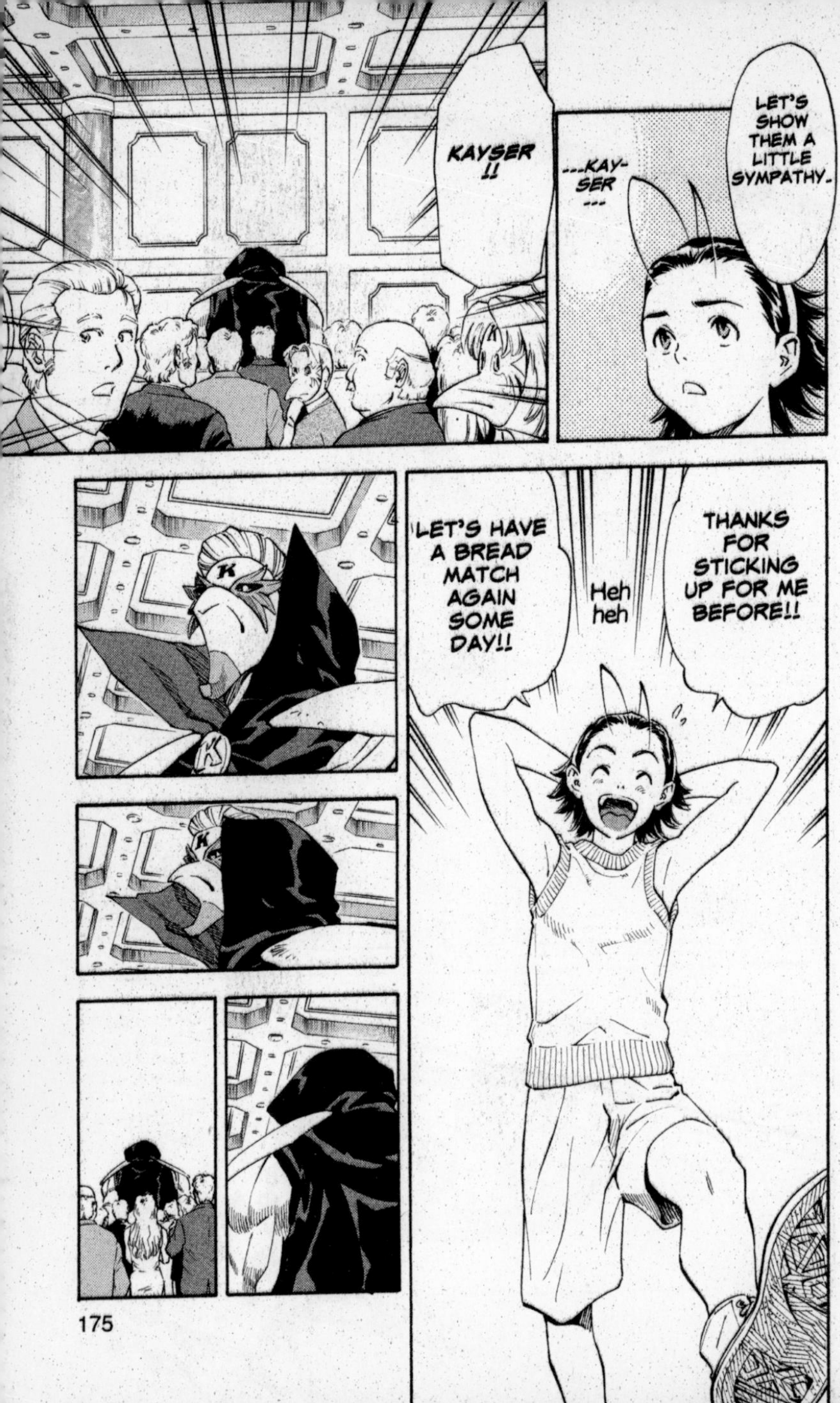
LET'S SHOW THEM A LITTLE SYMPATHY.
...KAY-SER...
KAYSER!!
THANKS FOR STICKING UP FOR ME BEFORE!!
Heh heh
LET'S HAVE A BREAD MATCH AGAIN SOME DAY!!

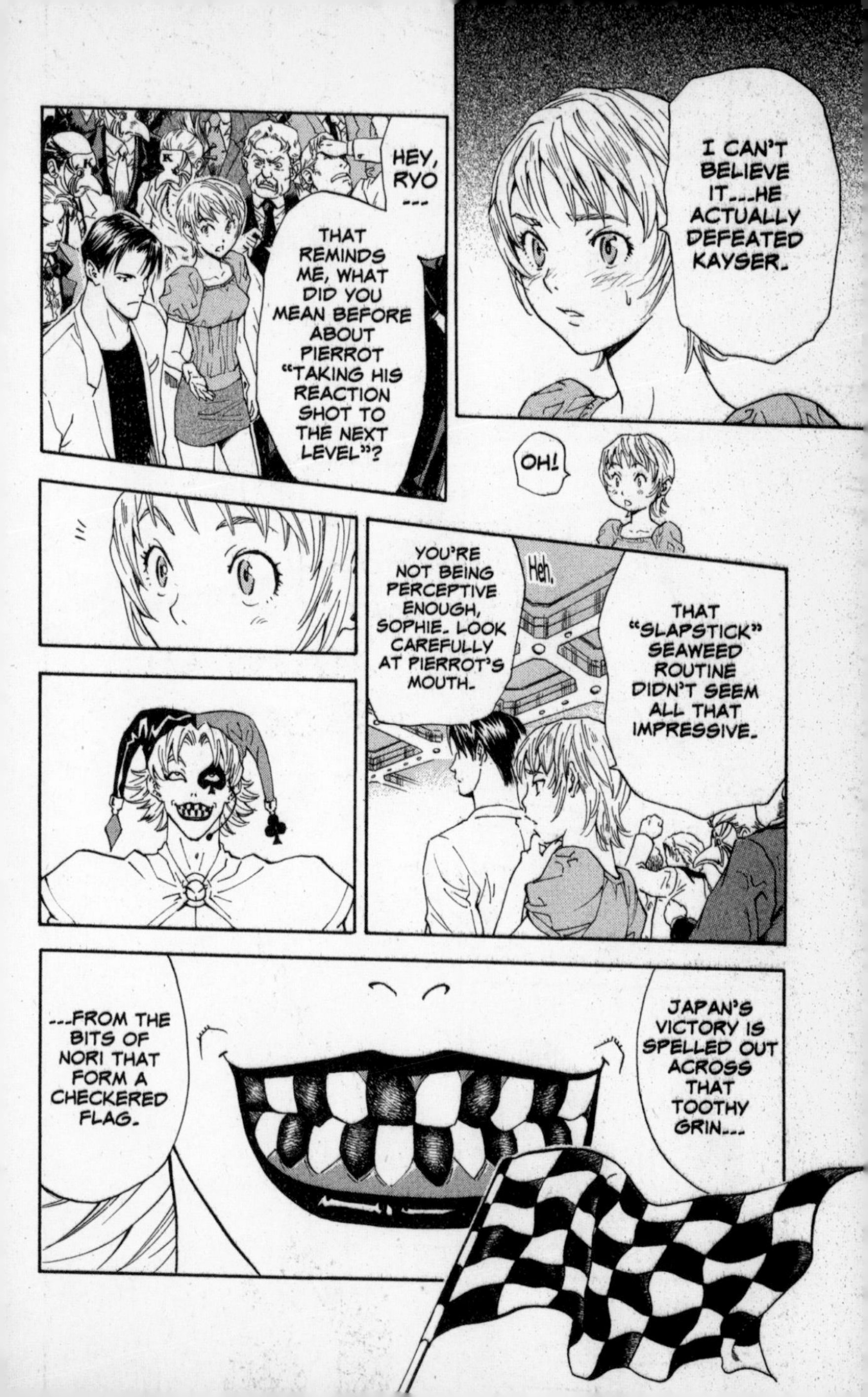
I CAN'T BELIEVE IT...HE ACTUALLY DEFEATED KAYSER.
HEY, RYO---
THAT REMINDS ME, WHAT DID YOU MEAN BEFORE ABOUT PIERROT "TAKING HIS REACTION SHOT TO THE NEXT LEVEL"?
OH!
THAT "SLAPSTICK" SEAWEED ROUTINE DIDN'T SEEM ALL THAT IMPRESSIVE.
Heh.
YOU'RE NOT BEING PERCEPTIVE ENOUGH, SOPHIE. LOOK CAREFULLY AT PIERROT'S MOUTH.
JAPAN'S VICTORY IS SPELLED OUT ACROSS THAT TOOTHY GRIN...
...FROM THE BITS OF NORI THAT FORM A CHECKERED FLAG.

Story 94: Shadow of a Doubt

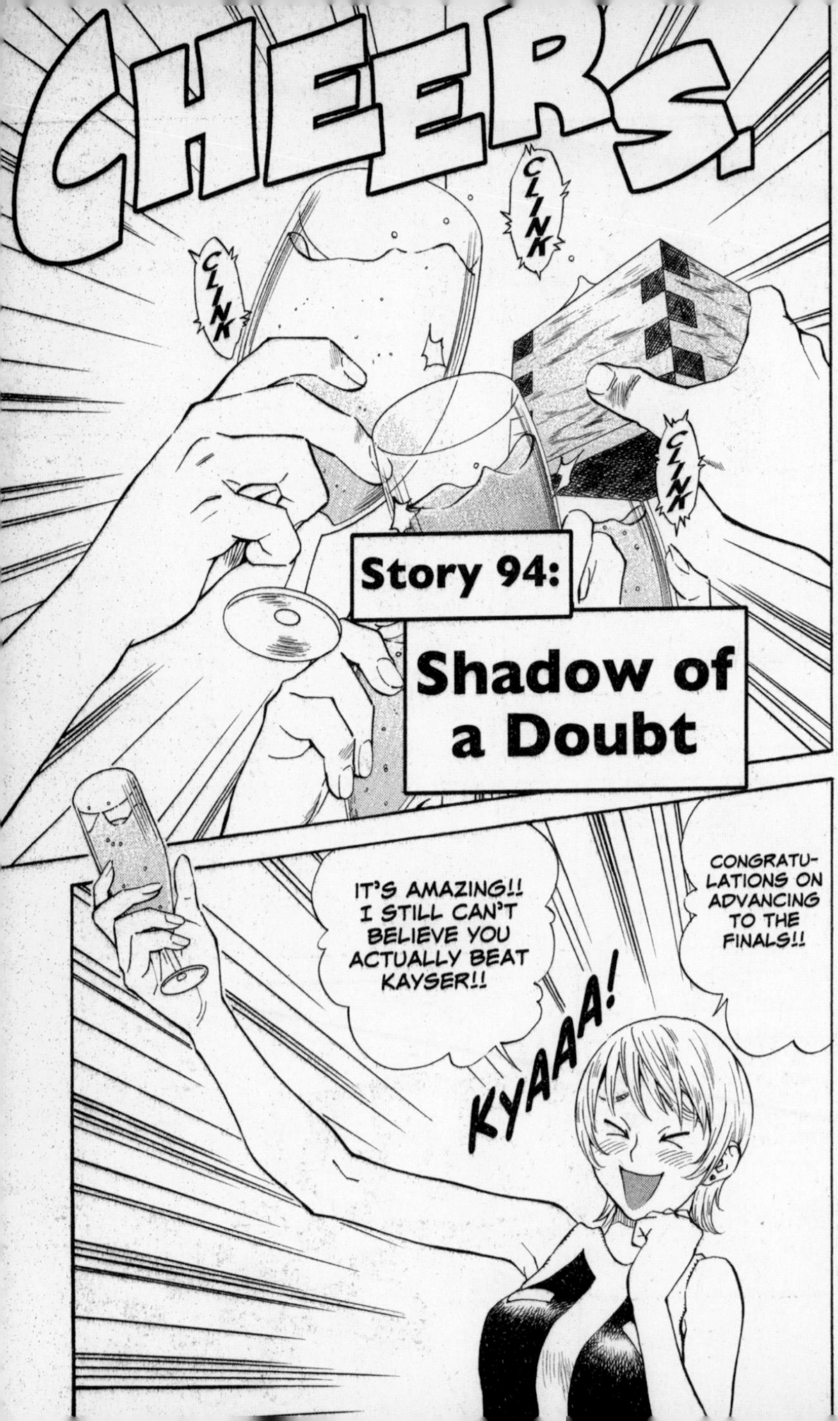
CHEERS!
CLINK
CLINK
CLINK
CONGRATULATIONS ON ADVANCING TO THE FINALS!!
IT'S AMAZING!! I STILL CAN'T BELIEVE YOU ACTUALLY BEAT KAYSER!!
KYAAA!

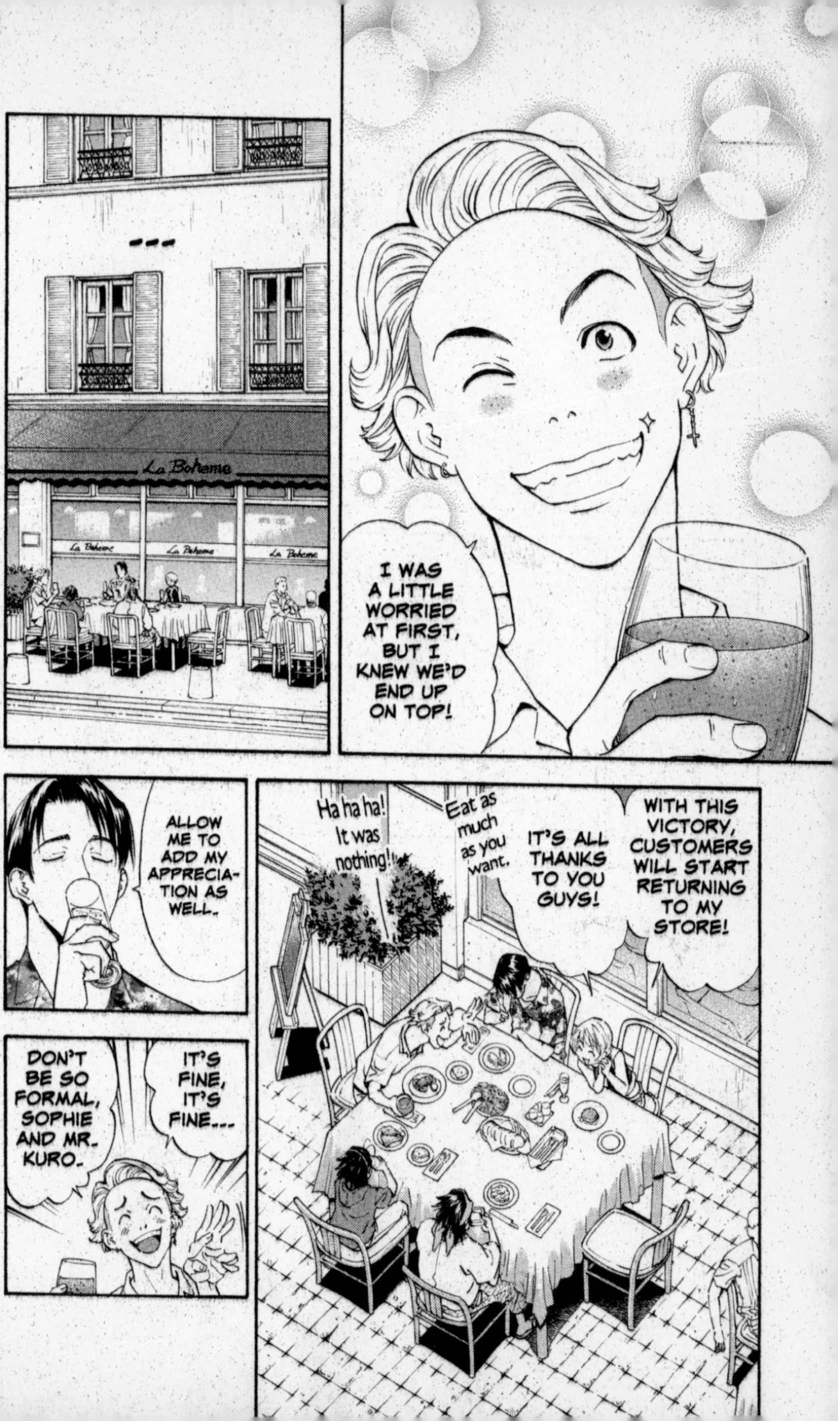
I WAS A LITTLE WORRIED AT FIRST, BUT I KNEW WE'D END UP ON TOP!
...
La Boheme
WITH THIS VICTORY, CUSTOMERS WILL START RETURNING TO MY STORE!
IT'S ALL THANKS TO YOU GUYS!
Eat as much as you want.
Ha ha ha! It was nothing!
ALLOW ME TO ADD MY APPRECIATION AS WELL.
IT'S FINE, IT'S FINE...
DON'T BE SO FORMAL, SOPHIE AND MR. KURO.

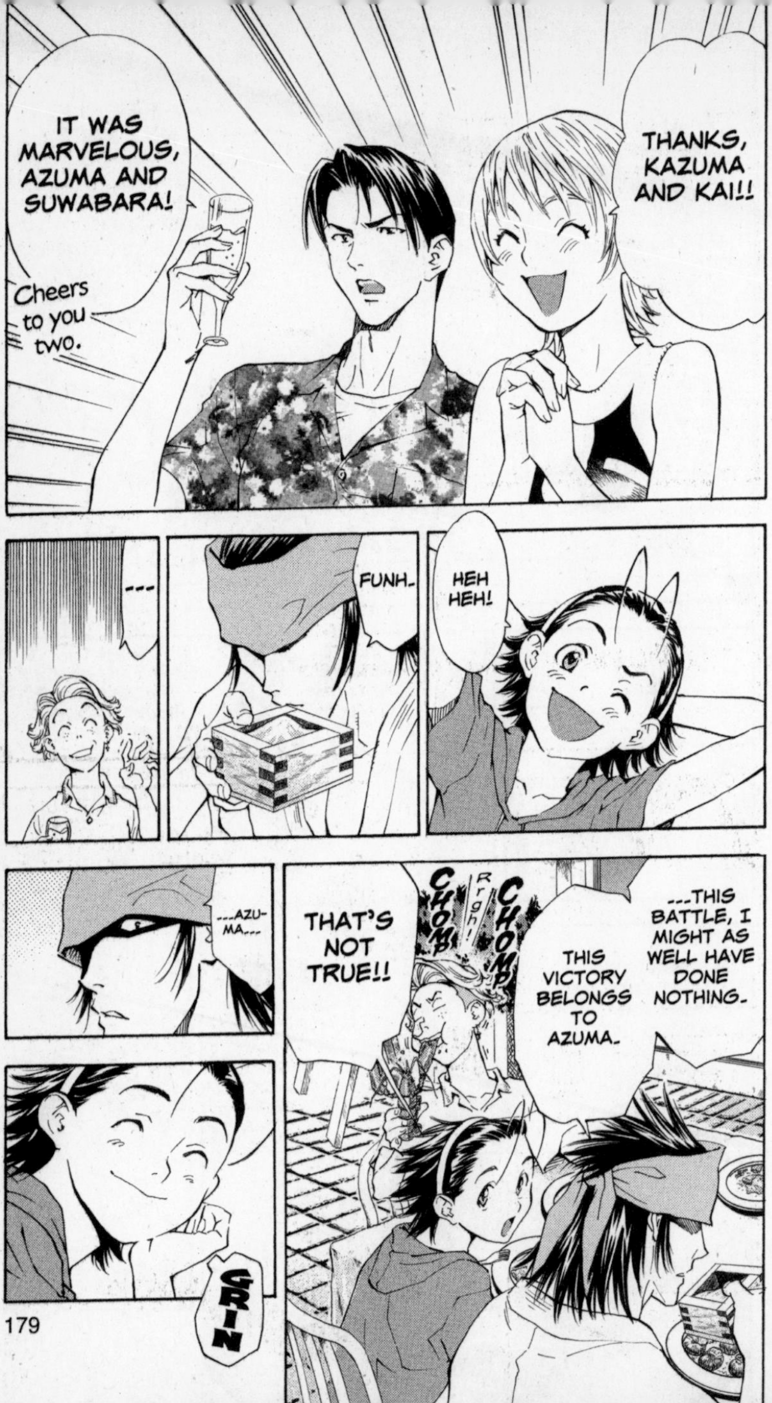
THANKS, KAZUMA AND KAI!!
IT WAS MARVELOUS, AZUMA AND SUWABARA!
Cheers to you two.
HEH HEH!
FUNH.

---THIS BATTLE, I MIGHT AS WELL HAVE DONE NOTHING.
THIS VICTORY BELONGS TO AZUMA.
CHOMP
Rrgh!
CHOMP
THAT'S NOT TRUE!!
---AZU-MA---
GRIN

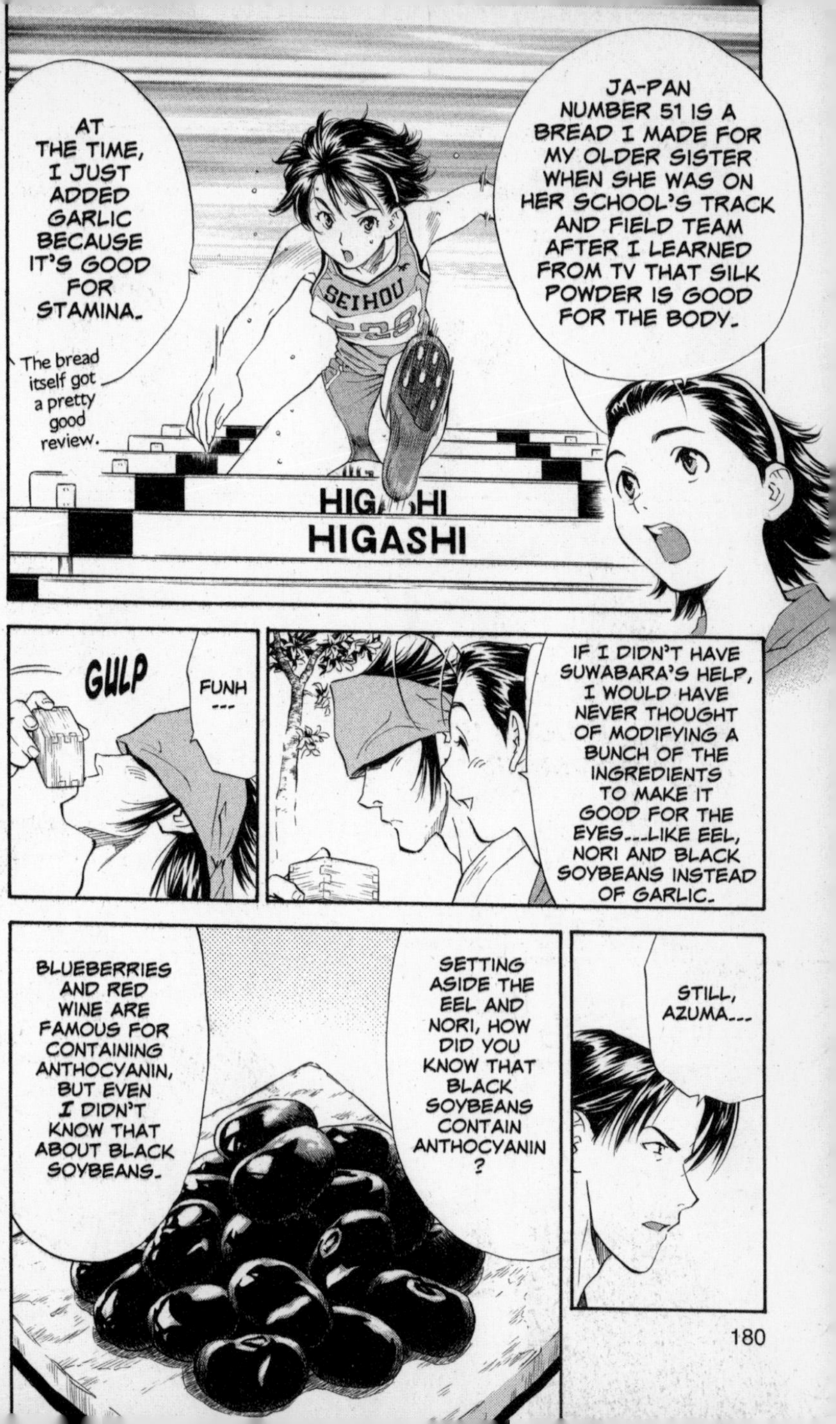

JA-PAN NUMBER 51 IS A BREAD I MADE FOR MY OLDER SISTER WHEN SHE WAS ON HER SCHOOL'S TRACK AND FIELD TEAM AFTER I LEARNED FROM TV THAT SILK POWDER IS GOOD FOR THE BODY.
AT THE TIME, I JUST ADDED GARLIC BECAUSE IT'S GOOD FOR STAMINA.
The bread itself got a pretty good review.
SEIHOU
HIGASHI
HIGASHI
IF I DIDN'T HAVE SUWABARA'S HELP, I WOULD HAVE NEVER THOUGHT OF MODIFYING A BUNCH OF THE INGREDIENTS TO MAKE IT GOOD FOR THE EYES...LIKE EEL, NORI AND BLACK SOYBEANS INSTEAD OF GARLIC.
FUNH ---
GULP
STILL, AZUMA...
SETTING ASIDE THE EEL AND NORI, HOW DID YOU KNOW THAT BLACK SOYBEANS CONTAIN ANTHOCYANIN ?
BLUEBERRIES AND RED WINE ARE FAMOUS FOR CONTAINING ANTHOCYANIN, BUT EVEN I DIDN'T KNOW THAT ABOUT BLACK SOYBEANS.

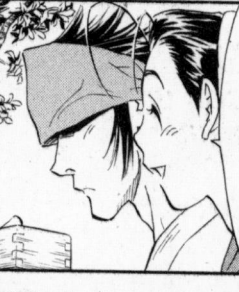

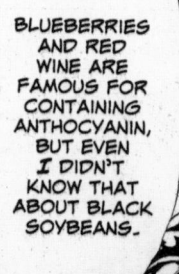

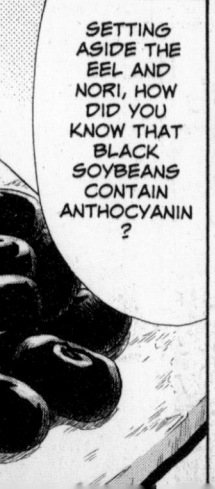

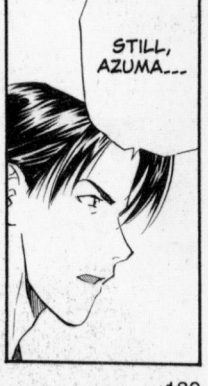

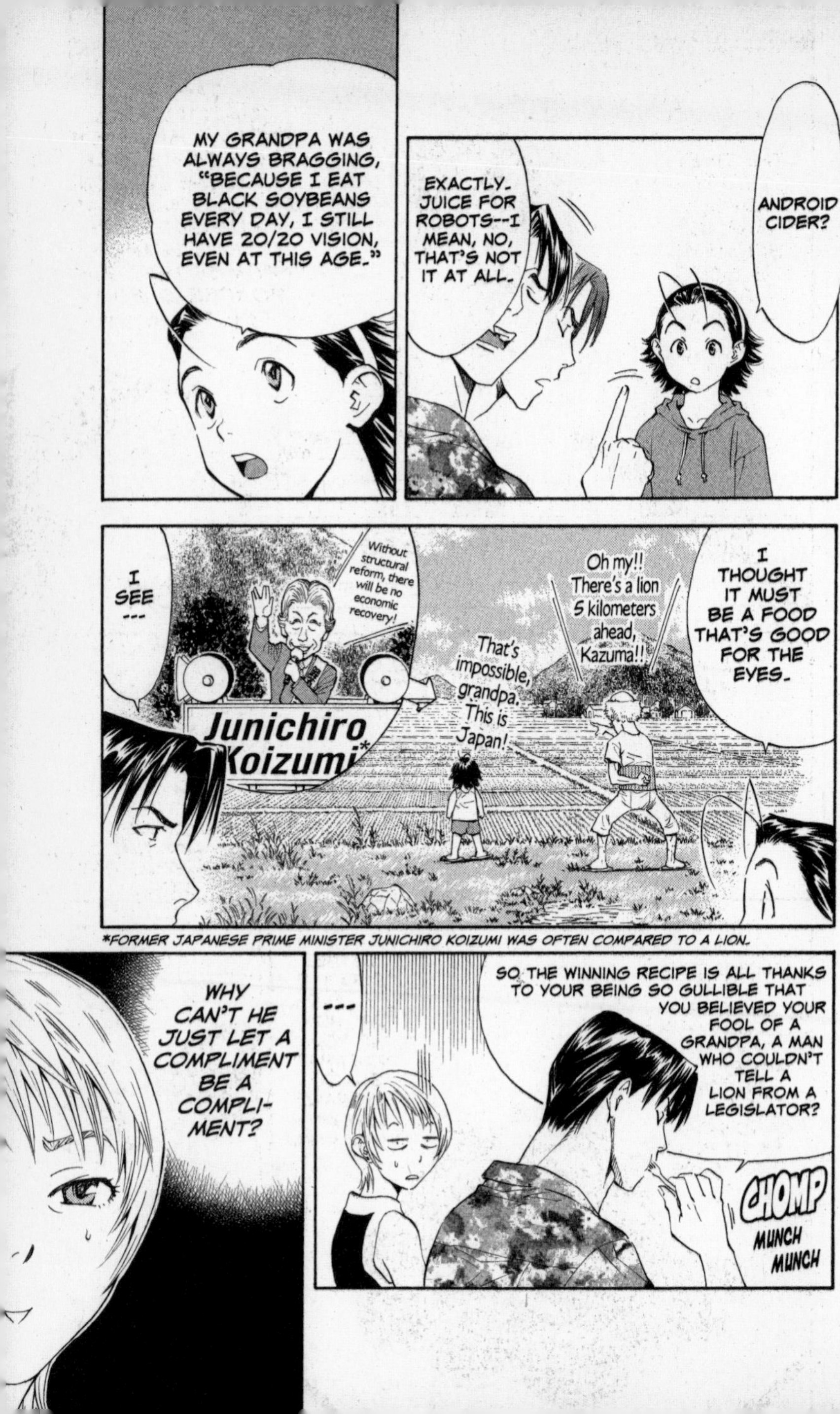
ANDROID CIDER?
EXACTLY. JUICE FOR ROBOTS--I MEAN, NO, THAT'S NOT IT AT ALL.
MY GRANDPA WAS ALWAYS BRAGGING, "BECAUSE I EAT BLACK SOYBEANS EVERY DAY, I STILL HAVE 20/20 VISION, EVEN AT THIS AGE."
I THOUGHT IT MUST BE A FOOD THAT'S GOOD FOR THE EYES.
Oh my!! There's a lion 5 kilometers ahead, Kazuma!!
That's impossible, grandpa. This is Japan!
Without structural reform, there will be no economic recovery!
Junichiro Koizumi*
I SEE ---
SO THE WINNING RECIPE IS ALL THANKS TO YOUR BEING SO GULLIBLE THAT YOU BELIEVED YOUR FOOL OF A GRANDPA, A MAN WHO COULDN'T TELL A LION FROM A LEGISLATOR?

CHOMP
MUNCH MUNCH
WHY CAN'T HE JUST LET A COMPLIMENT BE A COMPLI-MENT?
*FORMER JAPANESE PRIME MINISTER JUNICHIRO KOIZUMI WAS OFTEN COMPARED TO A LION.

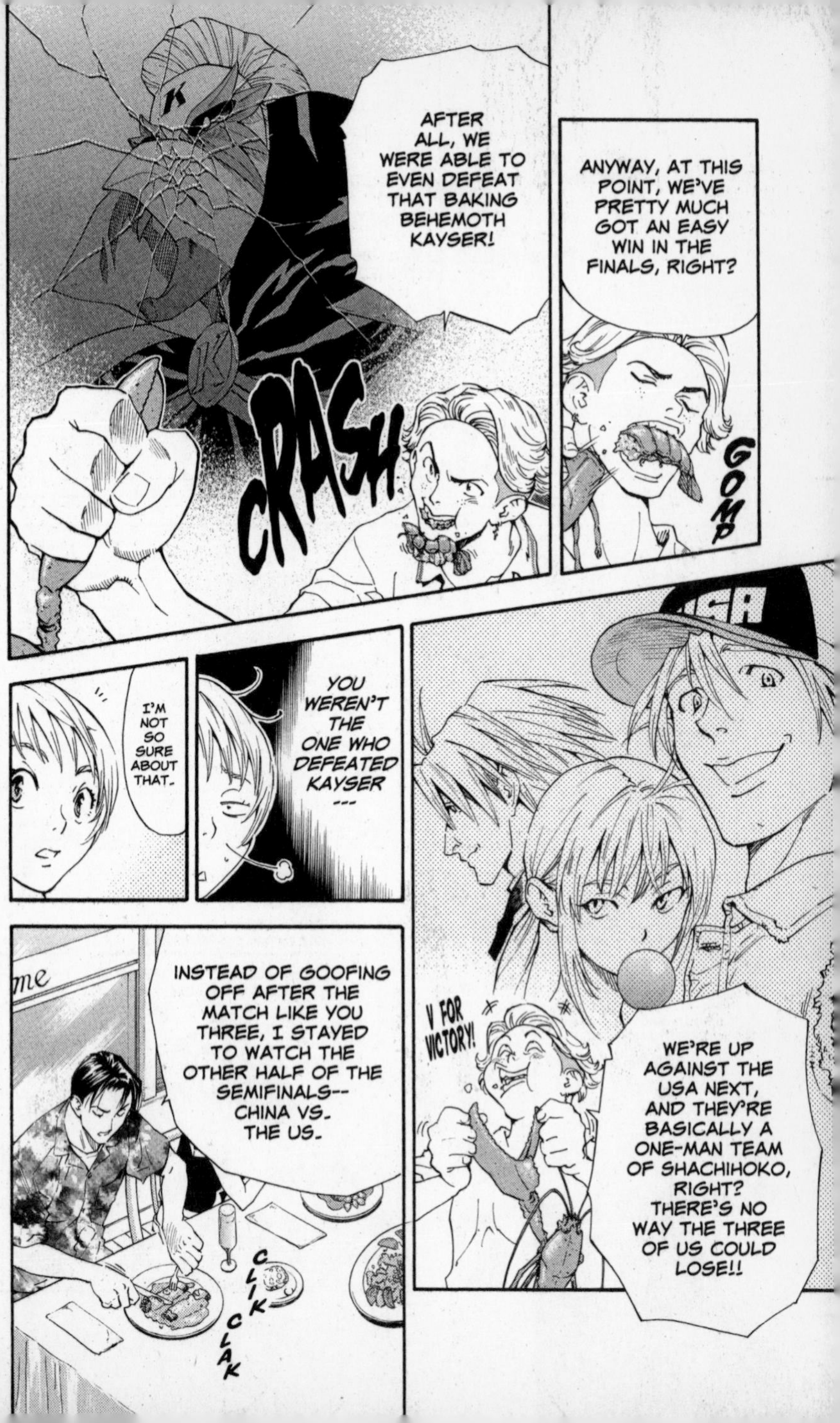
ANYWAY, AT THIS POINT, WE'VE PRETTY MUCH GOT AN EASY WIN IN THE FINALS, RIGHT?
GOMP
AFTER ALL, WE WERE ABLE TO EVEN DEFEAT THAT BAKING BEHEMOTH KAYSER!
CRASH
WE'RE UP AGAINST THE USA NEXT, AND THEY'RE BASICALLY A ONE-MAN TEAM OF SHACHIHOKO, RIGHT? THERE'S NO WAY THE THREE OF US COULD LOSE!!
V FOR VICTORY!
YOU WEREN'T THE ONE WHO DEFEATED KAYSER---
I'M NOT SO SURE ABOUT THAT.
INSTEAD OF GOOFING OFF AFTER THE MATCH LIKE YOU THREE, I STAYED TO WATCH THE OTHER HALF OF THE SEMIFINALS--CHINA VS. THE US.
CLIK CLAK

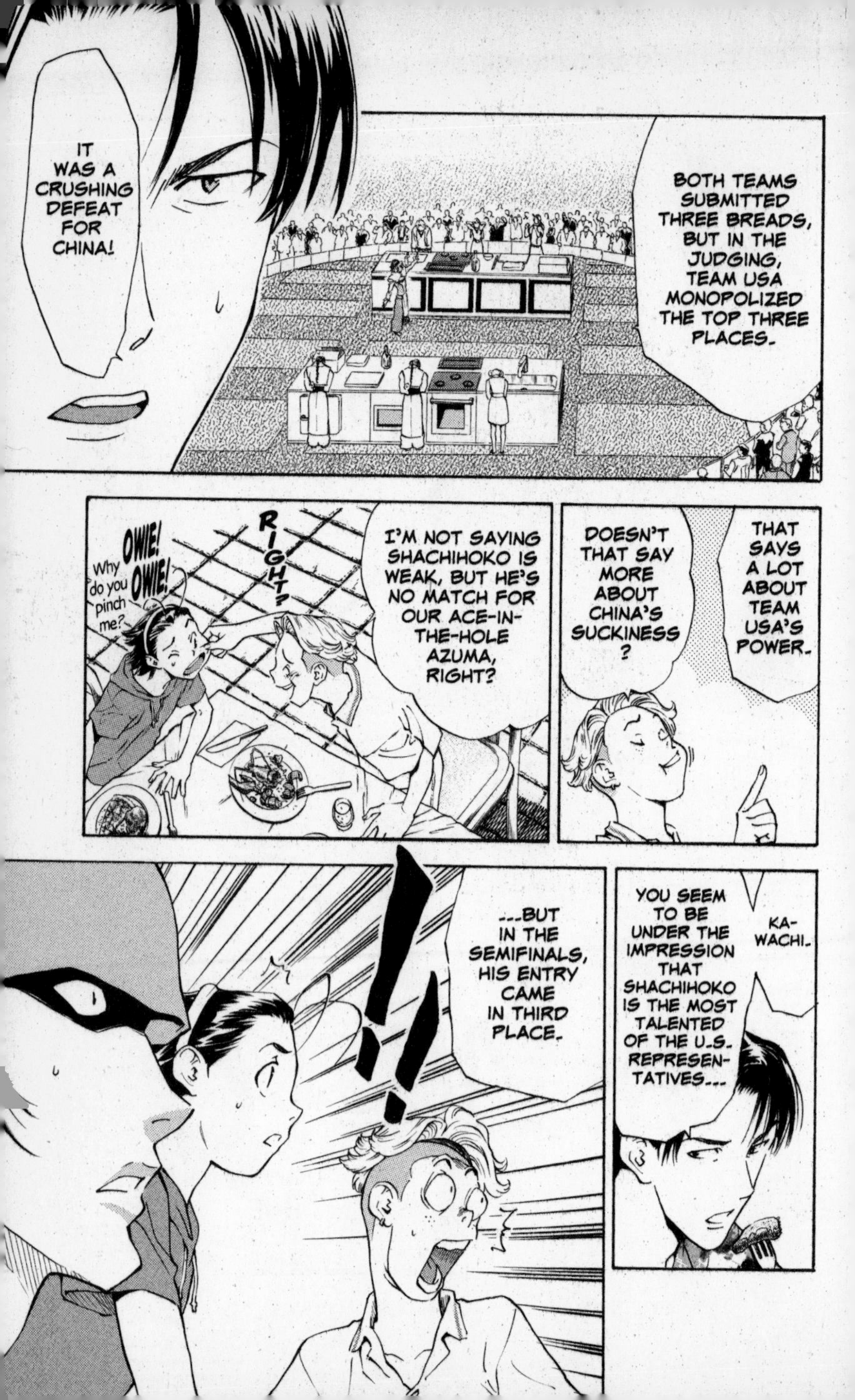
BOTH TEAMS SUBMITTED THREE BREADS, BUT IN THE JUDGING, TEAM USA MONOPOLIZED THE TOP THREE PLACES.
IT WAS A CRUSHING DEFEAT FOR CHINA!
THAT SAYS A LOT ABOUT TEAM USA'S POWER.
DOESN'T THAT SAY MORE ABOUT CHINA'S SUCKINESS?
I'M NOT SAYING SHACHIHOKO IS WEAK, BUT HE'S NO MATCH FOR OUR ACE-IN-THE-HOLE AZUMA, RIGHT?
RIGHT?
OWIE! OWIE!
Why do you pinch me?
KA-WACHI.
YOU SEEM TO BE UNDER THE IMPRESSION THAT SHACHIHOKO IS THE MOST TALENTED OF THE U.S. REPRESENTATIVES...
...BUT IN THE SEMIFINALS, HIS ENTRY CAME IN THIRD PLACE.
!!

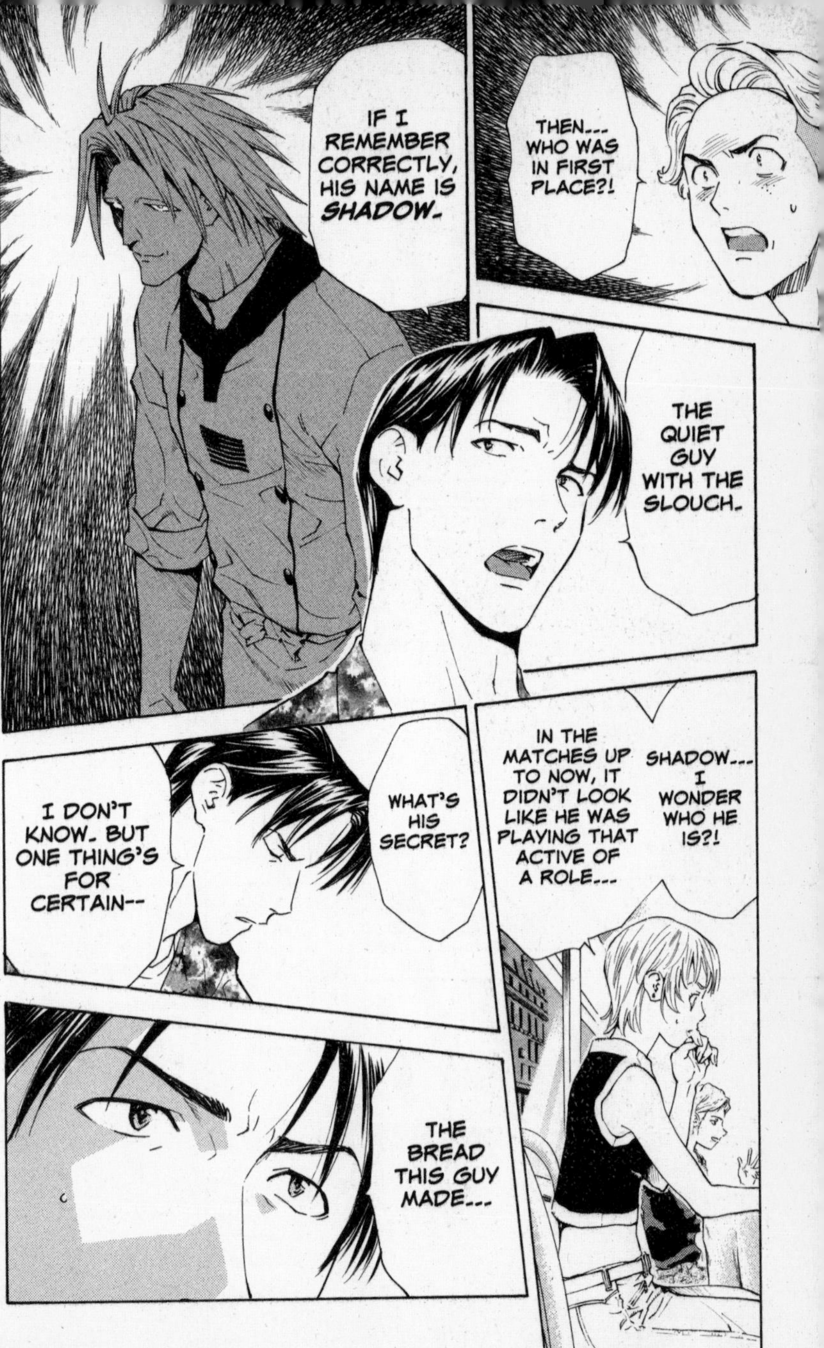
THEN... WHO WAS IN FIRST PLACE?!
THE QUIET GUY WITH THE SLOUCH.
IF I REMEMBER CORRECTLY, HIS NAME IS *SHADOW*.
SHADOW... I WONDER WHO HE IS?!
IN THE MATCHES UP TO NOW, IT DIDN'T LOOK LIKE HE WAS PLAYING THAT ACTIVE OF A ROLE...
WHAT'S HIS SECRET?
I DON'T KNOW. BUT ONE THING'S FOR CERTAIN--
THE BREAD THIS GUY MADE...

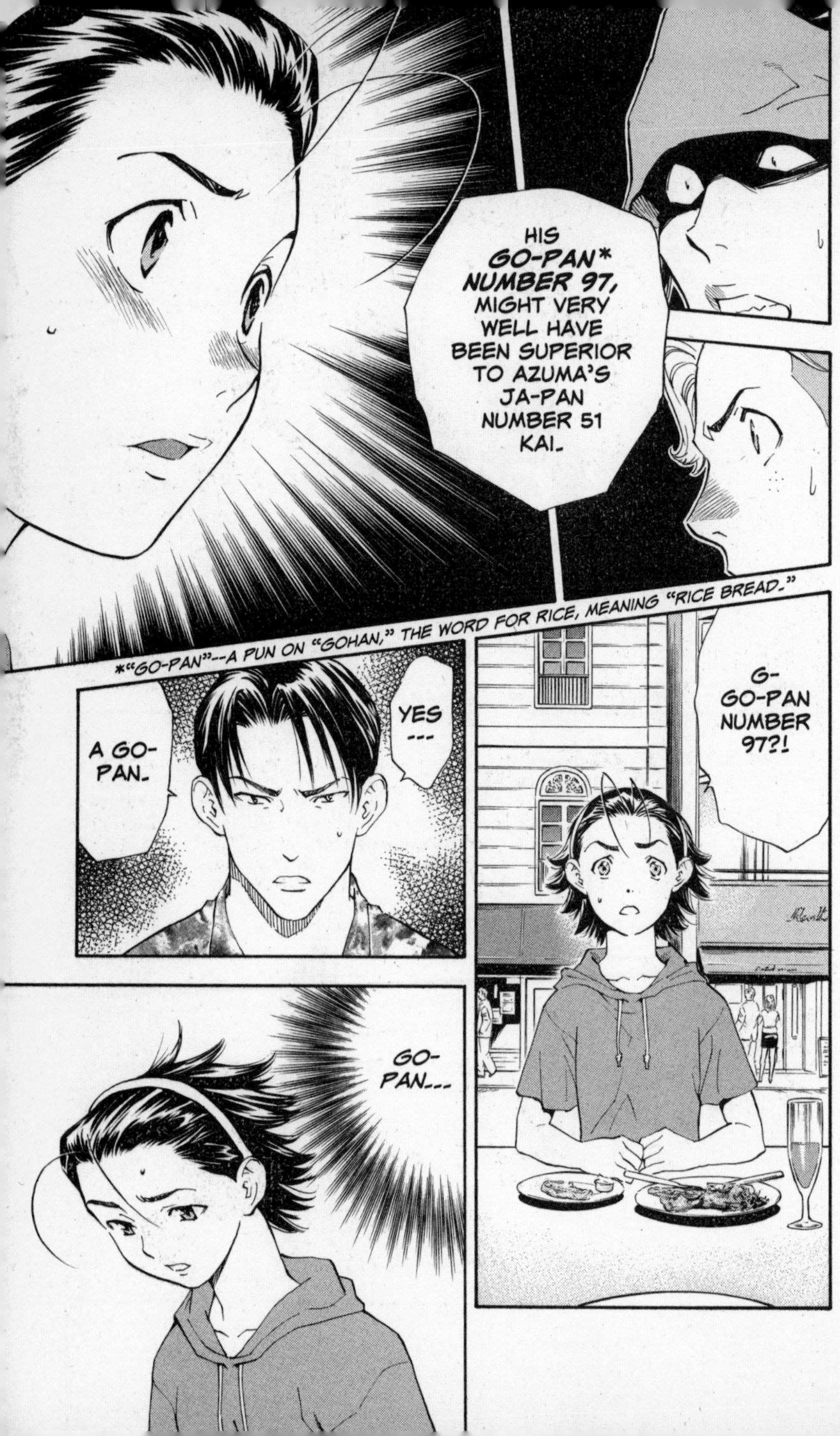
HIS GO-PAN* NUMBER 97, MIGHT VERY WELL HAVE BEEN SUPERIOR TO AZUMA'S JA-PAN NUMBER 51 KAI.
*"GO-PAN"--A PUN ON "GOHAN," THE WORD FOR RICE, MEANING "RICE BREAD."
G-GO-PAN NUMBER 97?!
YES---
A GO-PAN.
GO-PAN...

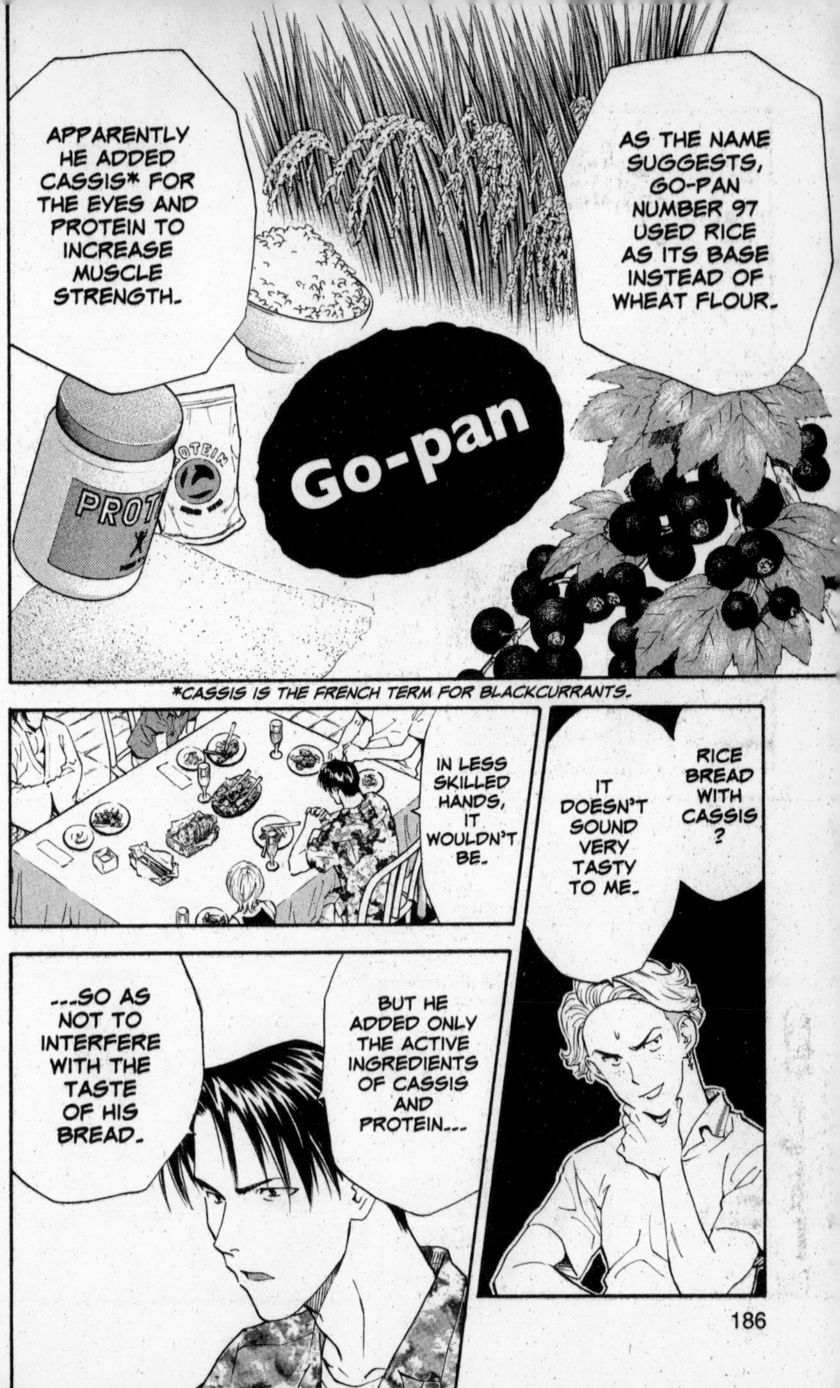
AS THE NAME SUGGESTS, GO-PAN NUMBER 97 USED RICE AS ITS BASE INSTEAD OF WHEAT FLOUR.
Go-pan
APPARENTLY HE ADDED CASSIS* FOR THE EYES AND PROTEIN TO INCREASE MUSCLE STRENGTH.
*CASSIS IS THE FRENCH TERM FOR BLACKCURRANTS.
RICE BREAD WITH CASSIS?
IT DOESN'T SOUND VERY TASTY TO ME.
IN LESS SKILLED HANDS, IT WOULDN'T BE.
BUT HE ADDED ONLY THE ACTIVE INGREDIENTS OF CASSIS AND PROTEIN...
...SO AS NOT TO INTERFERE WITH THE TASTE OF HIS BREAD.

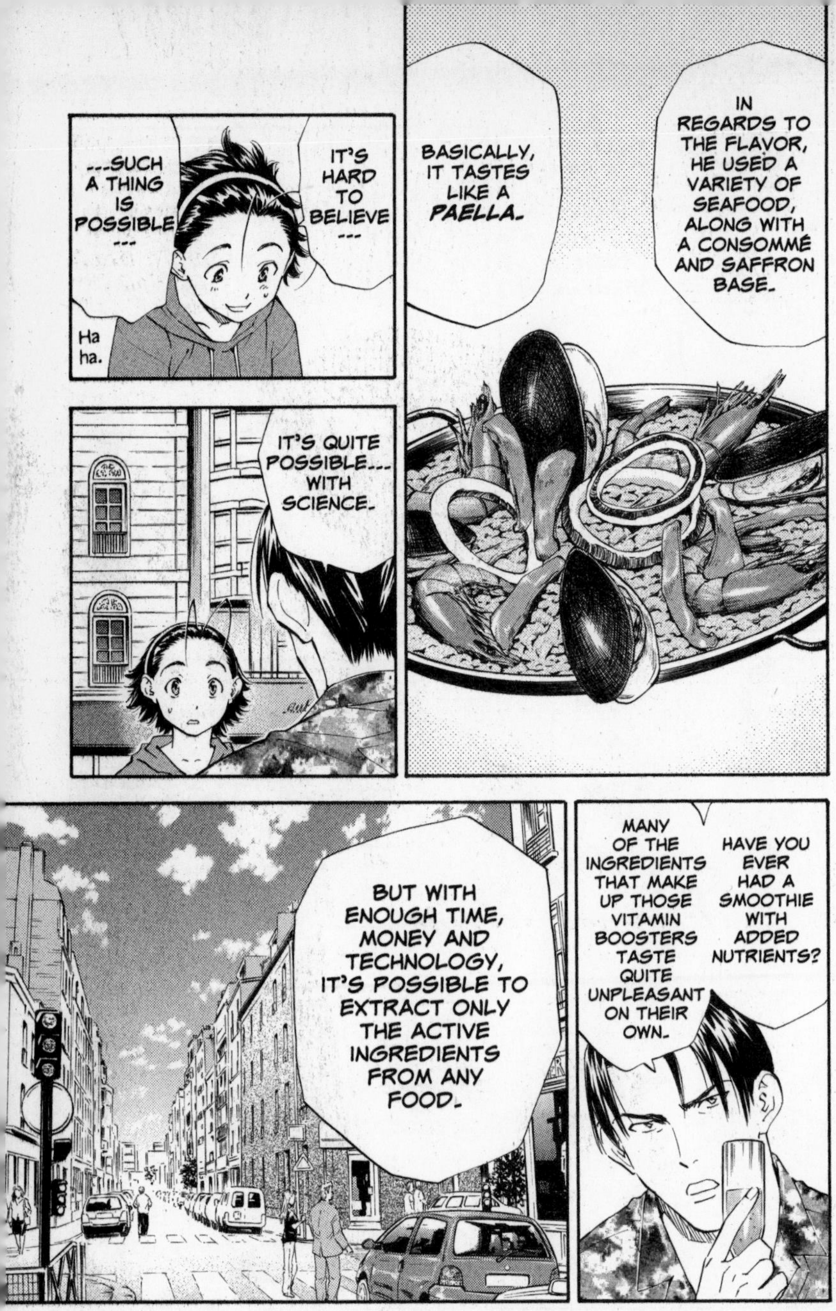
IN REGARDS TO THE FLAVOR, HE USED A VARIETY OF SEAFOOD, ALONG WITH A CONSOMMÉ AND SAFFRON BASE.
BASICALLY, IT TASTES LIKE A *PAELLA*.
IT'S HARD TO BELIEVE ---
---SUCH A THING IS POSSIBLE ---
Ha ha.
IT'S QUITE POSSIBLE--- WITH SCIENCE.
HAVE YOU EVER HAD A SMOOTHIE WITH ADDED NUTRIENTS?
MANY OF THE INGREDIENTS THAT MAKE UP THOSE VITAMIN BOOSTERS TASTE QUITE UNPLEASANT ON THEIR OWN.
BUT WITH ENOUGH TIME, MONEY AND TECHNOLOGY, IT'S POSSIBLE TO EXTRACT ONLY THE ACTIVE INGREDIENTS FROM ANY FOOD.

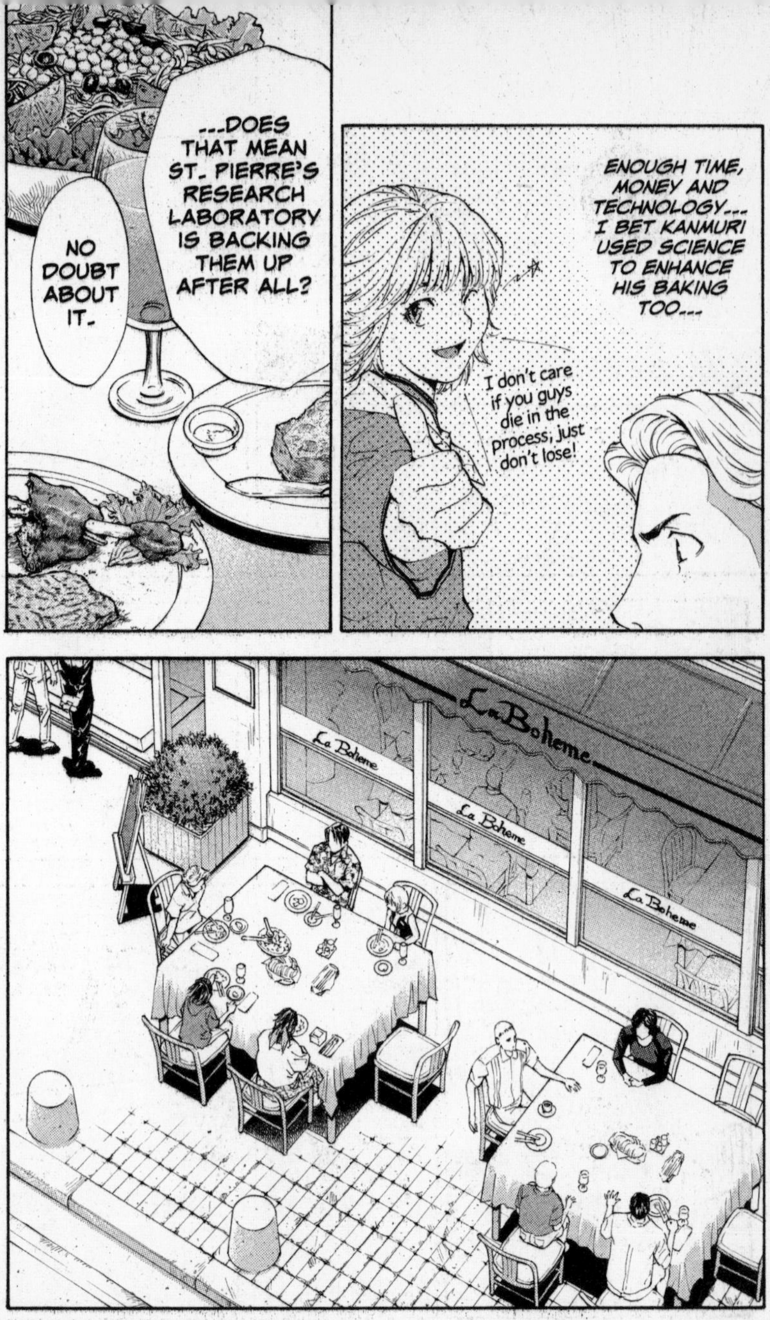
ENOUGH TIME, MONEY AND TECHNOLOGY... I BET KANMURI USED SCIENCE TO ENHANCE HIS BAKING TOO...
I don't care if you guys die in the process, just don't lose!
...DOES THAT MEAN ST. PIERRE'S RESEARCH LABORATORY IS BACKING THEM UP AFTER ALL?
NO DOUBT ABOUT IT.
La Boheme
La Boheme
La Boheme
La Boheme

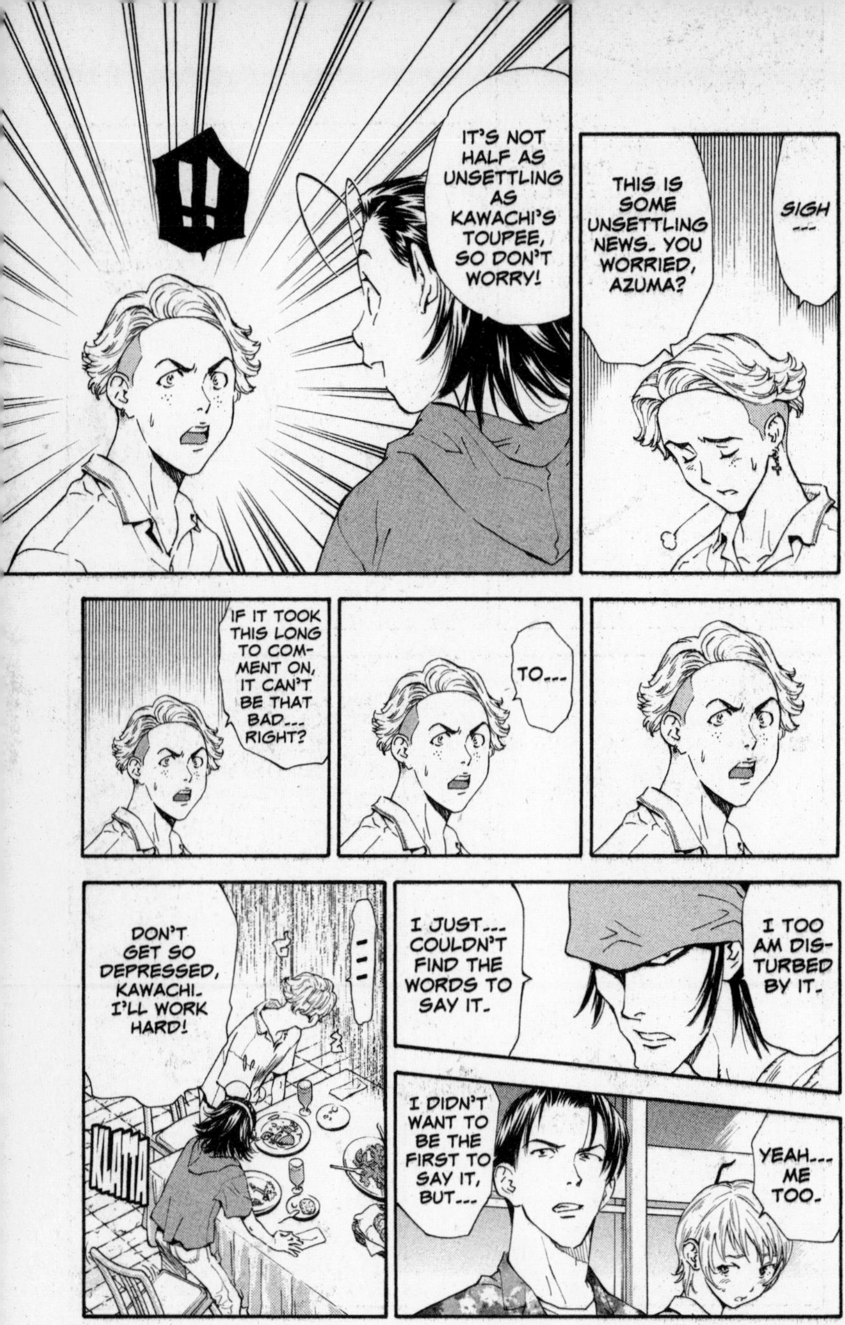
SIGH ---
THIS IS SOME UNSETTLING NEWS. YOU WORRIED, AZUMA?
IT'S NOT HALF AS UNSETTLING AS KAWACHI'S TOUPEE, SO DON'T WORRY!
!!
TO---
IF IT TOOK THIS LONG TO COMMENT ON, IT CAN'T BE THAT BAD--- RIGHT?
I TOO AM DISTURBED BY IT.
I JUST--- COULDN'T FIND THE WORDS TO SAY IT.
YEAH--- ME TOO.
I DIDN'T WANT TO BE THE FIRST TO SAY IT, BUT---
DON'T GET SO DEPRESSED, KAWACHI. I'LL WORK HARD!
KLATTA

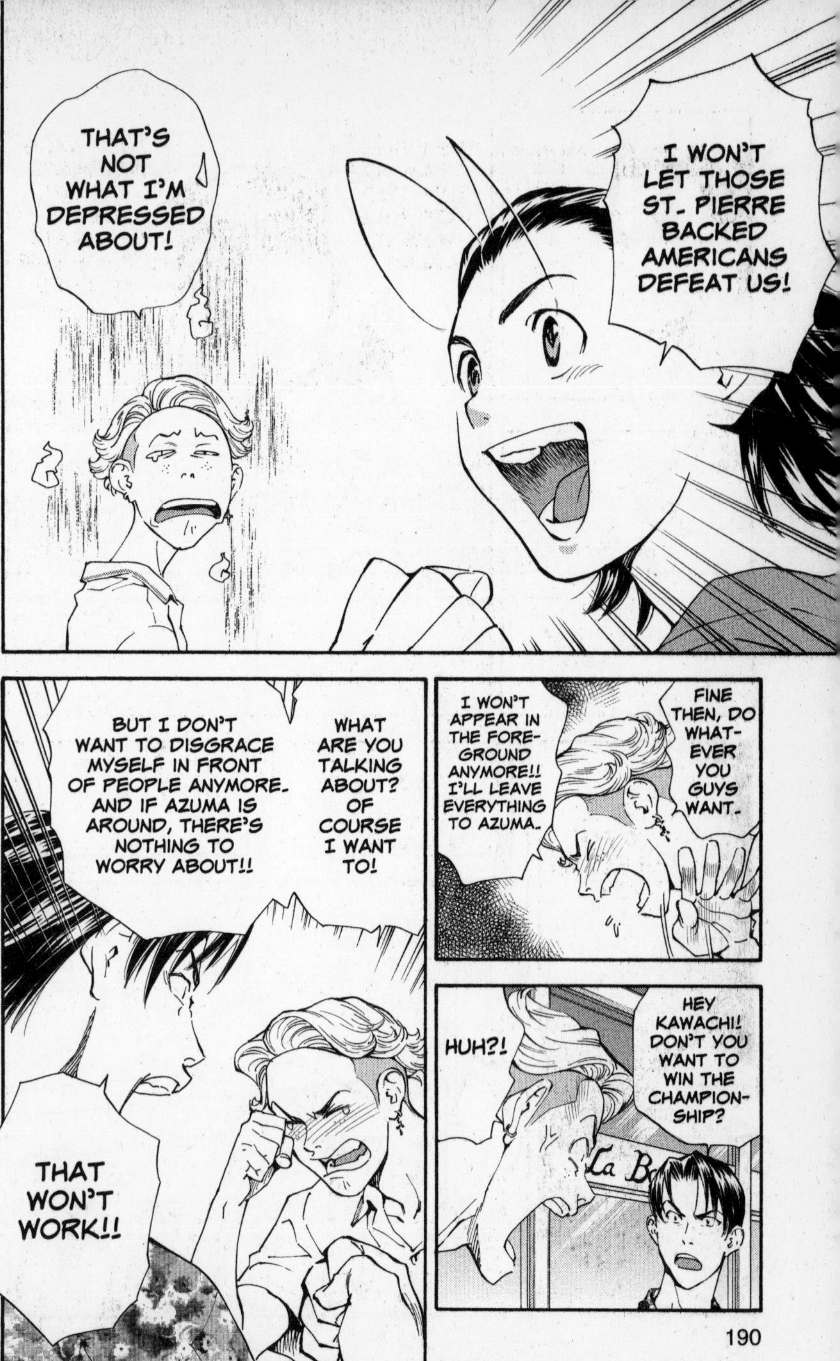
I WON'T LET THOSE ST. PIERRE BACKED AMERICANS DEFEAT US!
THAT'S NOT WHAT I'M DEPRESSED ABOUT!
FINE THEN, DO WHAT-EVER YOU GUYS WANT.
I WON'T APPEAR IN THE FORE-GROUND ANYMORE!! I'LL LEAVE EVERYTHING TO AZUMA.
HEY KAWACHI! DON'T YOU WANT TO WIN THE CHAMPION-SHIP?
HUH?!
WHAT ARE YOU TALKING ABOUT? OF COURSE I WANT TO!
BUT I DON'T WANT TO DISGRACE MYSELF IN FRONT OF PEOPLE ANYMORE. AND IF AZUMA IS AROUND, THERE'S NOTHING TO WORRY ABOUT!!
THAT WON'T WORK!!

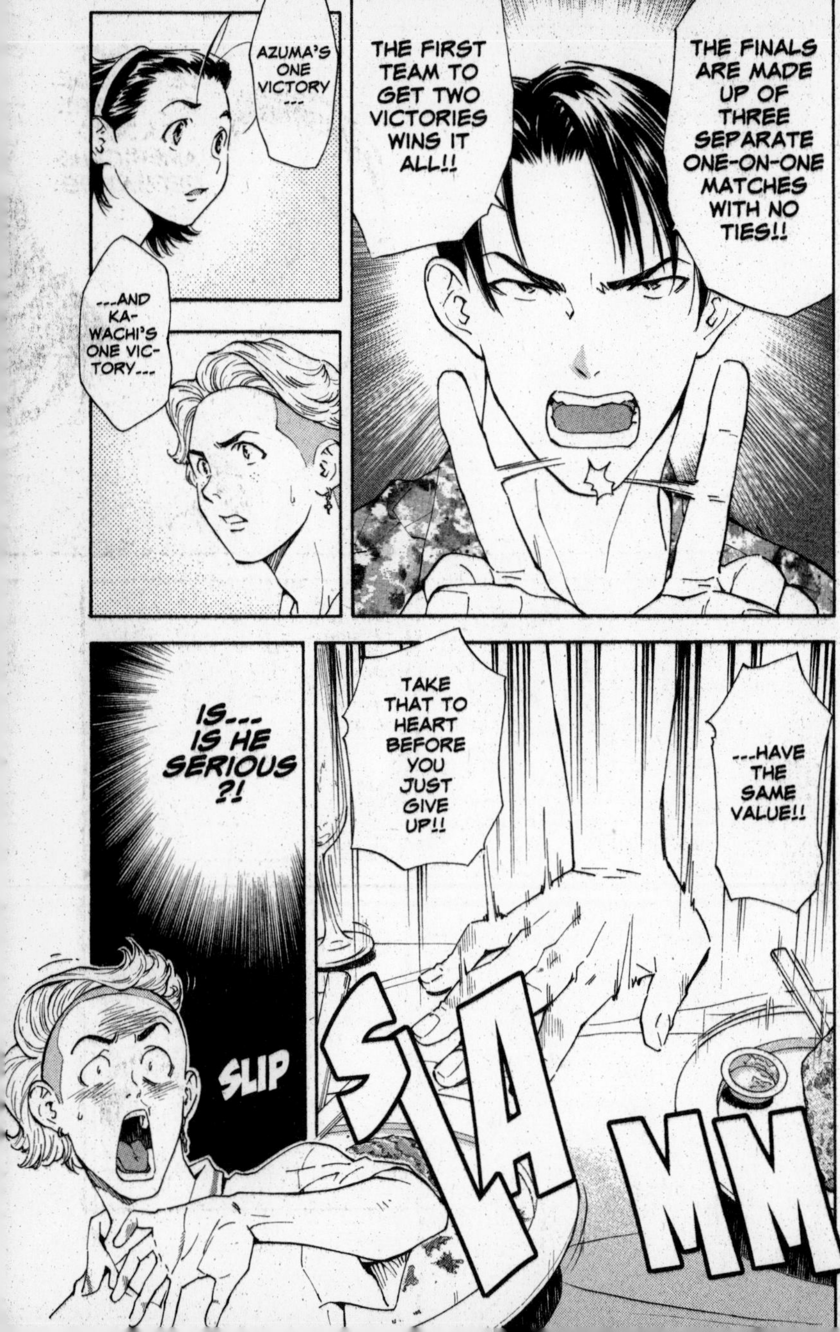
THE FINALS ARE MADE UP OF THREE SEPARATE ONE-ON-ONE MATCHES WITH NO TIES!!
THE FIRST TEAM TO GET TWO VICTORIES WINS IT ALL!!
AZUMA'S ONE VICTORY ---
---AND KA-WACHI'S ONE VIC-TORY---
---HAVE THE SAME VALUE!!
TAKE THAT TO HEART BEFORE YOU JUST GIVE UP!!
SLAMM
IS--- IS HE SERIOUS ?!
SLIP

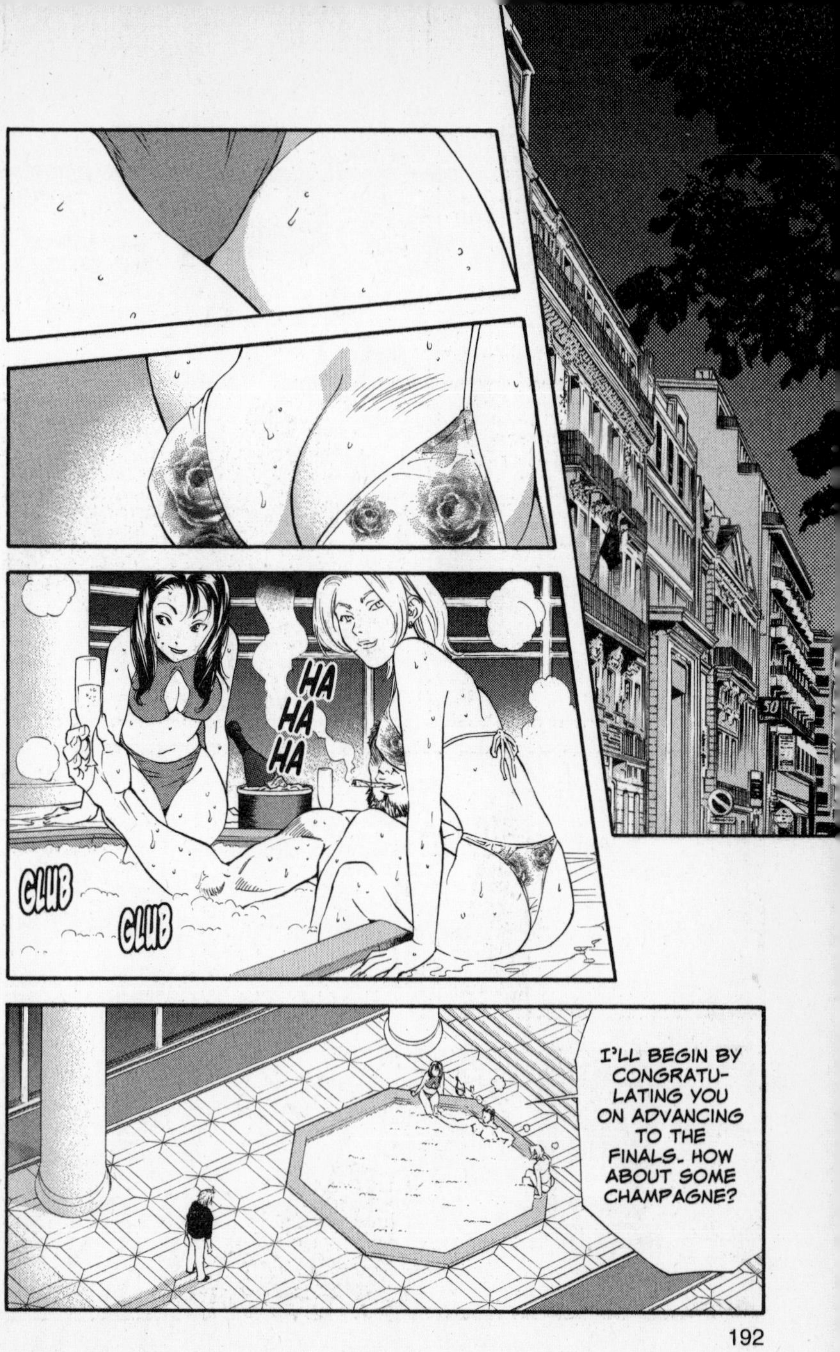
HA
HA
HA
GLUB
GLUB
I'LL BEGIN BY CONGRATU- LATING YOU ON ADVANCING TO THE FINALS. HOW ABOUT SOME CHAMPAGNE?

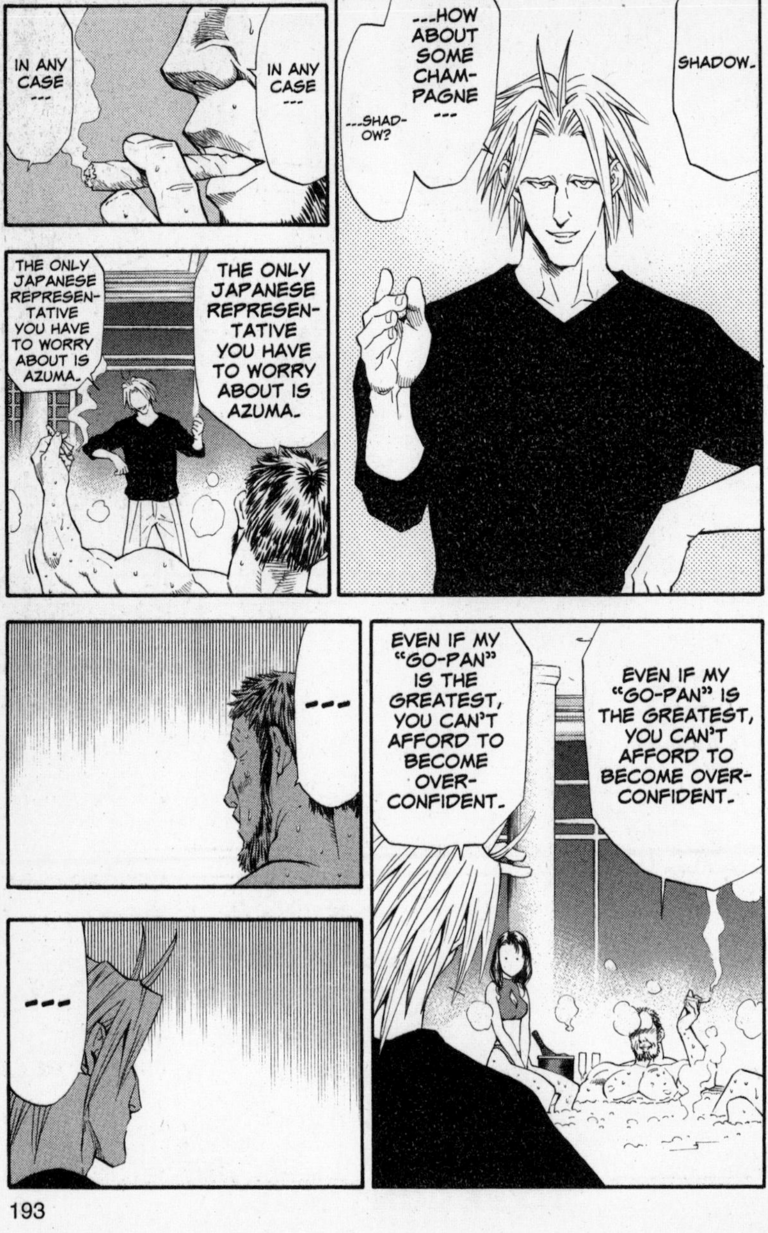
SHADOW.
...HOW ABOUT SOME CHAMPAGNE...
...SHADOW?
IN ANY CASE...
IN ANY CASE...
THE ONLY JAPANESE REPRESENTATIVE YOU HAVE TO WORRY ABOUT IS AZUMA.
THE ONLY JAPANESE REPRESENTATIVE YOU HAVE TO WORRY ABOUT IS AZUMA.
EVEN IF MY "GO-PAN" IS THE GREATEST, YOU CAN'T AFFORD TO BECOME OVER-CONFIDENT.
EVEN IF MY "GO-PAN" IS THE GREATEST, YOU CAN'T AFFORD TO BECOME OVER-CONFIDENT.
...
...

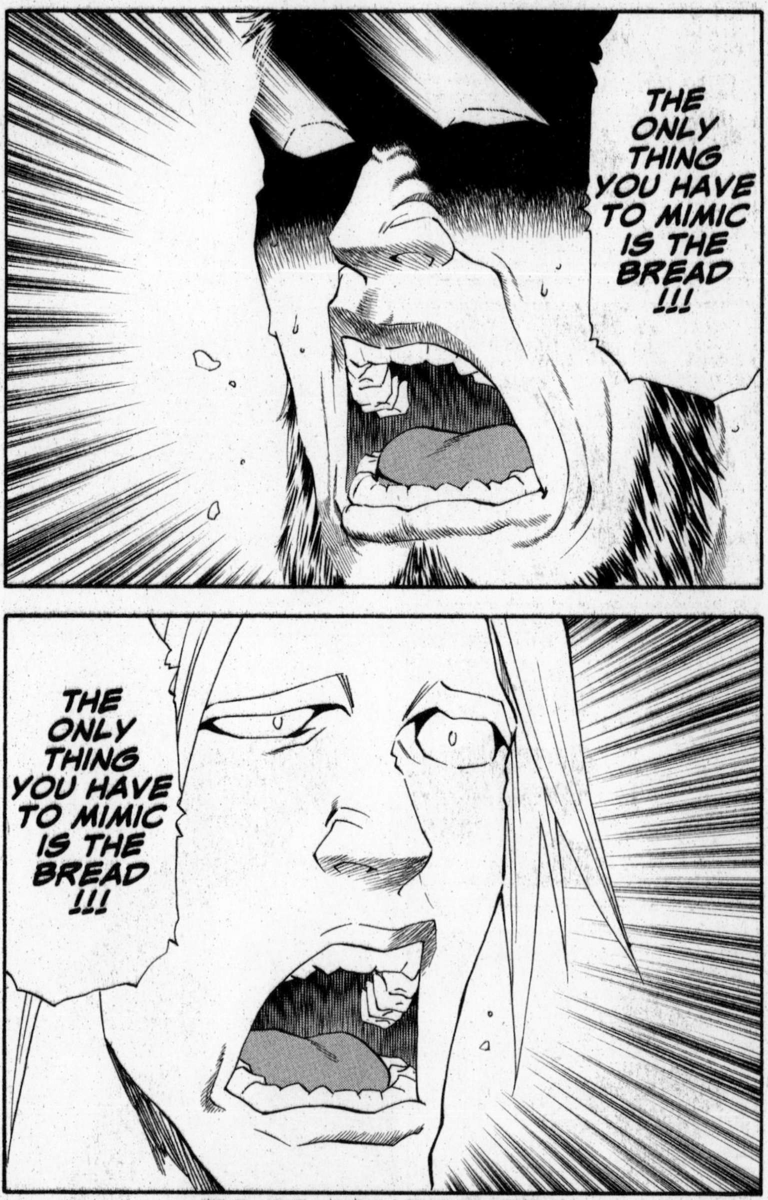
THE ONLY THING YOU HAVE TO MIMIC IS THE BREAD !!!
THE ONLY THING YOU HAVE TO MIMIC IS THE BREAD !!!

TO BE CONTINUED!

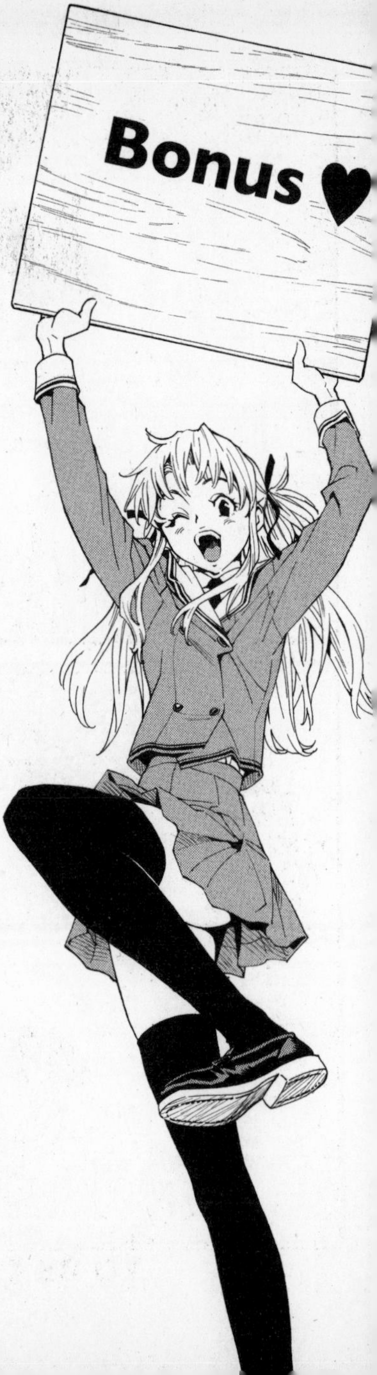
Bonus ♥

Extra Service

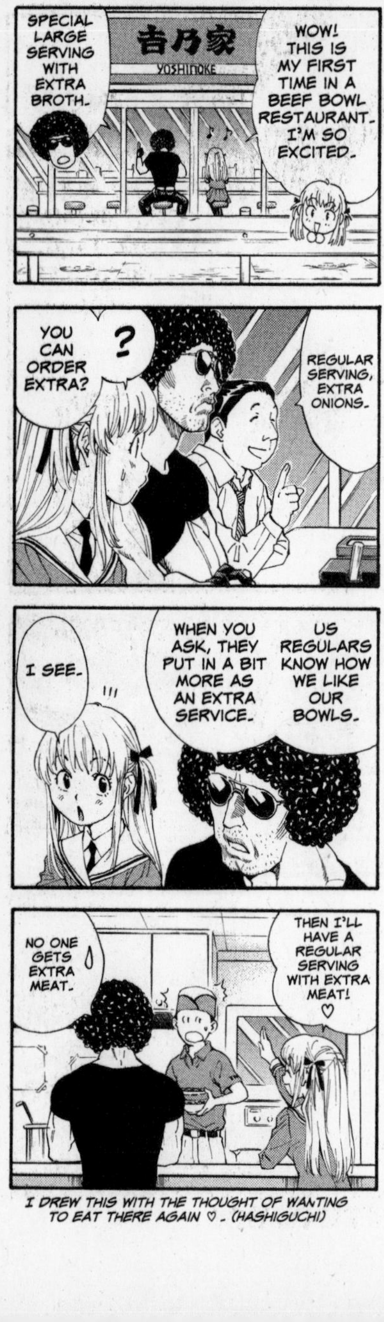
吉乃家
YOSHINOKE
WOW! THIS IS MY FIRST TIME IN A BEEF BOWL RESTAURANT. I'M SO EXCITED.
SPECIAL LARGE SERVING WITH EXTRA BROTH.
REGULAR SERVING, EXTRA ONIONS.
?
YOU CAN ORDER EXTRA?
US REGULARS KNOW HOW WE LIKE OUR BOWLS.
WHEN YOU ASK, THEY PUT IN A BIT MORE AS AN EXTRA SERVICE.
I SEE.
THEN I'LL HAVE A REGULAR SERVING WITH EXTRA MEAT! ♡
NO ONE GETS EXTRA MEAT.

I DREW THIS WITH THE THOUGHT OF WANTING TO EAT THERE AGAIN ♡. (HASHIGUCHI)

Love Letter

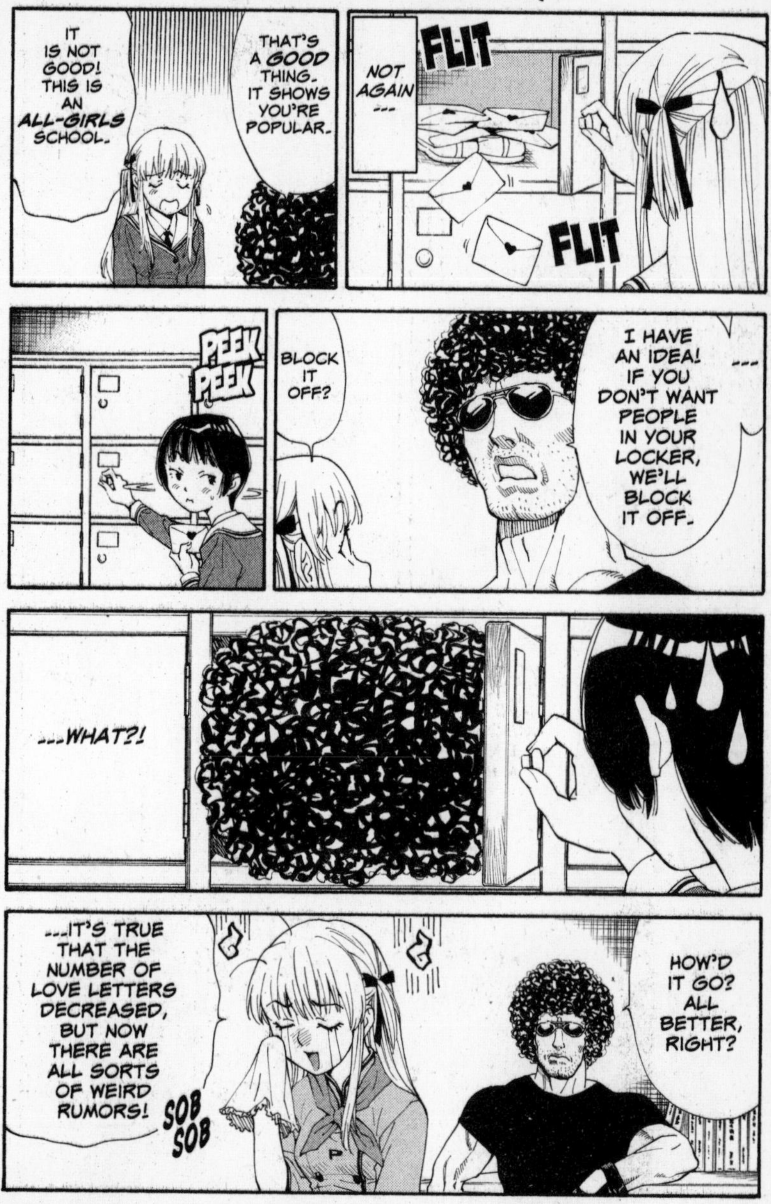
FLIT
NOT AGAIN ...
FLIT
THAT'S A GOOD THING. IT SHOWS YOU'RE POPULAR.
IT IS NOT GOOD! THIS IS AN ALL-GIRLS SCHOOL.
...
I HAVE AN IDEA! IF YOU DON'T WANT PEOPLE IN YOUR LOCKER, WE'LL BLOCK IT OFF.
BLOCK IT OFF?
PEEK PEEK
...WHAT?!
HOW'D IT GO? ALL BETTER, RIGHT?
...IT'S TRUE THAT THE NUMBER OF LOVE LETTERS DECREASED, BUT NOW THERE ARE ALL SORTS OF WEIRD RUMORS!
SOB SOB

Homework

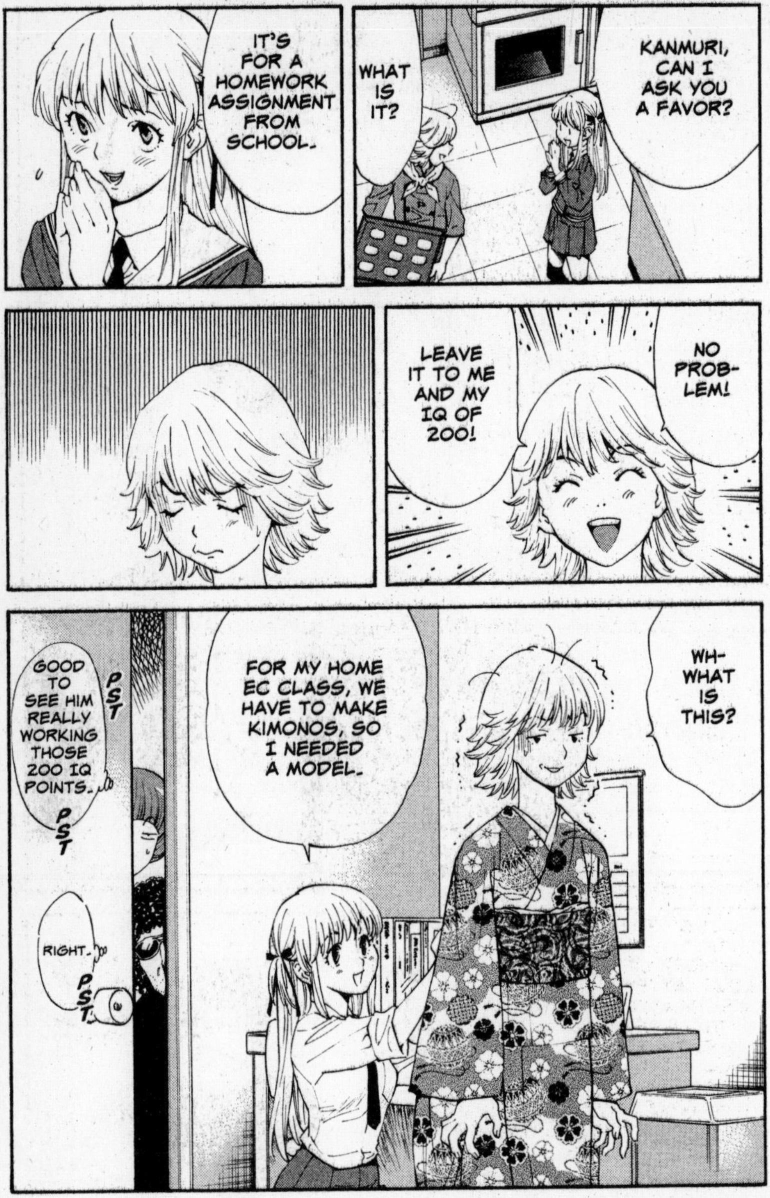
KANMURI, CAN I ASK YOU A FAVOR?
WHAT IS IT?
IT'S FOR A HOMEWORK ASSIGNMENT FROM SCHOOL…
NO PROBLEM!
LEAVE IT TO ME AND MY IQ OF 200!
WH-WHAT IS THIS?
FOR MY HOME EC CLASS, WE HAVE TO MAKE KIMONOS, SO I NEEDED A MODEL…
PST
GOOD TO SEE HIM REALLY WORKING THOSE 200 IQ POINTS…
PST
RIGHT…
PST

Freshly Baked!!
Mini Information

Amacha

In the original magazine run, the ingredient that's kneaded into Kayser's bread was just identified as hydrangea extract, but in the graphic novel form, we specified it as Amacha.

This is because normal hydrangea flowers can be quite toxic. There are methods for drawing out the toxin, of course, but we decided it would be safer to just change the text to the nontoxic variety just to be safe.

Amacha is a type of hydrangea, but unlike other varieties, it has no toxin for some reason. Plants sure are interesting!

YAKITATE!! JAPAN
VOL. 11

STORY AND ART BY
TAKASHI HASHIGUCHI

English Adaptation/Jake Forbes
Translation/Noritaka Minami
Touch-up Art & Lettering/Steve Dutro
Cover Design/Yukiko Whitley
Editor/Kit Fox

Editor in Chief, Books/Alvin Lu
Editor in Chief, Magazines/Marc Weidenbaum
VP of Publishing Licensing/Rika Inouye
VP of Sales/Gonzalo Ferreyra
Sr. VP of Marketing/Liza Coppola
Publisher/Hyoe Narita

Printed in the U.S.A.

Published by VIZ Media, LLC
P.O. Box 77010
San Francisco, CA 94107

10 9 8 7 6 5 4 3 2 1
First printing, May 2008

www.viz.com   store.viz.com

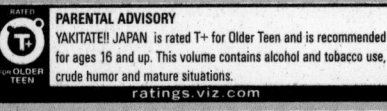